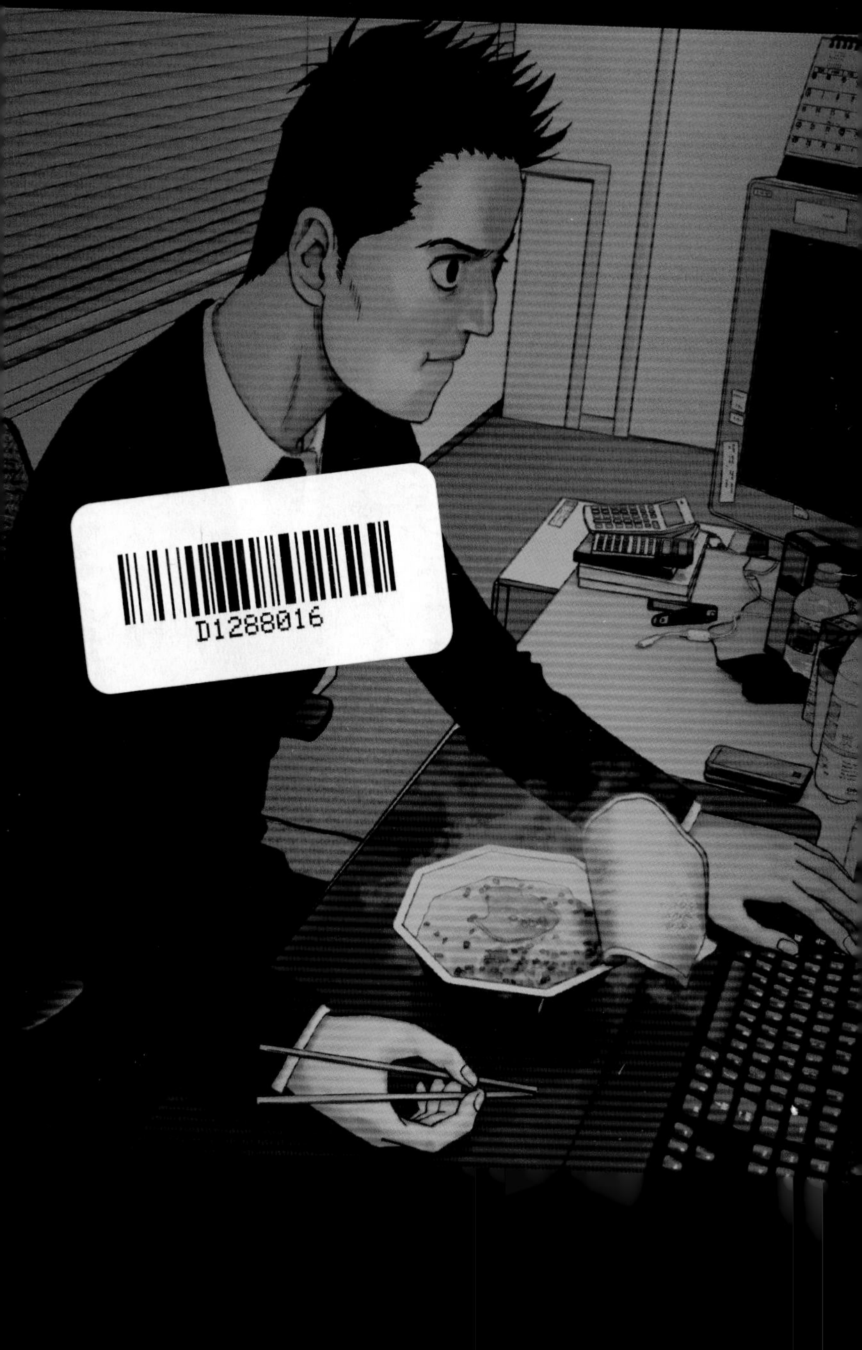

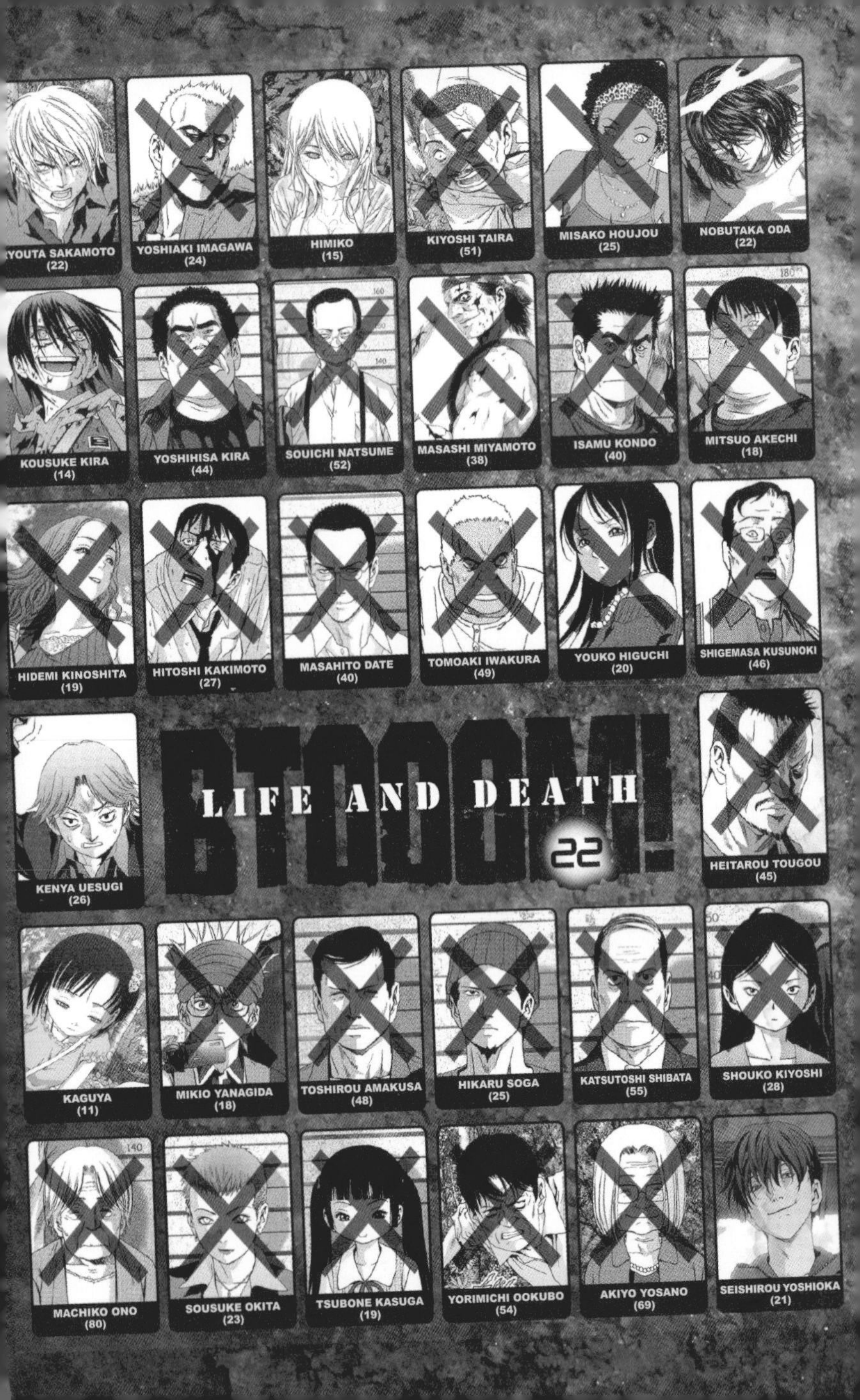
YOUTA SAKAMOTO (22)
YOSHIAKI IMAGAWA (24)
HIMIKO (15)
KIYOSHI TAIRA (51)
MISAKO HOUJOU (25)
NOBUTAKA ODA (22)
KOUSUKE KIRA (14)
YOSHIHISA KIRA (44)
SOUICHI NATSUME (52)
MASASHI MIYAMOTO (38)
ISAMU KONDO (40)
MITSUO AKECHI (18)
HIDEMI KINOSHITA (19)
HITOSHI KAKIMOTO (27)
MASAHITO DATE (40)
TOMOAKI IWAKURA (49)
YOUKO HIGUCHI (20)
SHIGEMASA KUSUNOKI (46)
KENYA UESUGI (26)
BTOOOM!
LIFE AND DEATH
22
HEITAROU TOUGOU (45)
KAGUYA (11)
MIKIO YANAGIDA (18)
TOSHIROU AMAKUSA (48)
HIKARU SOGA (25)
KATSUTOSHI SHIBATA (55)
SHOUKO KIYOSHI (28)
MACHIKO ONO (80)
SOUSUKE OKITA (23)
TSUBONE KASUGA (19)
YORIMICHI OOKUBO (54)
AKIYO YOSANO (69)
SEISHIROU YOSHIOKA (21)

BTOOOM!

JUNYA INOUE

22

CHARACTER

YOUKO HIGUCHI

GENDER: Female
AGE: 20
BLOOD TYPE: A
JOB: Actress
HOME: Kanagawa

Before she was taken to the island, she was active as a popular porn star who went by the name of "Kazuha." She has the uncanny ability to tell when someone's lying. She's a member of Tougou's team and likes strong men. When she made advances on Tougou, he turned her down due to his impotence.

KOUSUKE KIRA

GENDER: Male
AGE: 14
BLOOD TYPE: AB
JOB: Junior high student
HOME: Tokyo

This junior high student harbors a dark, brutal, murderous past. On the island, he blew up his own father and is genuinely enjoying this murderous game of "BTOOOM!". He's always been a big fan of the online version of the game, and his dream is to defeat "SAKAMOTO," a top world ranker. Unfortunately, he keeps failing at it. He joins Tougou's team and has grown up a little by doing so.

RYOUTA SAKAMOTO

GENDER: Male
AGE: 22
BLOOD TYPE: B
JOB: Unemployed
HOME: Tokyo

After spending every day cooped up in his home gaming online, he suddenly finds himself forced to participate in "BTOOOM! GAMERS," a killing game taking place on a mysterious uninhabited island. As a world ranker in the online third-person shooter "BTOOOM!", he uses his experience and natural instincts to survive and concoct a plan to get off the island along with his comrades, only for it to end in failure. While wallowing in despair, he arrives at the Sanctuary alone, where he teams up with Kaguya and Soga to beat Torio.

KAGUYA

GENDER: Female
AGE: 11
BLOOD TYPE: AB
JOB: Grade schooler
HOME: Tokyo

A mysterious little girl who came across Sakamoto when he washed ashore. She doesn't speak and uses a tablet to communicate. She's the figurehead of the Order of Moonlight, a religious cult. She can see dead people. In the Sanctuary, she worked with Sakamoto and Soga to defeat the real villain behind the tragedies, Torio.

KENYA UESUGI

GENDER: Male
AGE: 26
BLOOD TYPE: AB
JOB: Office worker
HOME: Tokyo

A cowardly and easily flattered young man who used to dream of becoming an actor. He was almost killed by Kira, but he escaped thanks to Higuchi's lie-detecting ability. He was previously a part of Tougou's team.

HIMIKO

GENDER: Female
AGE: 15
BLOOD TYPE: B
JOB: High school student
HOME: Tokyo

A foreign high school girl who has teamed up with Sakamoto. She harbors a deep resentment against men after a sordid experience in her past, but after surviving some battles thanks to Sakamoto, she begins to trust him. Her character in the online version of "BTOOOM!" is actually married to Sakamoto's character, and she has fallen in love with the real Sakamoto too.

LONGER SCHWARITZ

GENDER: Male
AGE: 77
BLOOD TYPE: O
JOB: Capitalist
HOME: New York

A descendant of European aristocracy, he is a man of power who controls the world behind the scenes with his considerable capital. In order to more thoroughly control the online realm, he founds the THEMIS project and has high hopes for "BTOOOM! GAMERS."

TAKANOHASHI

GENDER: Male
AGE: 45
BLOOD TYPE: AB
JOB: Game planner
HOME: Hokkaido

An executive staff member at Tyrannos Japan, he is the leader behind all the development of the online and real-life versions of "BTOOOM! GAMERS." He considers Sakamoto a valuable player and debugger. As a result of Sakamoto's plan to hijack the helicopter, Takanohashi's precious game was almost forced to come to a premature end.

SEISHIROU YOSHIOKA

GENDER: Male
AGE: 21
BLOOD TYPE: A
JOB: Musician
HOME: Tokyo

Himiko's childhood friend and the lead vocalist of a popular band. He and his bandmates lured their fans — Himiko's classmates — into his apartment and raped them. He was later arrested. He is the reason behind both Himiko's distrust of men and her nomination for the island.

HISANOBU

GENDER: Male
AGE: 55
BLOOD TYPE: A
JOB: Unemployed
HOME: Tokyo

Yukie's new husband and Sakamoto's stepfather. He's worried about how much time his stepson spends up in his room and scolds him, only to be attacked. Having just been laid off, he racks up debt because of his praiseworthy efforts to preserve his family's lifestyle. However, Yukie is frail in body and mind and attempts to kill herself. Fate has dealt him an unfair card in life.

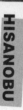

TSUNEAKI IIDA

GENDER: Male
AGE: 24
BLOOD TYPE: A
JOB: Programmer
HOME: Tokyo

An employee at Tyrannos Japan and Sakamoto's senpai from college. He's an excellent programmer and works under Takanohashi on the development of "BTOOOM! GAMERS." But he doesn't agree with the inhumane nature of the game and strategy and approached Sakamoto with the proposal to put a stop to the game's development, only for the plan to fall apart.

MATTHEW PERRIER

GENDER: Male
AGE: 27
BLOOD TYPE: O
JOB: Ex-NSA programmer, political refugee
HOME: Washington (location unknown after exile)

A former programmer with the NSA (U.S. National Security Agency), he's a capable hacker and curbed a number of cyber-crimes while with the NSA. But after learning about the government's darker side, he made off with sensitive data about the THEMIS project — in a way, the evidence of their nefarious plans — and defected to another country.

CONTENTS

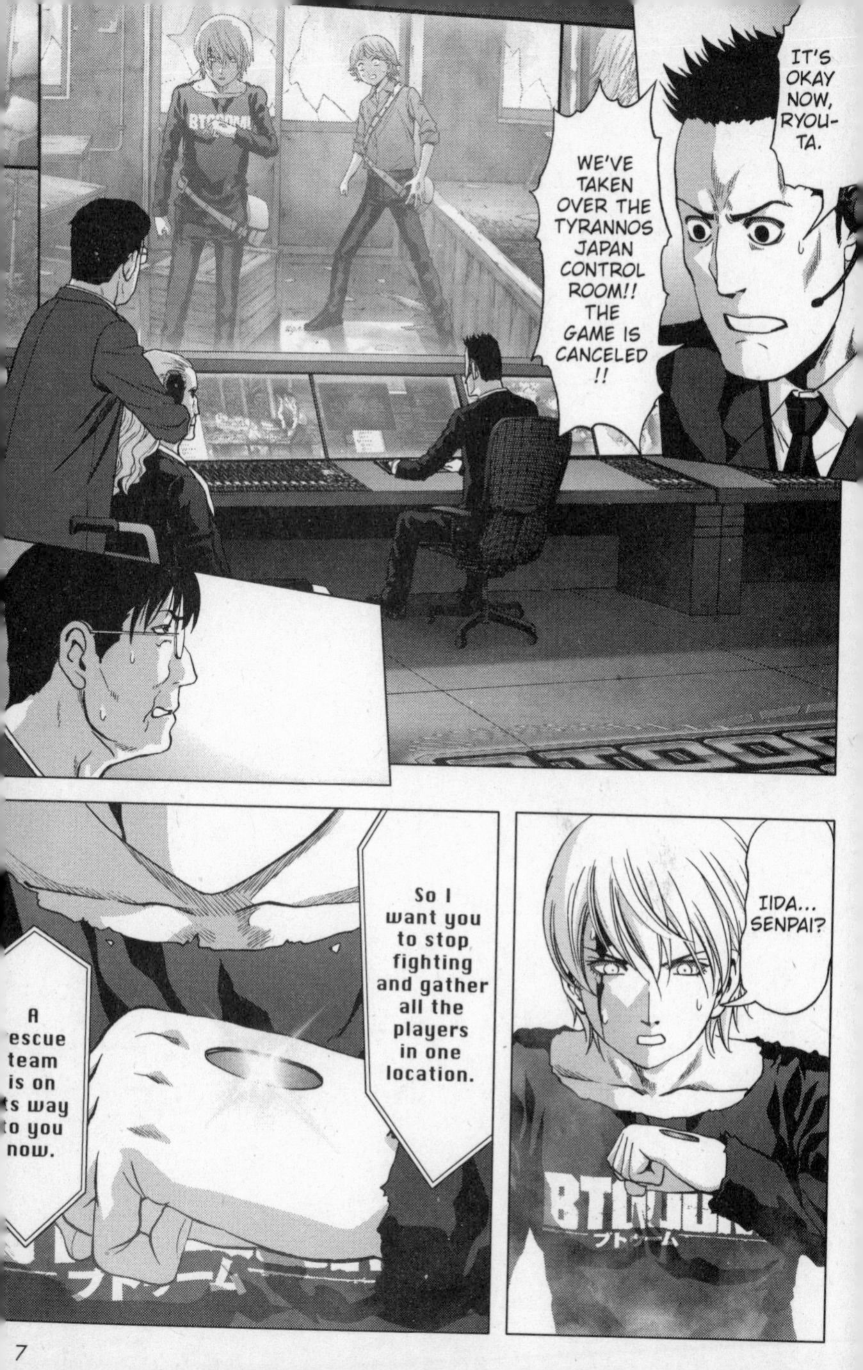
IT'S OKAY NOW, RYOUTA.
WE'VE TAKEN OVER THE TYRANNOS JAPAN CONTROL ROOM!! THE GAME IS CANCELED!!
IIDA... SENPAI?
A escue team is on ts way o you now.
So I want you to stop fighting and gather all the players in one location.

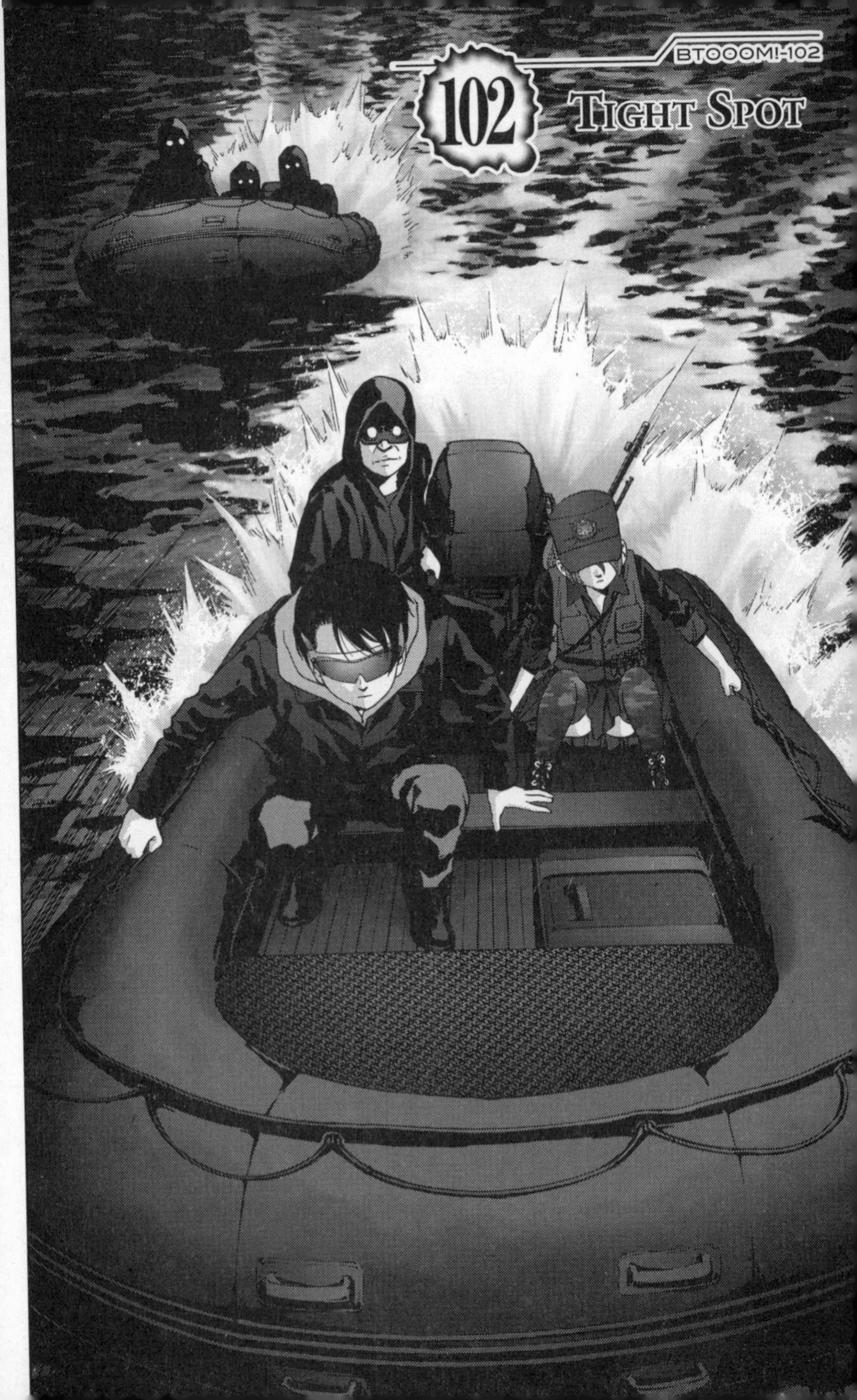
BTOOOM!-102
102
TIGHT SPOT

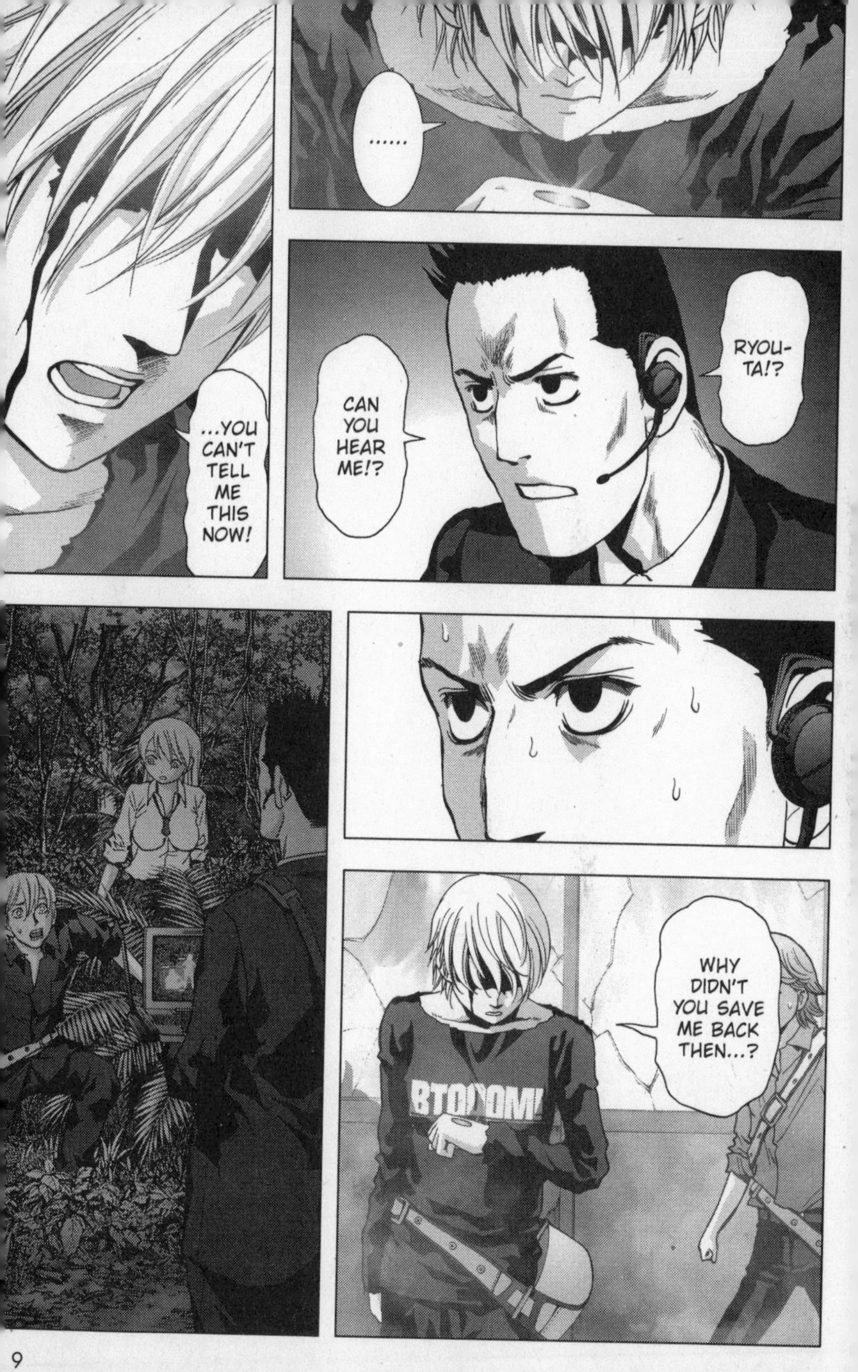
......
RYOU-TA!?
CAN YOU HEAR ME!?
...YOU CAN'T TELL ME THIS NOW!
WHY DIDN'T YOU SAVE ME BACK THEN...?

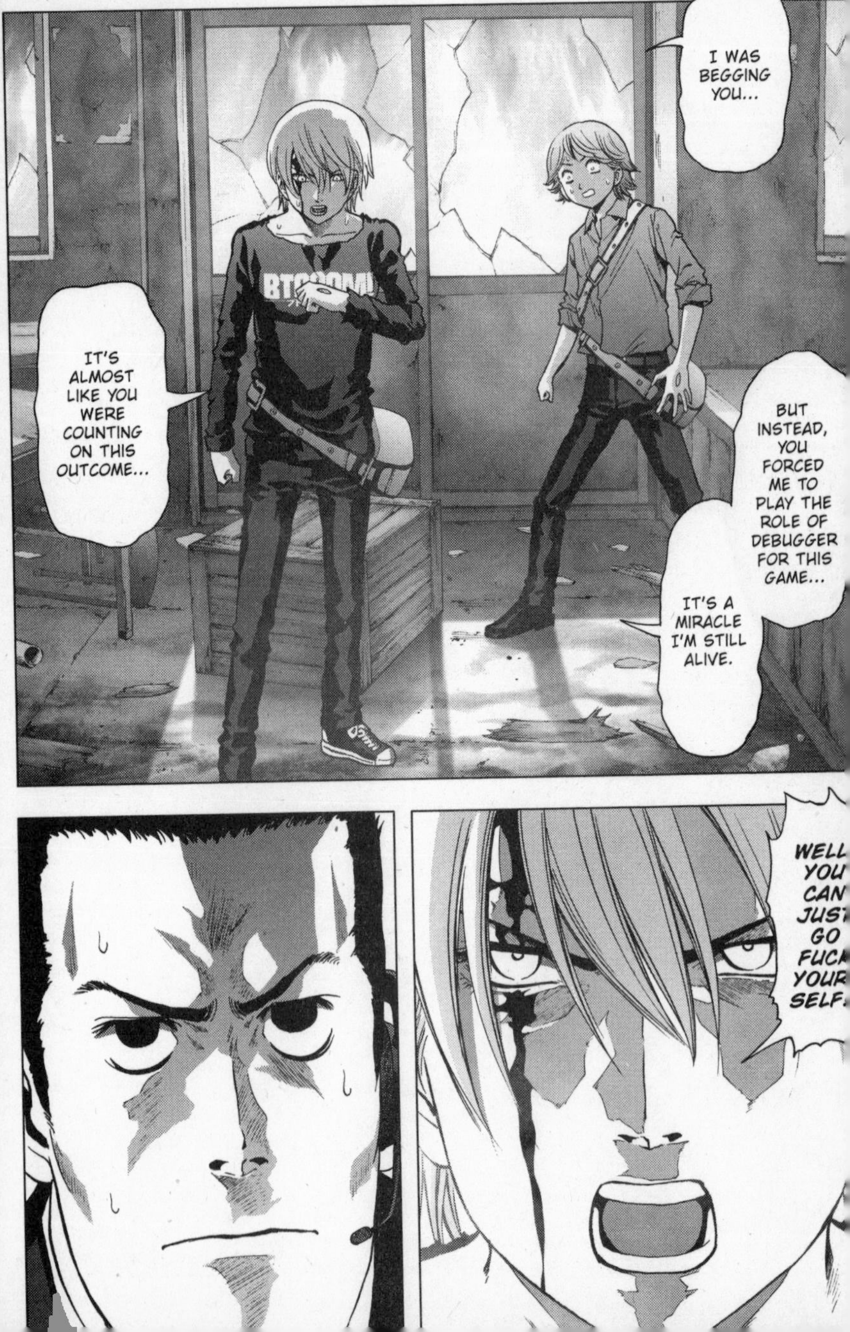
I WAS BEGGING YOU...
BUT INSTEAD, YOU FORCED ME TO PLAY THE ROLE OF DEBUGGER FOR THIS GAME...
IT'S A MIRACLE I'M STILL ALIVE.
IT'S ALMOST LIKE YOU WERE COUNTING ON THIS OUTCOME...
WELL YOU CAN JUST GO FUCK YOURSELF.

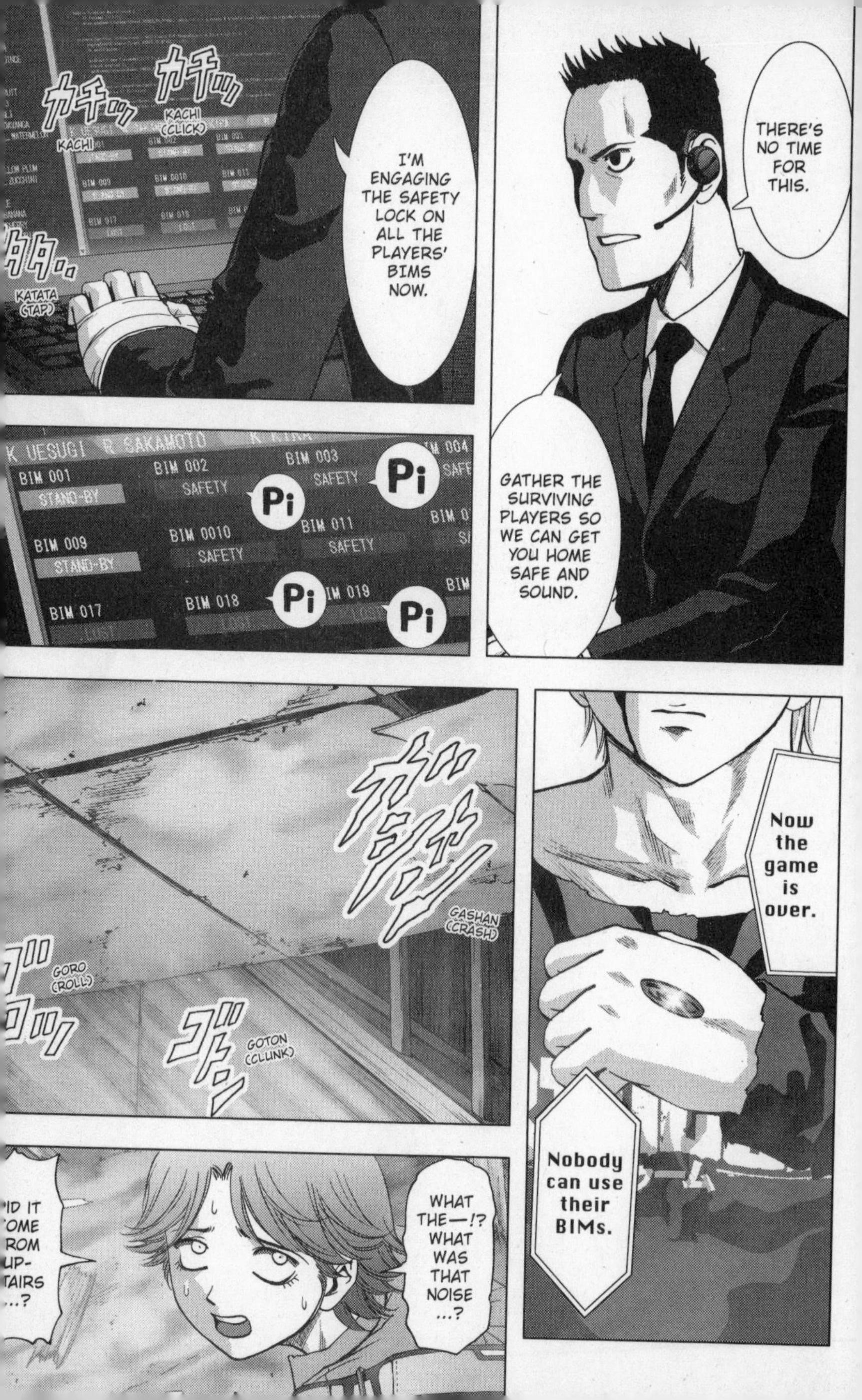
THERE'S NO TIME FOR THIS.
GATHER THE SURVIVING PLAYERS SO WE CAN GET YOU HOME SAFE AND SOUND.
KACHI (CLICK)
KACHI
I'M ENGAGING THE SAFETY LOCK ON ALL THE PLAYERS' BIMS NOW.
KATATA (TAP)
K UESUGI R SAKAMOTO
BIM 001 STAND-BY
BIM 002 SAFETY
BIM 003 SAFETY
BIM 009 STAND-BY
BIM 0010 SAFETY
BIM 011 SAFETY
BIM 017 LOST
BIM 018 LOST
BIM 019 LOST
Pi
Pi
Pi
Pi
Now the game is over.
Nobody can use their BIMs.
GASHAN (CRASH)
GORO (ROLL)
GOTON (CLUNK)
WHAT THE—!? WHAT WAS THAT NOISE ...?
DID IT COME FROM UP-STAIRS ...?

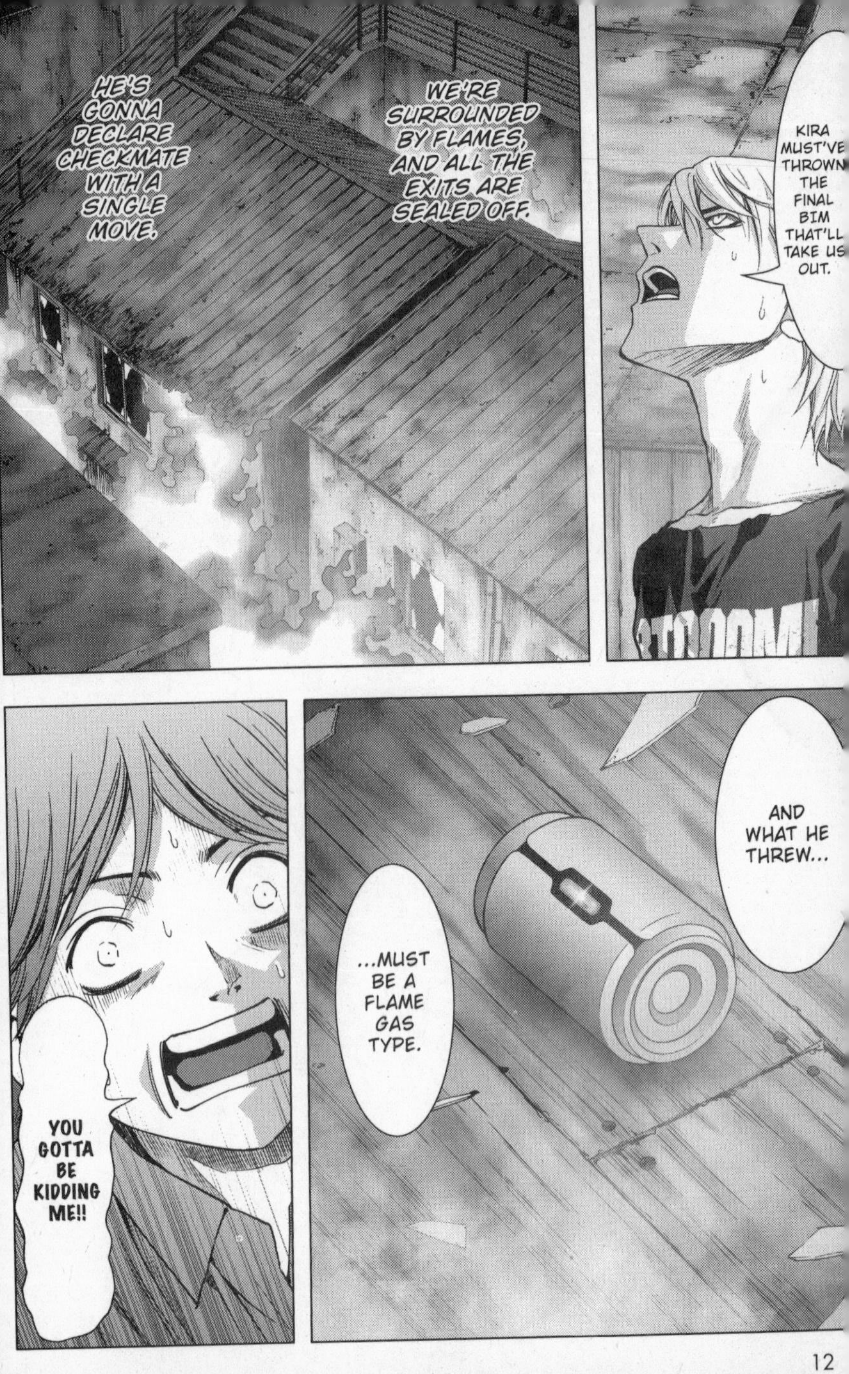
KIRA MUST'VE THROWN THE FINAL BIM THAT'LL TAKE US OUT.
WE'RE SURROUNDED BY FLAMES, AND ALL THE EXITS ARE SEALED OFF.
HE'S GONNA DECLARE CHECKMATE WITH A SINGLE MOVE.
AND WHAT HE THREW...
...MUST BE A FLAME GAS TYPE.
YOU GOTTA BE KIDDING ME!!

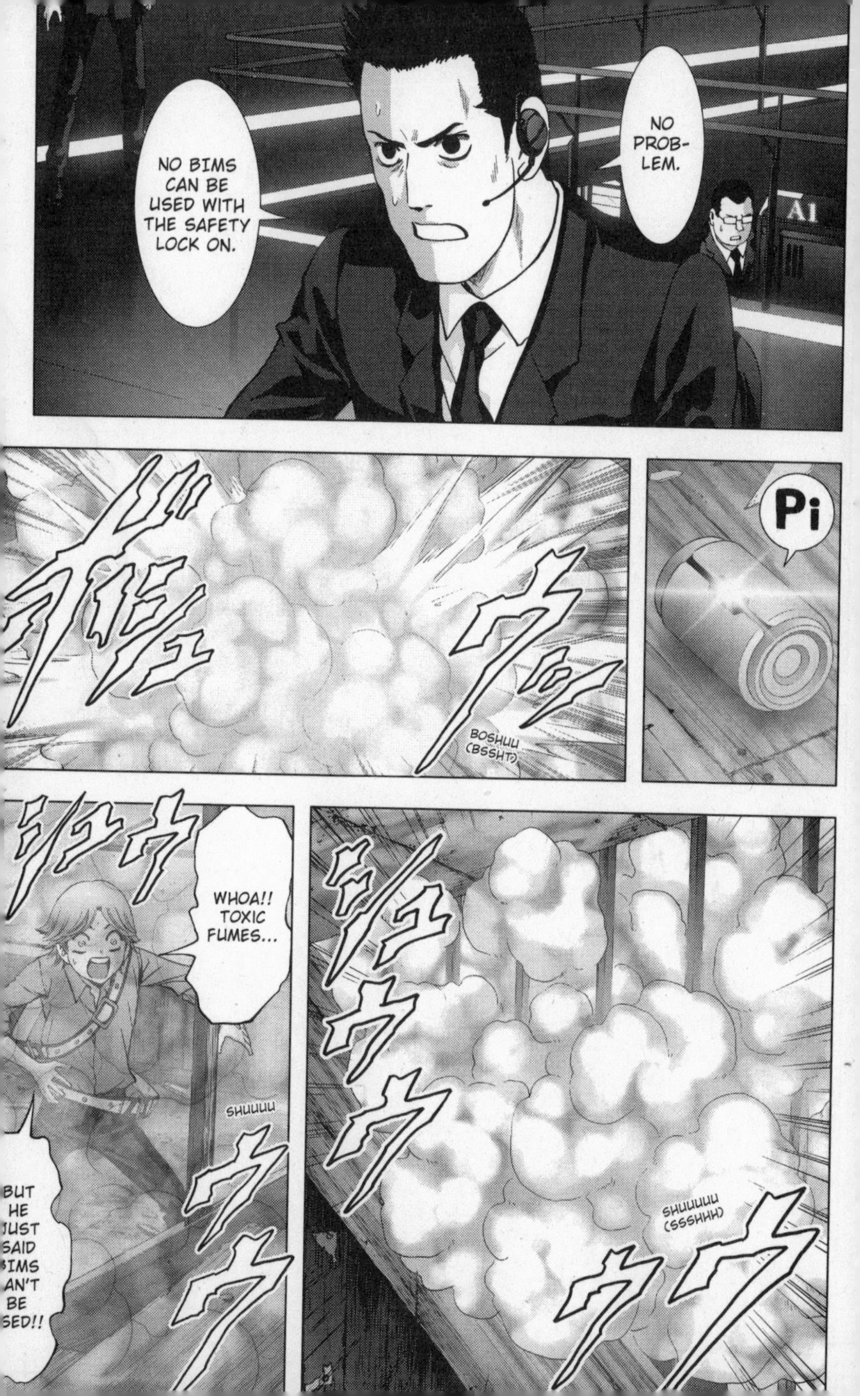
NO PROBLEM.
NO BIMS CAN BE USED WITH THE SAFETY LOCK ON.
Pi
BOSHUU (BSSHT)
SHUUUUU (SSSHHH)
WHOA!! TOXIC FUMES...
SHUUUU
BUT HE JUST SAID BIMS AN'T BE SED!!

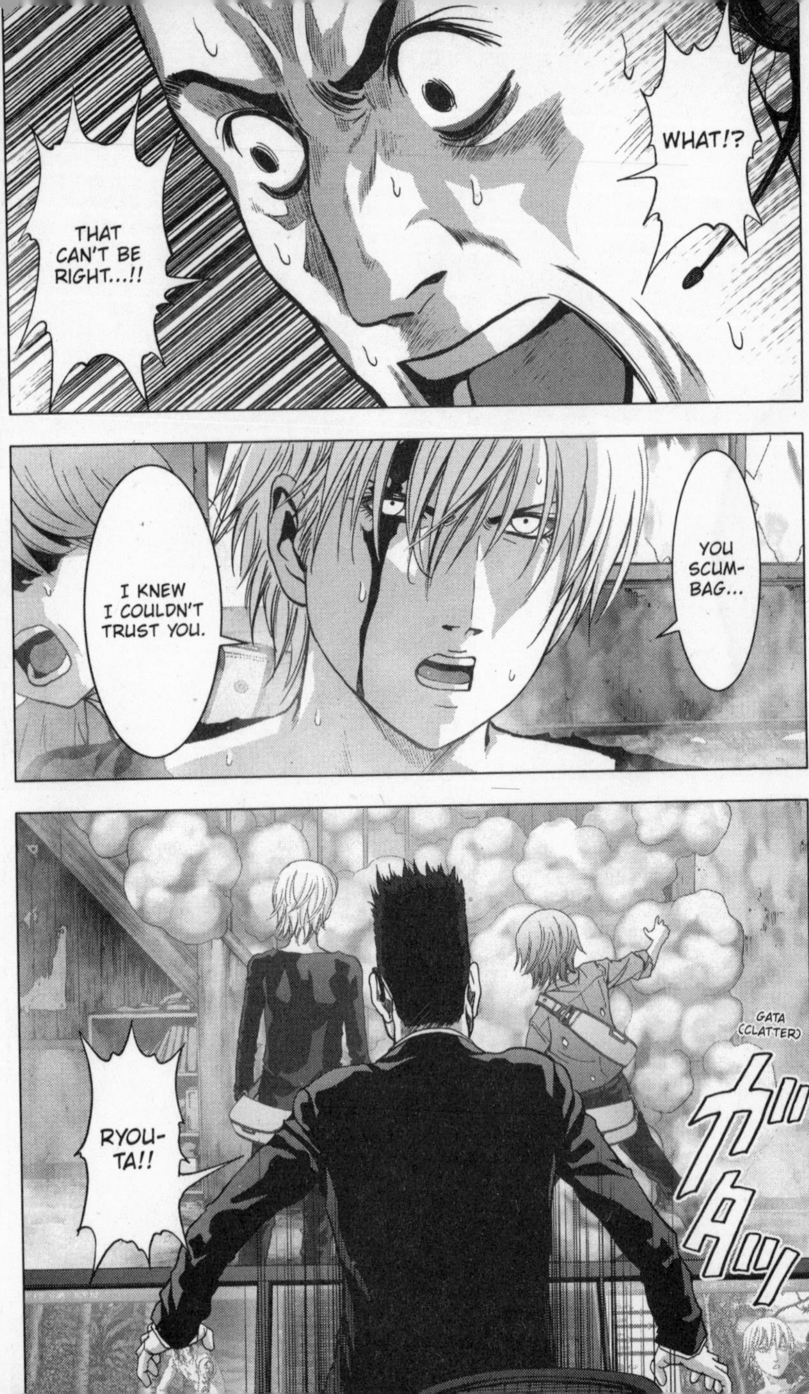
WHAT!?
THAT CAN'T BE RIGHT...!!
YOU SCUM-BAG...
I KNEW I COULDN'T TRUST YOU.
GATA (CLATTER)
RYOU-TA!!

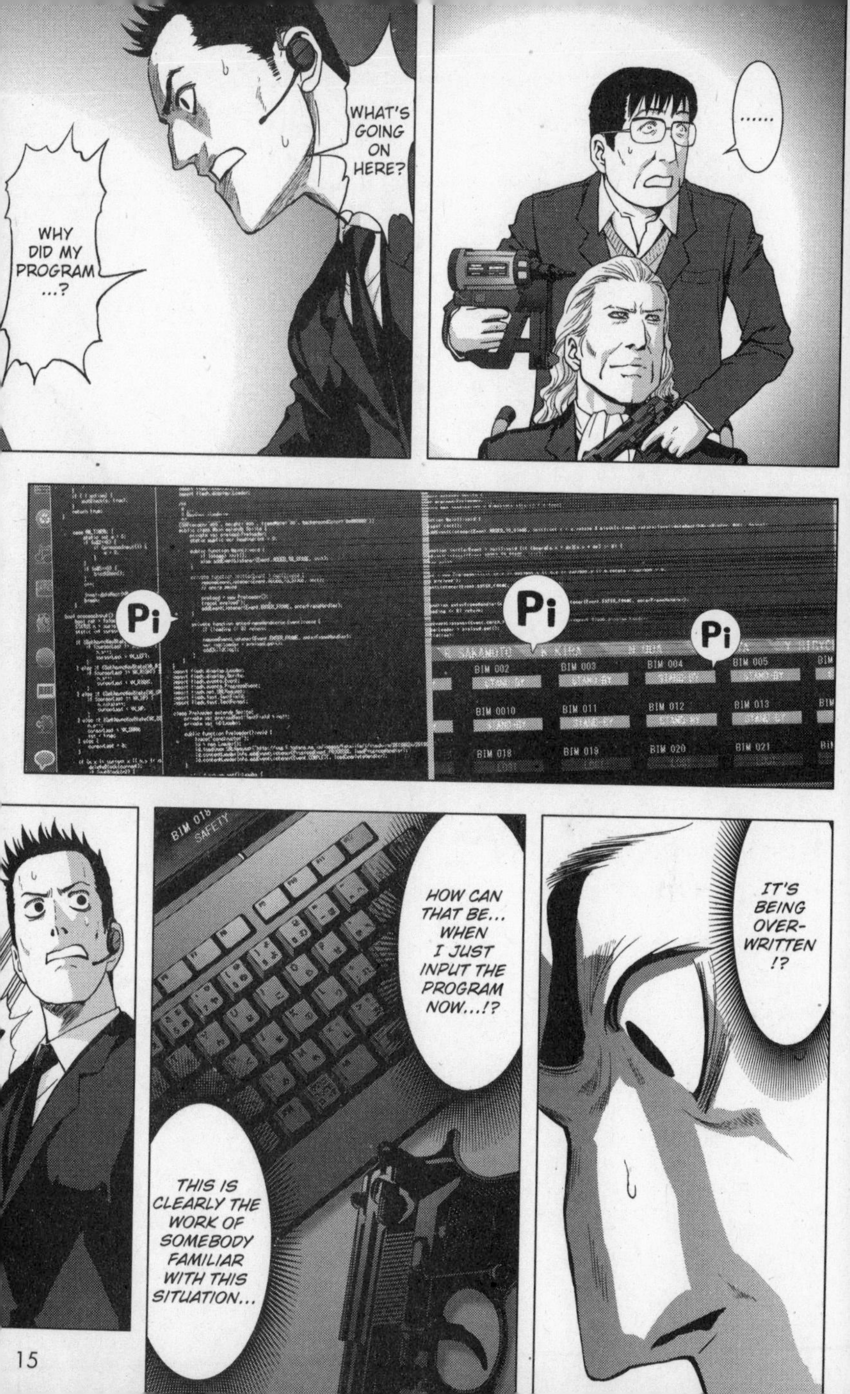
......
WHAT'S GOING ON HERE?
WHY DID MY PROGRAM ...?
Pi
Pi
Pi
IT'S BEING OVER-WRITTEN !?
BIM 018 SAFETY
HOW CAN THAT BE... WHEN I JUST INPUT THE PROGRAM NOW...!?
THIS IS CLEARLY THE WORK OF SOMEBODY FAMILIAR WITH THIS SITUATION...

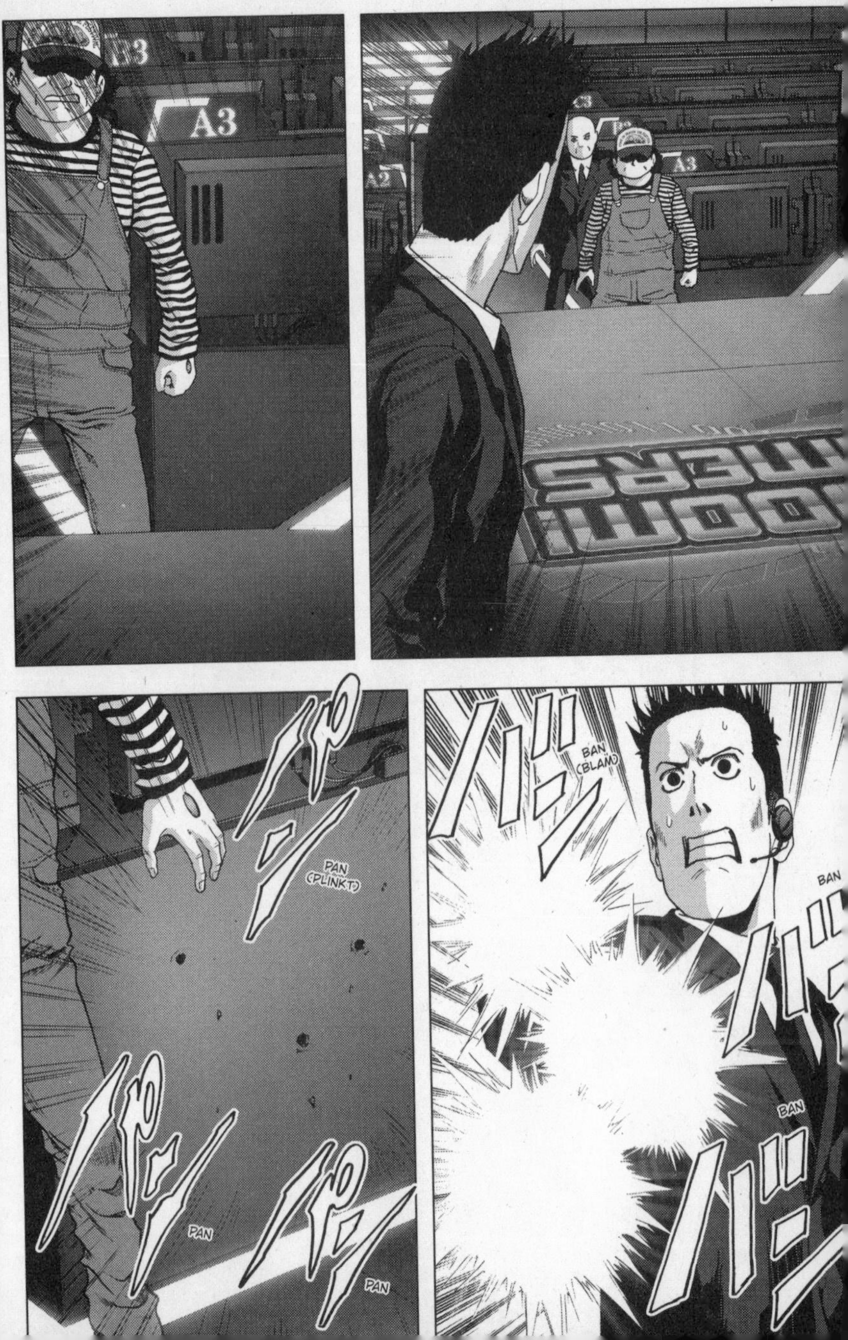
BAN (BLAM)
BAN
BAN
PAN (PLINKT)
PAN
PAN

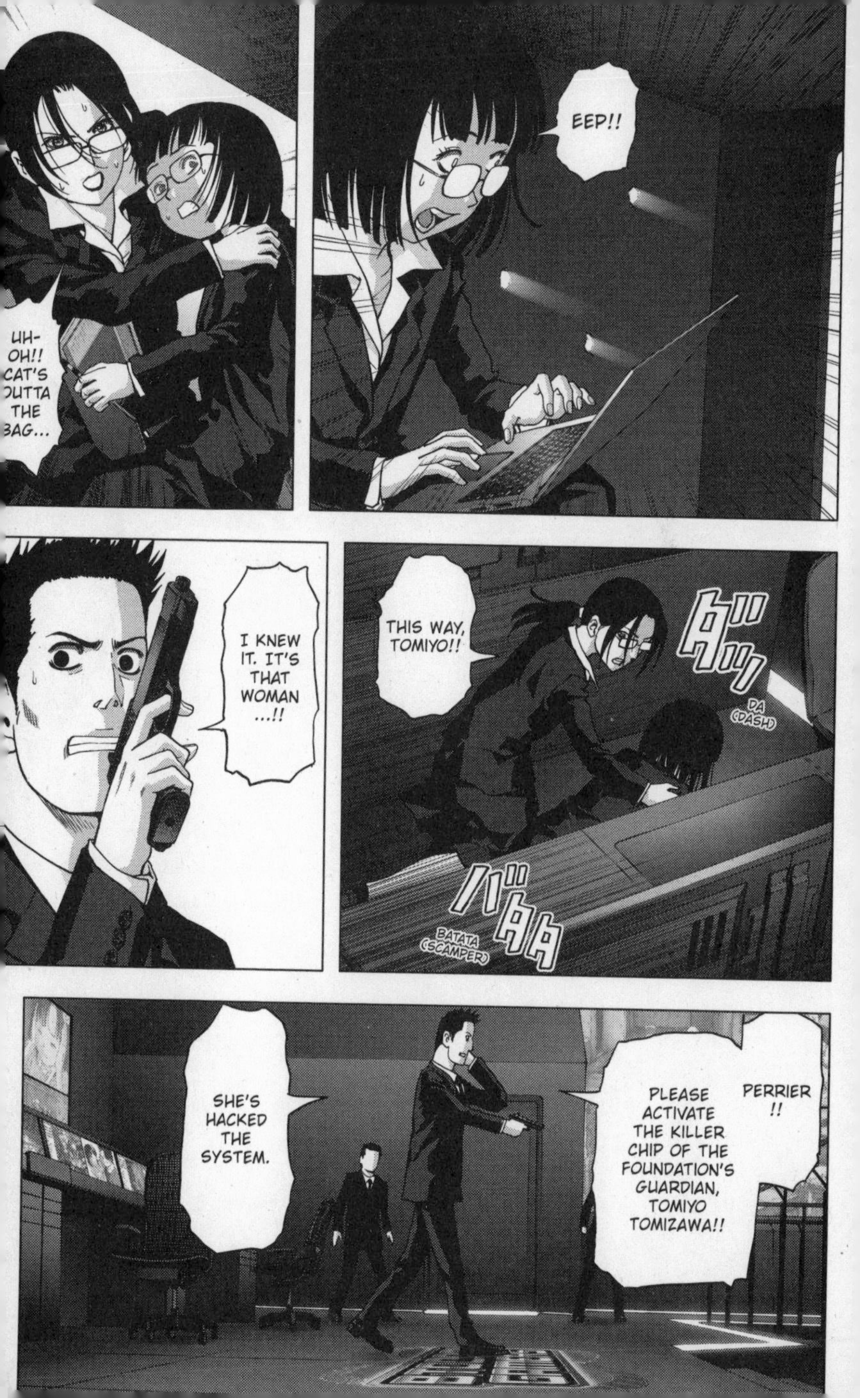
EEP!!
UH-OH!! CAT'S OUTTA THE BAG...
THIS WAY, TOMIYO!!
DA (DASH)
BATATA (SCAMPER)
I KNEW IT. IT'S THAT WOMAN ...!!
PERRIER !!
PLEASE ACTIVATE THE KILLER CHIP OF THE FOUNDATION'S GUARDIAN, TOMIYO TOMIZAWA!!
SHE'S HACKED THE SYSTEM.

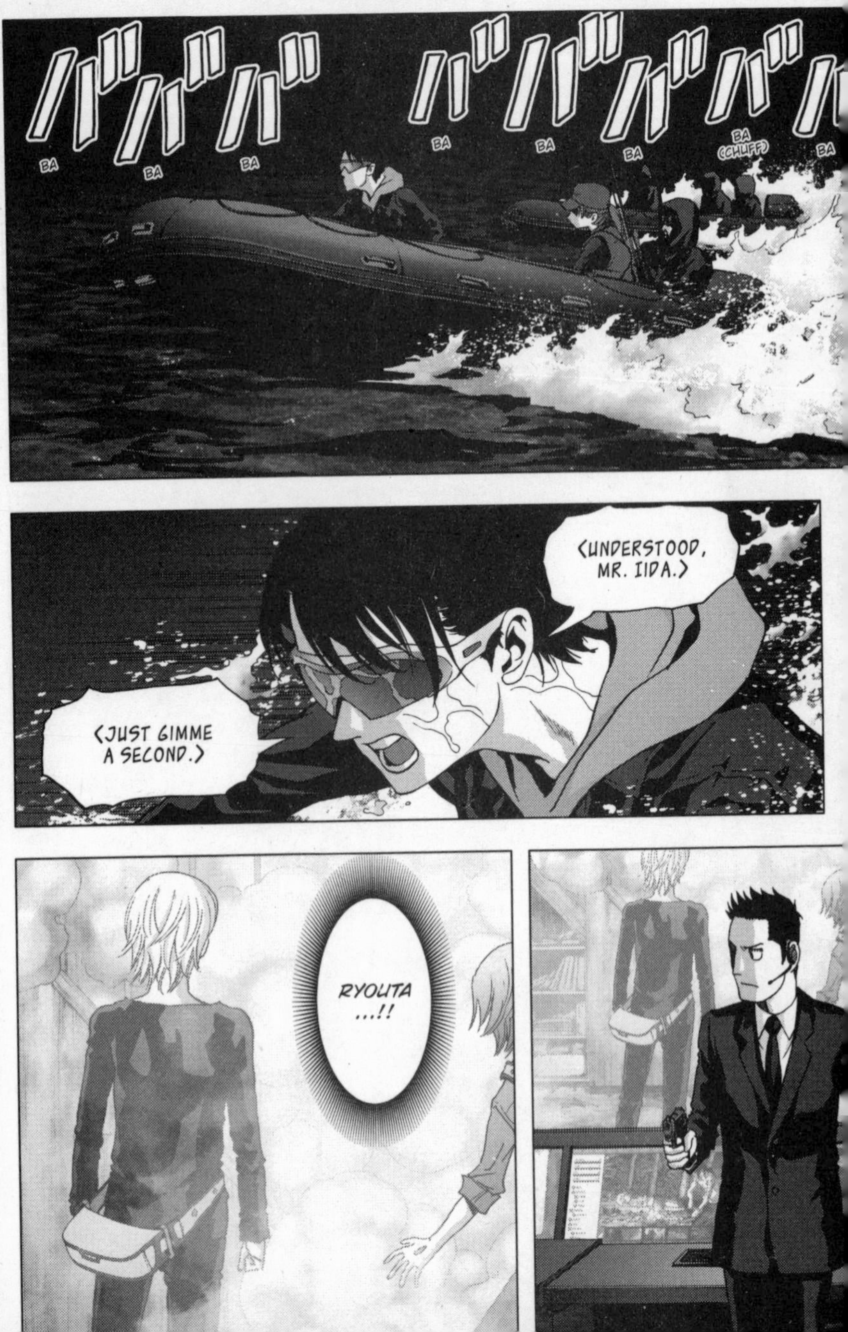
BA
BA
(CHUFF)
BA
BA
BA
BA
BA
BA
BA
<UNDERSTOOD, MR. IIDA.>
<JUST GIMME A SECOND.>
RYOUTA ...!!

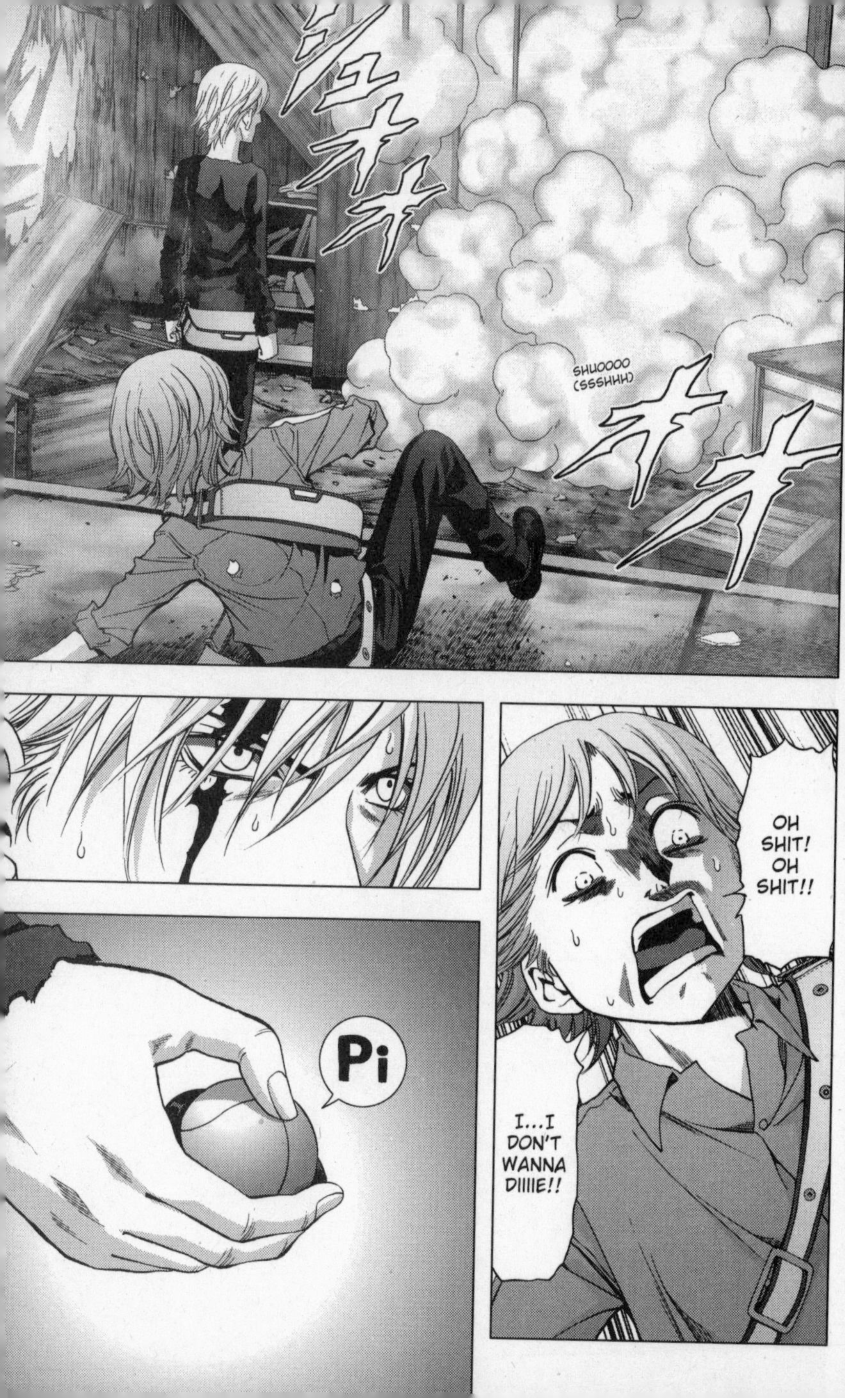
シュオォォ
オォ
SHUOOOO (SSSHHH)
OH SHIT! OH SHIT!!
I...I DON'T WANNA DIIIIE!!
Pi

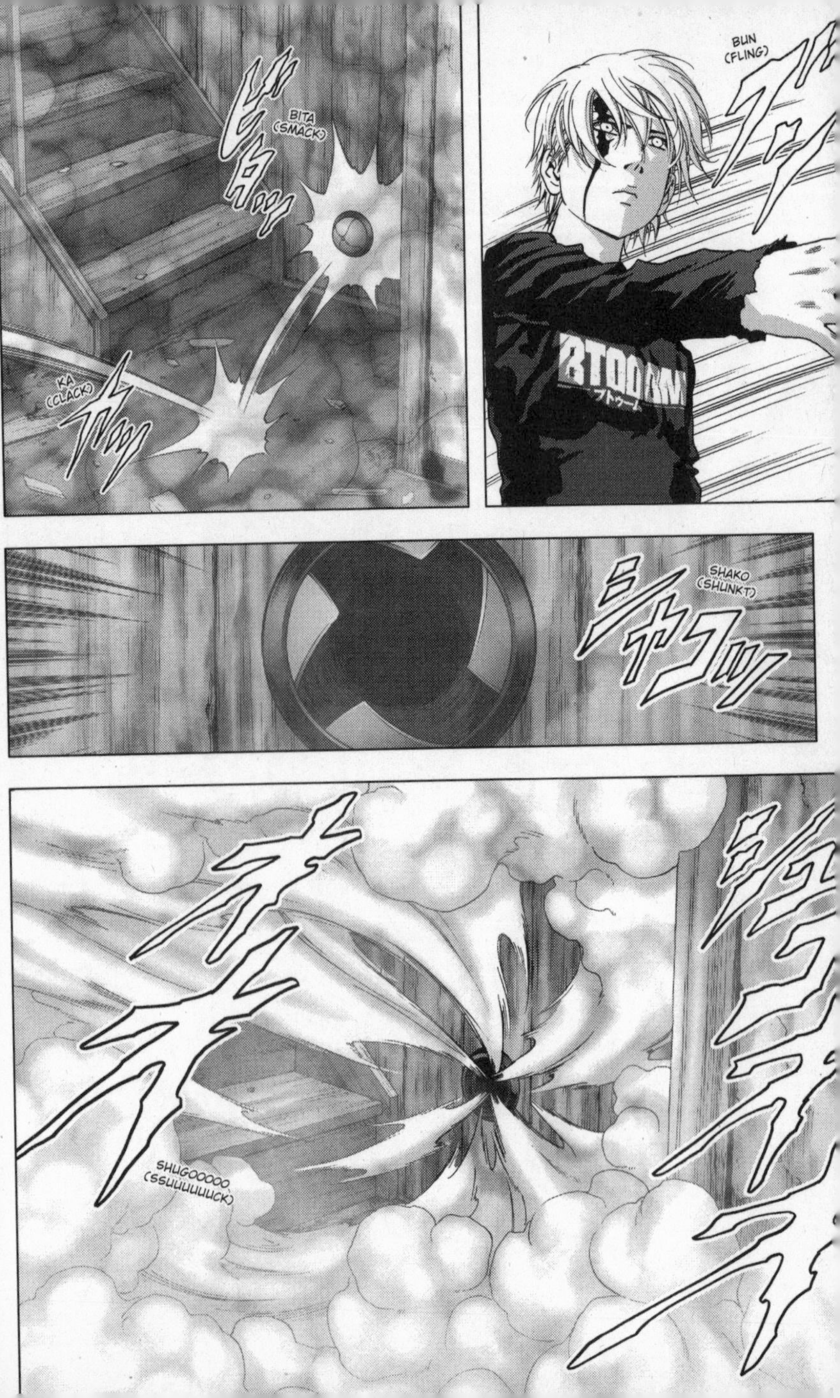
BUN
(FLING)
BITA
(SMACK)
KA
(CLACK)
SHAKO
(SHUNKT)
SHUGOOOOO
(SSUUUUUUUCK)

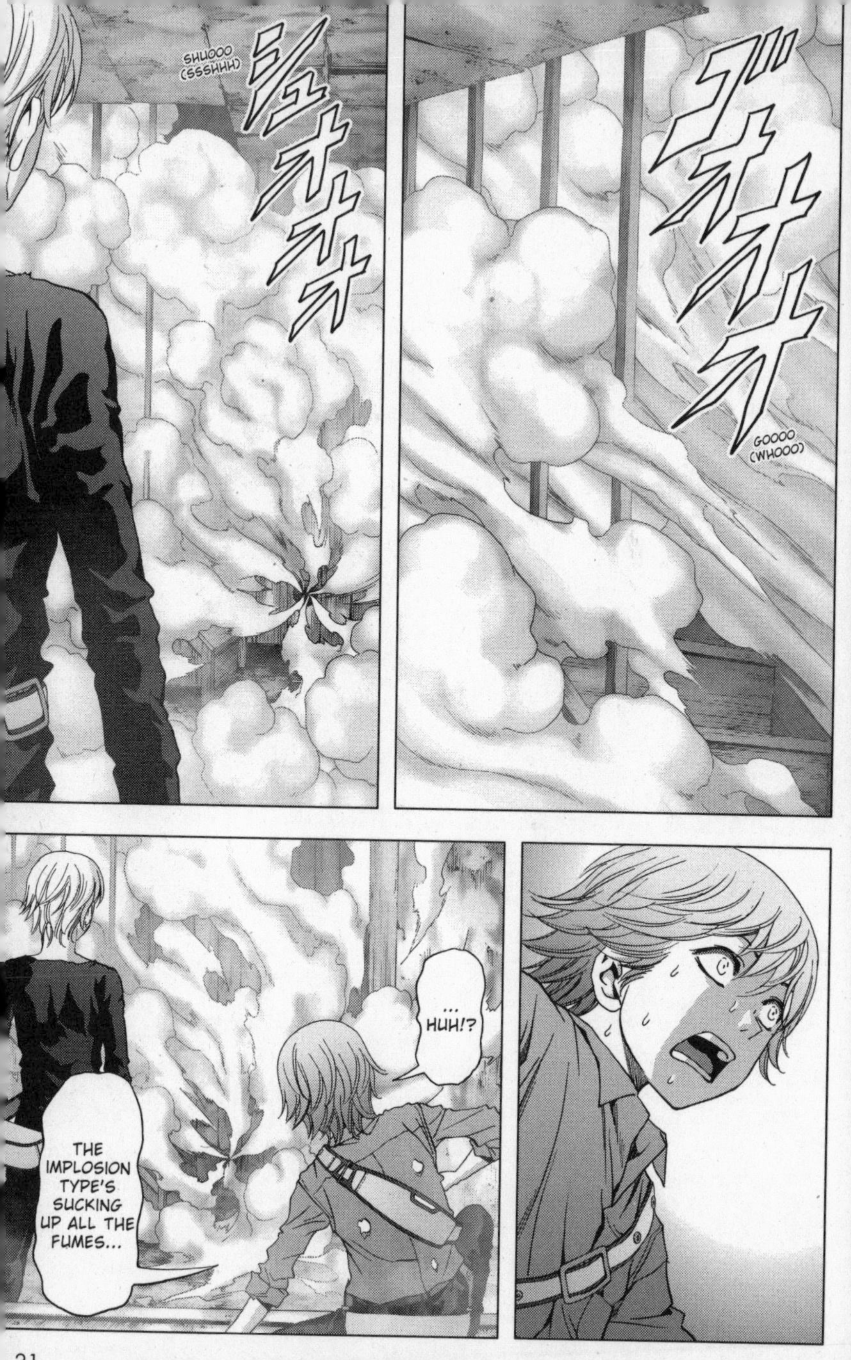
ゴオオオ
GOOOO (WHOOO)
シュオオオ
SHUOOO (SSSHHH)
... HUH!?
THE IMPLOSION TYPE'S SUCKING UP ALL THE FUMES...

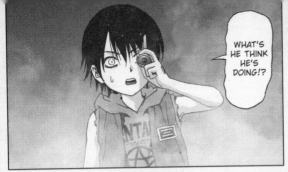

WHAT'S HE THINK HE'S DOING!?
SAKA-MOTO...
WHY ISN'T HE RUNNING AWAY?
HAS HE GIVEN UP...?
NO... HE'S NOT THAT KINDA GUY.
HIS STANCE LOOKS SO TRIUMPHANT...
WHAT'S HE UP TO?

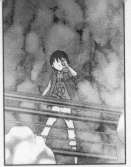

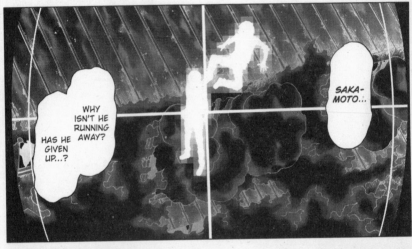

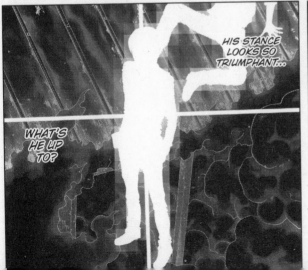

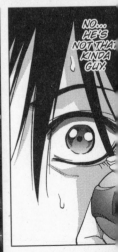

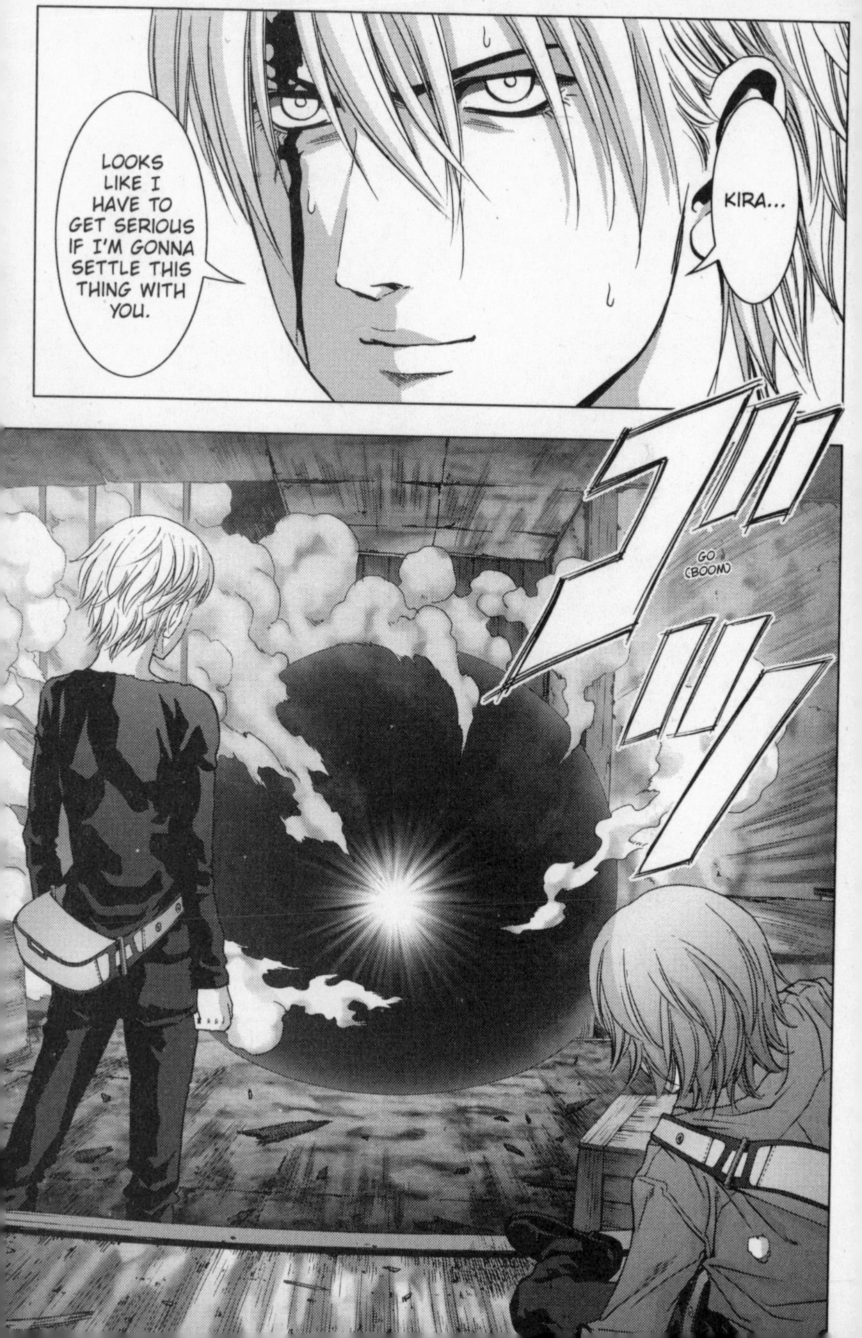
KIRA...
LOOKS LIKE I HAVE TO GET SERIOUS IF I'M GONNA SETTLE THIS THING WITH YOU.
GO (BOOM)

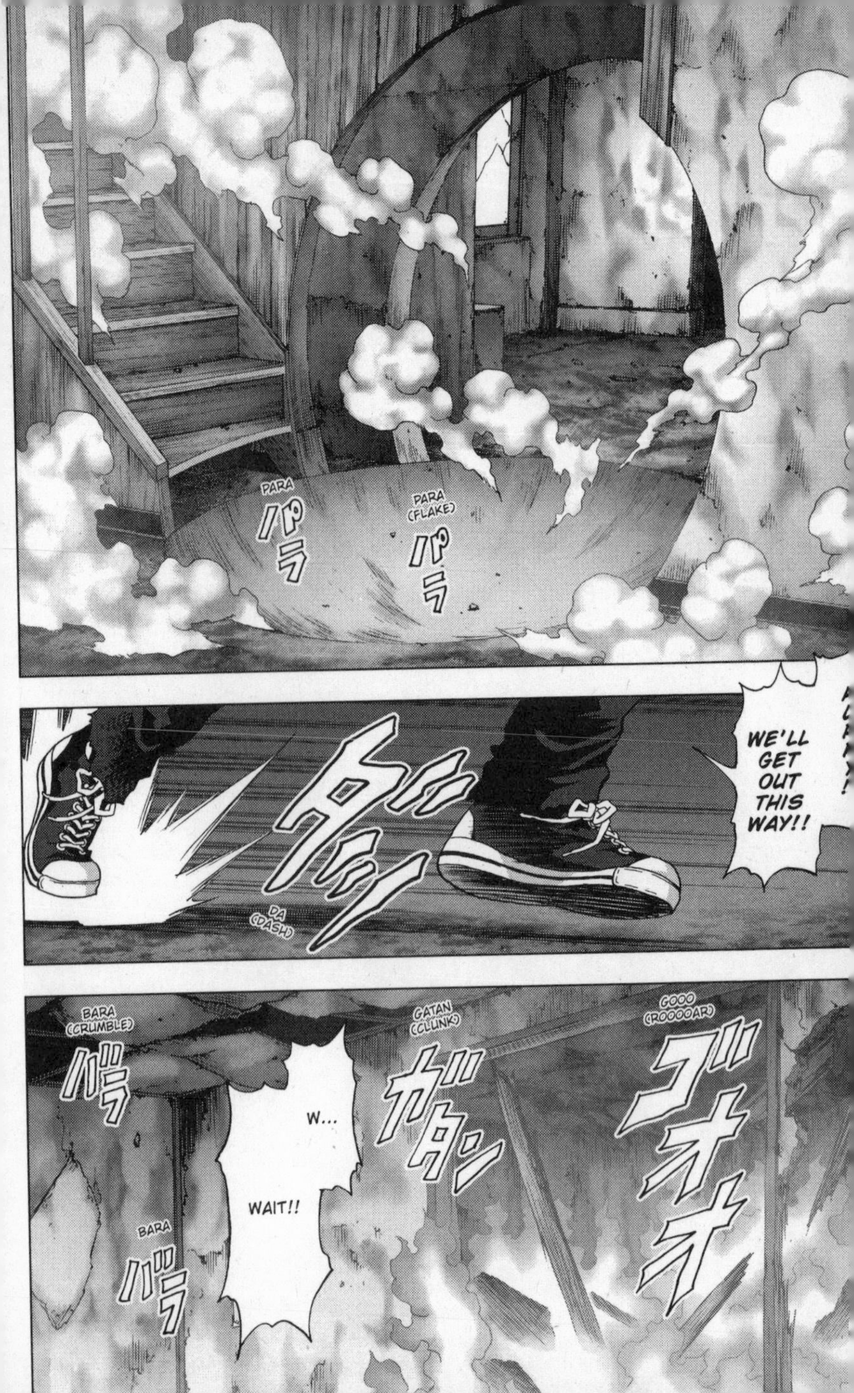
PARA (FLAKE)
パラ
PARA
パラ
WE'LL GET OUT THIS WAY!!
ダッ
DA (DASH)
GOOO (ROOOOAR)
ゴオオ
GATAN (CLUNK)
ガタン
W...
WAIT!!
BARA (CRUMBLE)
バラ
BARA
バラ

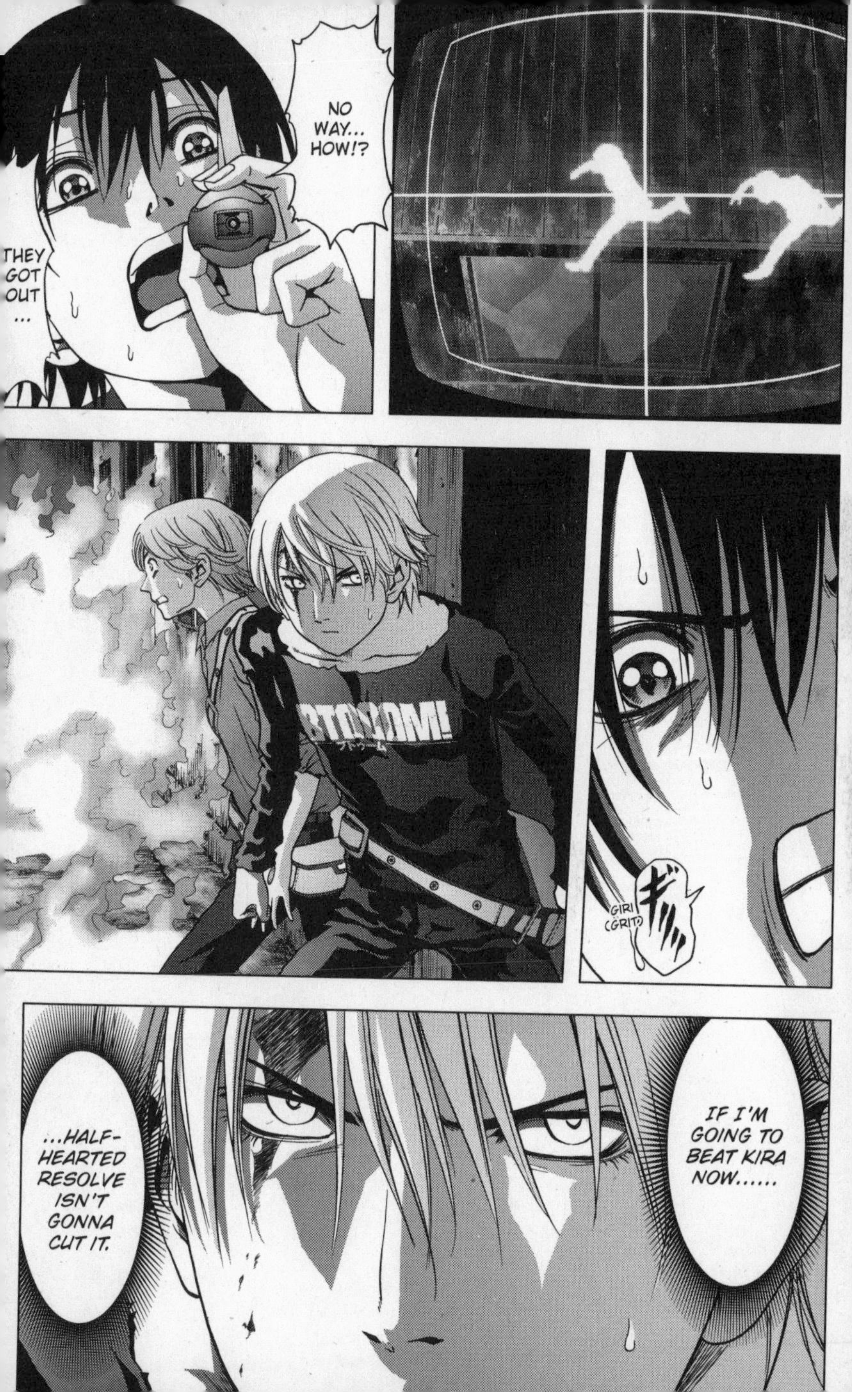
NO WAY... HOW!?
THEY GOT OUT ...
GIRI (GRIT)
IF I'M GOING TO BEAT KIRA NOW......
...HALF-HEARTED RESOLVE ISN'T GONNA CUT IT.

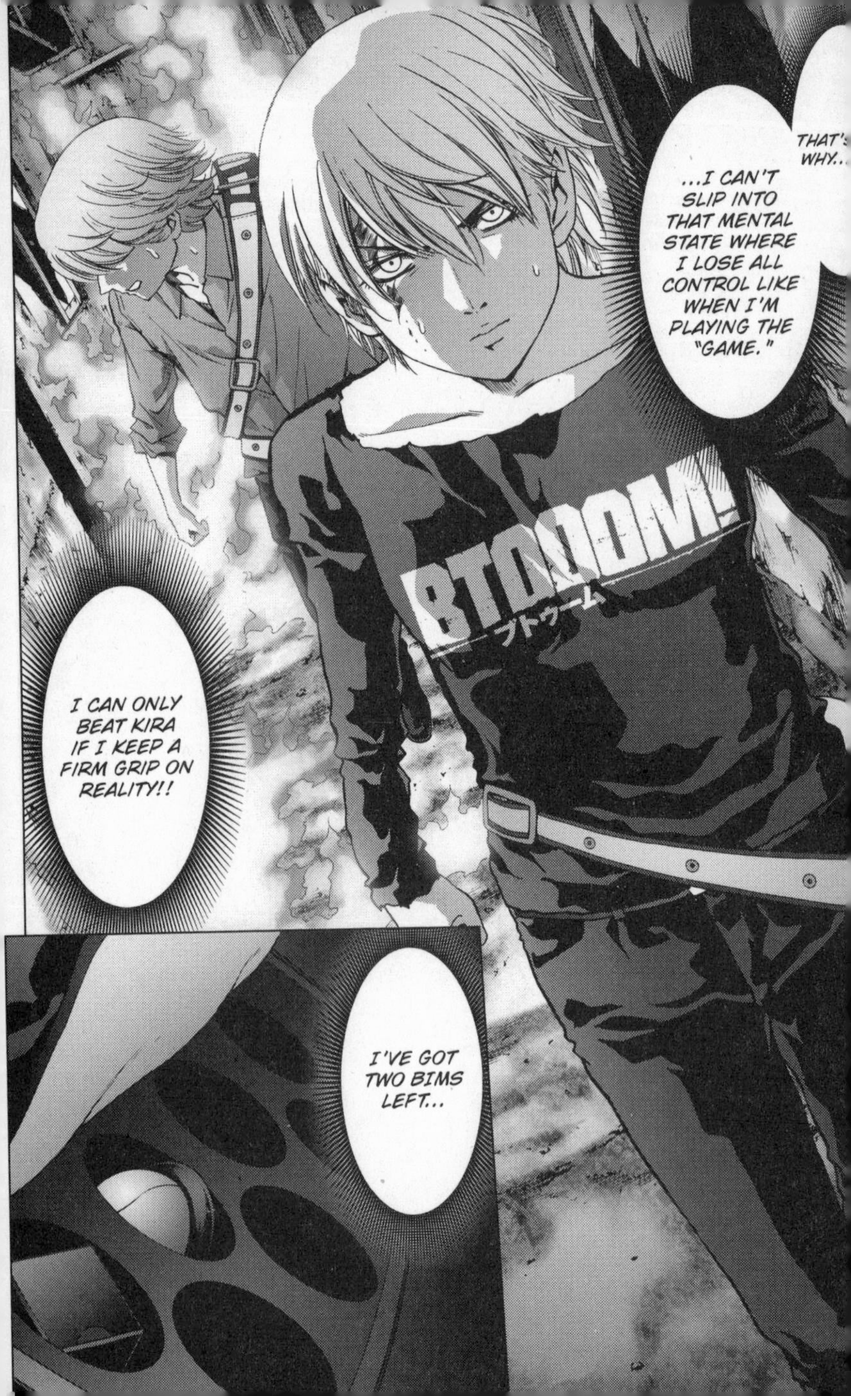
THAT'S WHY...
...I CAN'T SLIP INTO THAT MENTAL STATE WHERE I LOSE ALL CONTROL LIKE WHEN I'M PLAYING THE "GAME."
I CAN ONLY BEAT KIRA IF I KEEP A FIRM GRIP ON REALITY!!
I'VE GOT TWO BIMS LEFT...

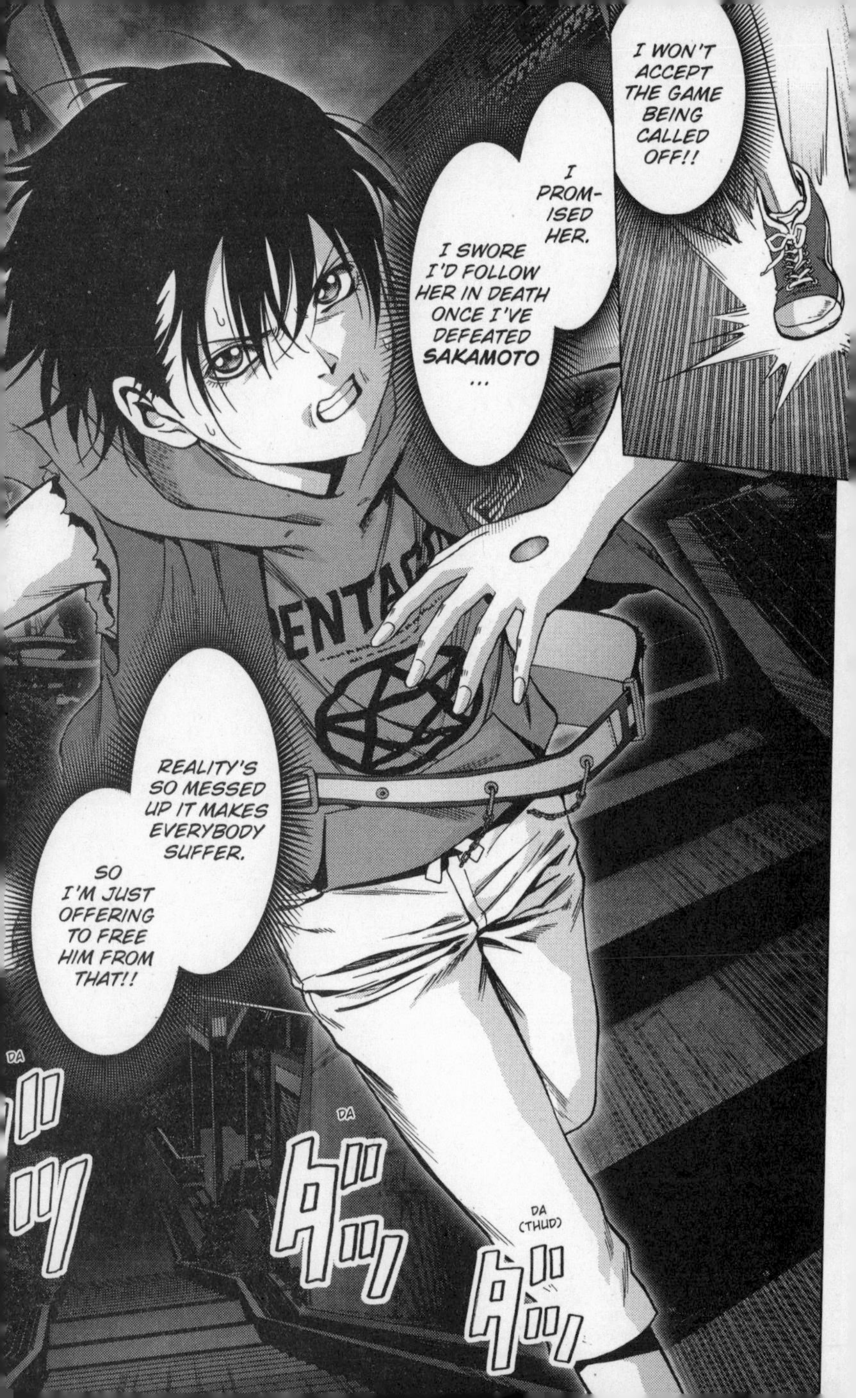
I WON'T ACCEPT THE GAME BEING CALLED OFF!!
I PROMISED HER.
I SWORE I'D FOLLOW HER IN DEATH ONCE I'VE DEFEATED SAKAMOTO...
REALITY'S SO MESSED UP IT MAKES EVERYBODY SUFFER.
SO I'M JUST OFFERING TO FREE HIM FROM THAT!!
DA
DA
DA (THUD)

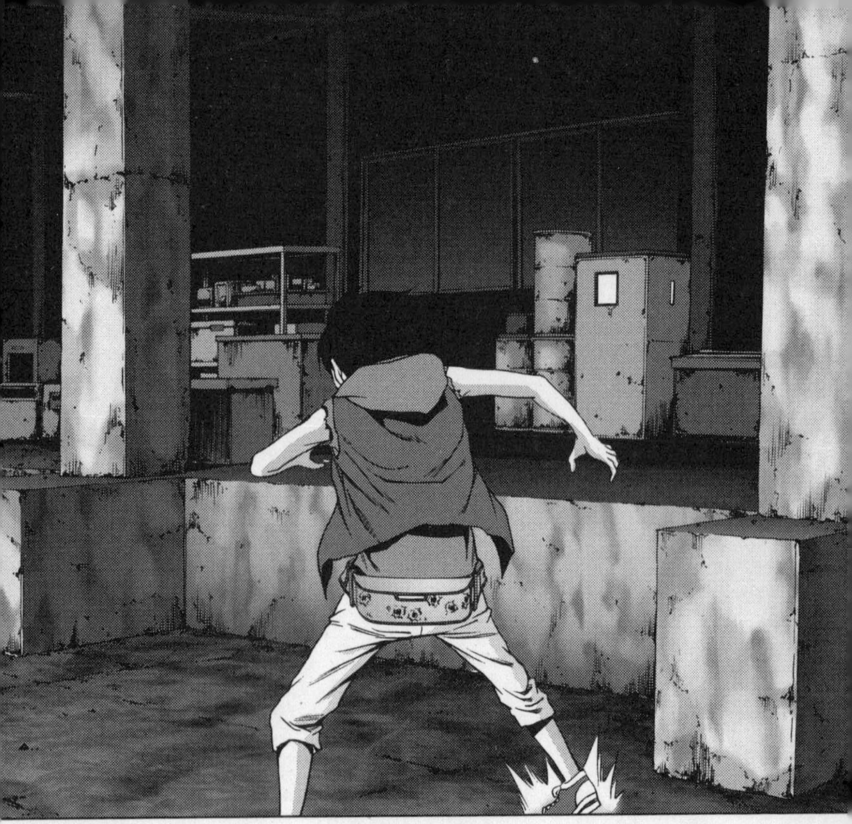

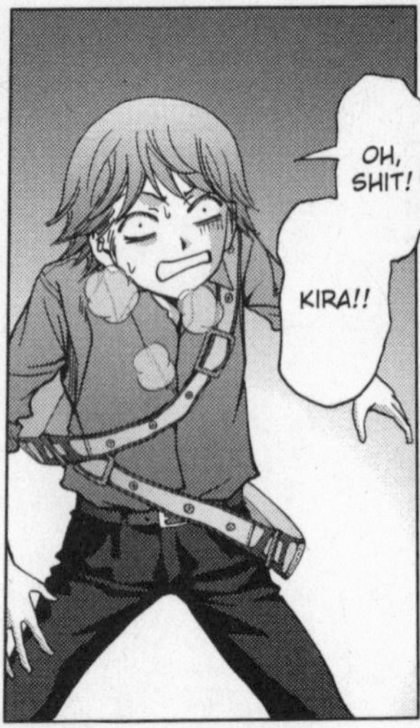
OH, SHIT!
KIRA!!

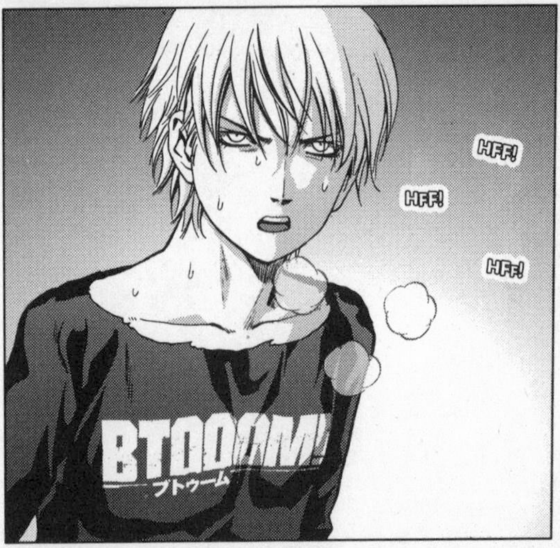
HFF!
HFF!
HFF!

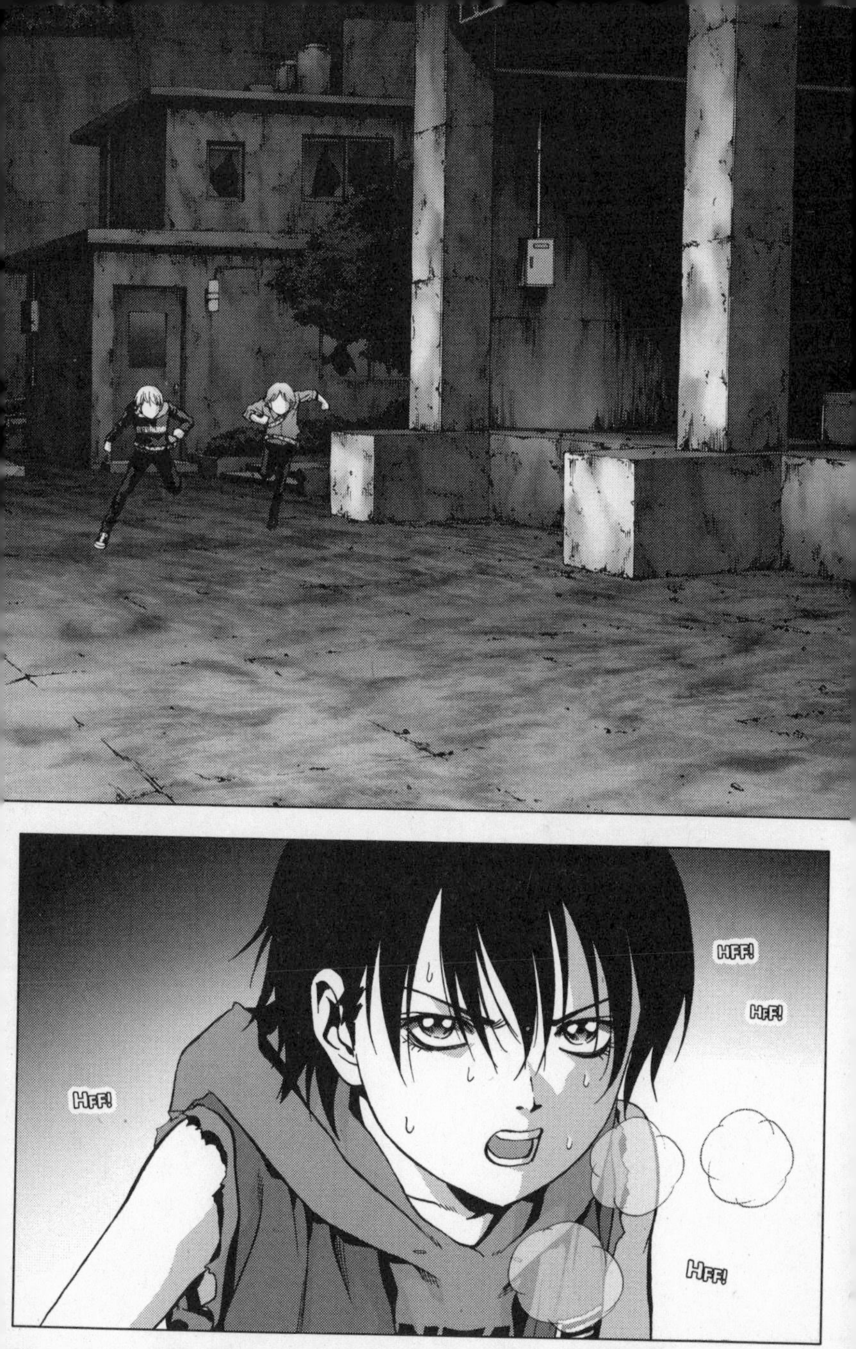
HFF!
HFF!
HFF!
HFF!

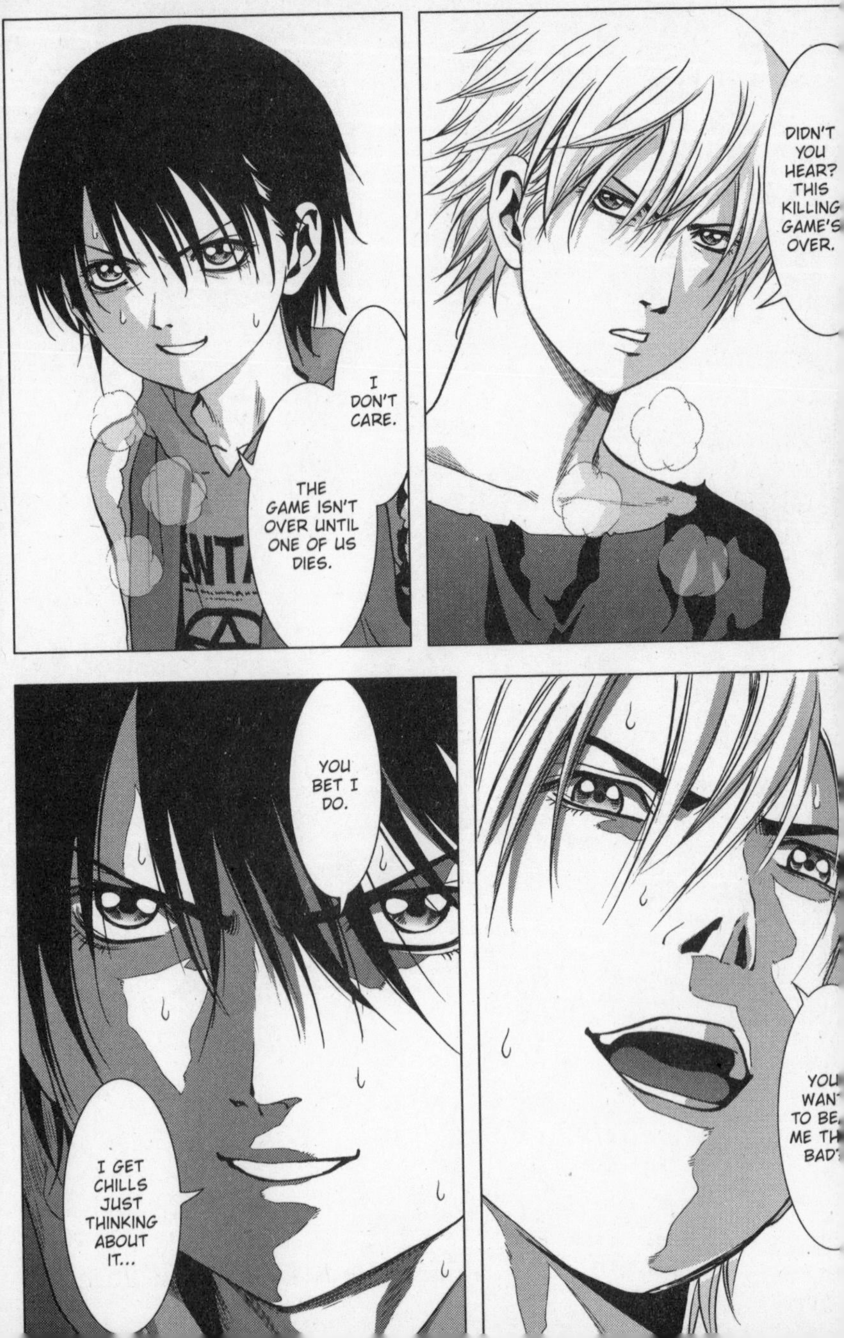
DIDN'T YOU HEAR? THIS KILLING GAME'S OVER.
I DON'T CARE.
THE GAME ISN'T OVER UNTIL ONE OF US DIES.
YOU WAN TO BE, ME TH BAD
YOU BET I DO.
I GET CHILLS JUST THINKING ABOUT IT...

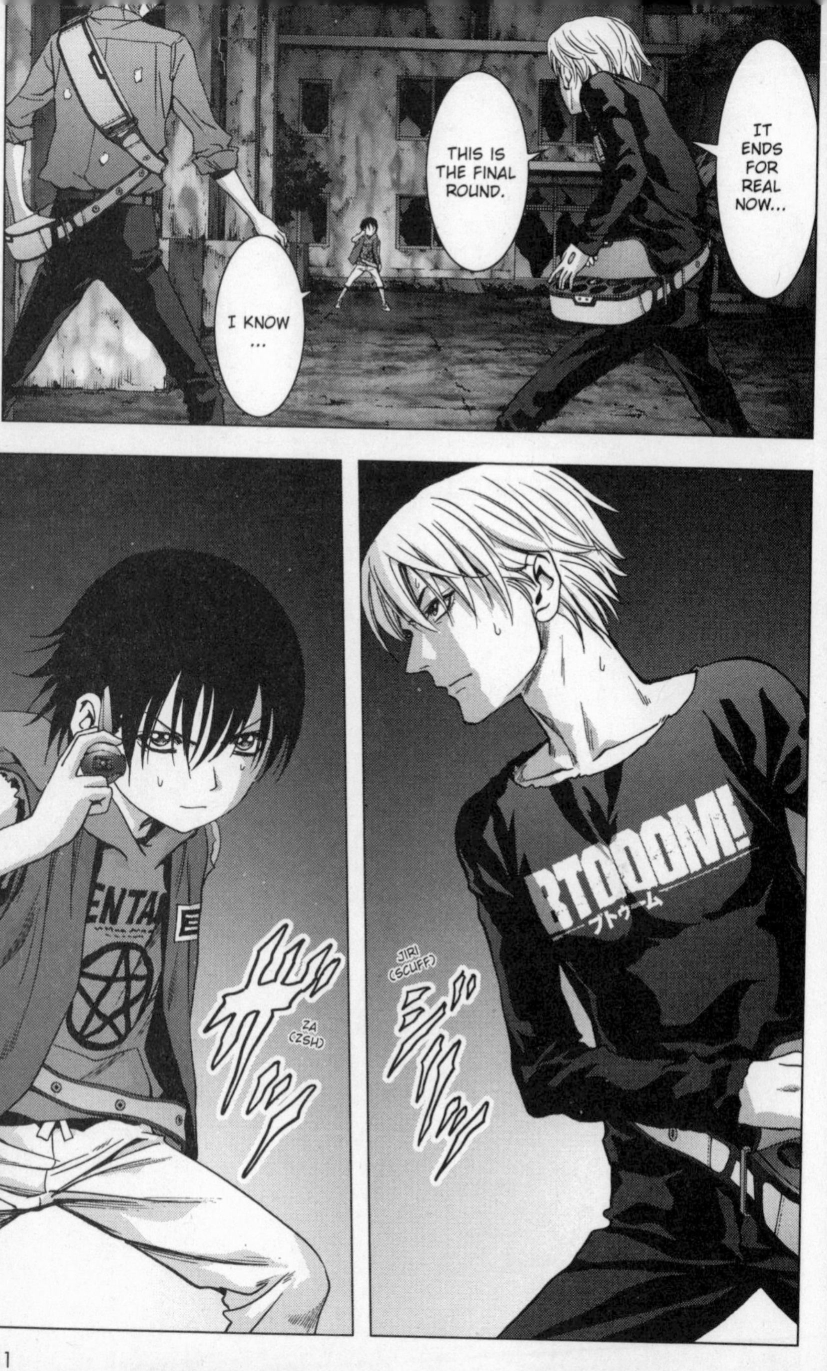

IT ENDS FOR REAL NOW...
THIS IS THE FINAL ROUND.
I KNOW ...
BTOOOM!
ブトゥーム
JIRI (SCUFF)
ZA (ZSH)

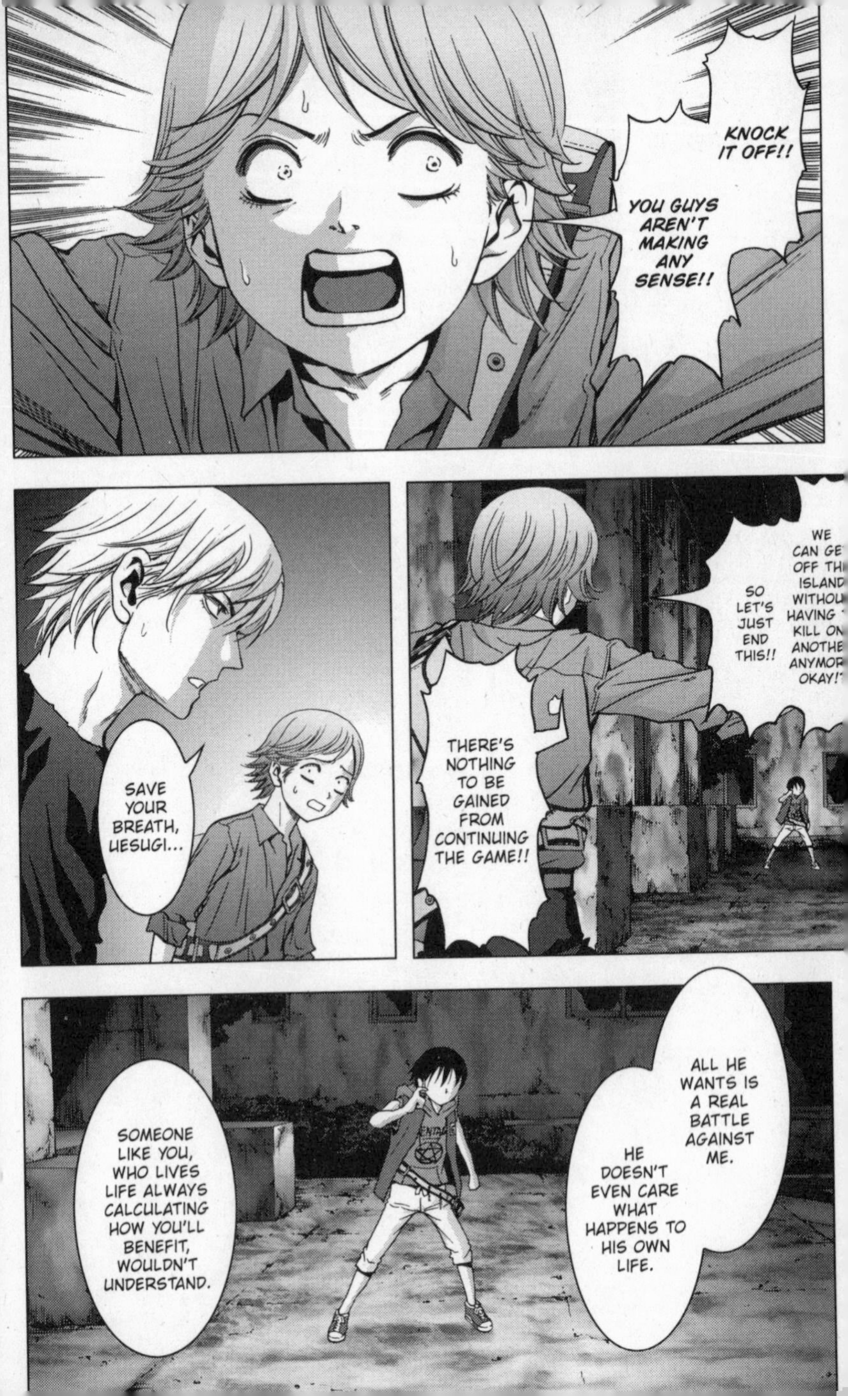
KNOCK IT OFF!!
YOU GUYS AREN'T MAKING ANY SENSE!!
WE CAN GE OFF TH ISLAND WITHOU HAVING KILL ON ANOTHE ANYMOR OKAY!
SO LET'S JUST END THIS!!
THERE'S NOTHING TO BE GAINED FROM CONTINUING THE GAME!!
SAVE YOUR BREATH, UESUGI...
ALL HE WANTS IS A REAL BATTLE AGAINST ME.
HE DOESN'T EVEN CARE WHAT HAPPENS TO HIS OWN LIFE.
SOMEONE LIKE YOU, WHO LIVES LIFE ALWAYS CALCULATING HOW YOU'LL BENEFIT, WOULDN'T UNDERSTAND.

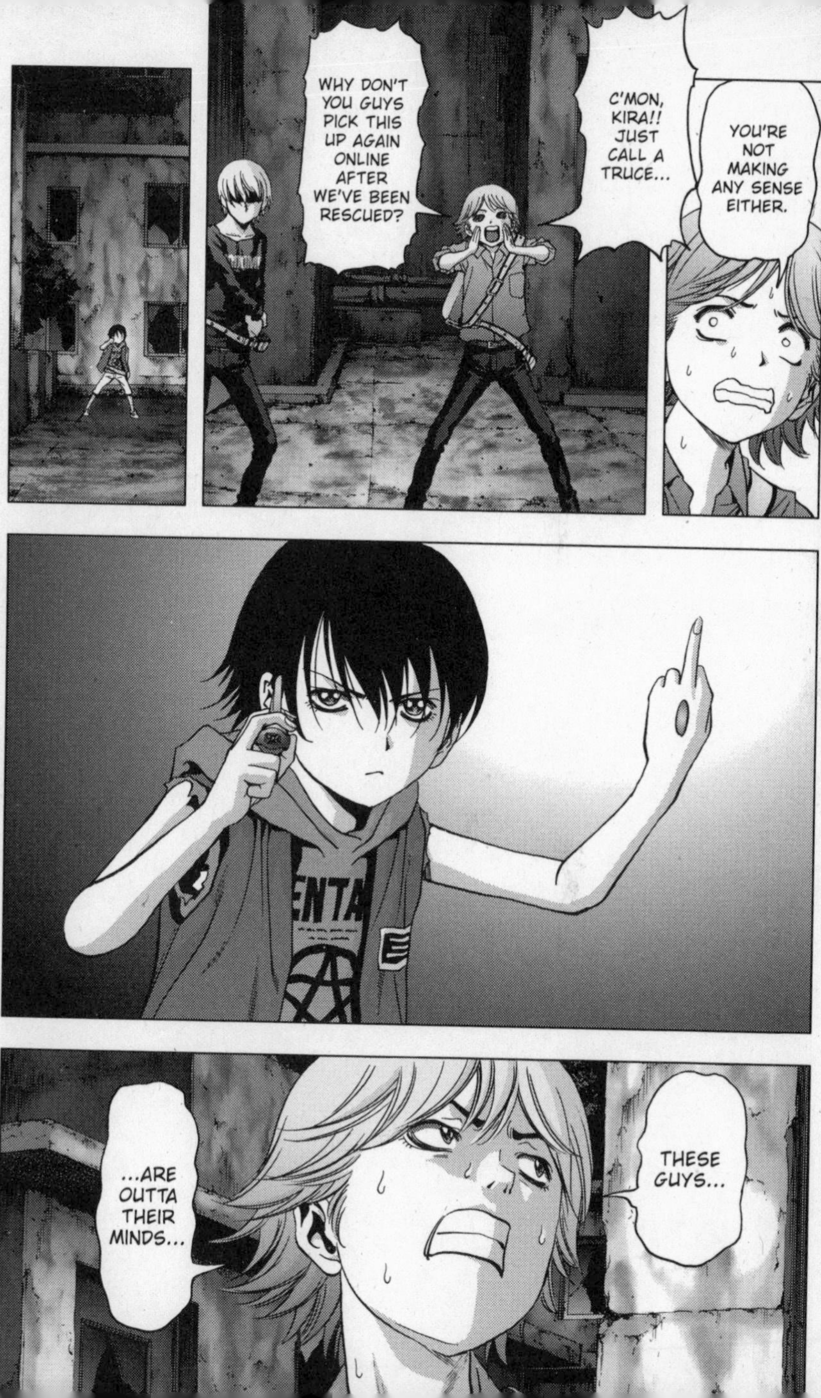
C'MON, KIRA!! JUST CALL A TRUCE...
WHY DON'T YOU GUYS PICK THIS UP AGAIN ONLINE AFTER WE'VE BEEN RESCUED?
YOU'RE NOT MAKING ANY SENSE EITHER.
THESE GUYS...
...ARE OUTTA THEIR MINDS...

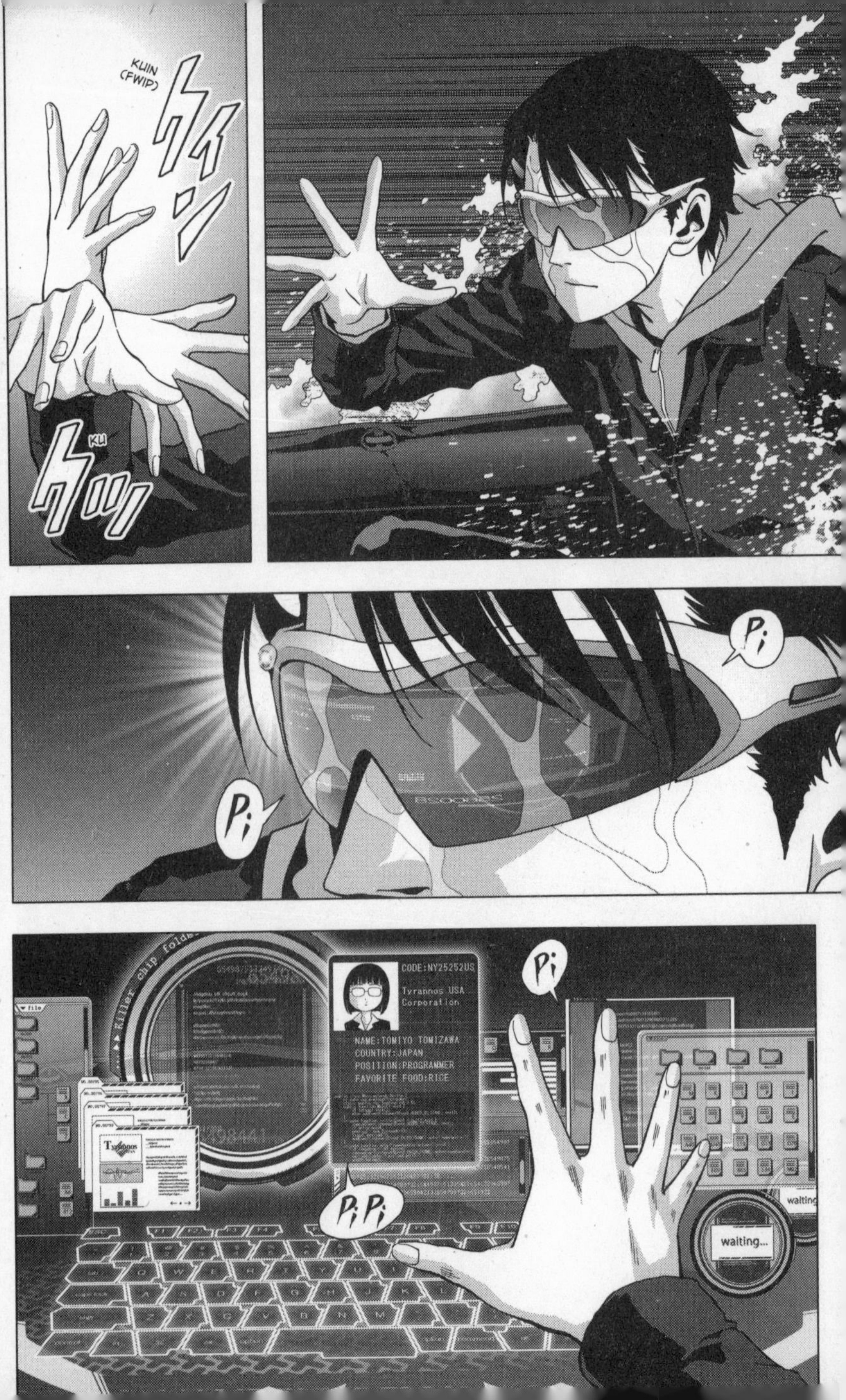
KUIN
(FWIP)
KU
Pi
Pi
Pi
CODE:NY25252US
Tyrannos USA Corporation
NAME:TOMIYO TOMIZAWA
COUNTRY:JAPAN
POSITION:PROGRAMMER
FAVORITE FOOD:RICE
waiting
waiting...
PiPi

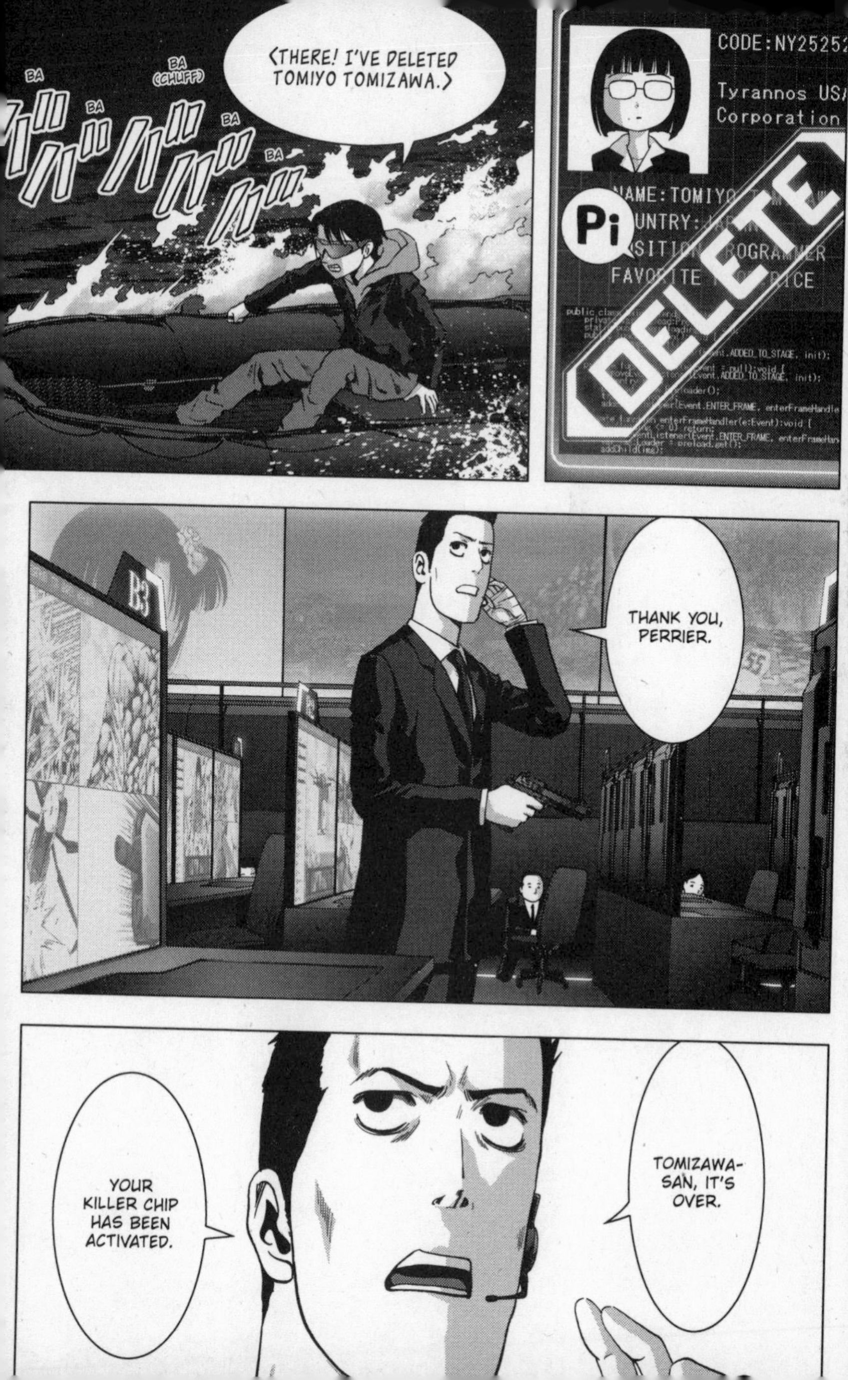
CODE:NY2525
Tyrannos US
Corporation
Pi
DELETE
⟨THERE! I'VE DELETED TOMIYO TOMIZAWA.⟩
BA
BA (CHUFF)
BA
BA
BA
THANK YOU, PERRIER.
TOMIZAWA-SAN, IT'S OVER.
YOUR KILLER CHIP HAS BEEN ACTIVATED.

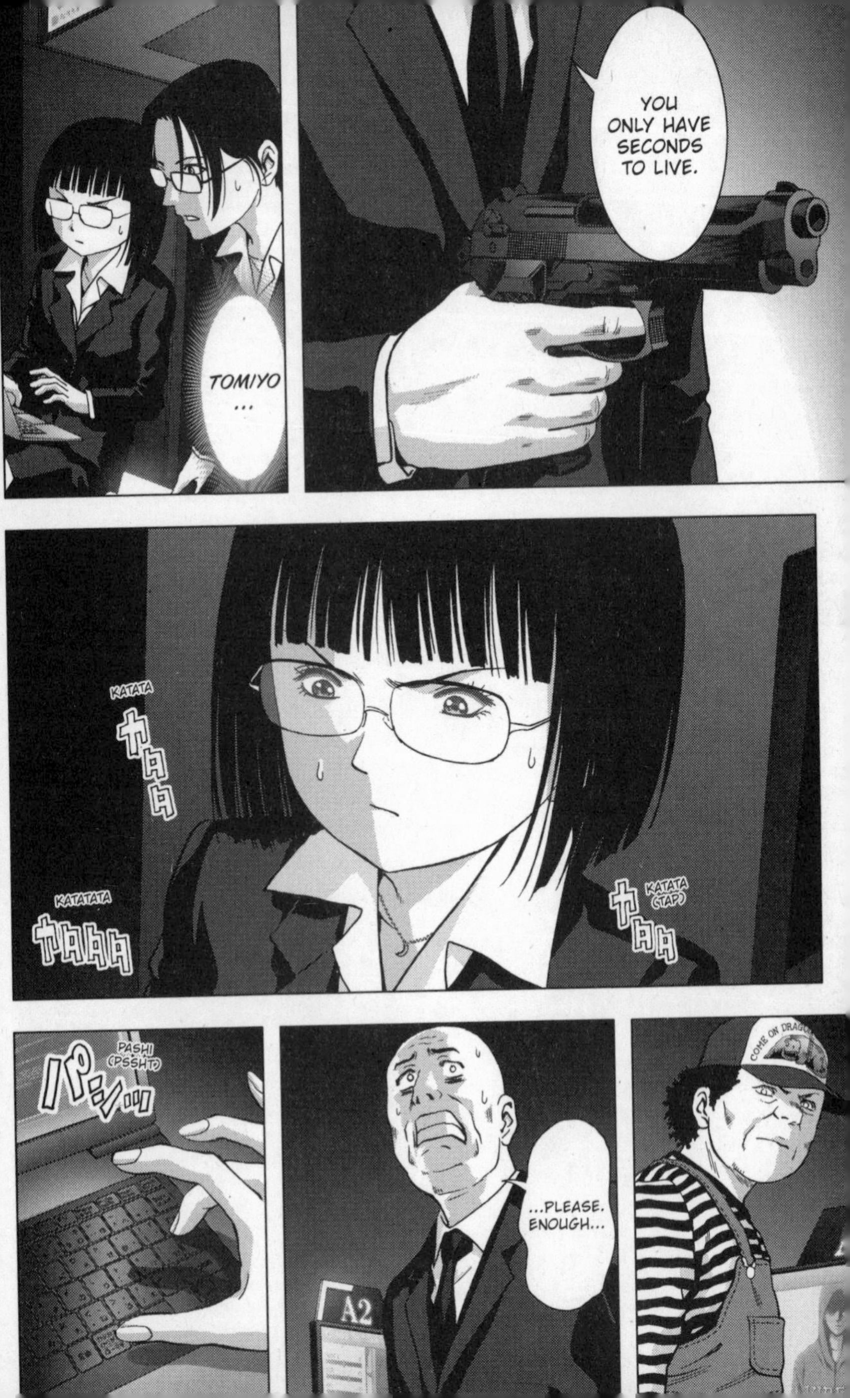
YOU ONLY HAVE SECONDS TO LIVE.
TOMIYO ...
KATATA (TAP)
KATATA
KATATATA
...PLEASE. ENOUGH...
PASHI (PSSHT)

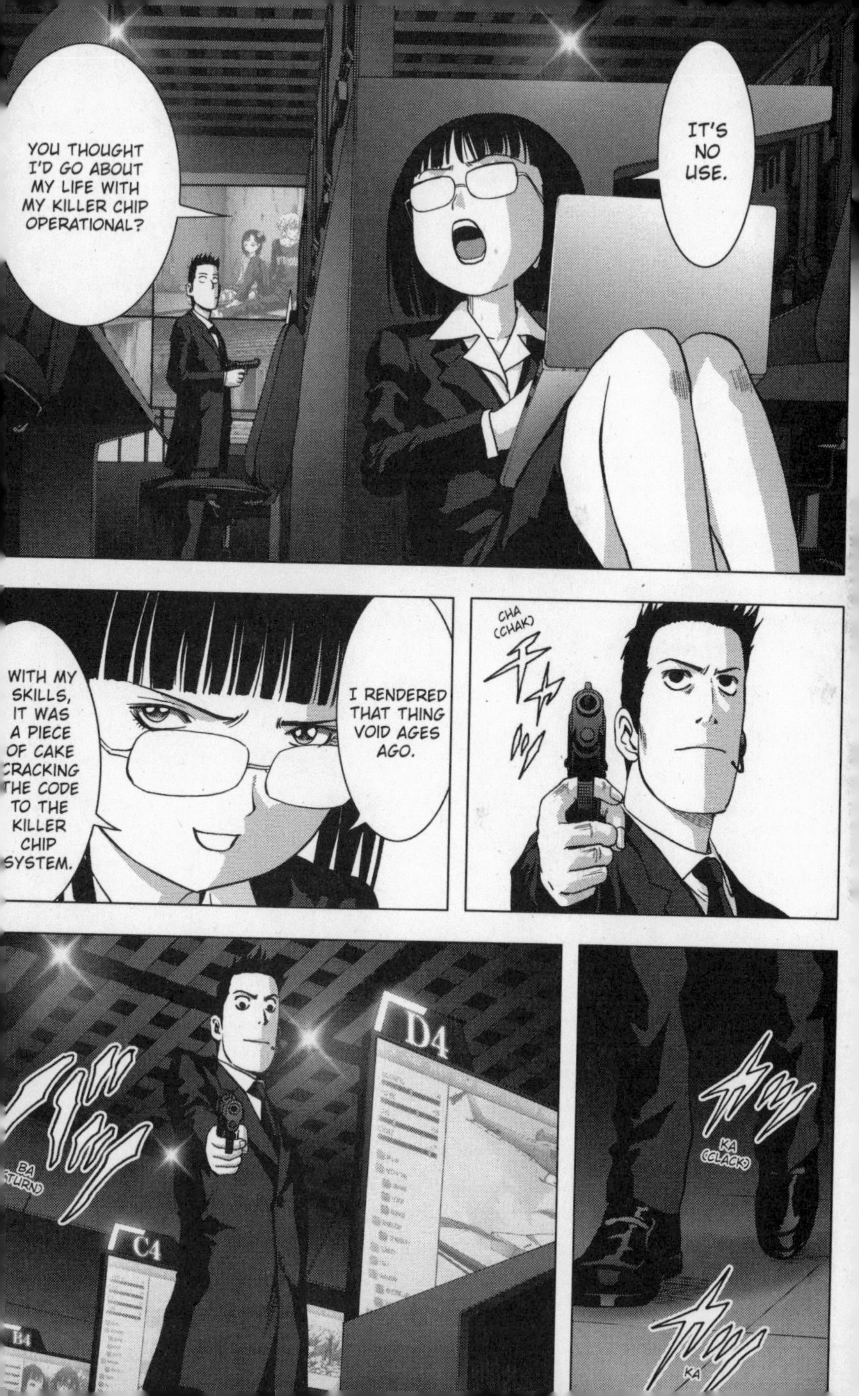
IT'S NO USE.
YOU THOUGHT I'D GO ABOUT MY LIFE WITH MY KILLER CHIP OPERATIONAL?
CHA (CHAK)
I RENDERED THAT THING VOID AGES AGO.
WITH MY SKILLS, IT WAS A PIECE OF CAKE CRACKING THE CODE TO THE KILLER CHIP SYSTEM.
KA (CLACK)
KA
D4
BA (TURN)
C4
B4

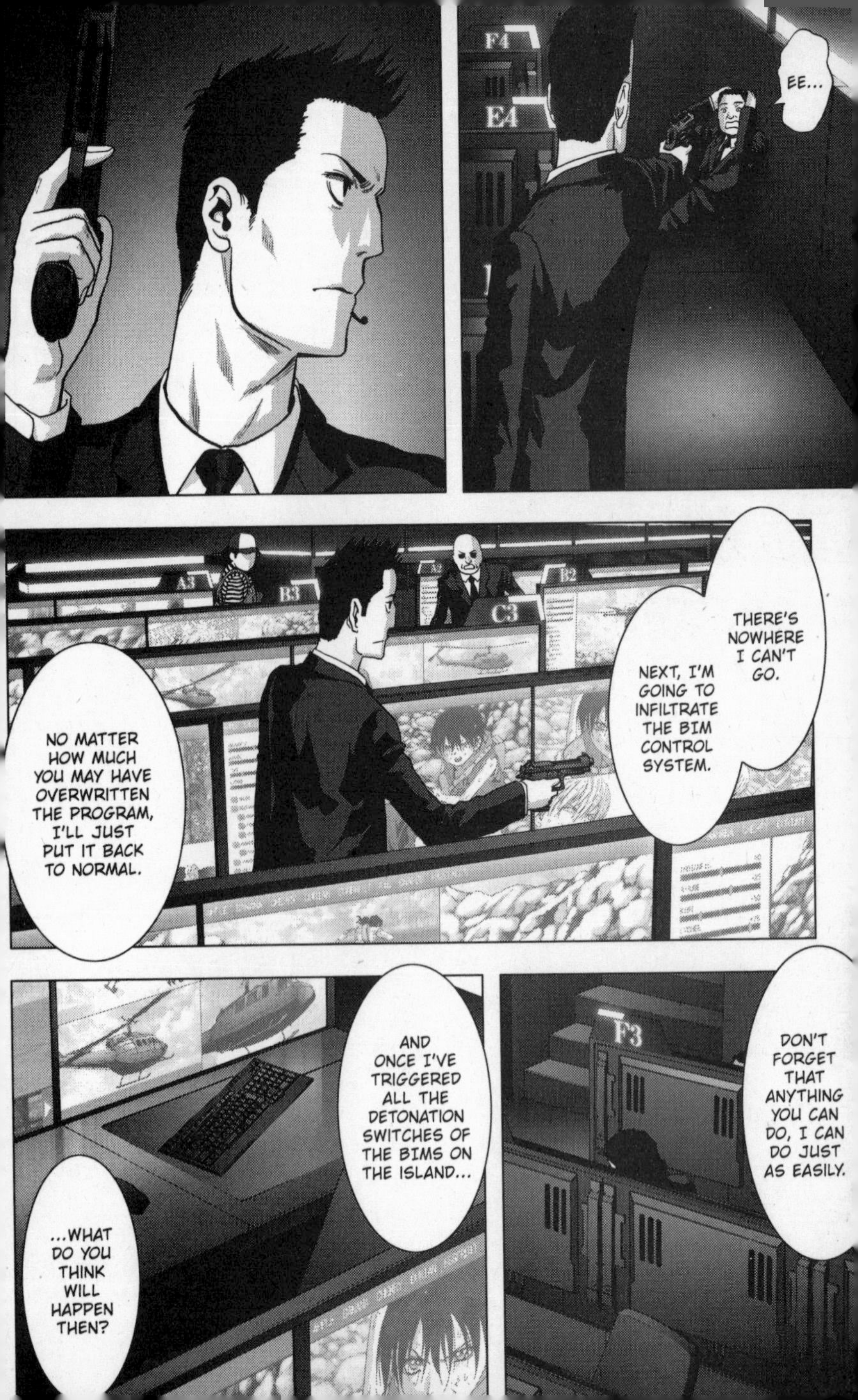
EE...
THERE'S NOWHERE I CAN'T GO.
NEXT, I'M GOING TO INFILTRATE THE BIM CONTROL SYSTEM.
NO MATTER HOW MUCH YOU MAY HAVE OVERWRITTEN THE PROGRAM, I'LL JUST PUT IT BACK TO NORMAL.
DON'T FORGET THAT ANYTHING YOU CAN DO, I CAN DO JUST AS EASILY.
AND ONCE I'VE TRIGGERED ALL THE DETONATION SWITCHES OF THE BIMS ON THE ISLAND...
...WHAT DO YOU THINK WILL HAPPEN THEN?

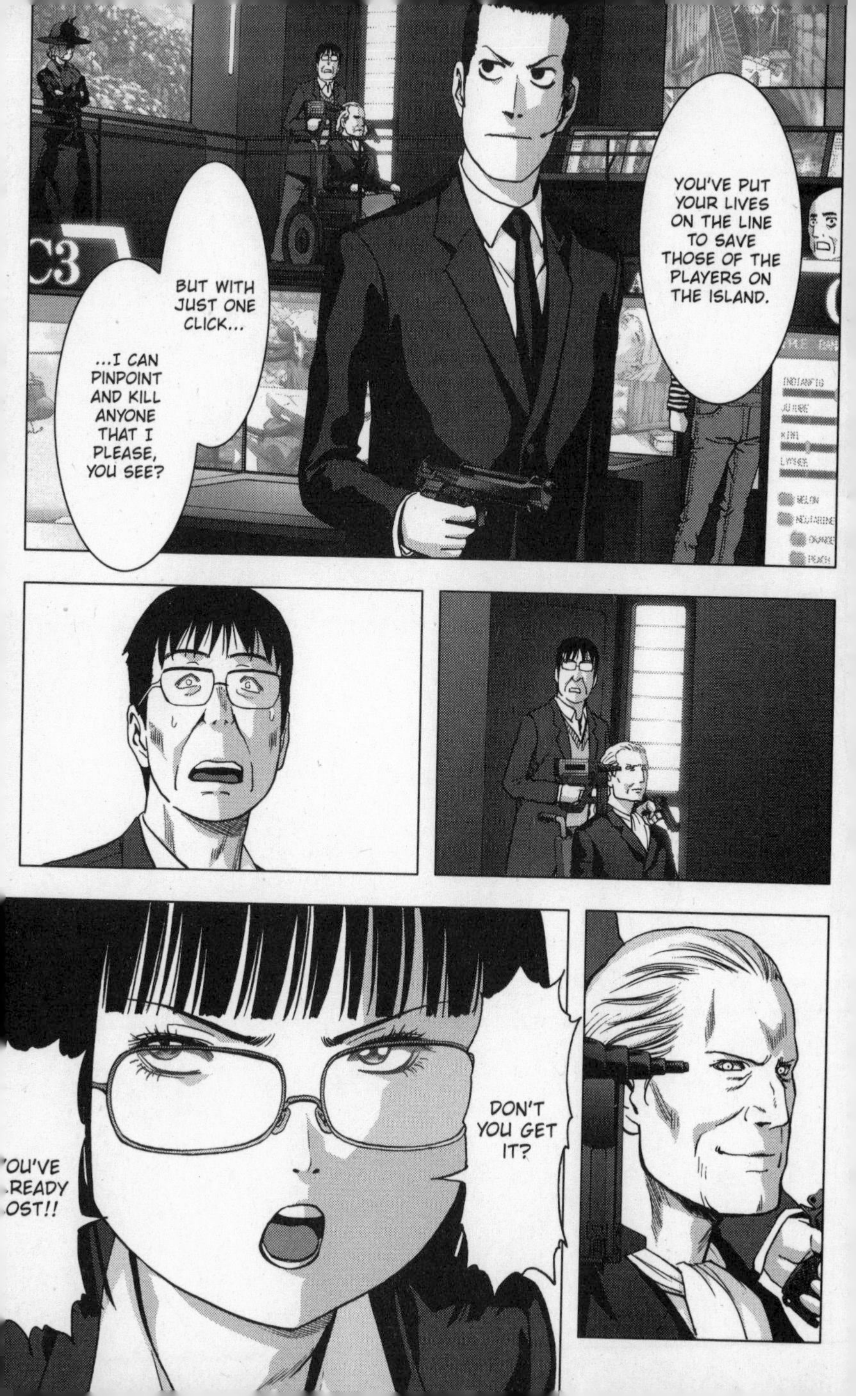
YOU'VE PUT YOUR LIVES ON THE LINE TO SAVE THOSE OF THE PLAYERS ON THE ISLAND.
BUT WITH JUST ONE CLICK...
...I CAN PINPOINT AND KILL ANYONE THAT I PLEASE, YOU SEE?
DON'T YOU GET IT?
OU'VE READY OST!!

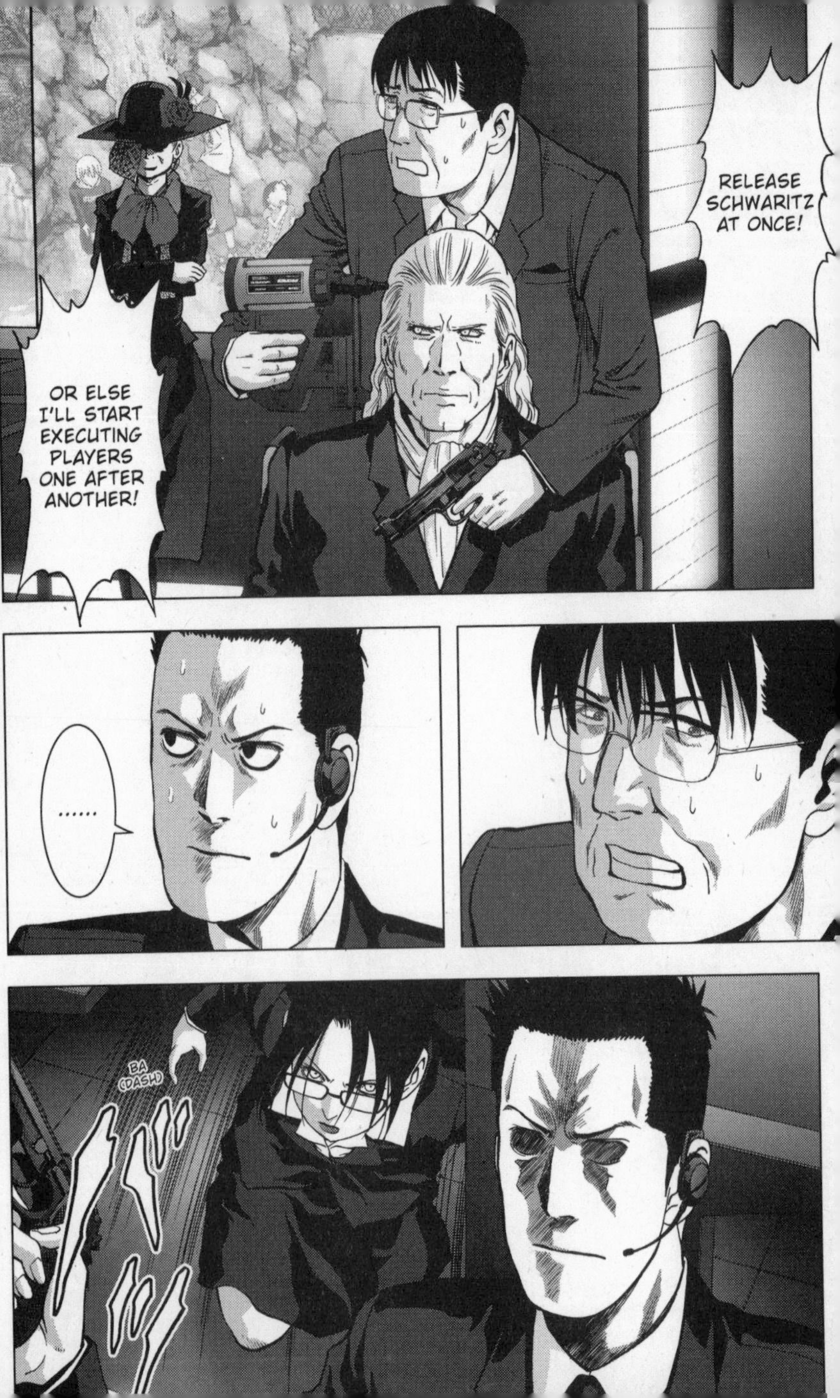
RELEASE SCHWARITZ AT ONCE!
OR ELSE I'LL START EXECUTING PLAYERS ONE AFTER ANOTHER!
......
BA (DASH)

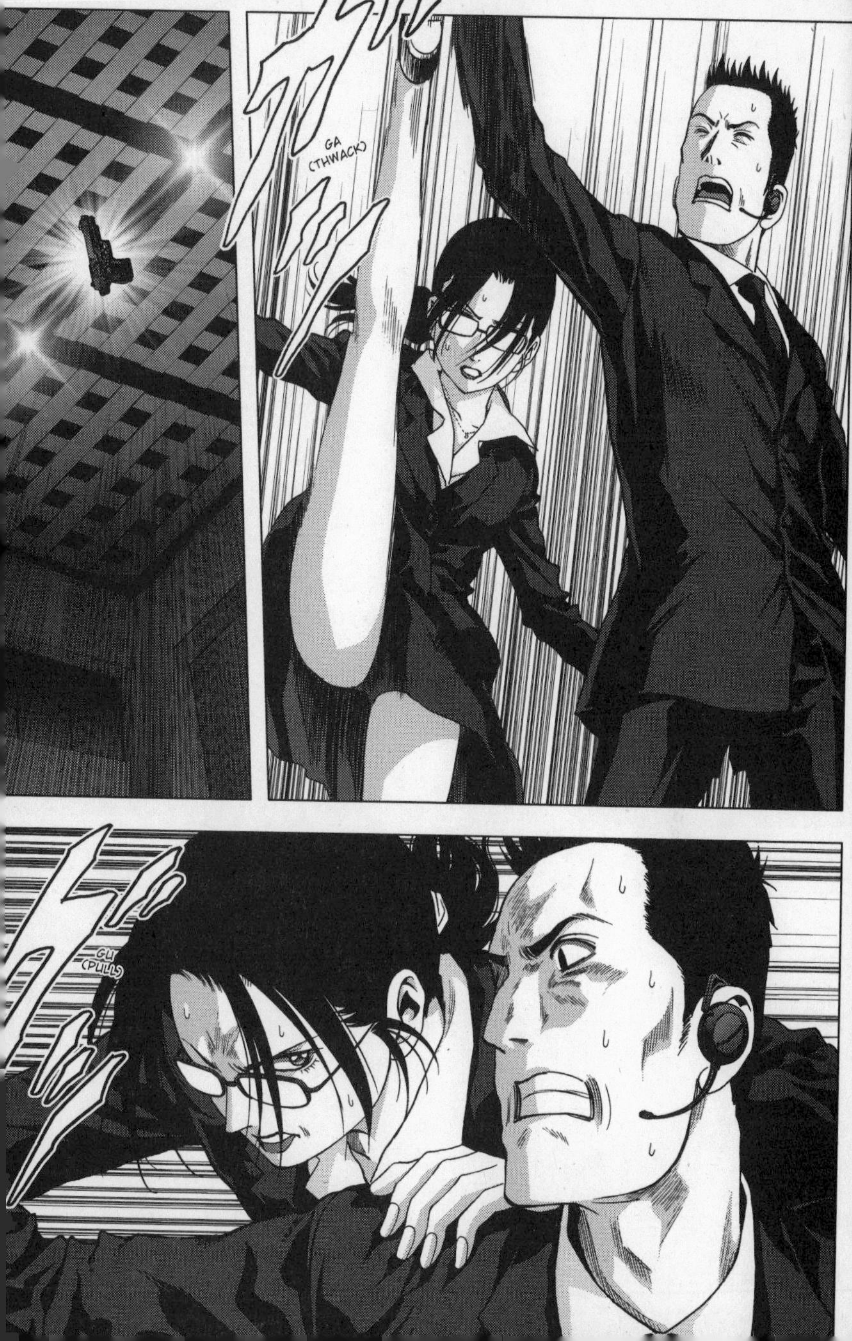
GA
(THWACK)
GU
(PULL)

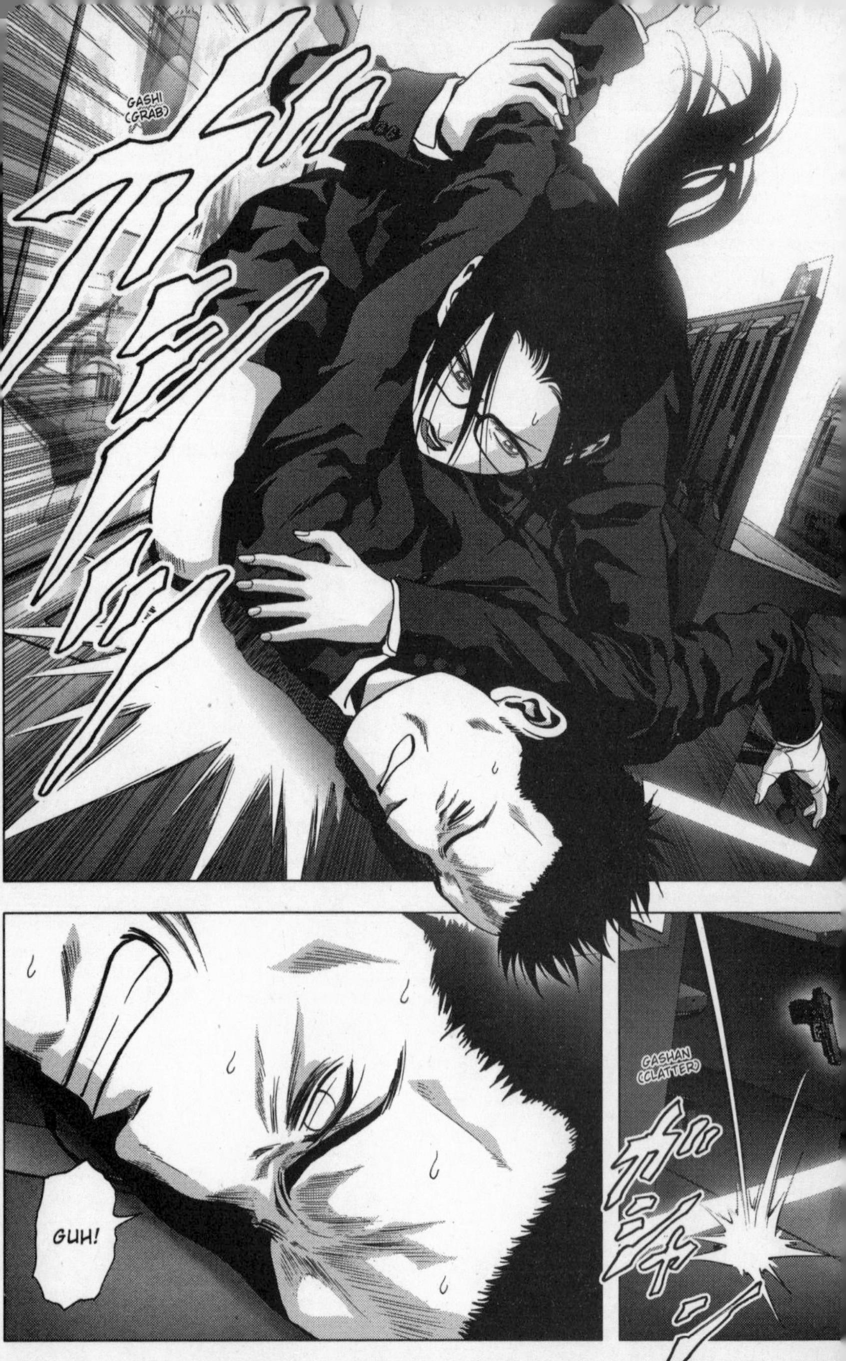
GASHI (GRAB)
GASHAN (CLATTER)
GUH!

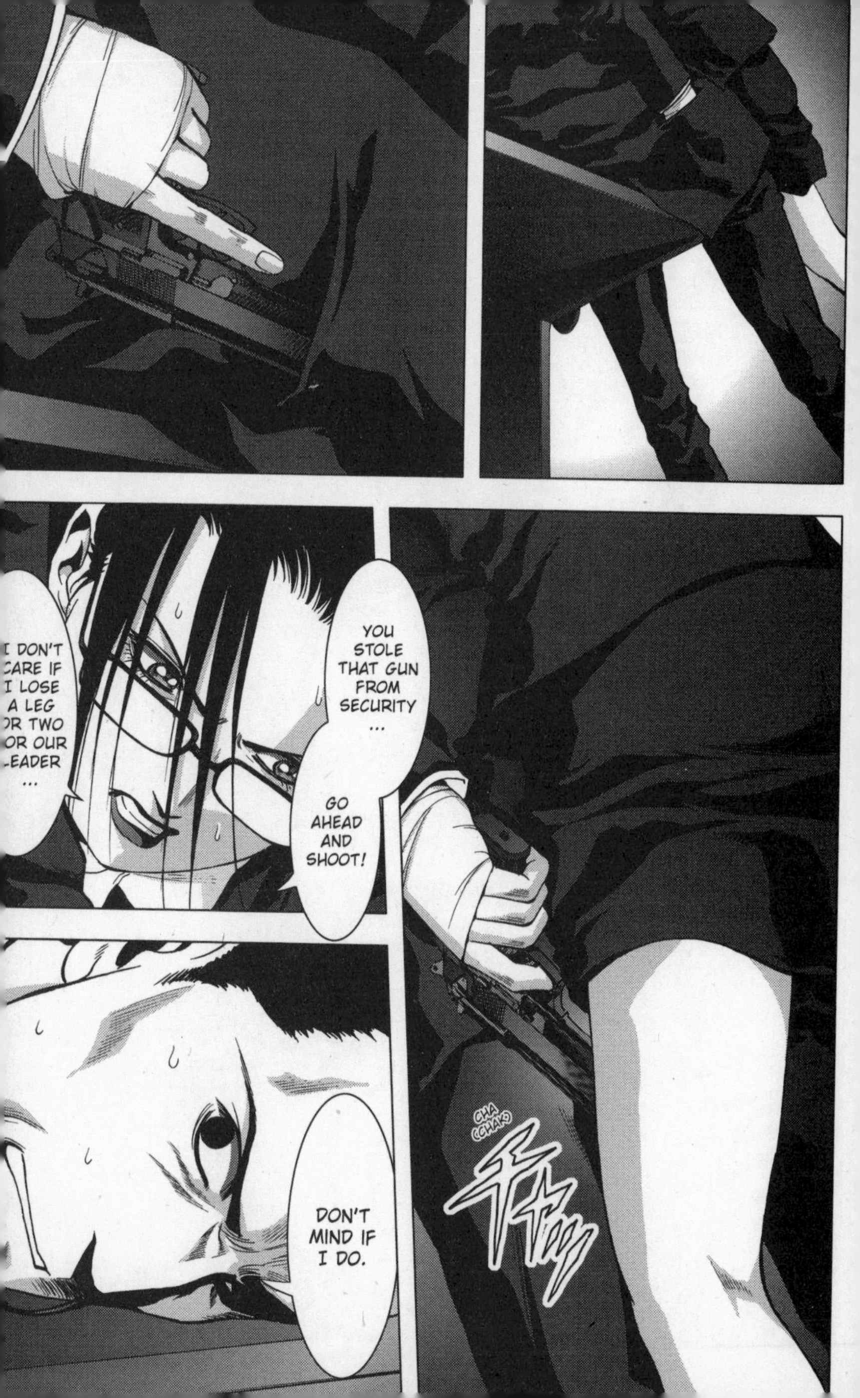
CHA (CHAK)
YOU STOLE THAT GUN FROM SECURITY ...
GO AHEAD AND SHOOT!
I DON'T CARE IF I LOSE A LEG OR TWO FOR OUR LEADER ...
DON'T MIND IF I DO.

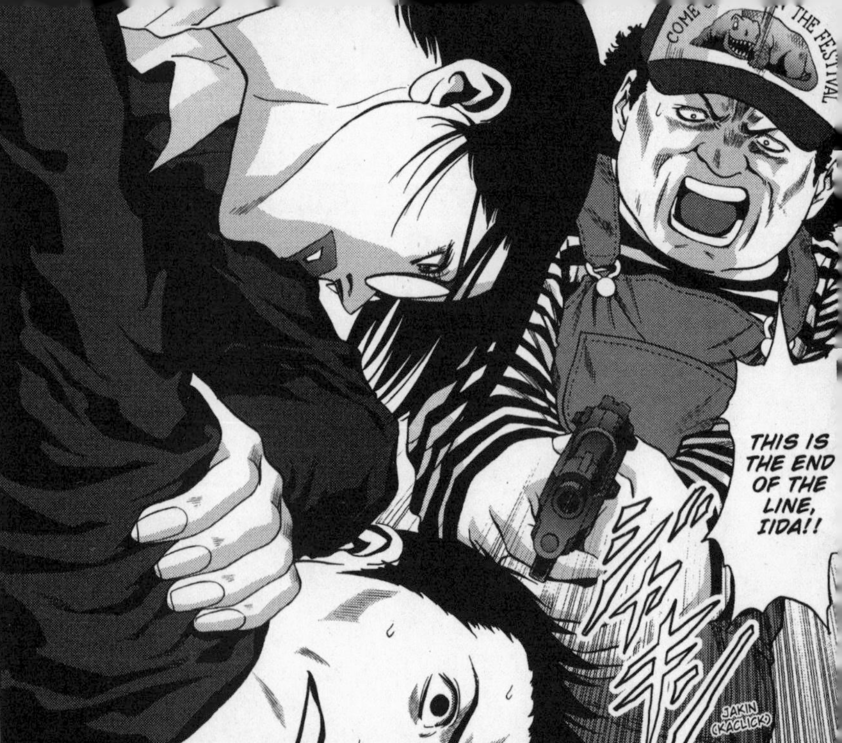
THIS IS THE END OF THE LINE, IIDA!!
JAKIN (KACLICK)

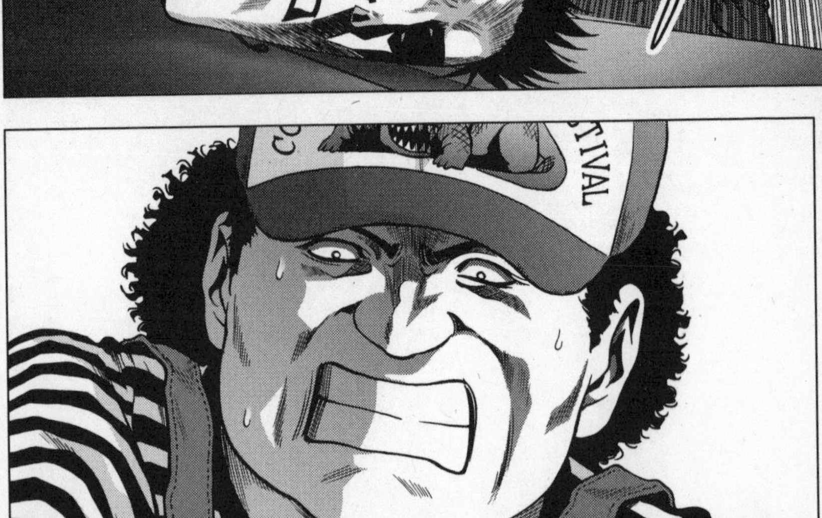

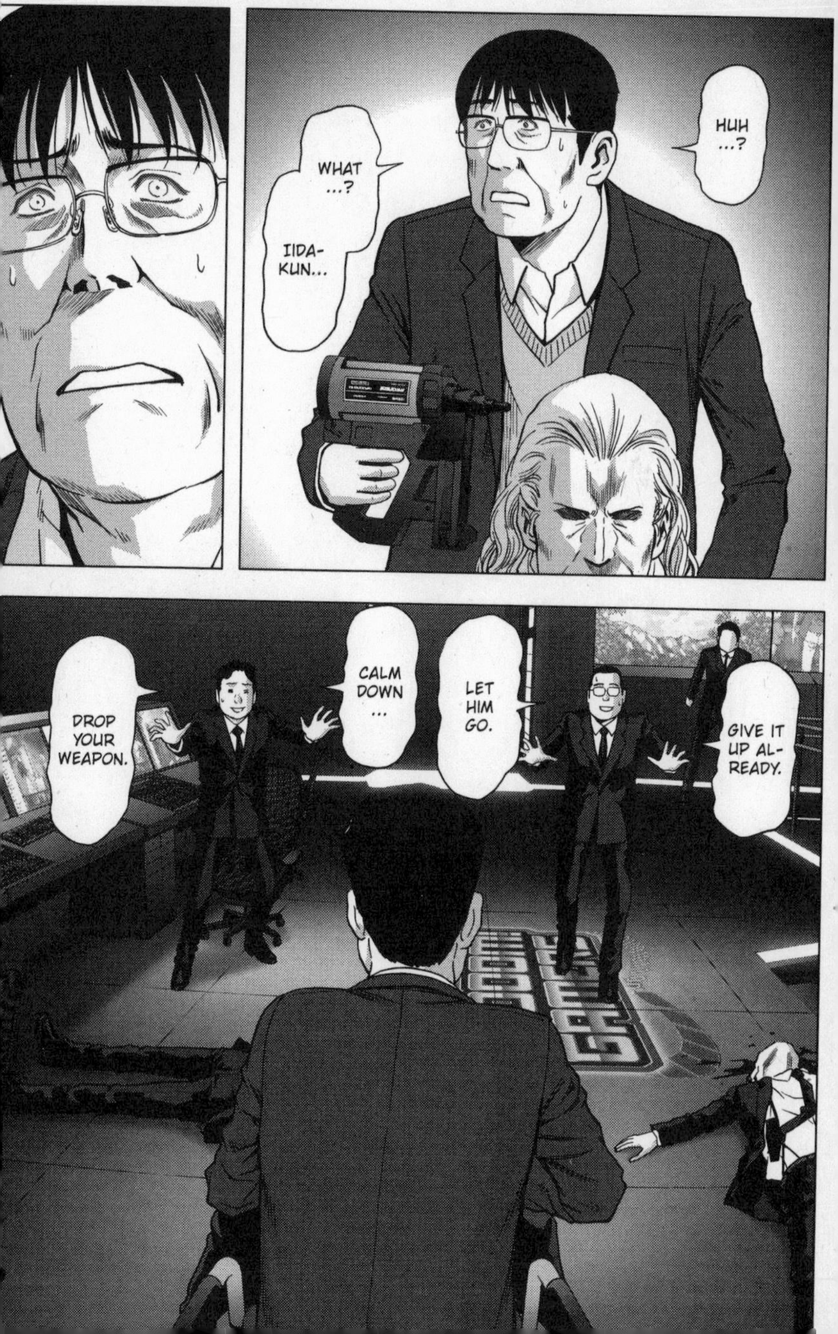
HUH ...?
WHAT ...?
IIDA-KUN...
GIVE IT UP AL-READY.
LET HIM GO.
CALM DOWN ...
DROP YOUR WEAPON.

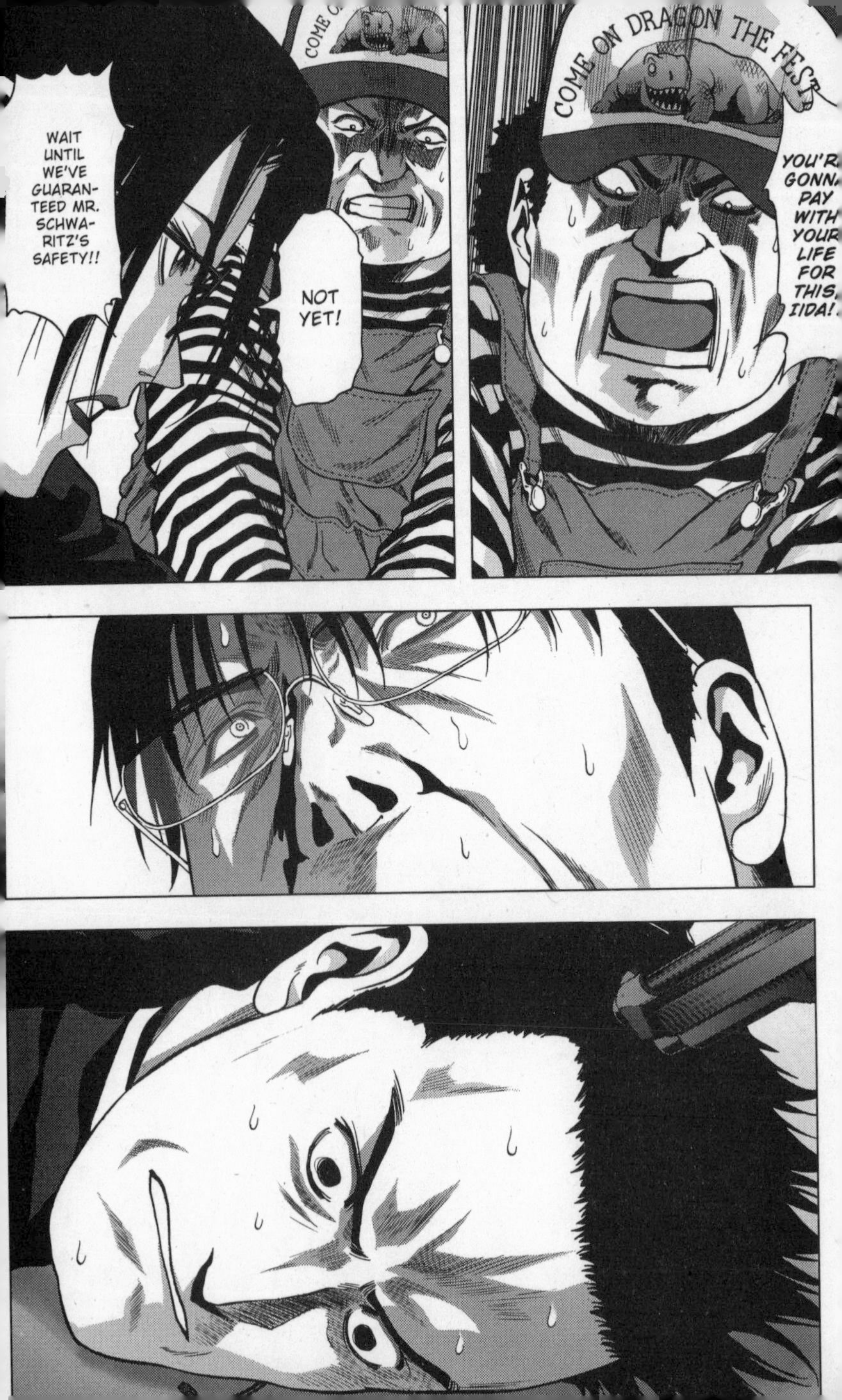
COME ON DRAGON THE FEST
YOU'R GONN PAY WITH YOUR LIFE FOR THIS, IIDA!!
COME O
NOT YET!
WAIT UNTIL WE'VE GUARAN-TEED MR. SCHWA-RITZ'S SAFETY!!

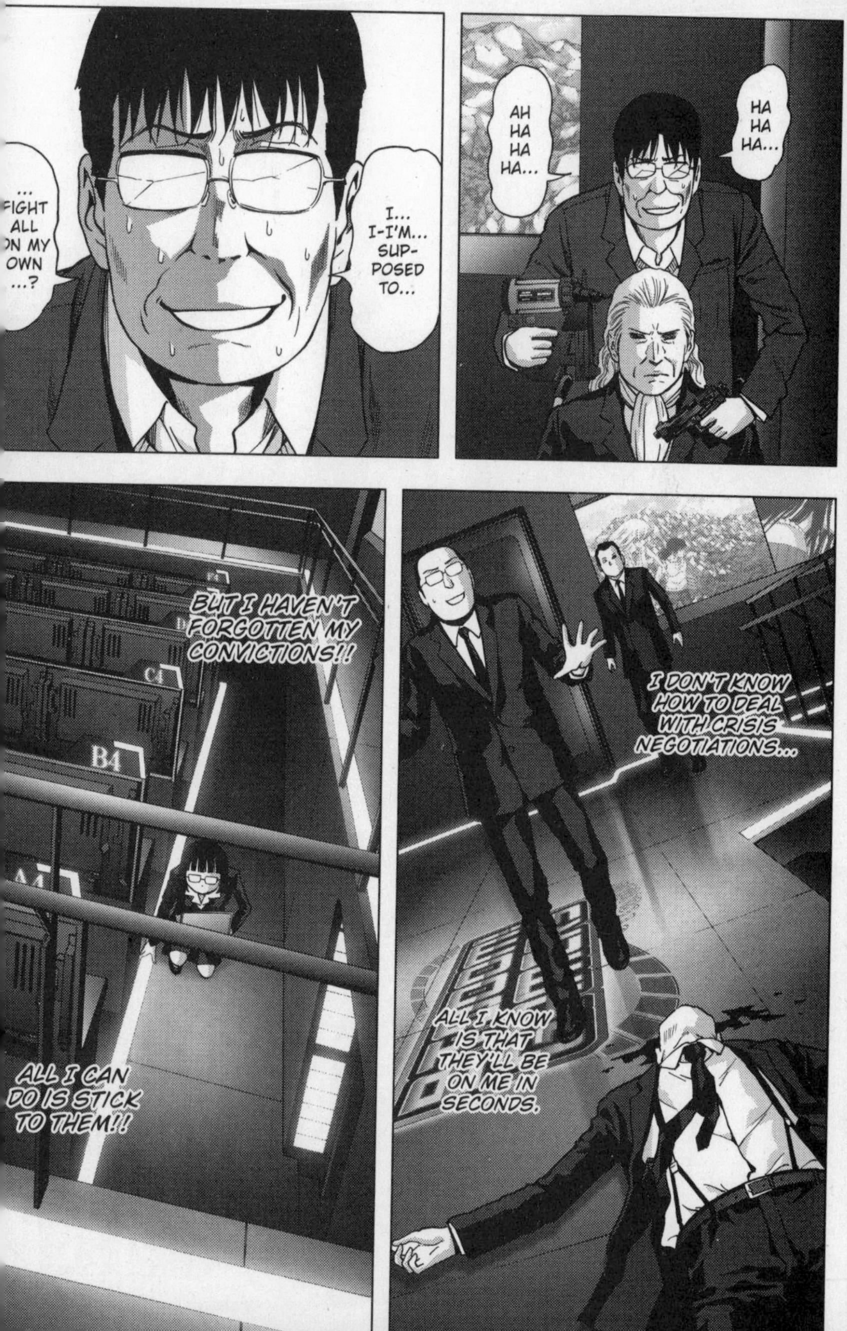
HA HA HA...
AH HA HA HA...
I... I-I'M... SUP-POSED TO...
...FIGHT ALL ON MY OWN ...?
I DON'T KNOW HOW TO DEAL WITH CRISIS NEGOTIATIONS...
ALL I KNOW IS THAT THEY'LL BE ON ME IN SECONDS.
BUT I HAVEN'T FORGOTTEN MY CONVICTIONS!!
ALL I CAN DO IS STICK TO THEM!!

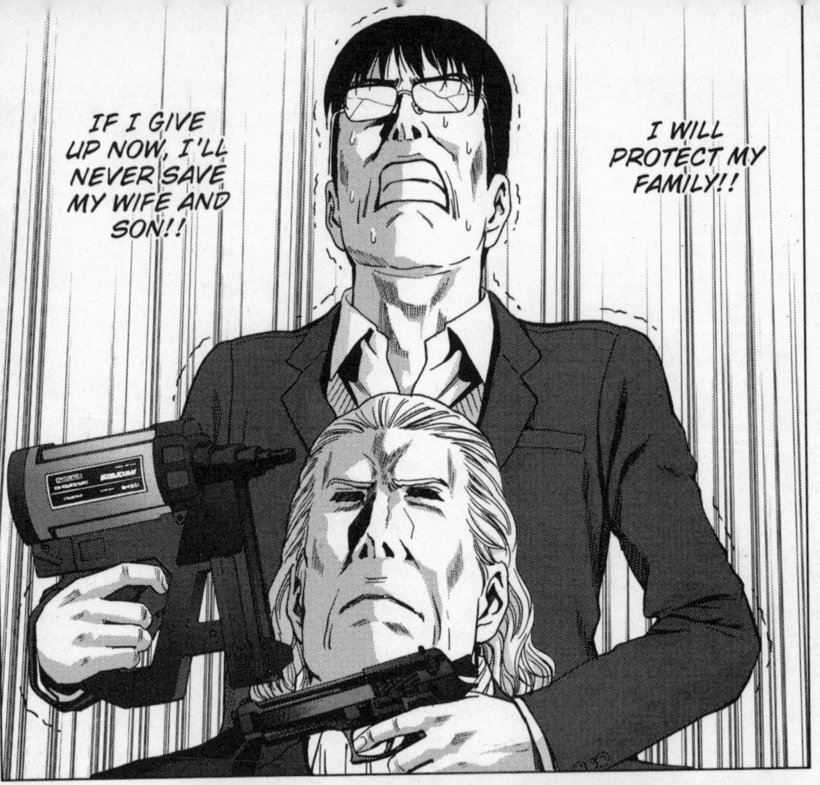
I WILL PROTECT MY FAMILY!!
IF I GIVE UP NOW, I'LL NEVER SAVE MY WIFE AND SON!!

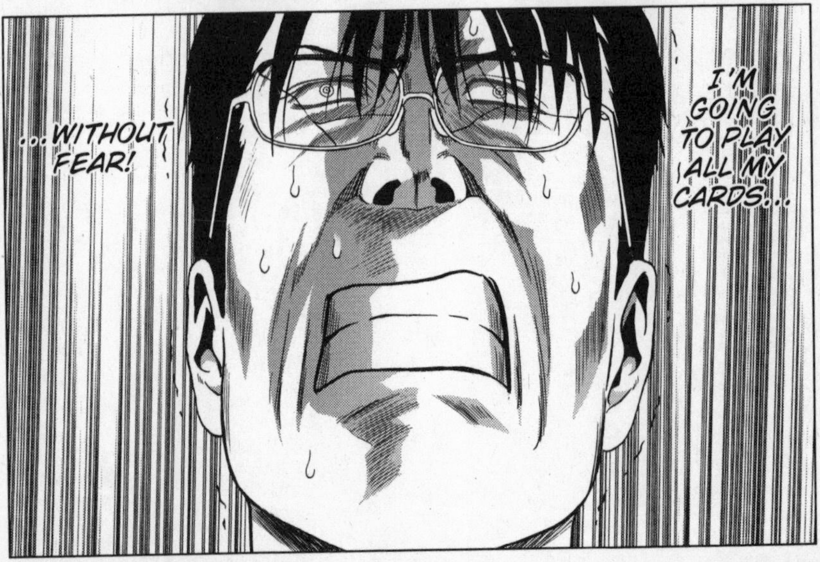
I'M GOING TO PLAY ALL MY CARDS...
...WITHOUT FEAR!

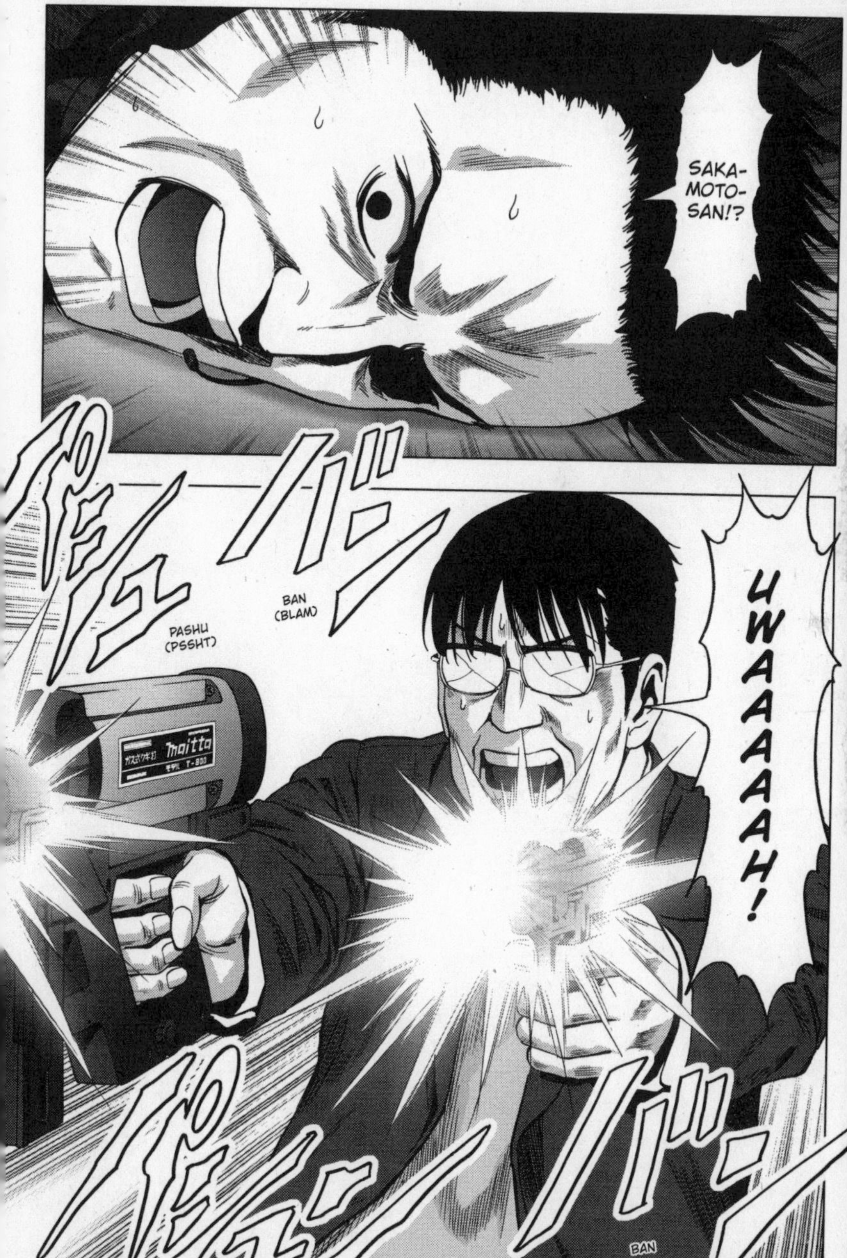
SAKA-MOTO-SAN!?
UWAAAAAAAH!
BAN (BLAM)
PASHU (PSSHT)
BAN
PASHUN

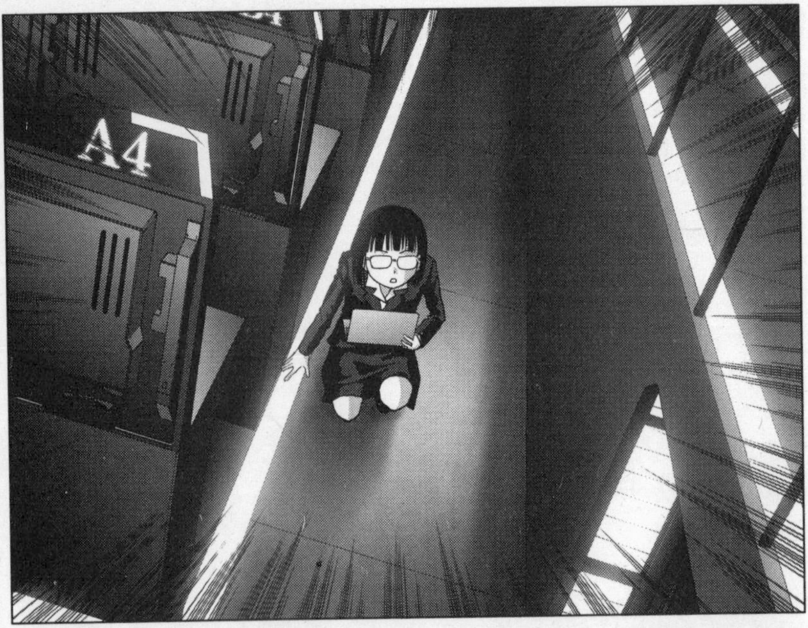
A4

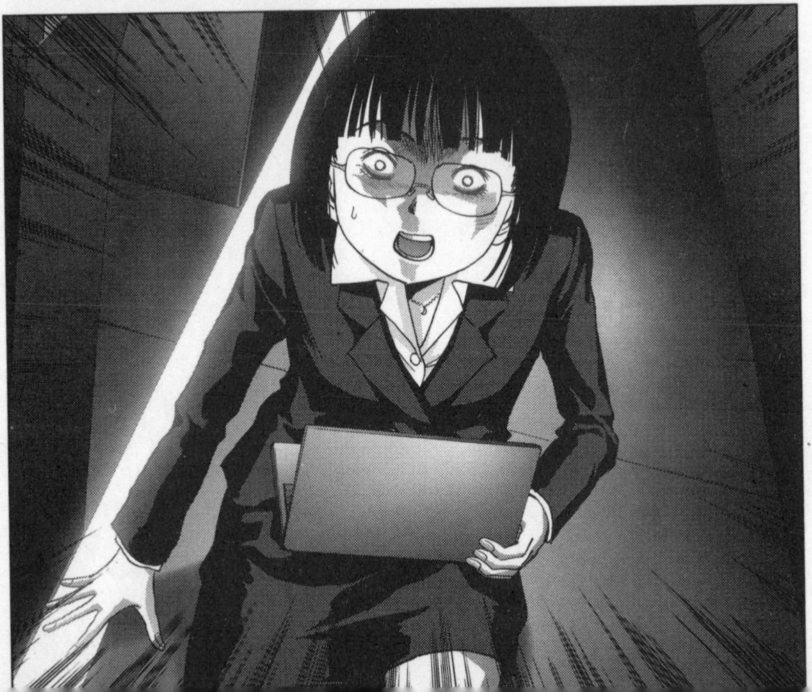

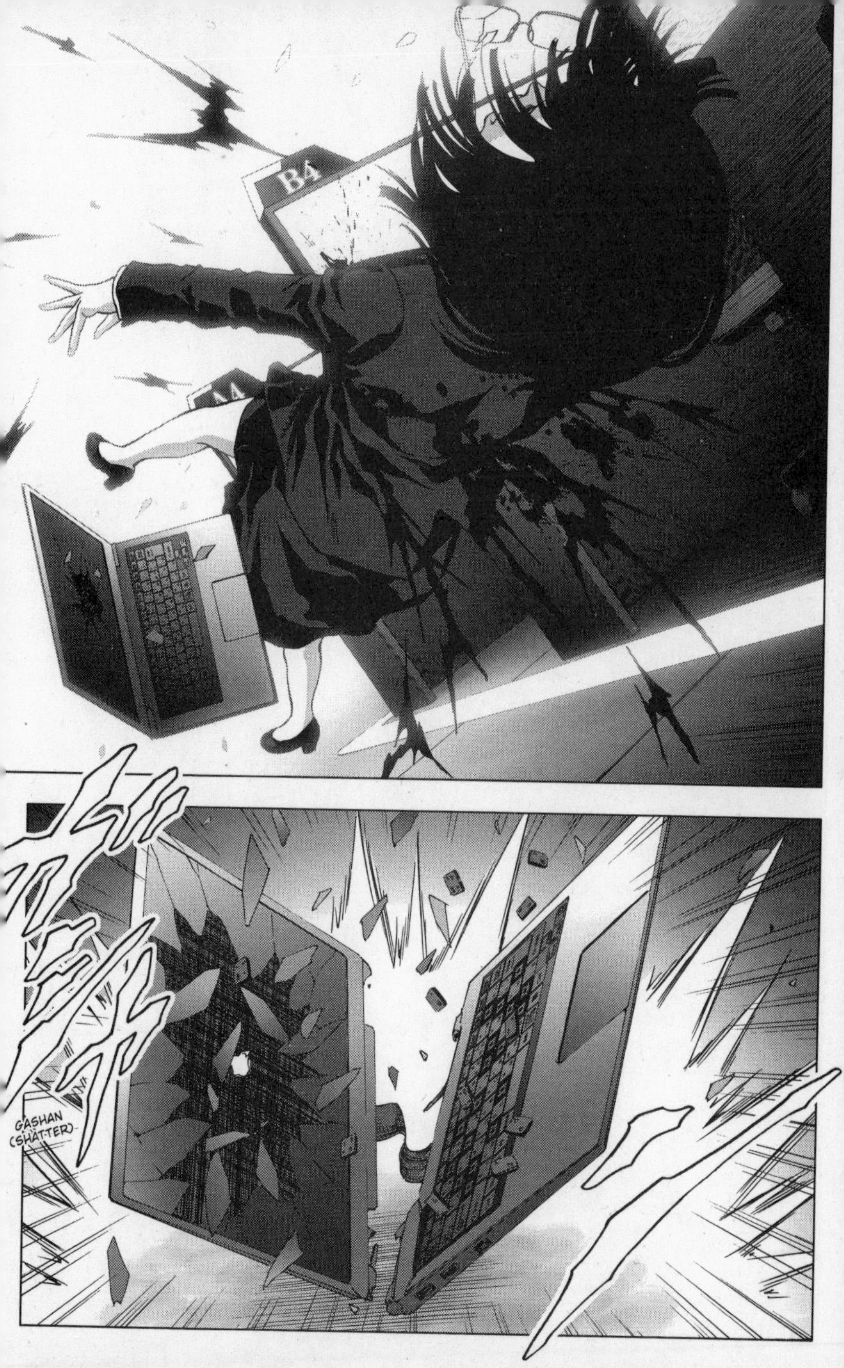
GASHAN
(SHAT-TER)

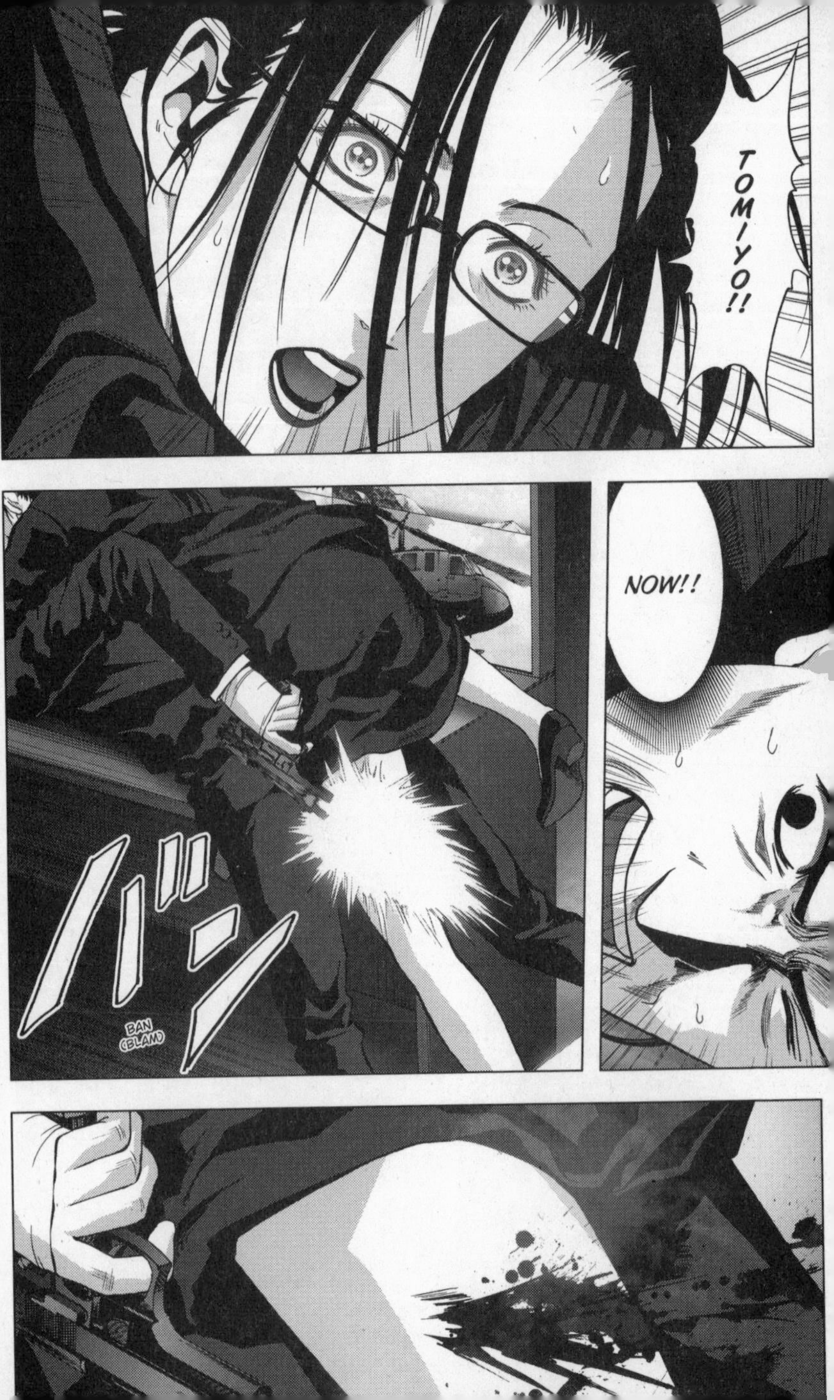
TOMIYO!!
NOW!!
BAN (BLAM)

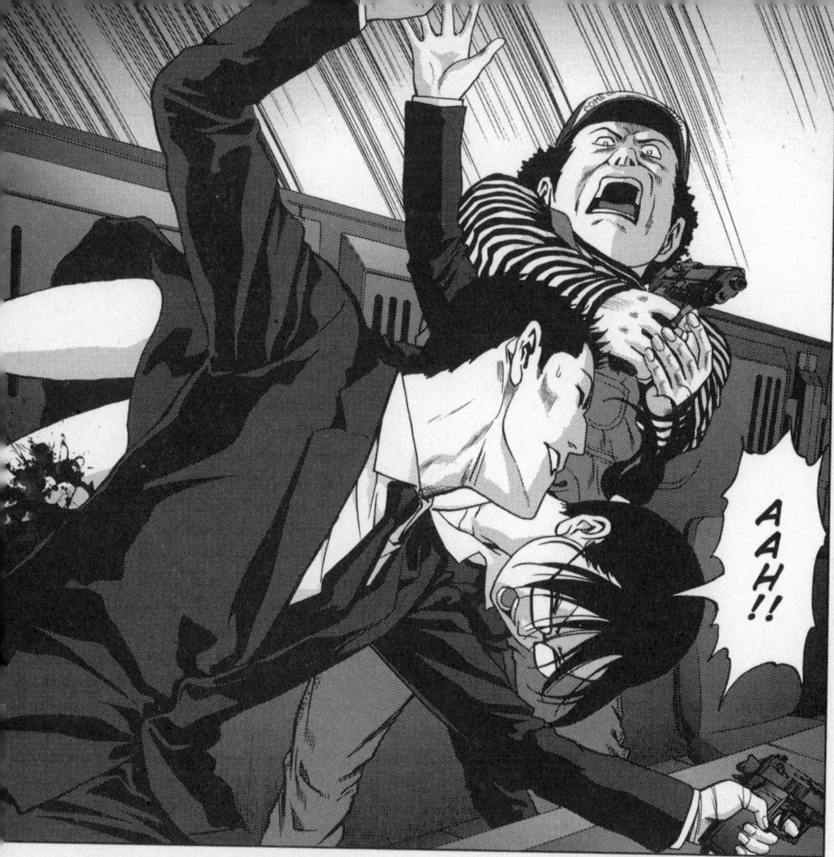
AAH!!

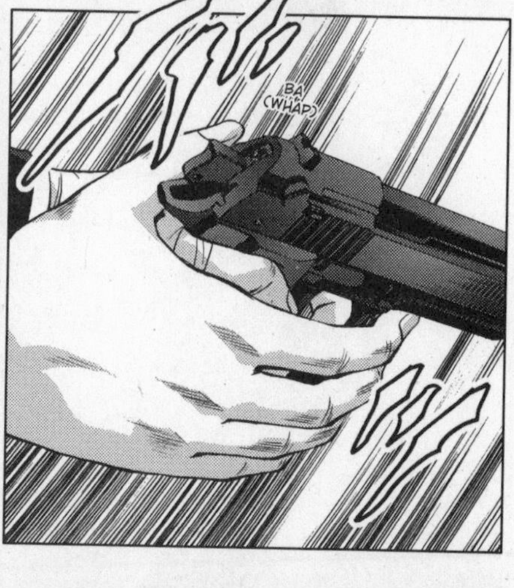
BA
(WHAP)

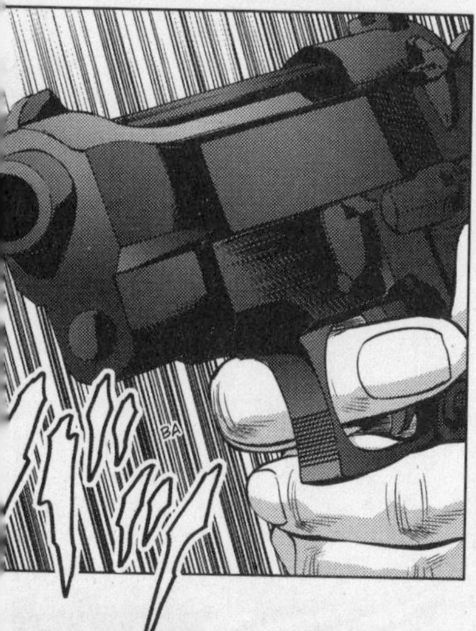
BA

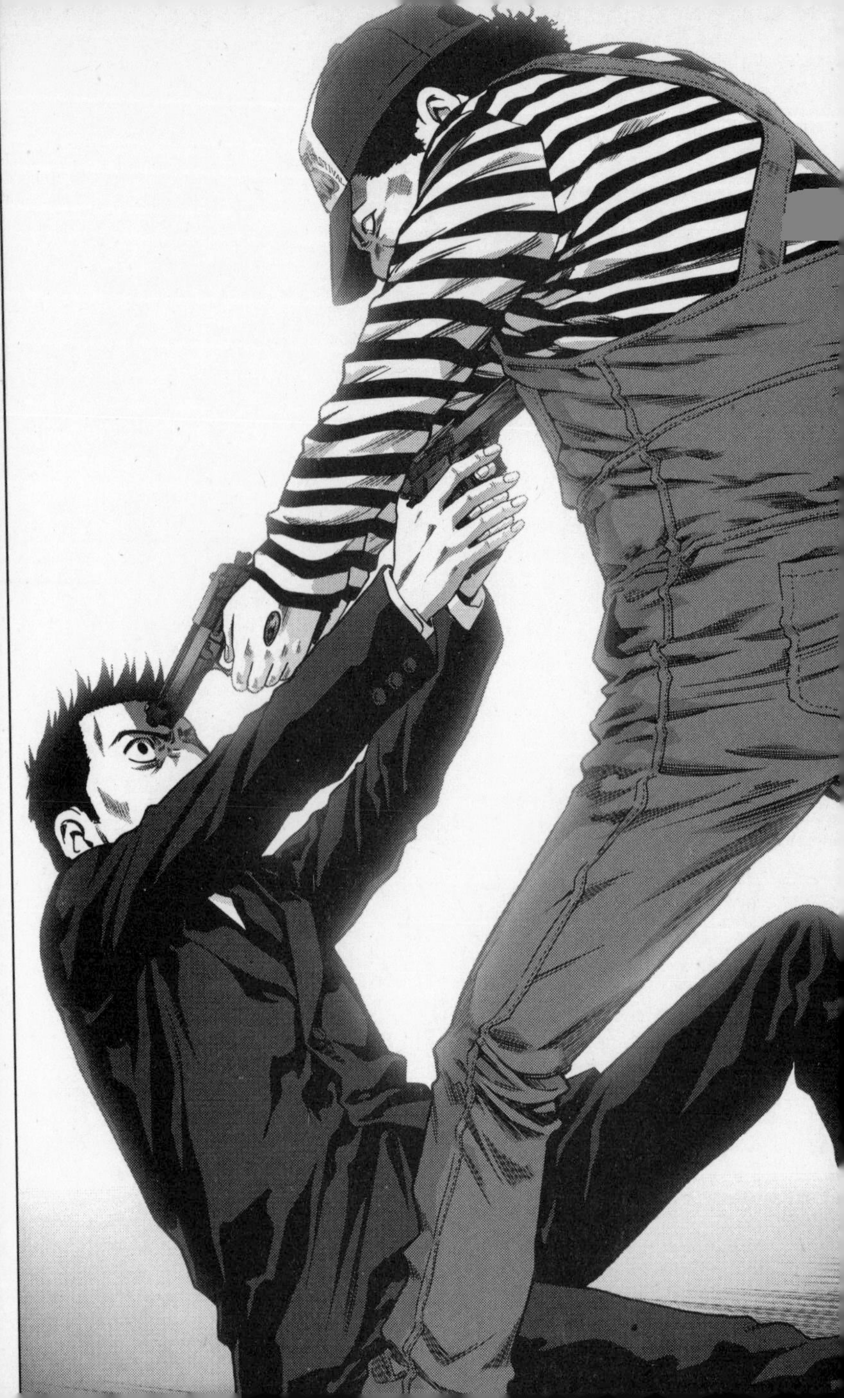

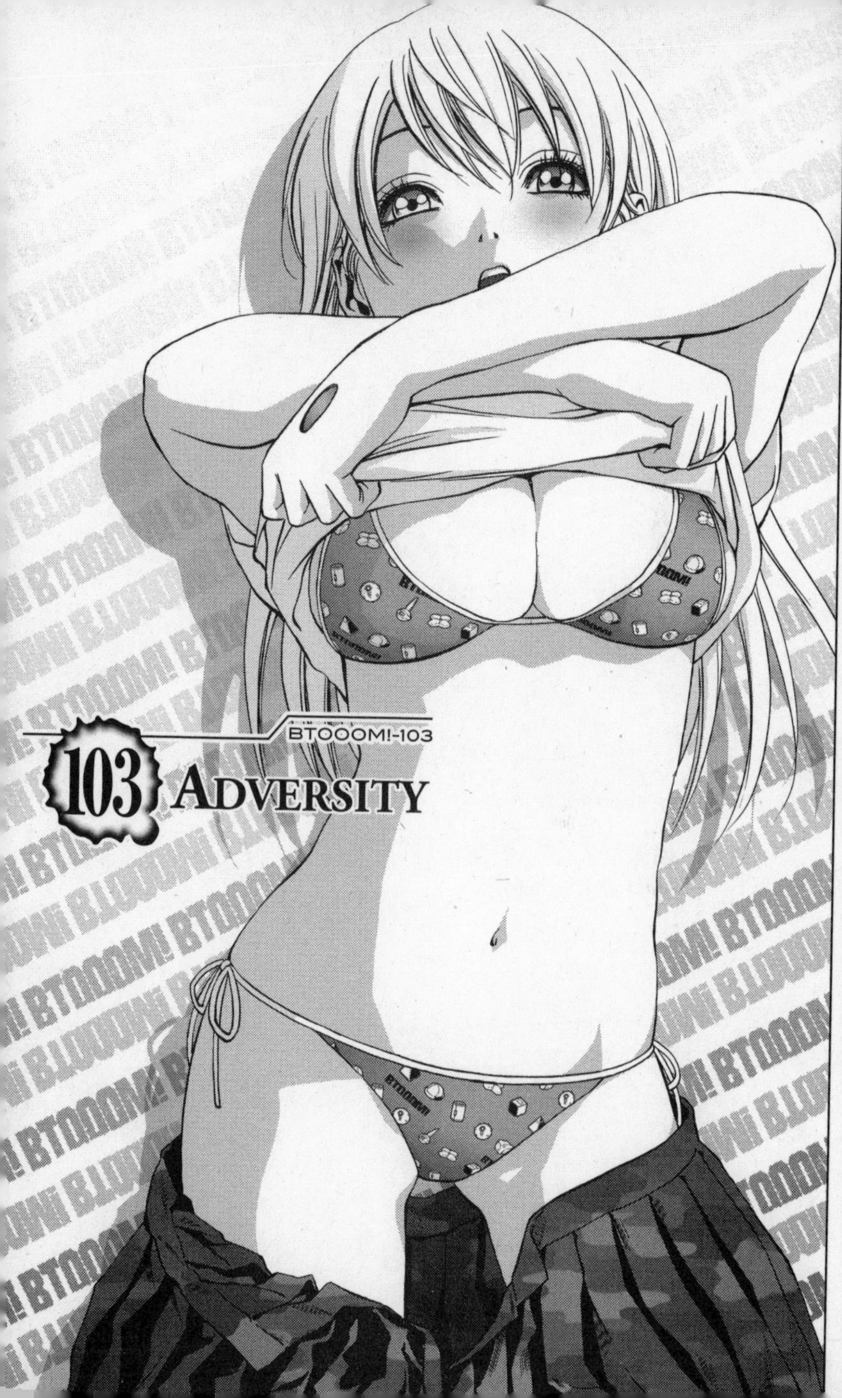
BTOOOM!-103
103 ADVERSITY

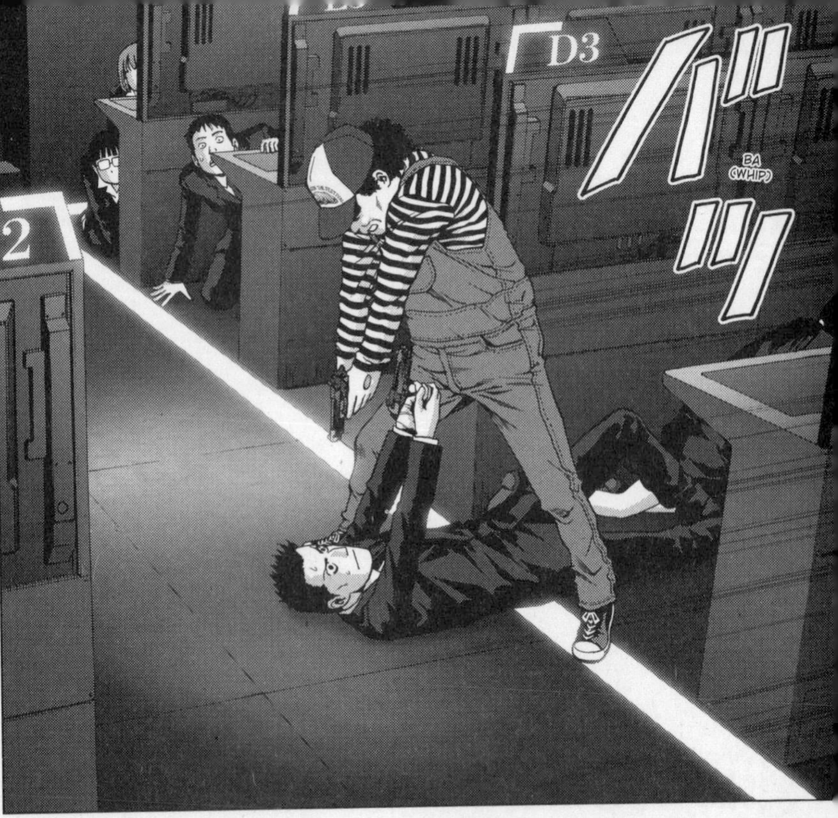
D3
バッ
BA (WHIP)

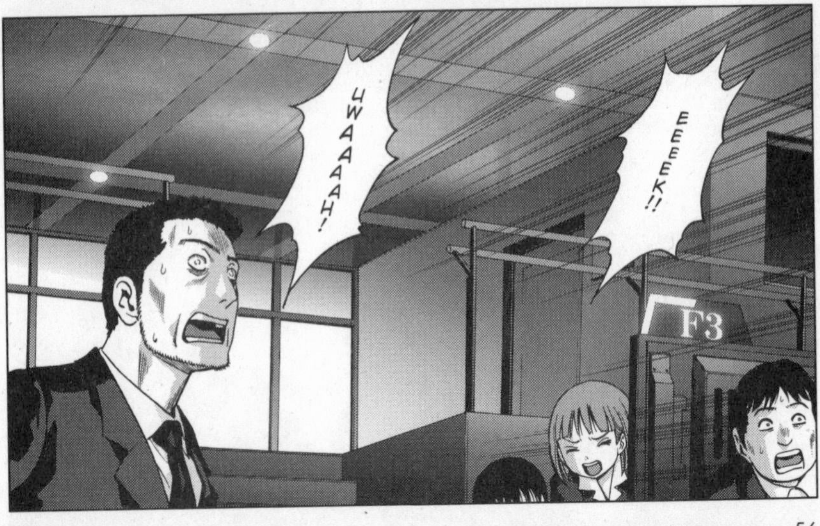
EEEEK!!
UWAAAAAH!
F3

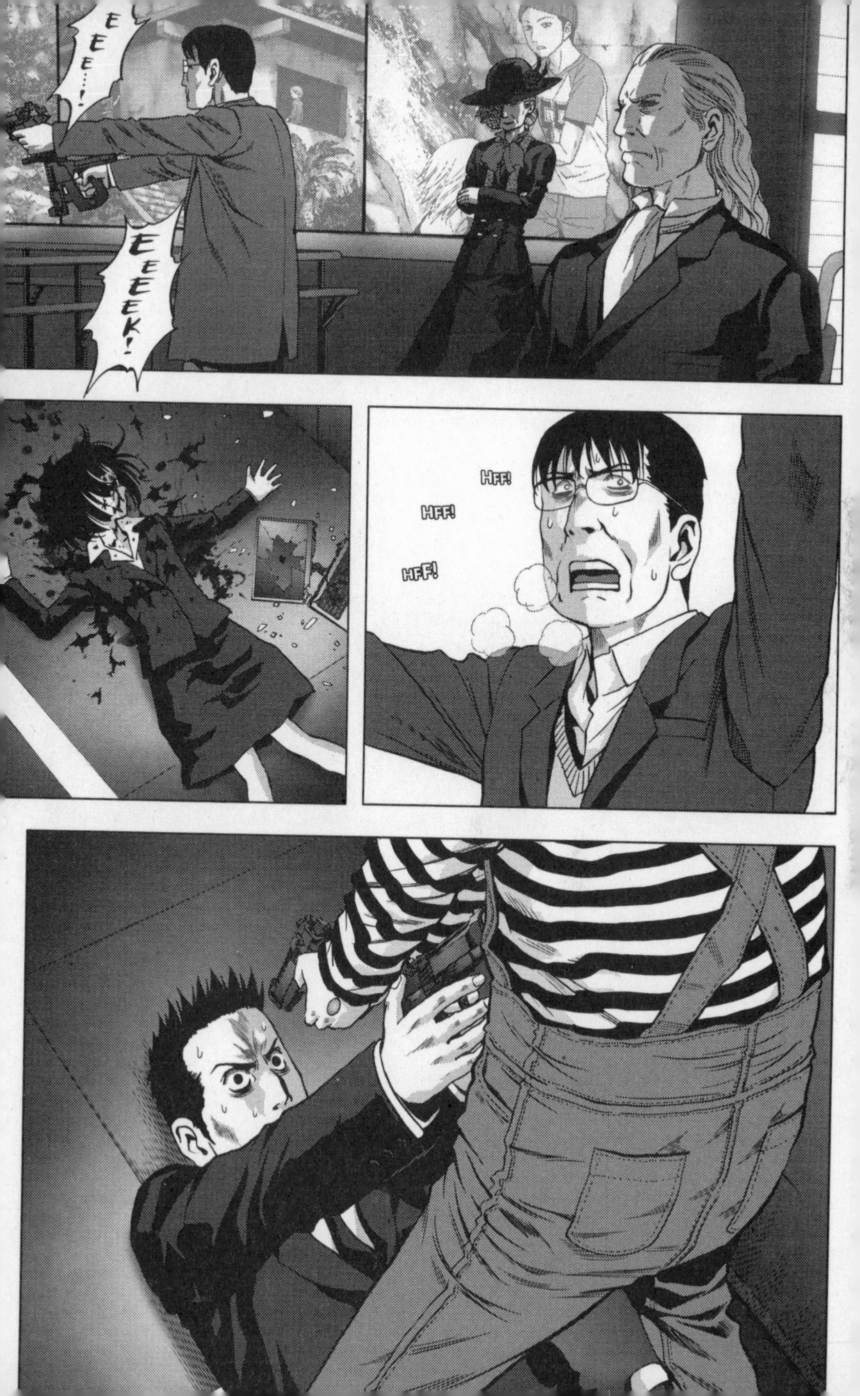
EEE...!
EEEEK!
HFF!
HFF!
HFF!

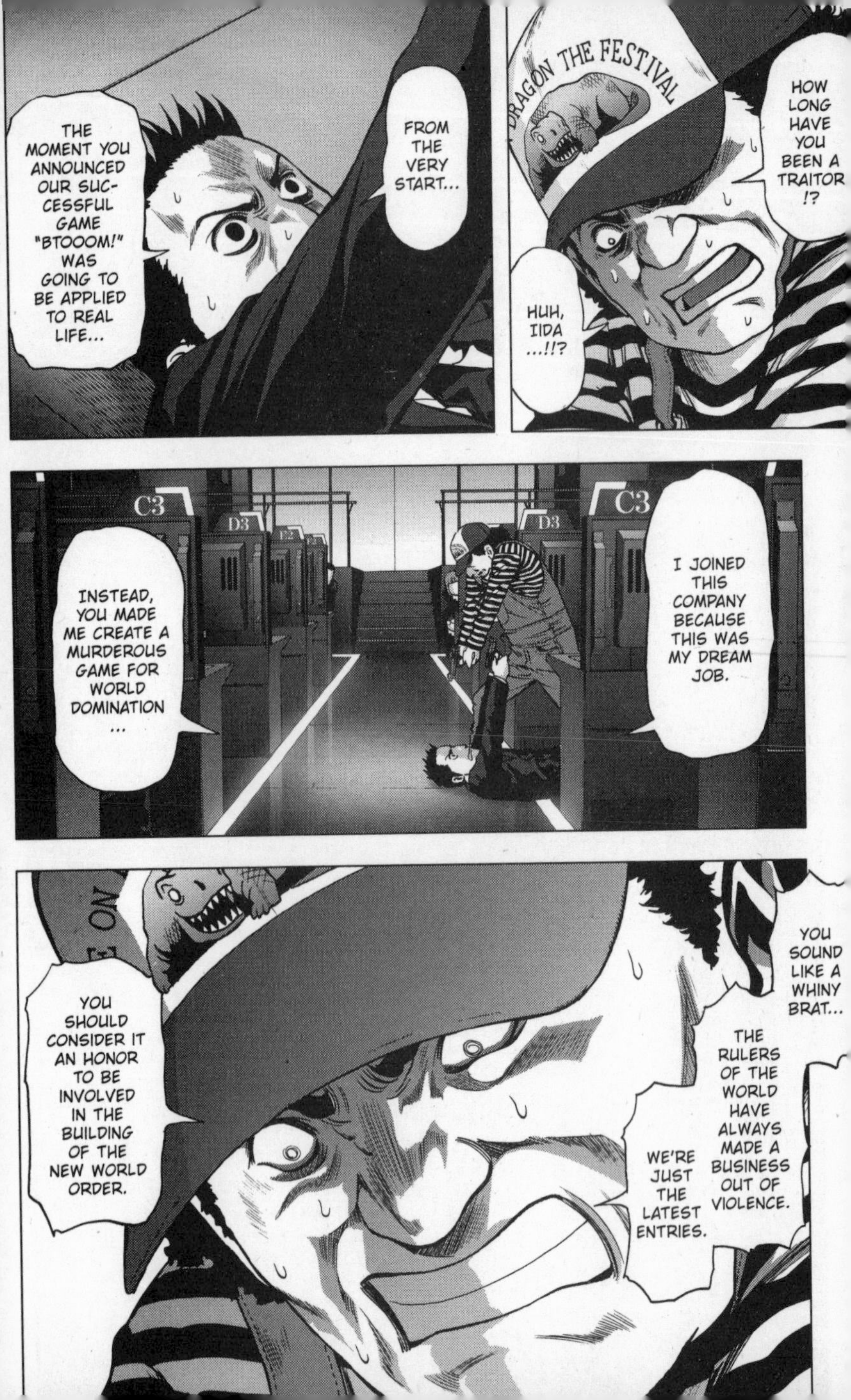
DRAGON THE FESTIVAL
HOW LONG HAVE YOU BEEN A TRAITOR !?
HUH, IIDA ...!!?
FROM THE VERY START...
THE MOMENT YOU ANNOUNCED OUR SUC-CESSFUL GAME "BTOOOM!" WAS GOING TO BE APPLIED TO REAL LIFE...
C3
D3
I JOINED THIS COMPANY BECAUSE THIS WAS MY DREAM JOB.
INSTEAD, YOU MADE ME CREATE A MURDEROUS GAME FOR WORLD DOMINATION ...
YOU SOUND LIKE A WHINY BRAT...
THE RULERS OF THE WORLD HAVE ALWAYS MADE A BUSINESS OUT OF VIOLENCE.
WE'RE JUST THE LATEST ENTRIES.
YOU SHOULD CONSIDER IT AN HONOR TO BE INVOLVED IN THE BUILDING OF THE NEW WORLD ORDER.

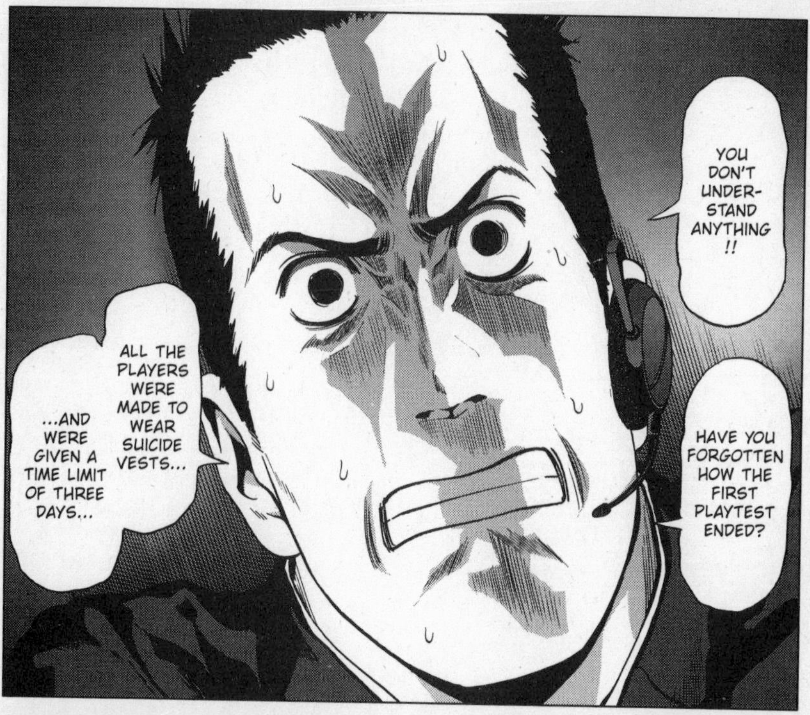
YOU DON'T UNDERSTAND ANYTHING!!
HAVE YOU FORGOTTEN HOW THE FIRST PLAYTEST ENDED?
ALL THE PLAYERS WERE MADE TO WEAR SUICIDE VESTS...
...AND WERE GIVEN A TIME LIMIT OF THREE DAYS...
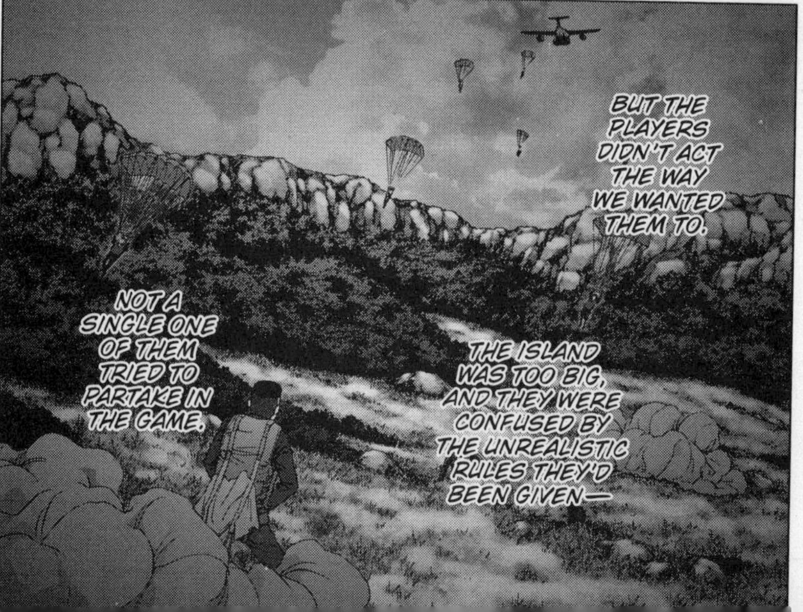
BUT THE PLAYERS DIDN'T ACT THE WAY WE WANTED THEM TO.
THE ISLAND WAS TOO BIG, AND THEY WERE CONFUSED BY THE UNREALISTIC RULES THEY'D BEEN GIVEN—
NOT A SINGLE ONE OF THEM TRIED TO PARTAKE IN THE GAME.

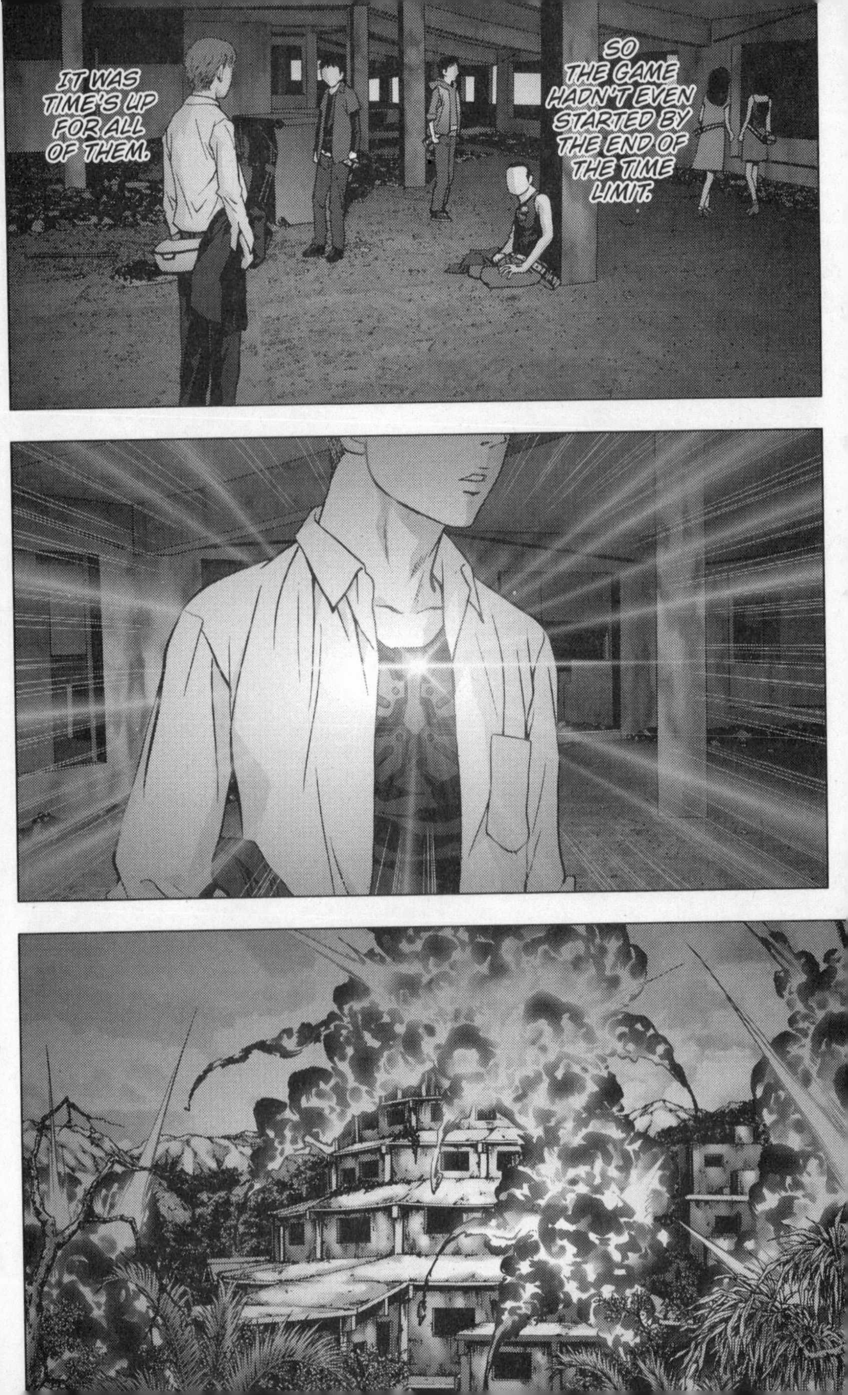
SO THE GAME HADN'T EVEN STARTED BY THE END OF THE TIME LIMIT.
IT WAS TIME'S UP FOR ALL OF THEM.

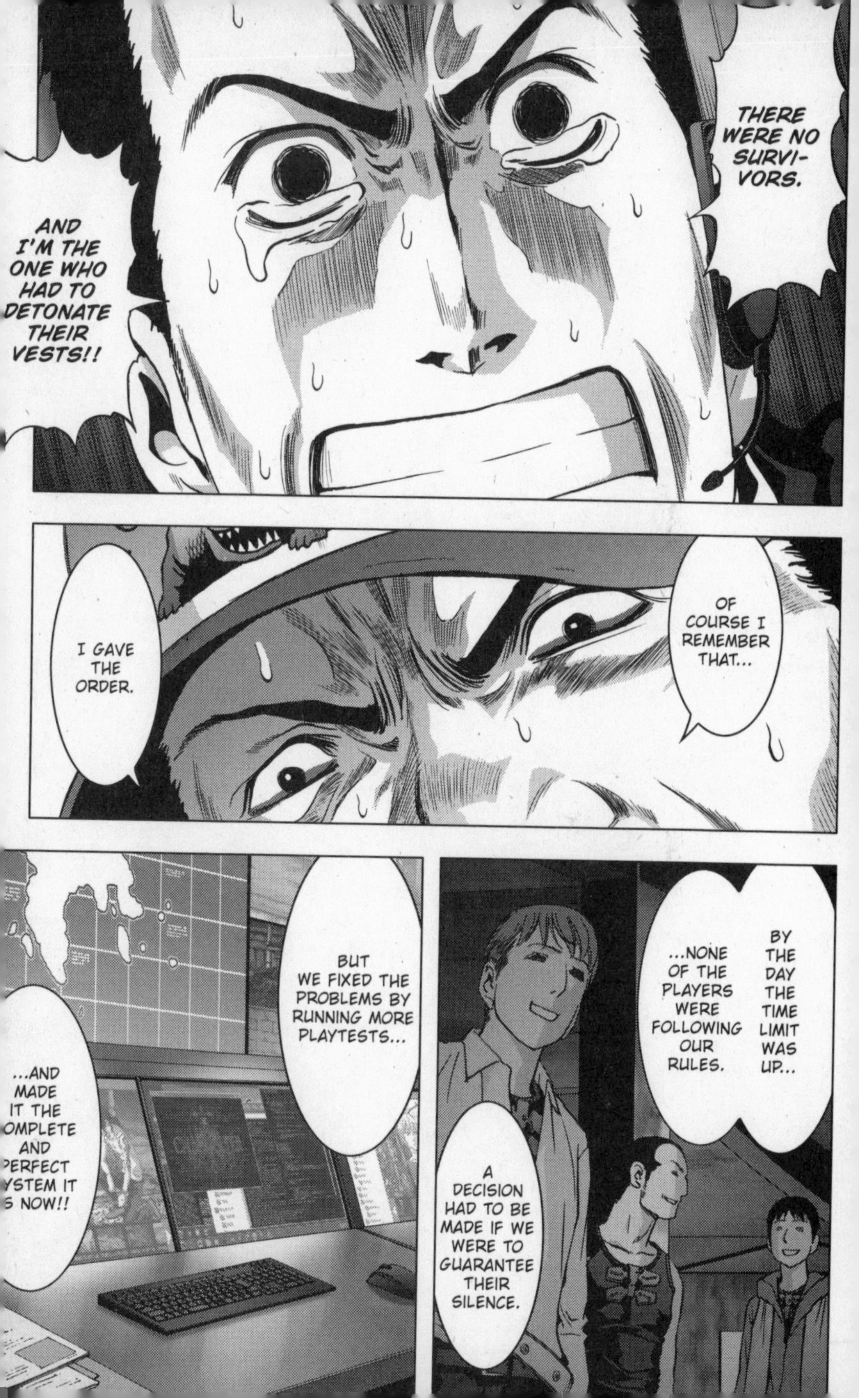
THERE WERE NO SURVIVORS.
AND I'M THE ONE WHO HAD TO DETONATE THEIR VESTS!!
OF COURSE I REMEMBER THAT...
I GAVE THE ORDER.
BY THE DAY THE TIME LIMIT WAS UP...
...NONE OF THE PLAYERS WERE FOLLOWING OUR RULES.
A DECISION HAD TO BE MADE IF WE WERE TO GUARANTEE THEIR SILENCE.
BUT WE FIXED THE PROBLEMS BY RUNNING MORE PLAYTESTS...
...AND MADE IT THE OMPLETE AND ERFECT YSTEM IT S NOW!!

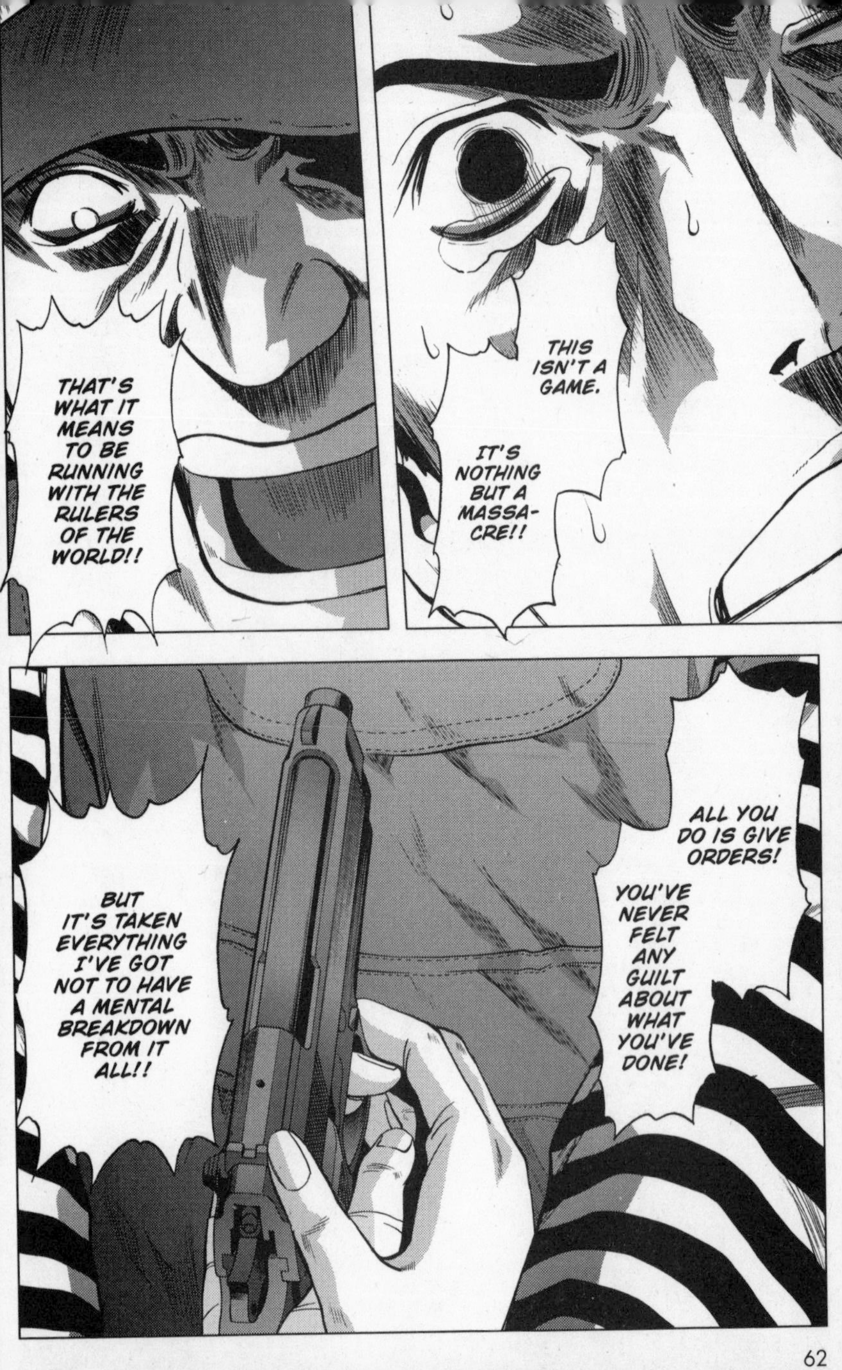
THIS ISN'T A GAME.
IT'S NOTHING BUT A MASSA-CRE!!
THAT'S WHAT IT MEANS TO BE RUNNING WITH THE RULERS OF THE WORLD!!
ALL YOU DO IS GIVE ORDERS!
YOU'VE NEVER FELT ANY GUILT ABOUT WHAT YOU'VE DONE!
BUT IT'S TAKEN EVERYTHING I'VE GOT NOT TO HAVE A MENTAL BREAKDOWN FROM IT ALL!!

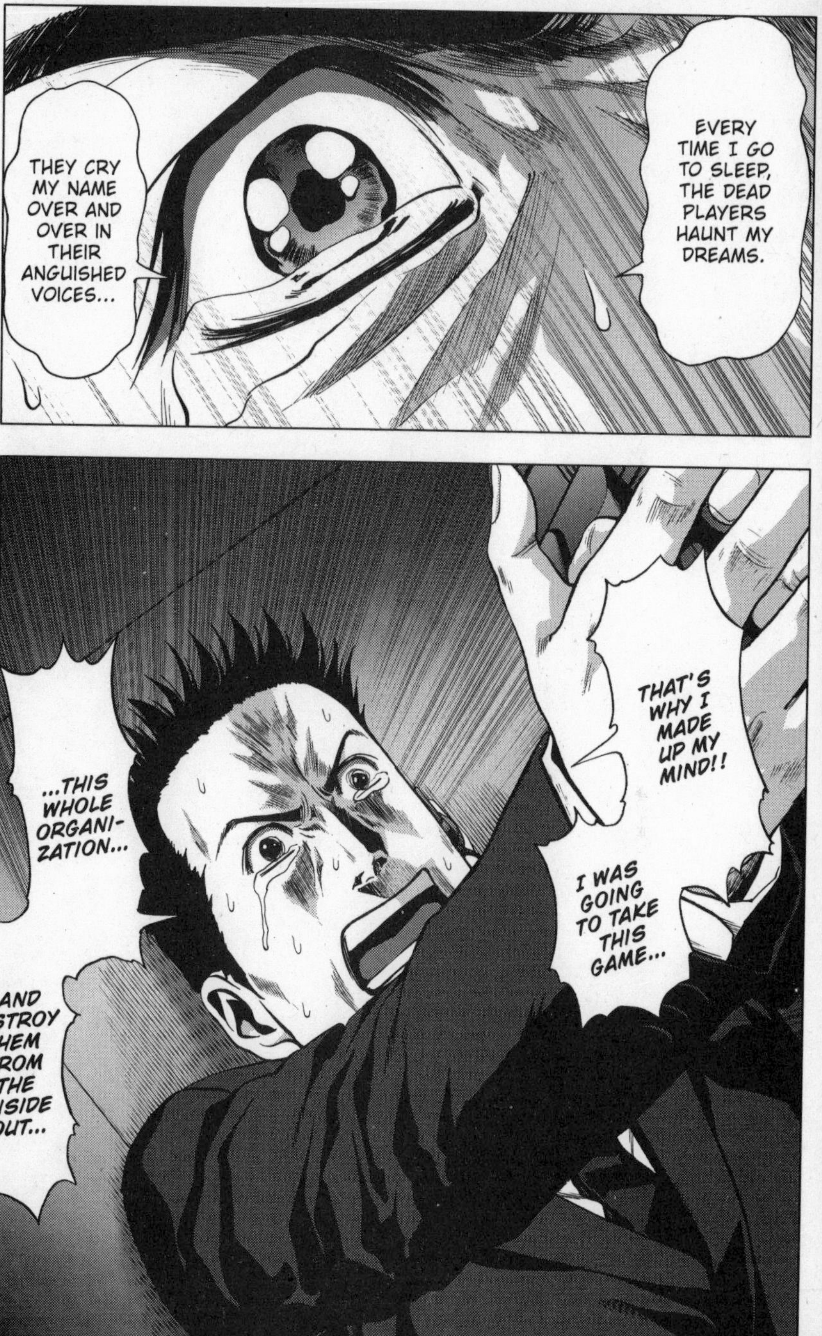
EVERY TIME I GO TO SLEEP, THE DEAD PLAYERS HAUNT MY DREAMS.
THEY CRY MY NAME OVER AND OVER IN THEIR ANGUISHED VOICES...
THAT'S WHY I MADE UP MY MIND!!
I WAS GOING TO TAKE THIS GAME...
...THIS WHOLE ORGANI-ZATION...
...AND ESTROY THEM FROM THE INSIDE OUT...

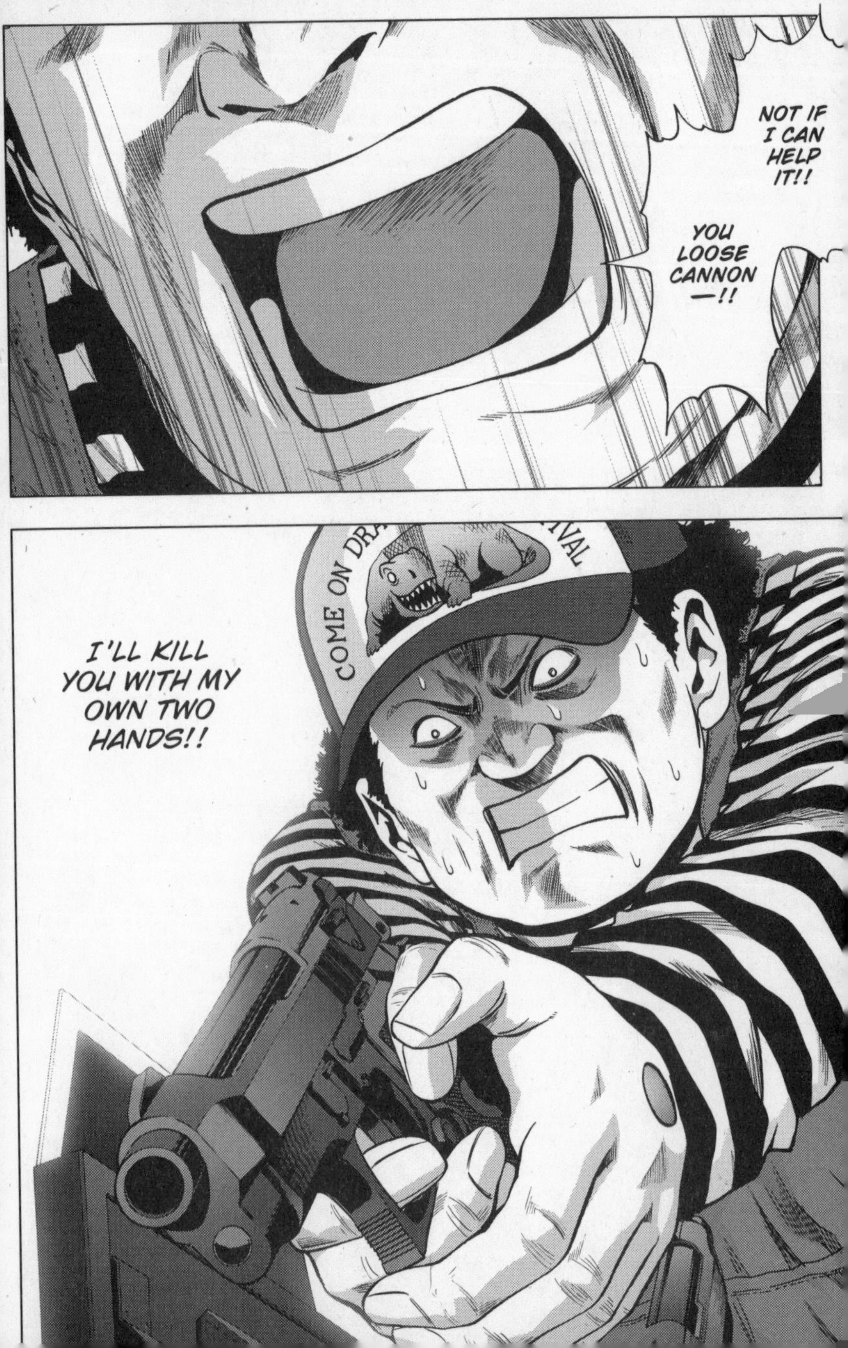
NOT IF I CAN HELP IT!!
YOU LOOSE CANNON —!!
I'LL KILL YOU WITH MY OWN TWO HANDS!!

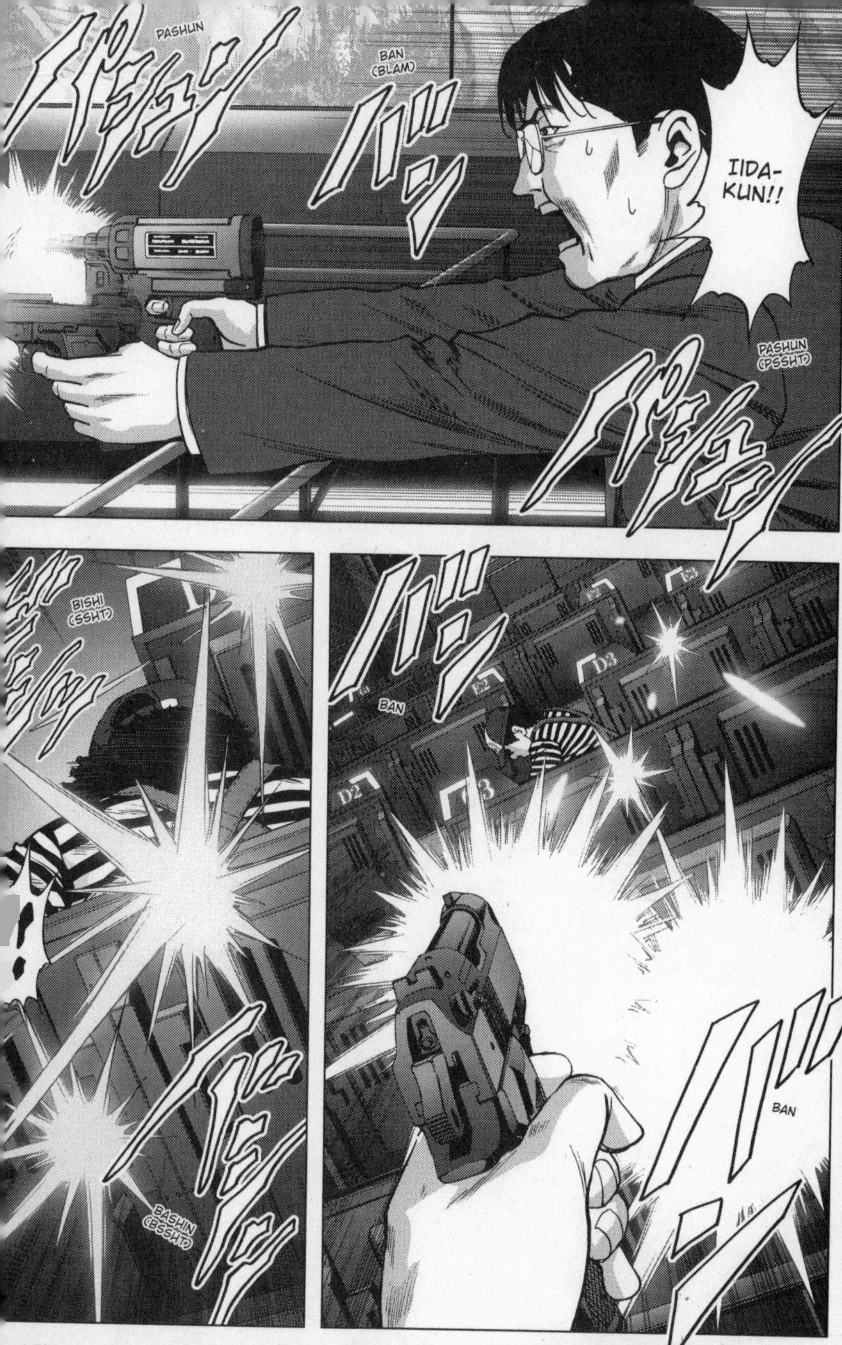
IIDA-KUN!!
PASHUN (PSSHT)
BAN (BLAM)
PASHUN
BAN
BAN
BISHI (SSHT)
BASHIN (BSSHT)

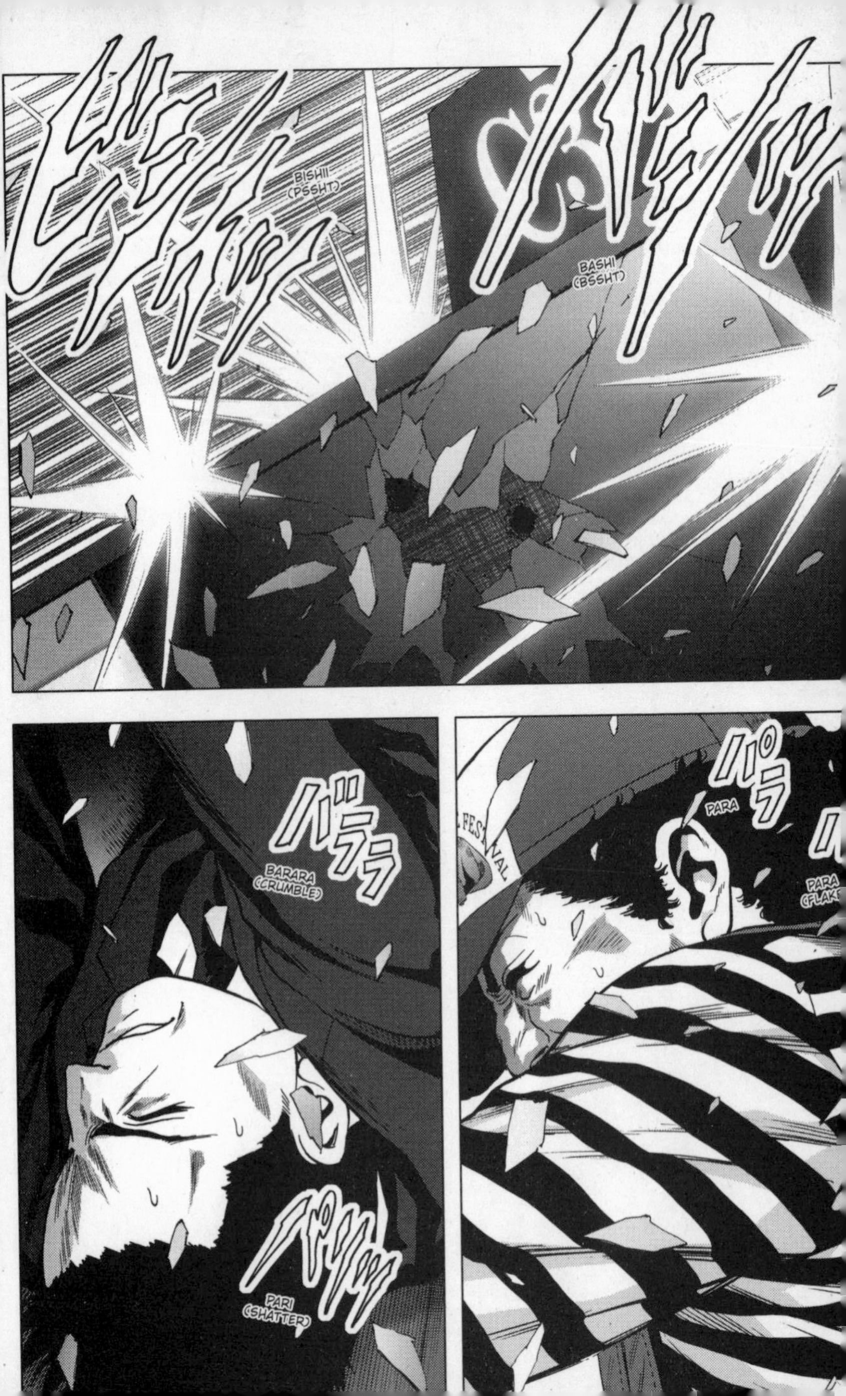
BASHI (BSSHT)
BISHII (PSSHT)
FESTIVAL
PARA
PARA
BARARA (CRUMBLE)
PARI (SHATTER)

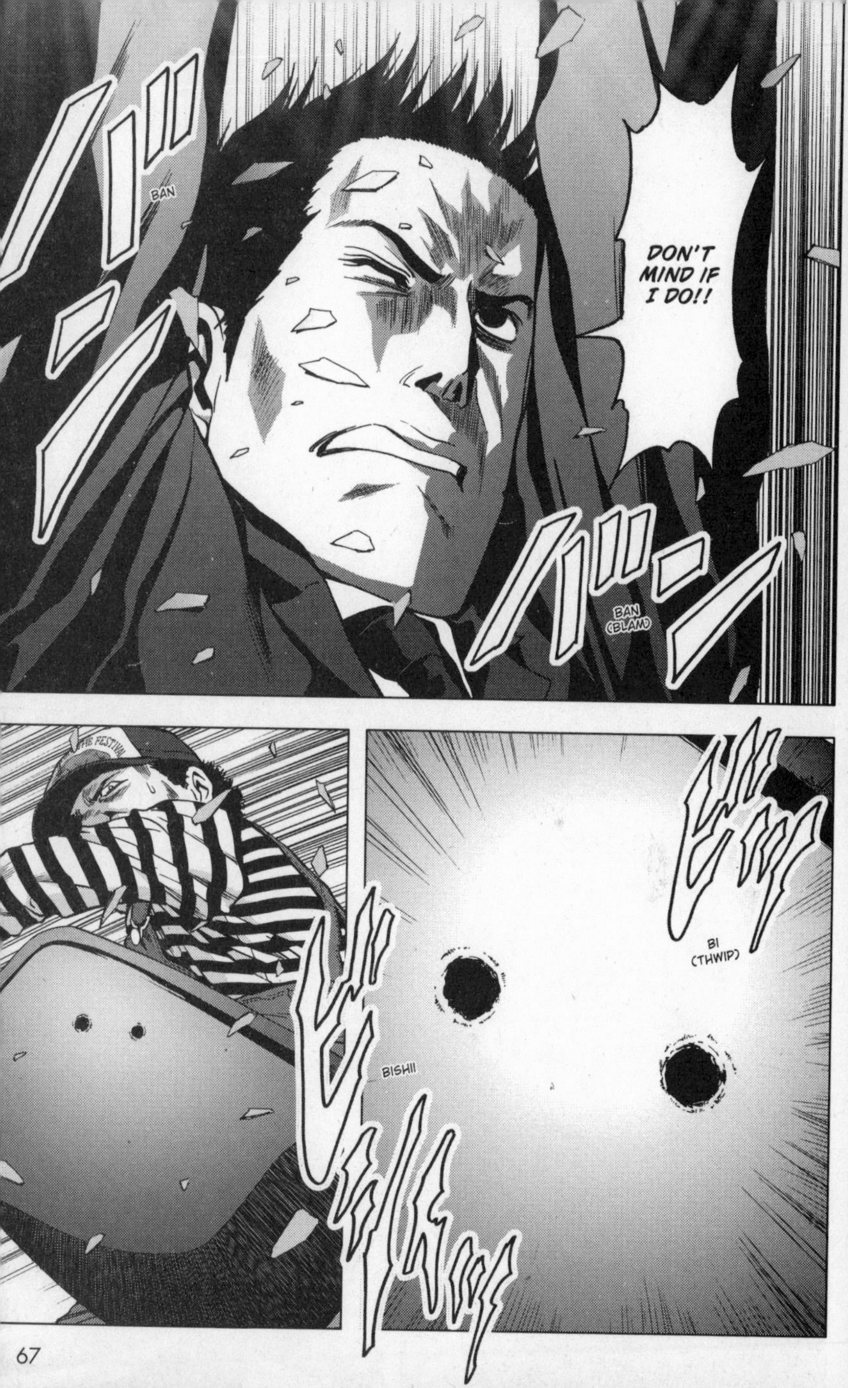
DON'T MIND IF I DO!!
BAN (BLAM)
BAN
BI (THWIP)
BISHII

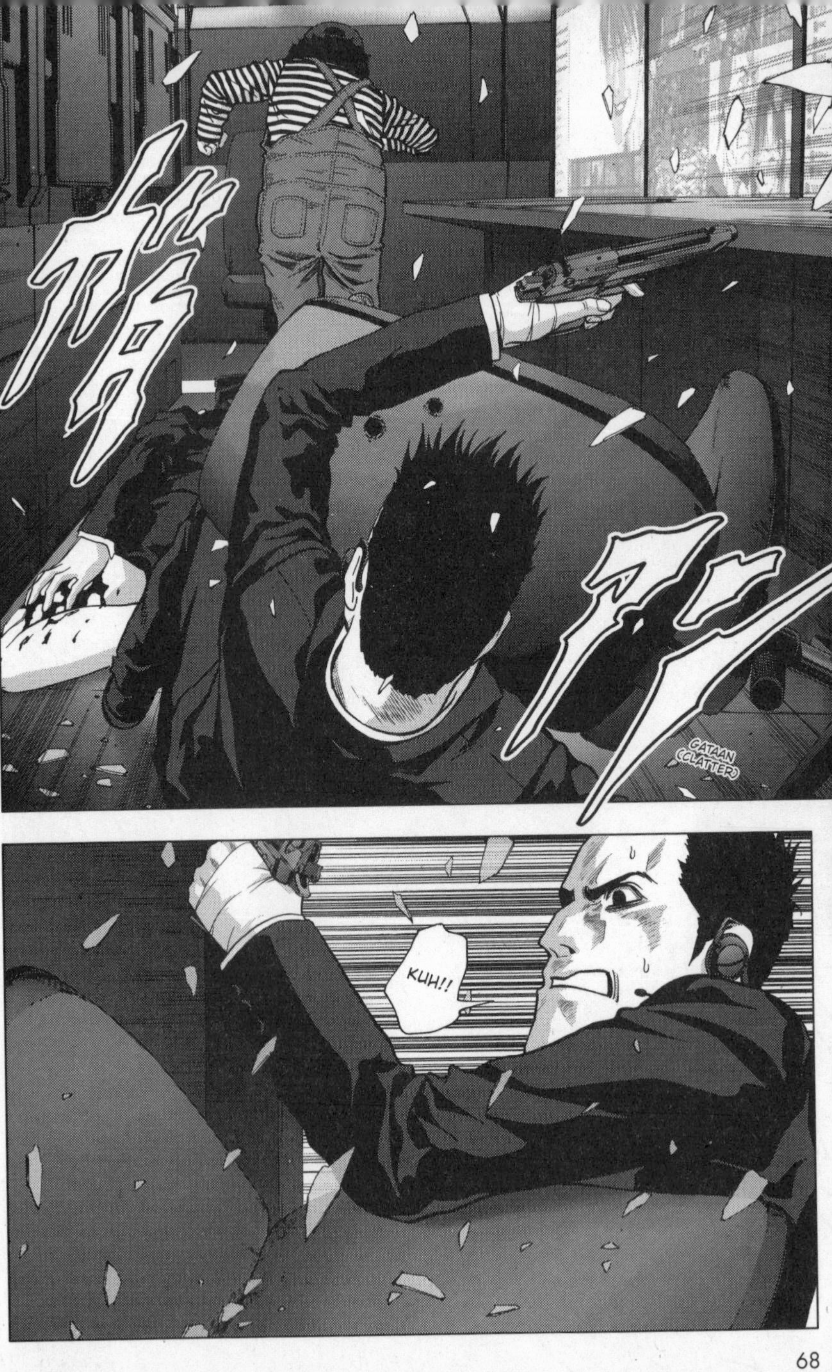
GATAAN
(CLATTER)
KUH!!

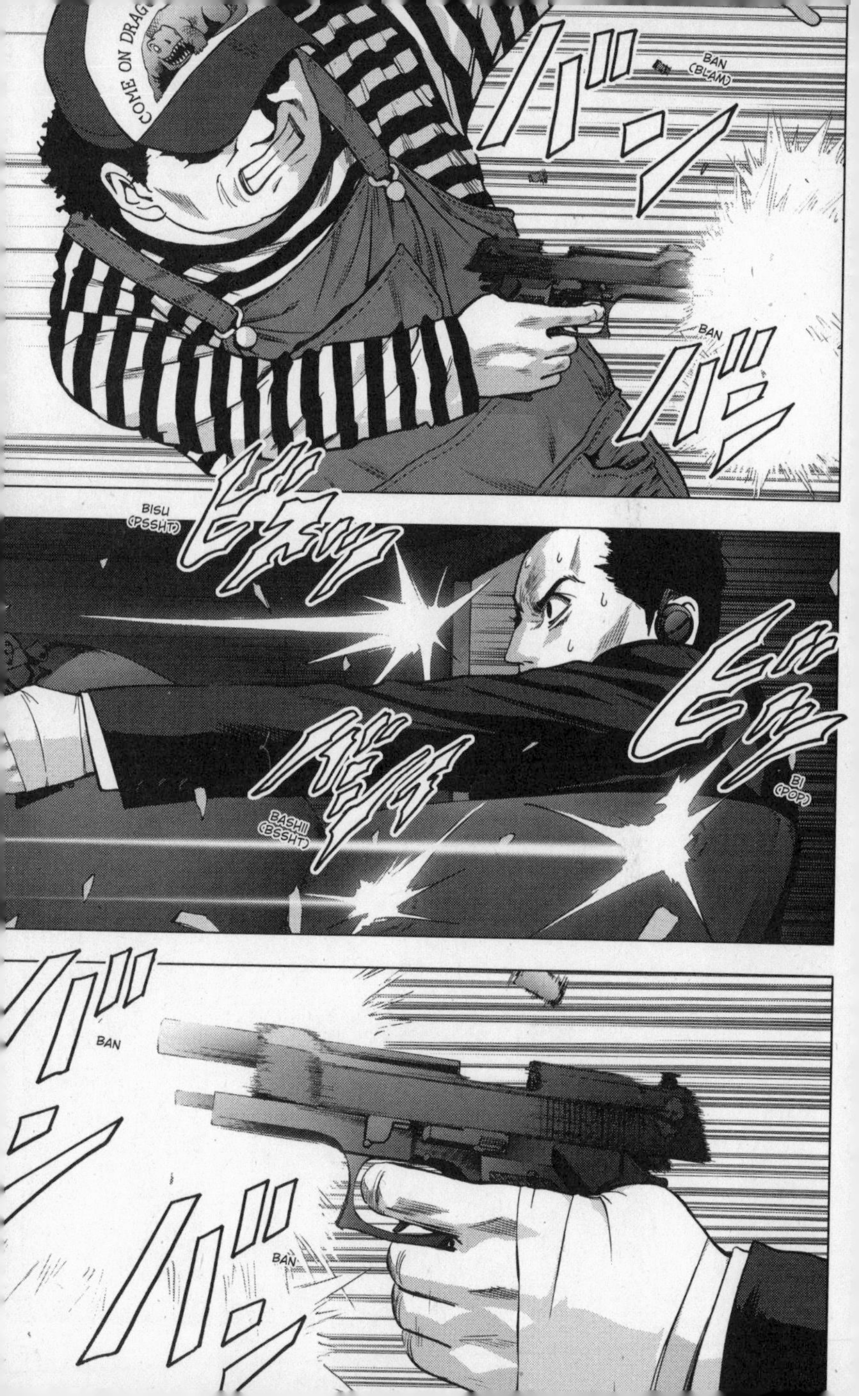
COME ON DRAG
BAN (BLAM)
BAN
BI (POP)
BASHII (BSSHT)
BISU (PSSHT)
BAN
BAN

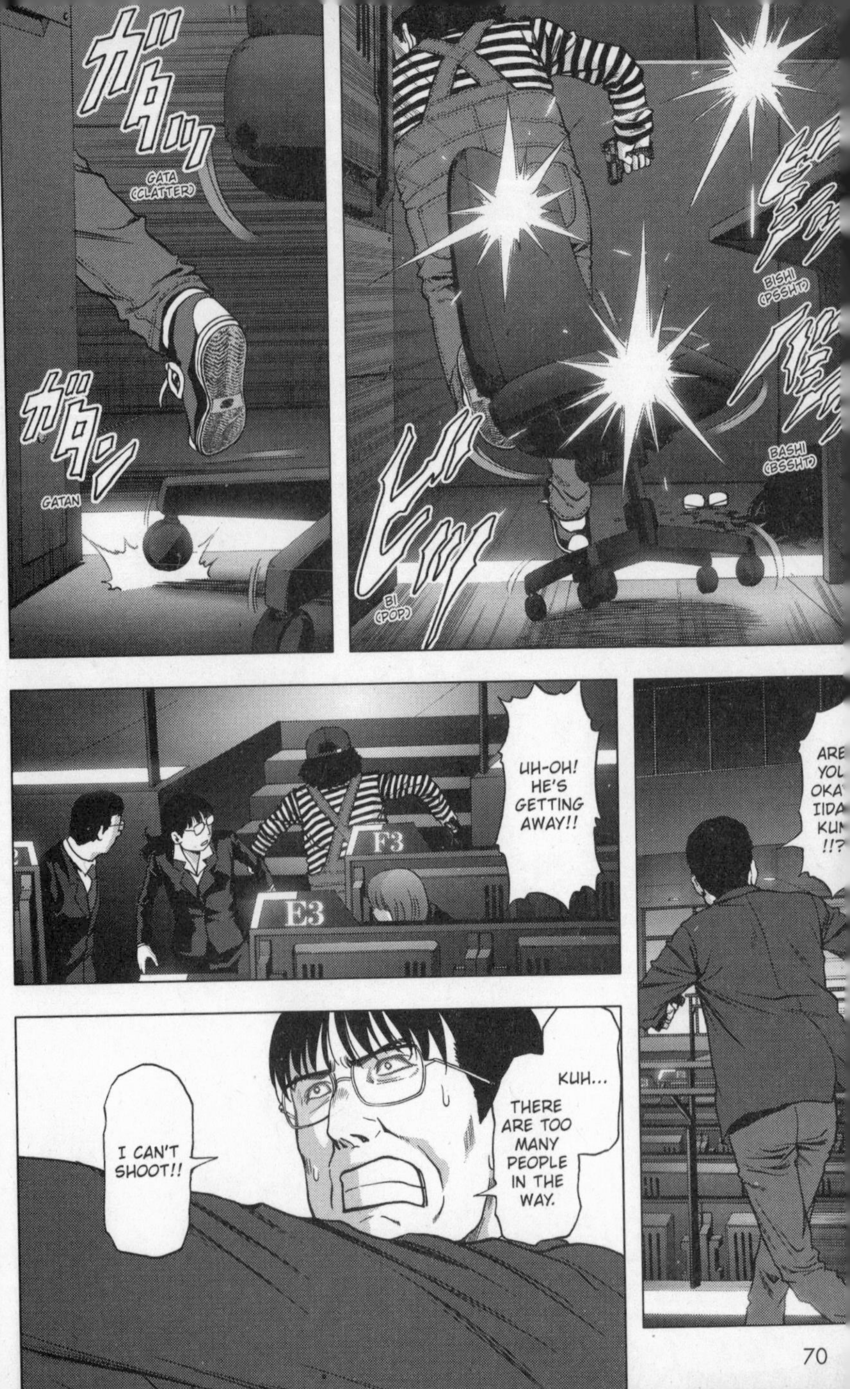
BISHI (PSSHT)
BASHI (BSSHT)
BI (POP)
GATA (CLATTER)
GATAN
ARE YOU OKA IIDA KUN !!?
UH-OH! HE'S GETTING AWAY!!
F3
E3
KUH...
THERE ARE TOO MANY PEOPLE IN THE WAY.
I CAN'T SHOOT!!

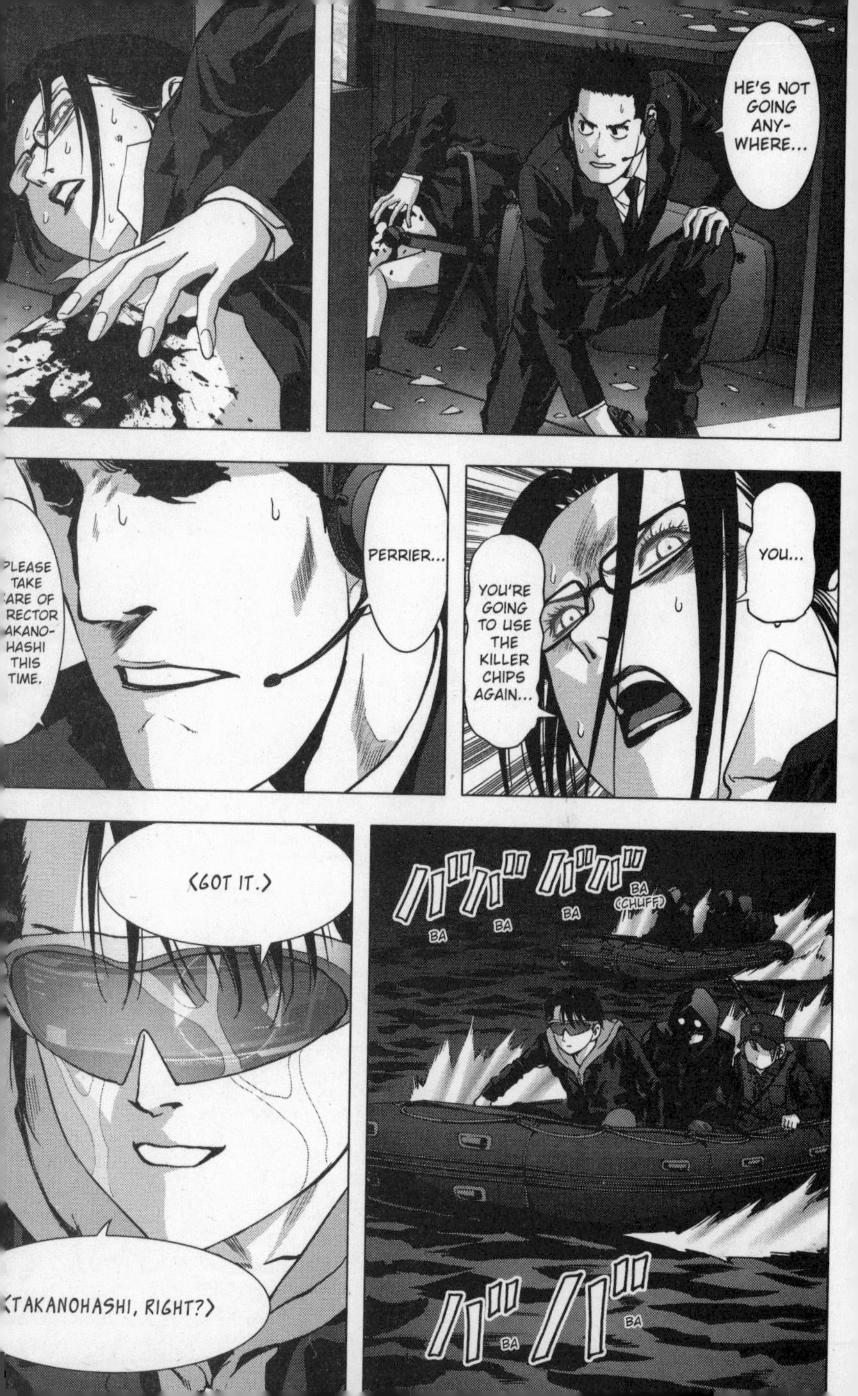

HE'S NOT GOING ANY-WHERE...
YOU...
YOU'RE GOING TO USE THE KILLER CHIPS AGAIN...
PERRIER...
PLEASE TAKE ARE OF RECTOR AKANO-HASHI THIS TIME.
BA BA BA BA (CHUFF)
BA BA
‹GOT IT.›
‹TAKANOHASHI, RIGHT?›

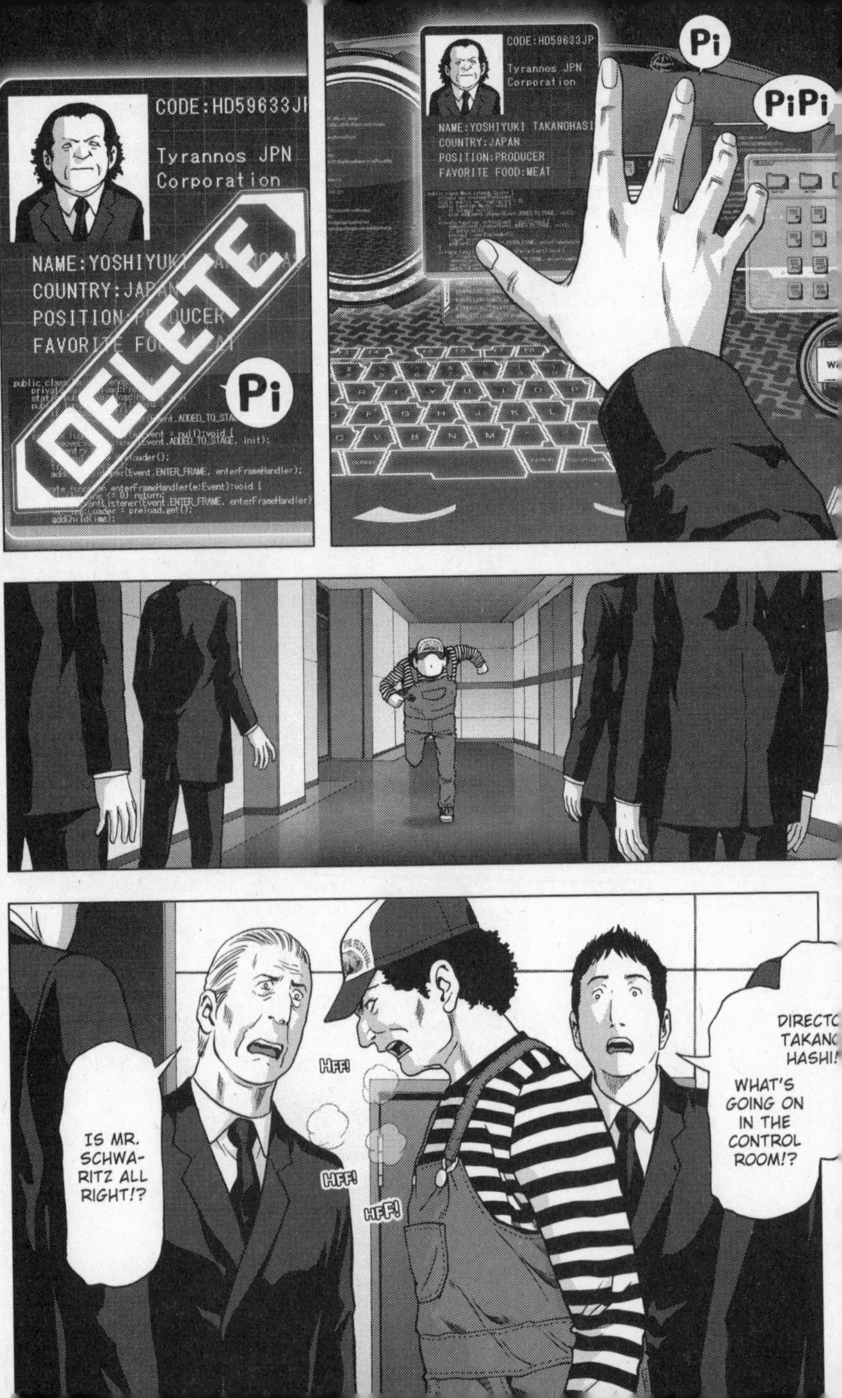
Pi
PiPi
CODE:HD59633JP
Tyrannos JPN
Corporation
NAME:YOSHIYUKI TAKANOHASI
COUNTRY:JAPAN
POSITION:PRODUCER
FAVORITE FOOD:MEAT
CODE:HD59633J
Tyrannos JPN
Corporation
DELETE
Pi
DIRECTO TAKANO HASHI!
WHAT'S GOING ON IN THE CONTROL ROOM!?
HFF!
HFF!
HFF!
IS MR. SCHWA-RITZ ALL RIGHT!?

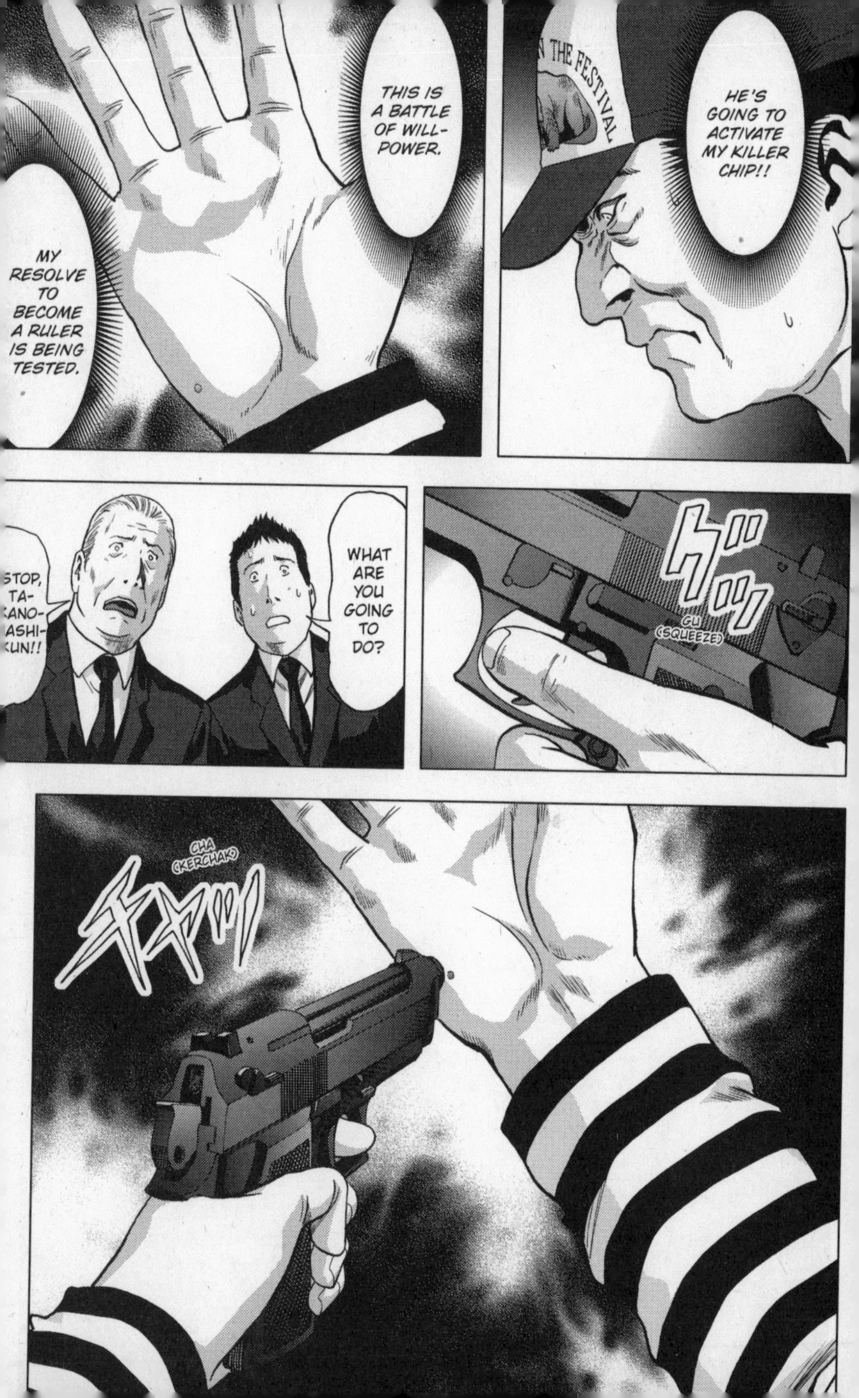
HE'S GOING TO ACTIVATE MY KILLER CHIP!!
N THE FESTIVAL
THIS IS A BATTLE OF WILL-POWER.
MY RESOLVE TO BECOME A RULER IS BEING TESTED.
GU (SQUEEZE)
WHAT ARE YOU GOING TO DO?
STOP, TA-KANO-ASHI-KUN!!
CHA (KERCHAK)

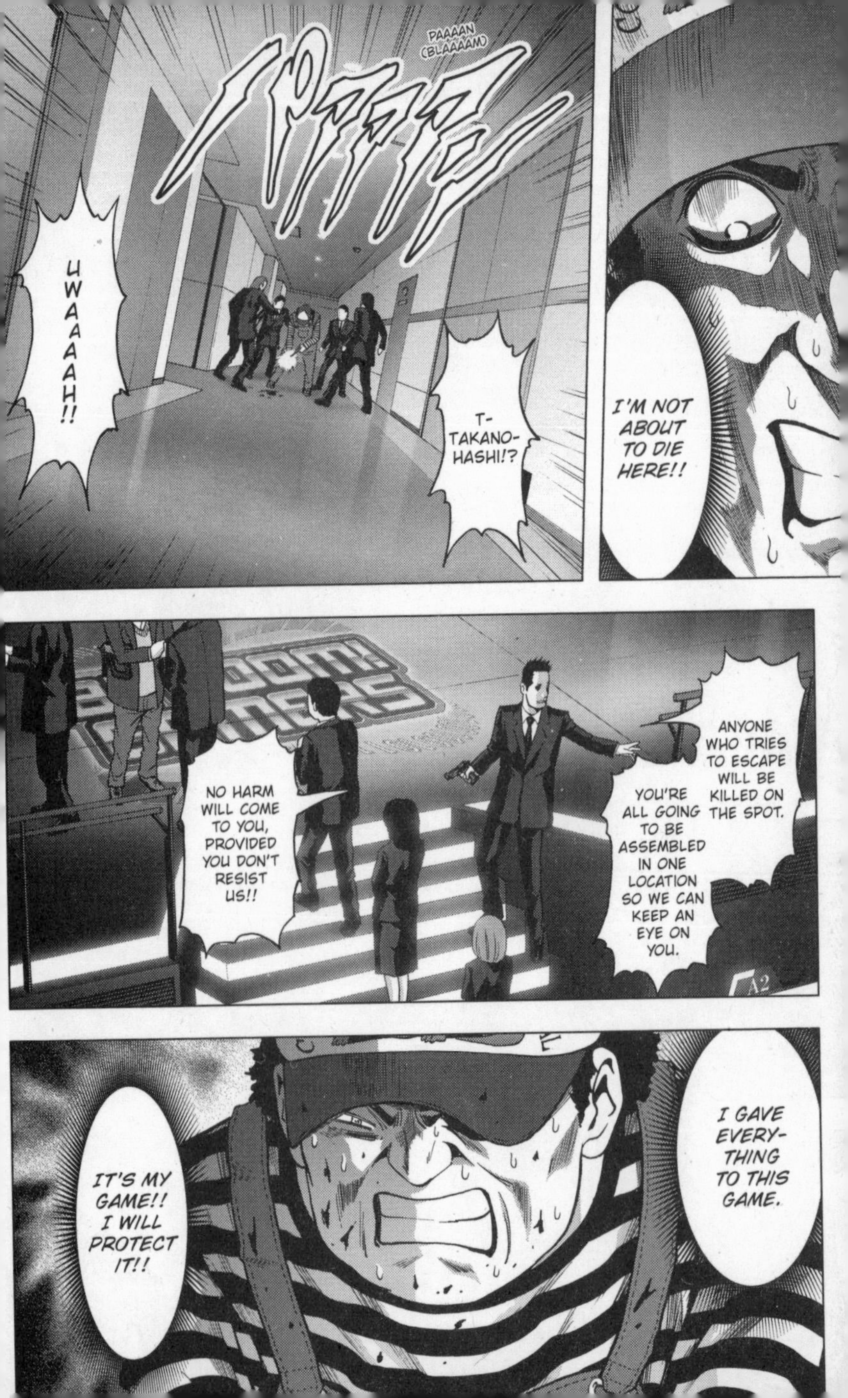
I'M NOT ABOUT TO DIE HERE!!
PAAAAN (BLAAAAM)
T-TAKANO-HASHI!?
UWAAAAAH!!
ANYONE WHO TRIES TO ESCAPE WILL BE KILLED ON THE SPOT.
YOU'RE ALL GOING TO BE ASSEMBLED IN ONE LOCATION SO WE CAN KEEP AN EYE ON YOU.
NO HARM WILL COME TO YOU, PROVIDED YOU DON'T RESIST US!!
A2
I GAVE EVERY-THING TO THIS GAME.
IT'S MY GAME!! I WILL PROTECT IT!!

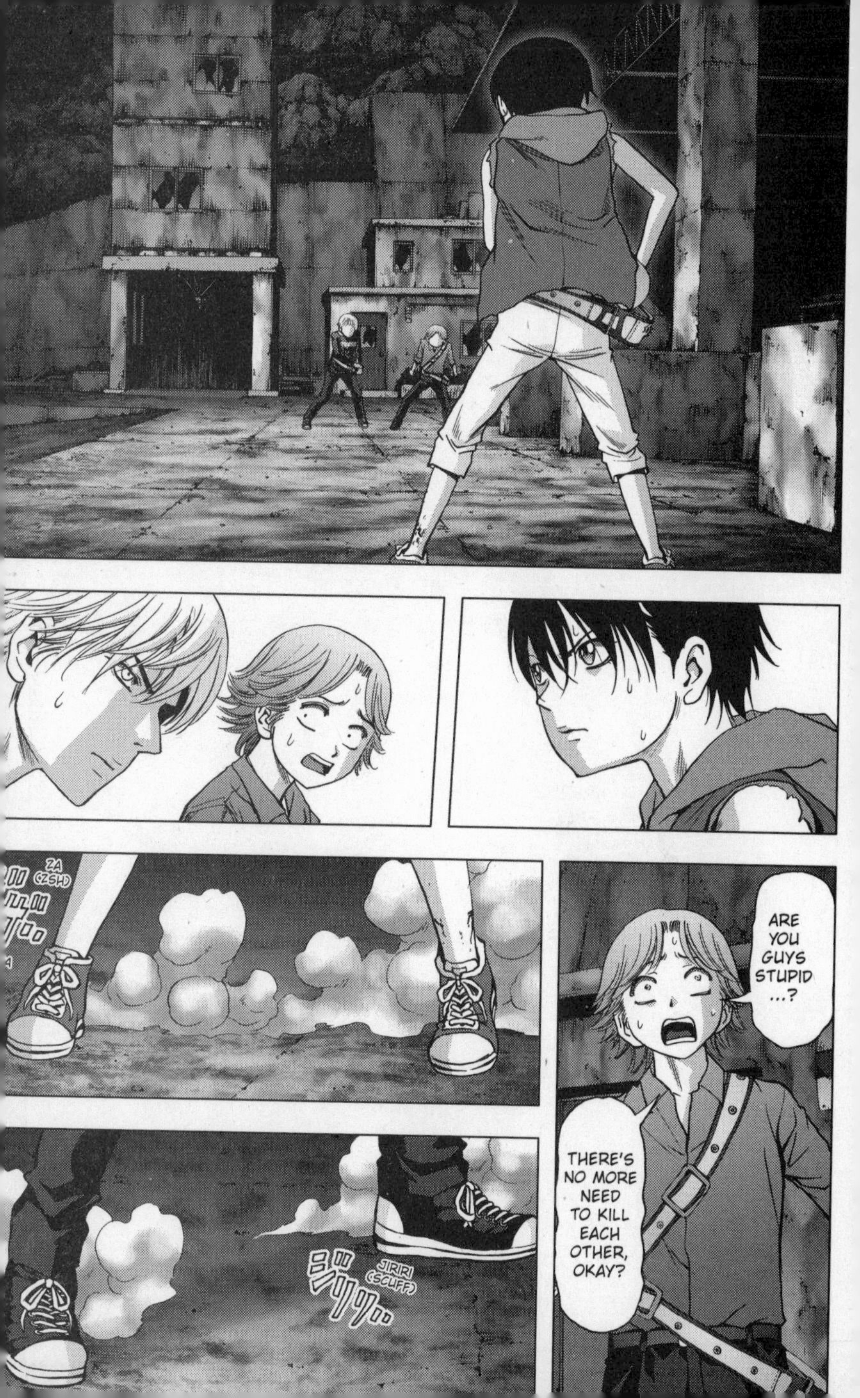
ARE YOU GUYS STUPID ...?
THERE'S NO MORE NEED TO KILL EACH OTHER, OKAY?
ZA (ZSH)
JIRIRI (SCUFF)

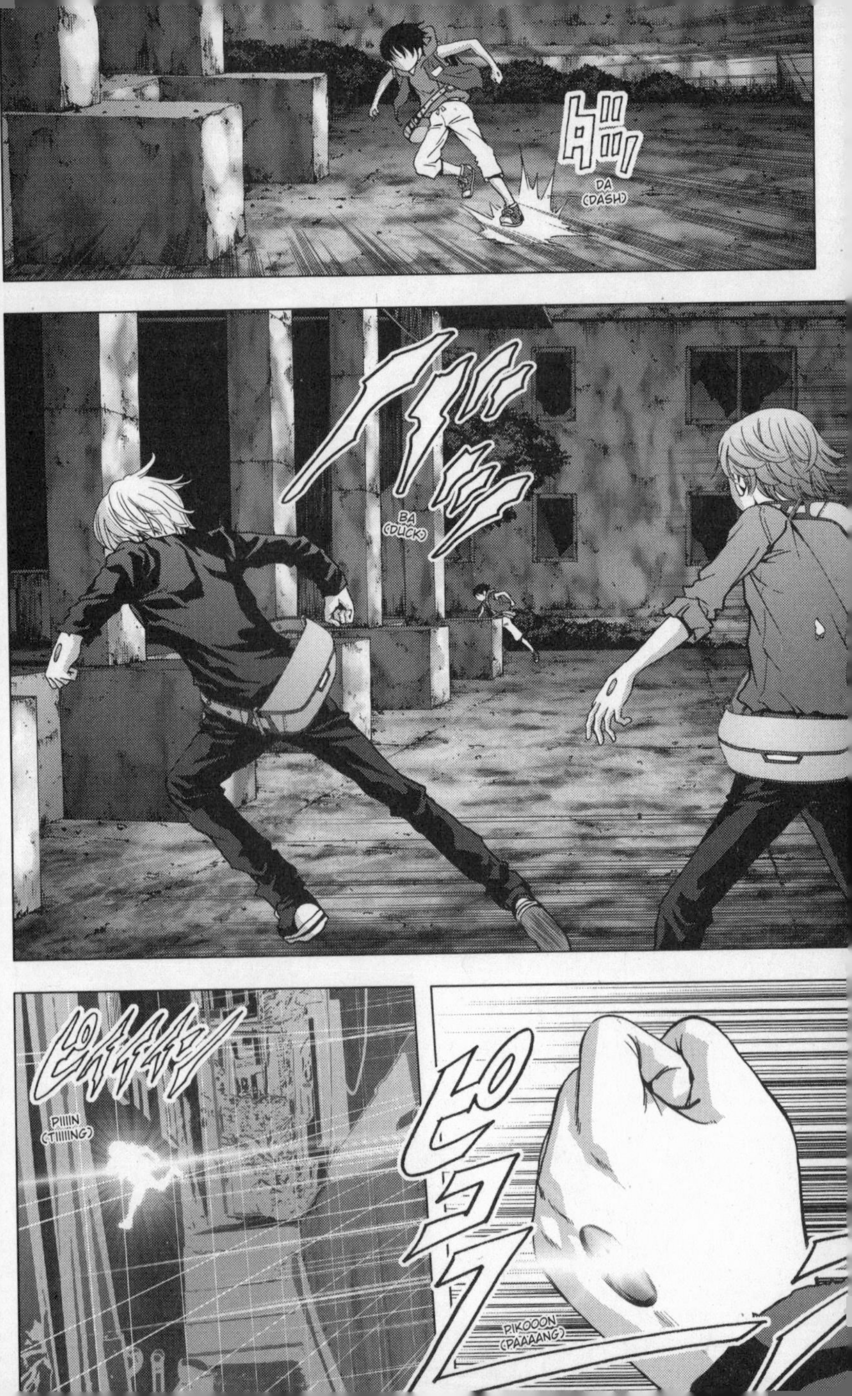
DA
(DASH)
BA
(DUCK)
PIKOOON
(PAAAANG)
PIIIIN
(TIIIIING)

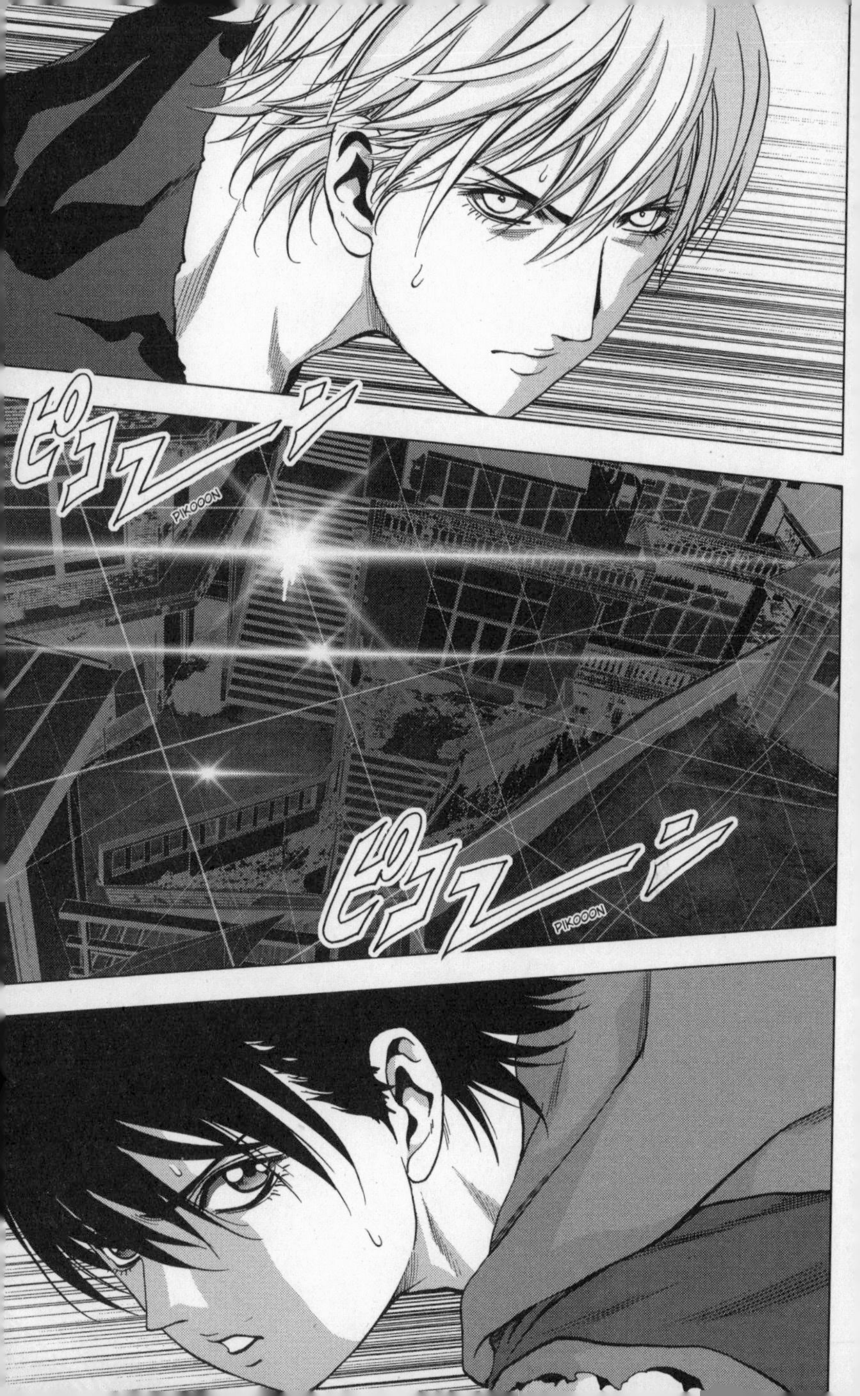
ピコーン
PIKOOON
ピコーン
PIKOOON

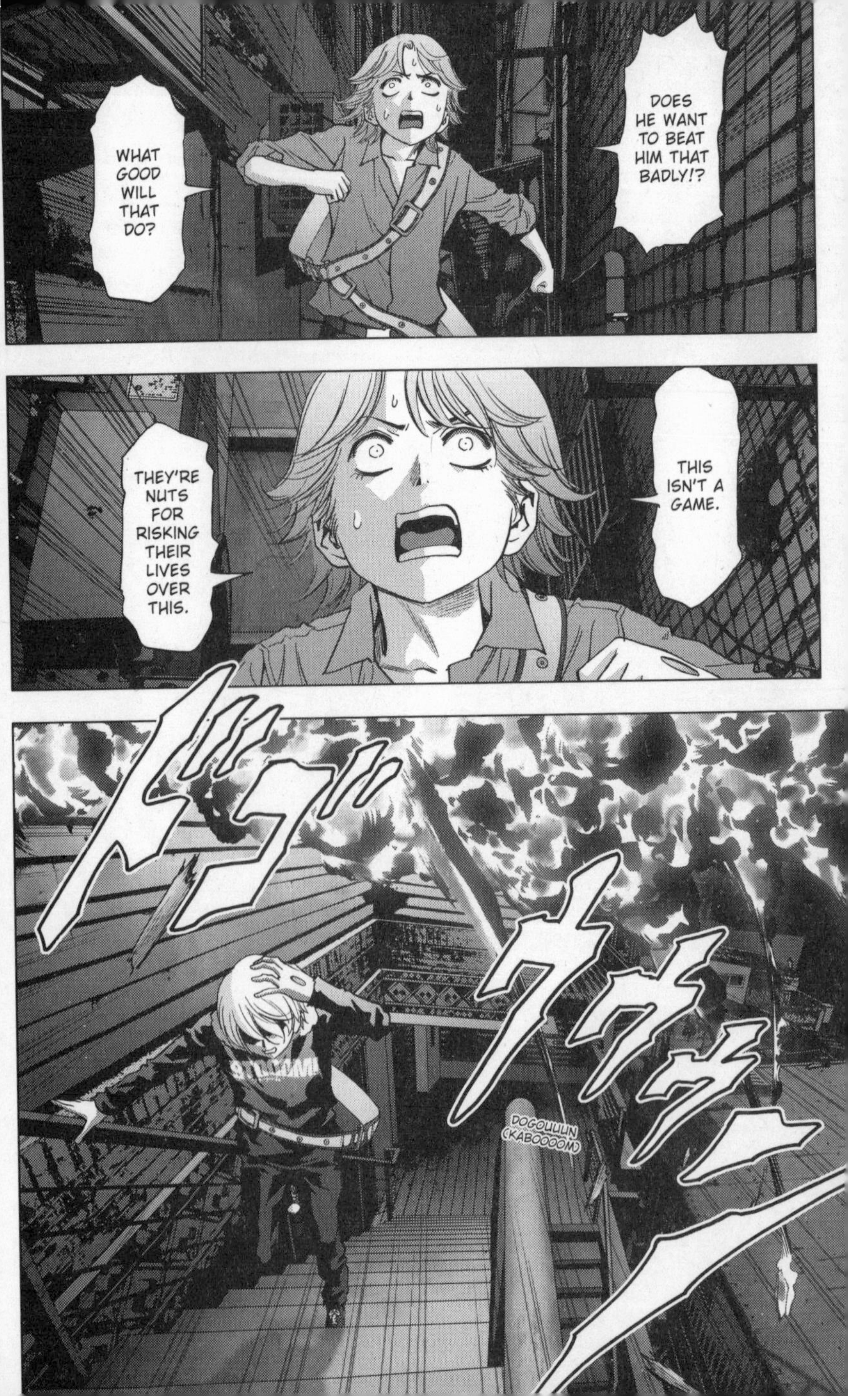
DOES HE WANT TO BEAT HIM THAT BADLY!?
WHAT GOOD WILL THAT DO?
THIS ISN'T A GAME.
THEY'RE NUTS FOR RISKING THEIR LIVES OVER THIS.
DOGOUUUN (KABOOOOM)

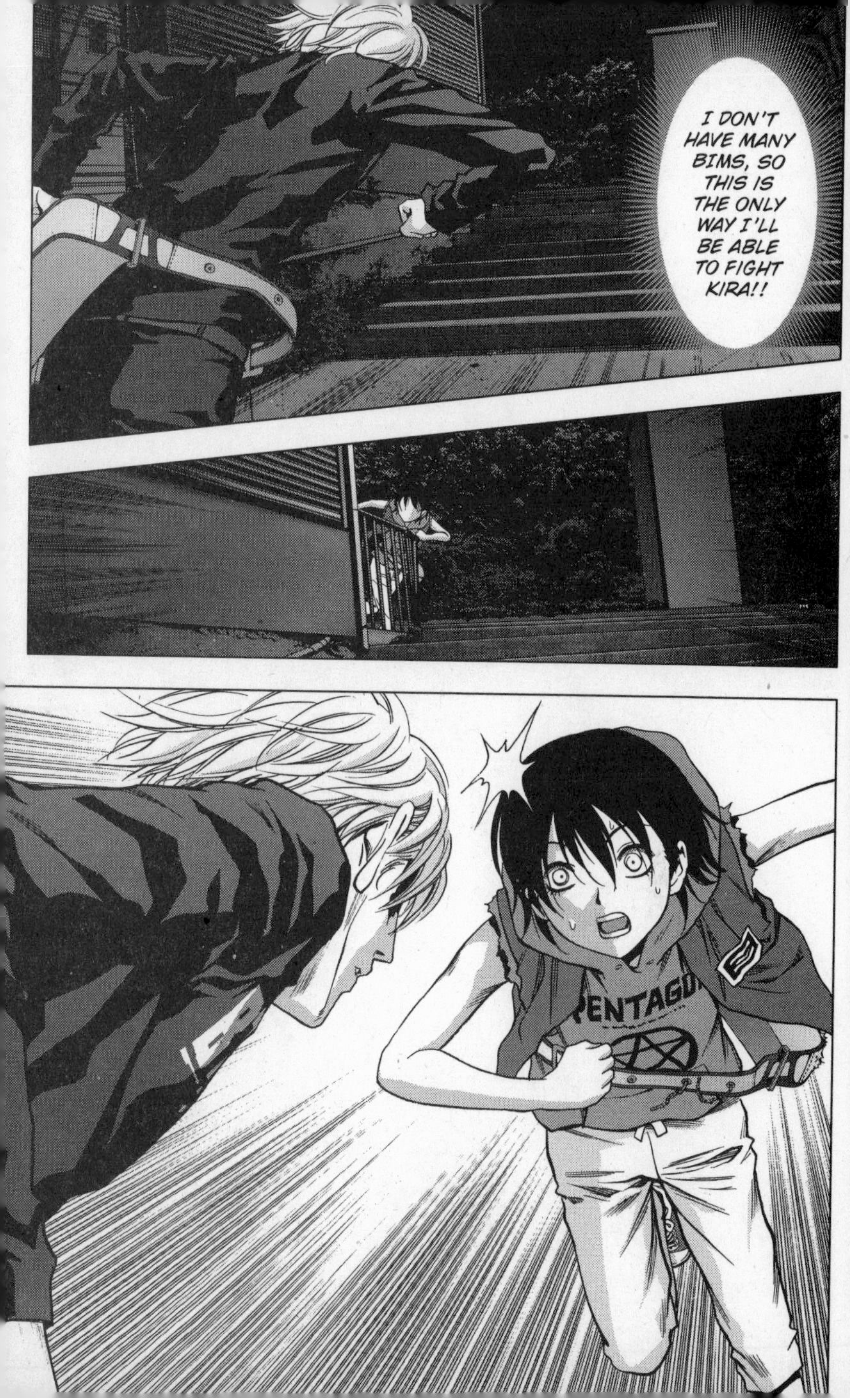
I DON'T HAVE MANY BIMS, SO THIS IS THE ONLY WAY I'LL BE ABLE TO FIGHT KIRA!!
PENTAGO

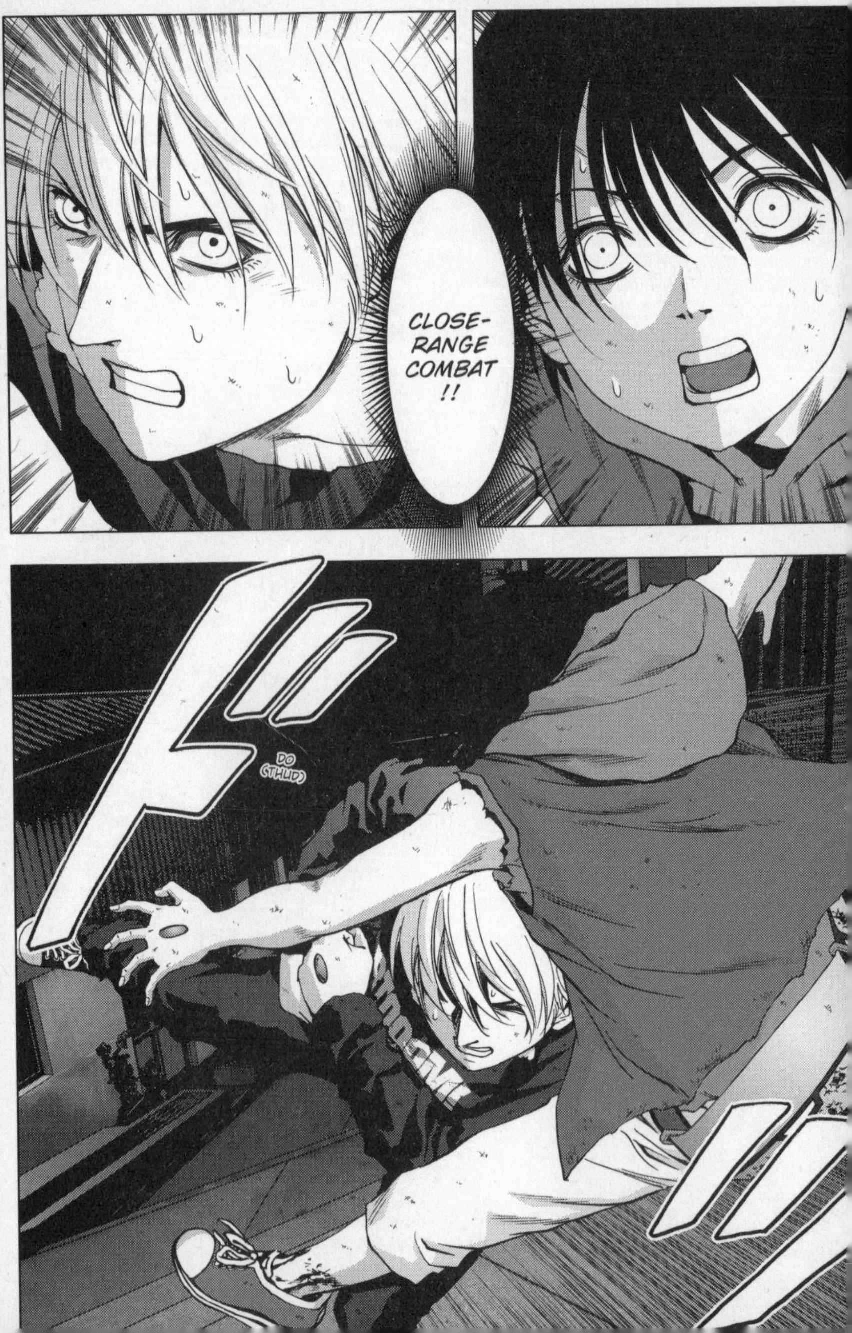
CLOSE-RANGE COMBAT !!
DO (THUD)

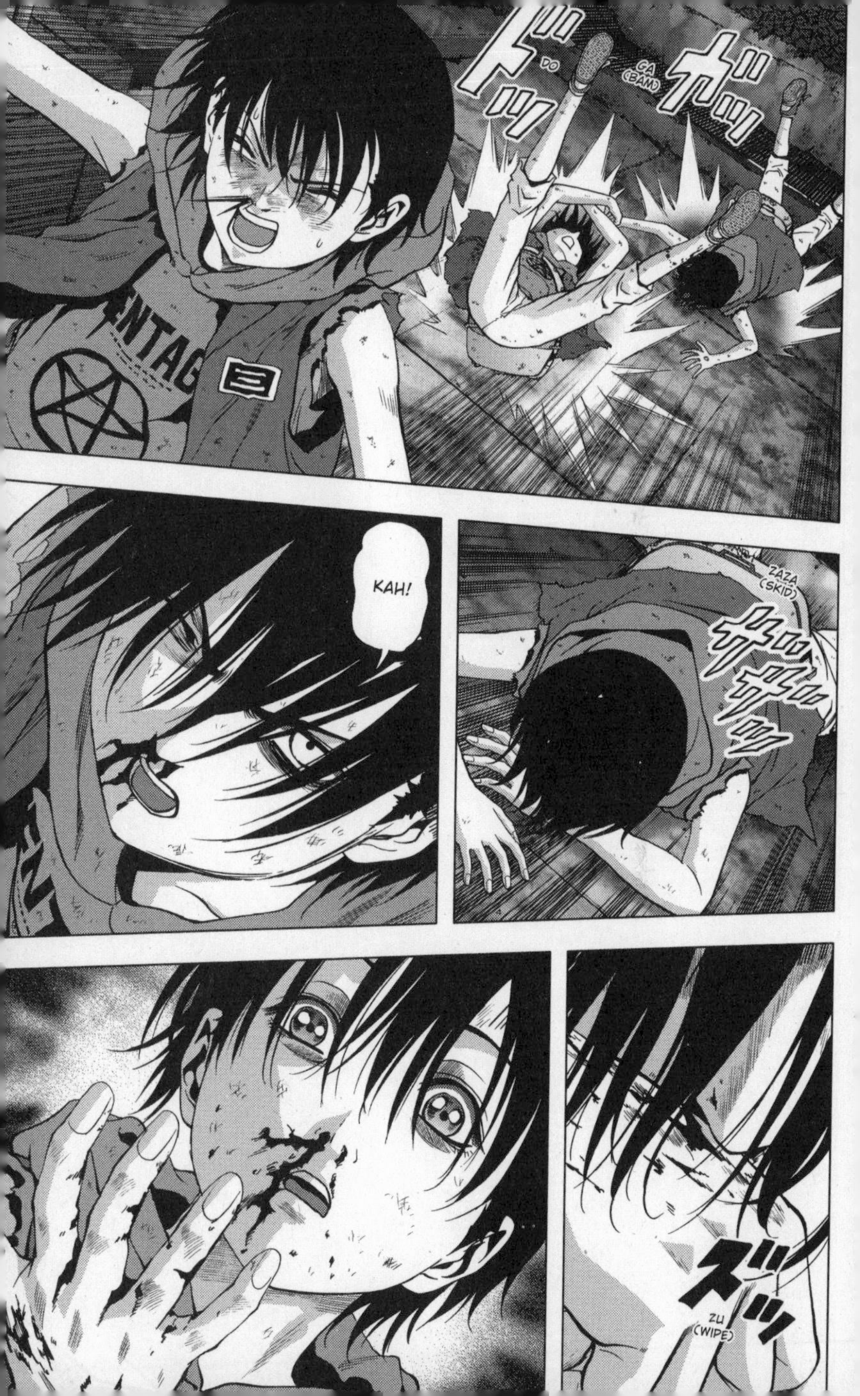
GA (BAM)
DO
ZAZA (SKID)
KAH!
ZU (WIPE)

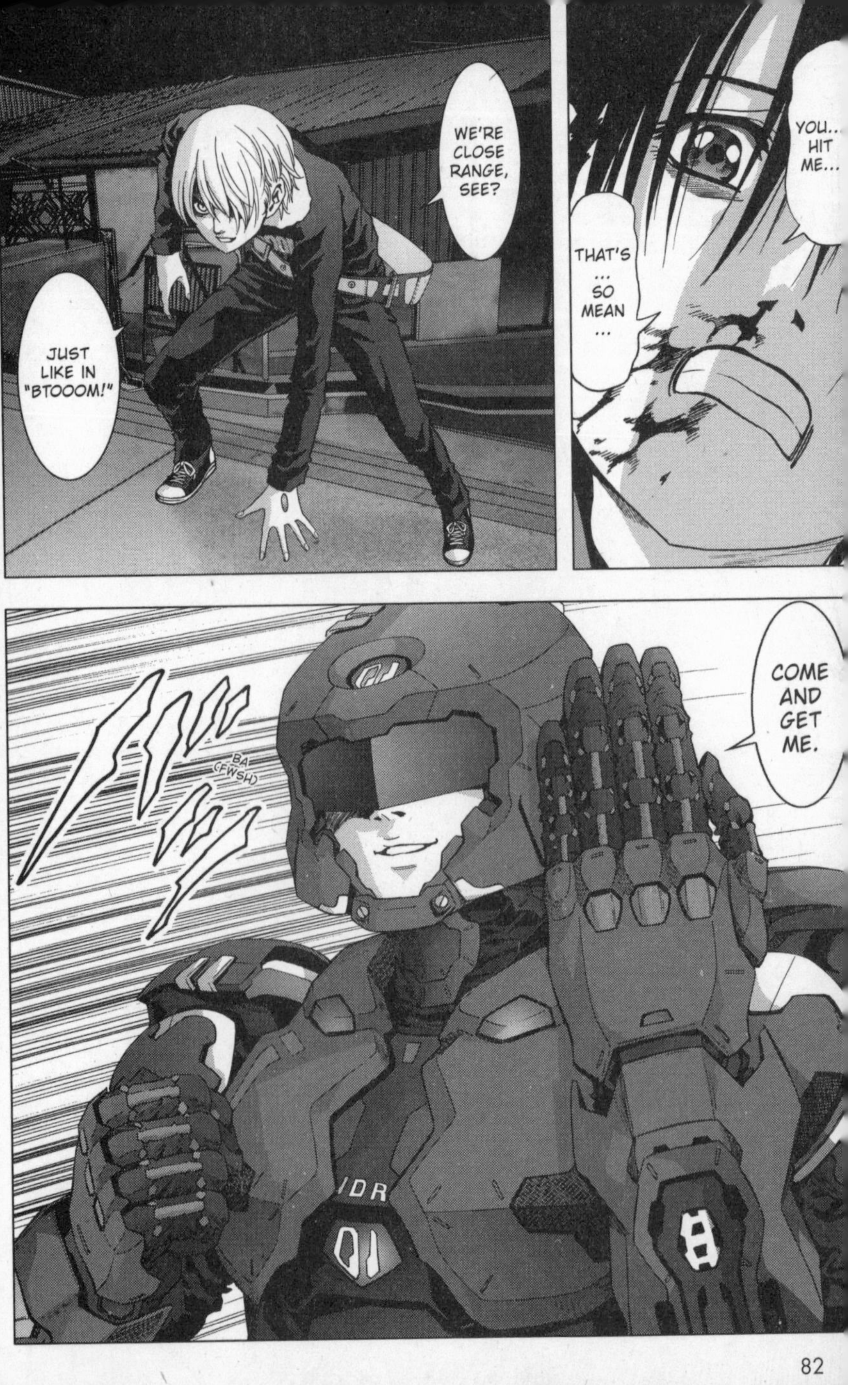
YOU... HIT ME...
THAT'S ... SO MEAN ...
WE'RE CLOSE RANGE, SEE?
JUST LIKE IN "BTOOOM!"
COME AND GET ME.
BA (FWSH)

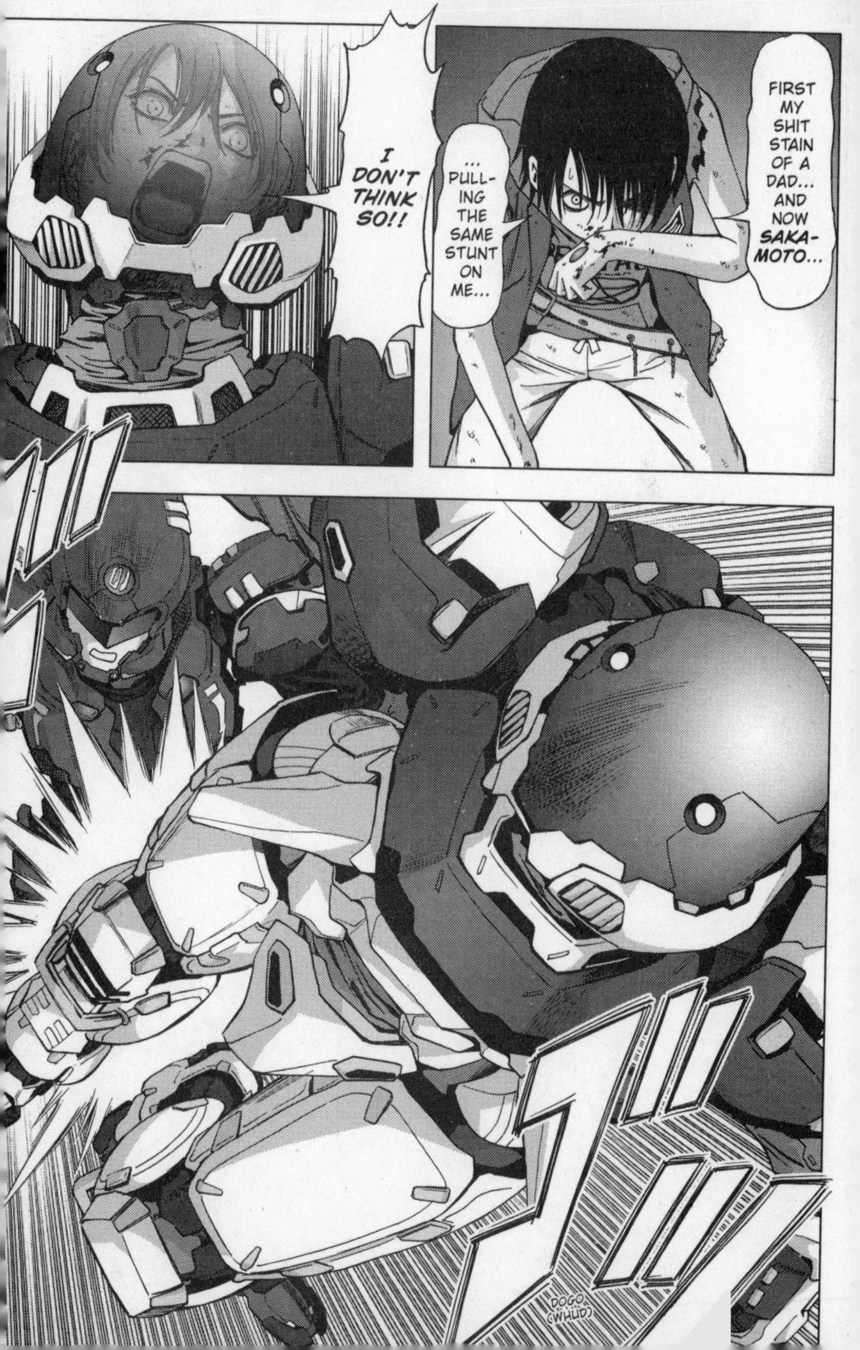
FIRST MY SHIT STAIN OF A DAD... AND NOW SAKAMOTO...
...PULLING THE SAME STUNT ON ME...
I DON'T THINK SO!!
DOGO (WHUD)

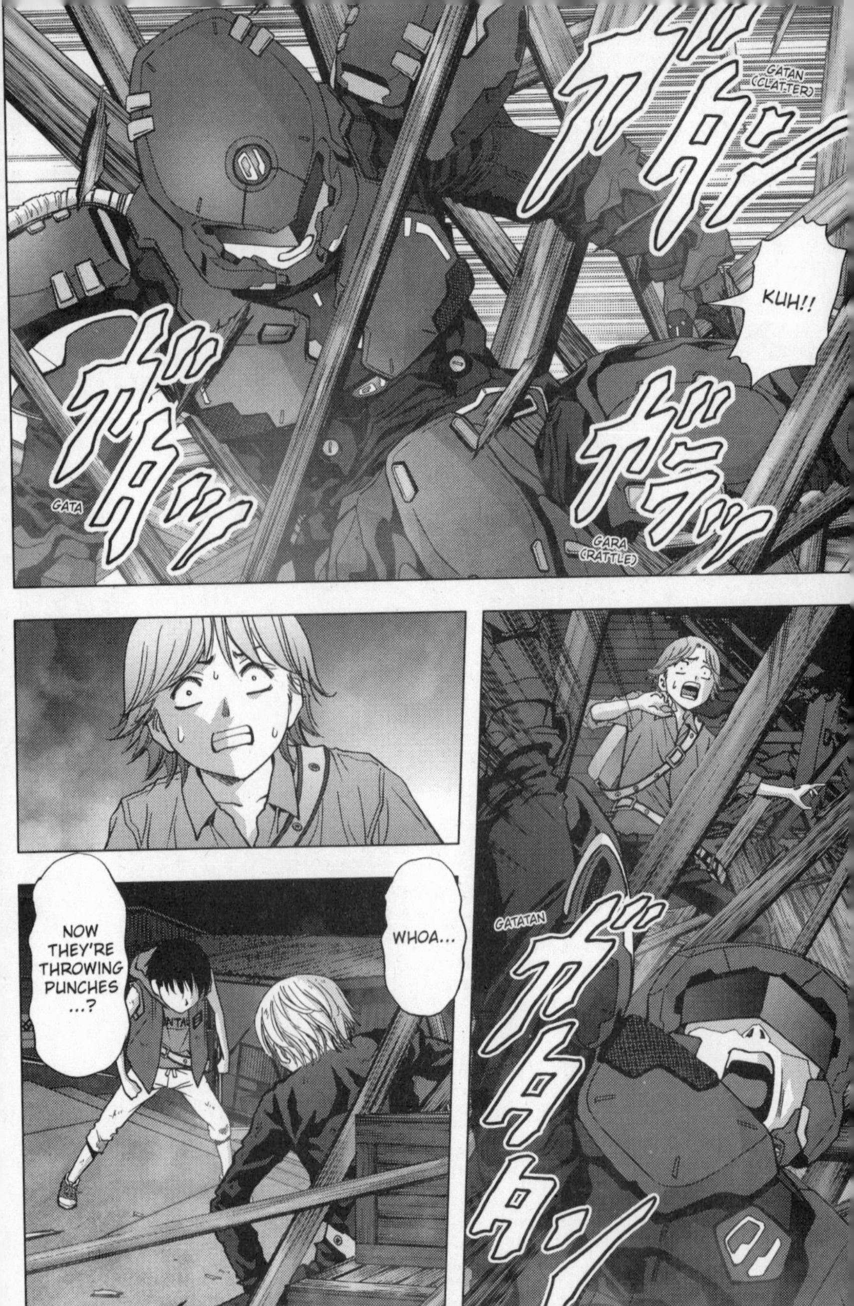
GATAN (CLATTER)
KUH!!
GARA (RATTLE)
GATA
GATATAN
WHOA...
NOW THEY'RE THROWING PUNCHES ...?

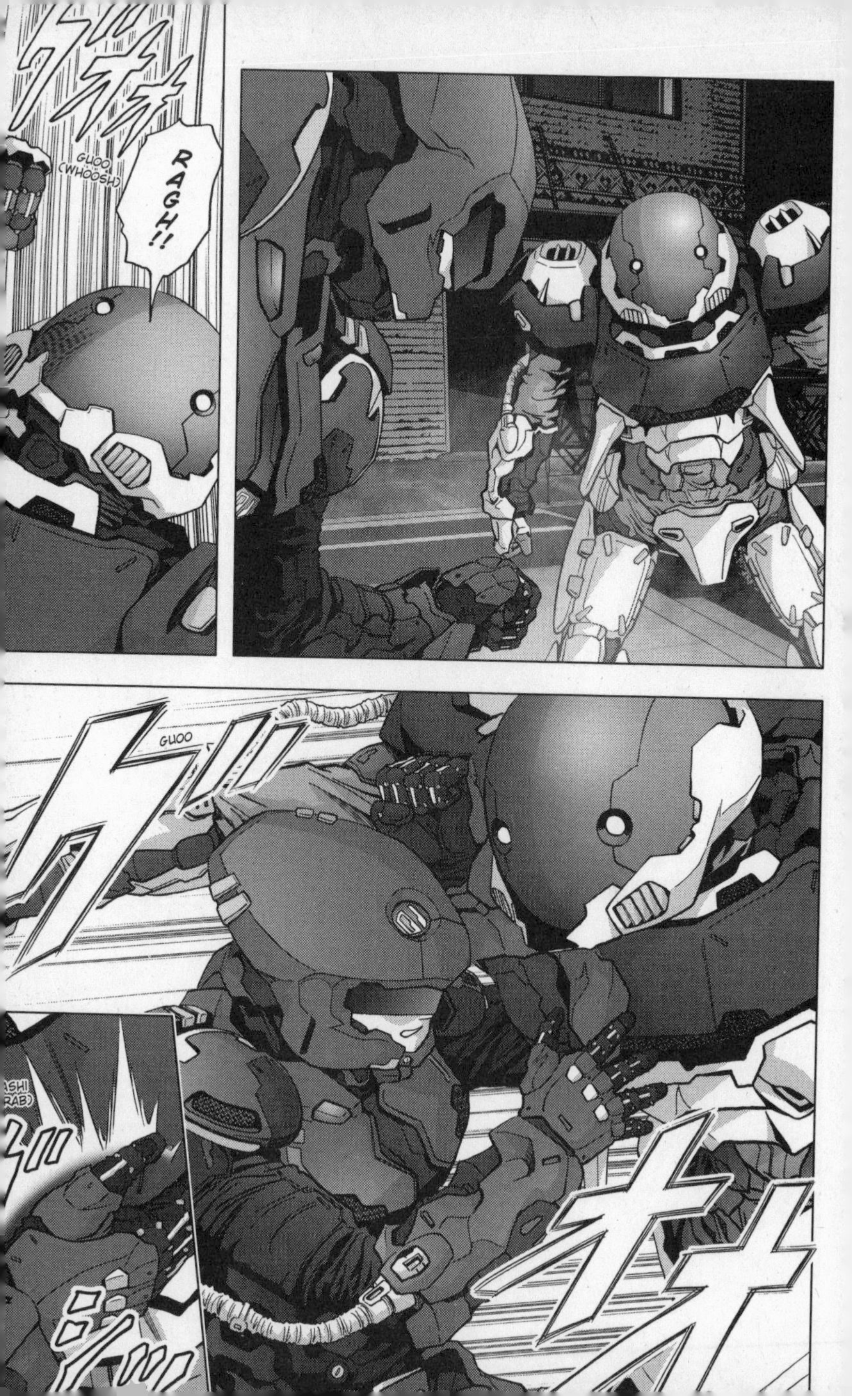
RAGH!!
GUOO (WHOOSH)
GUOO
ASHI!
RAB)

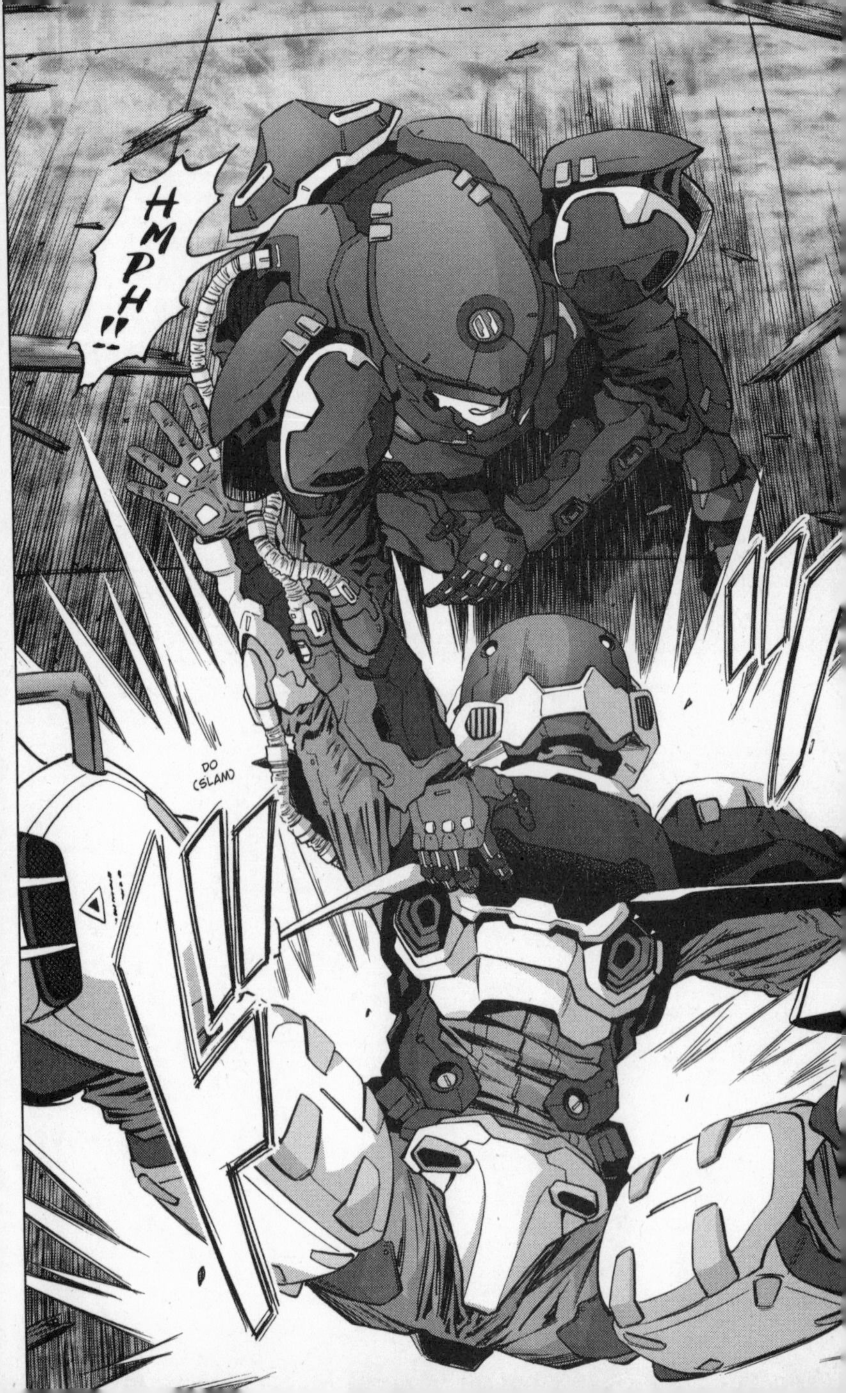
HMPH!!
DO (SLAM)

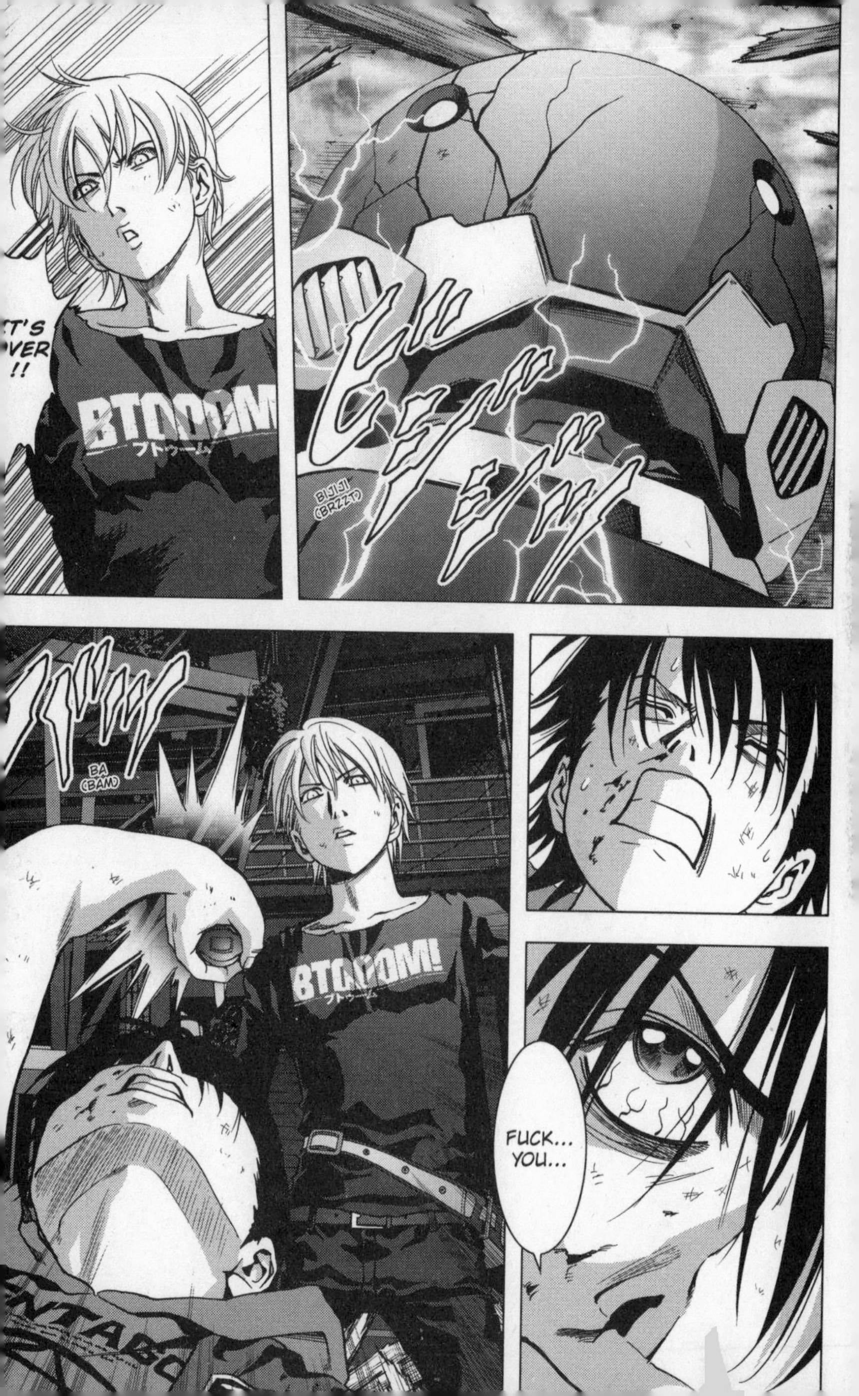
BIJIJI (BRZZT)
T'S OVER!!
BTOOOM!
ブトゥーム
FUCK... YOU...
BA (BAM)
BTOOOM!
ブトゥーム

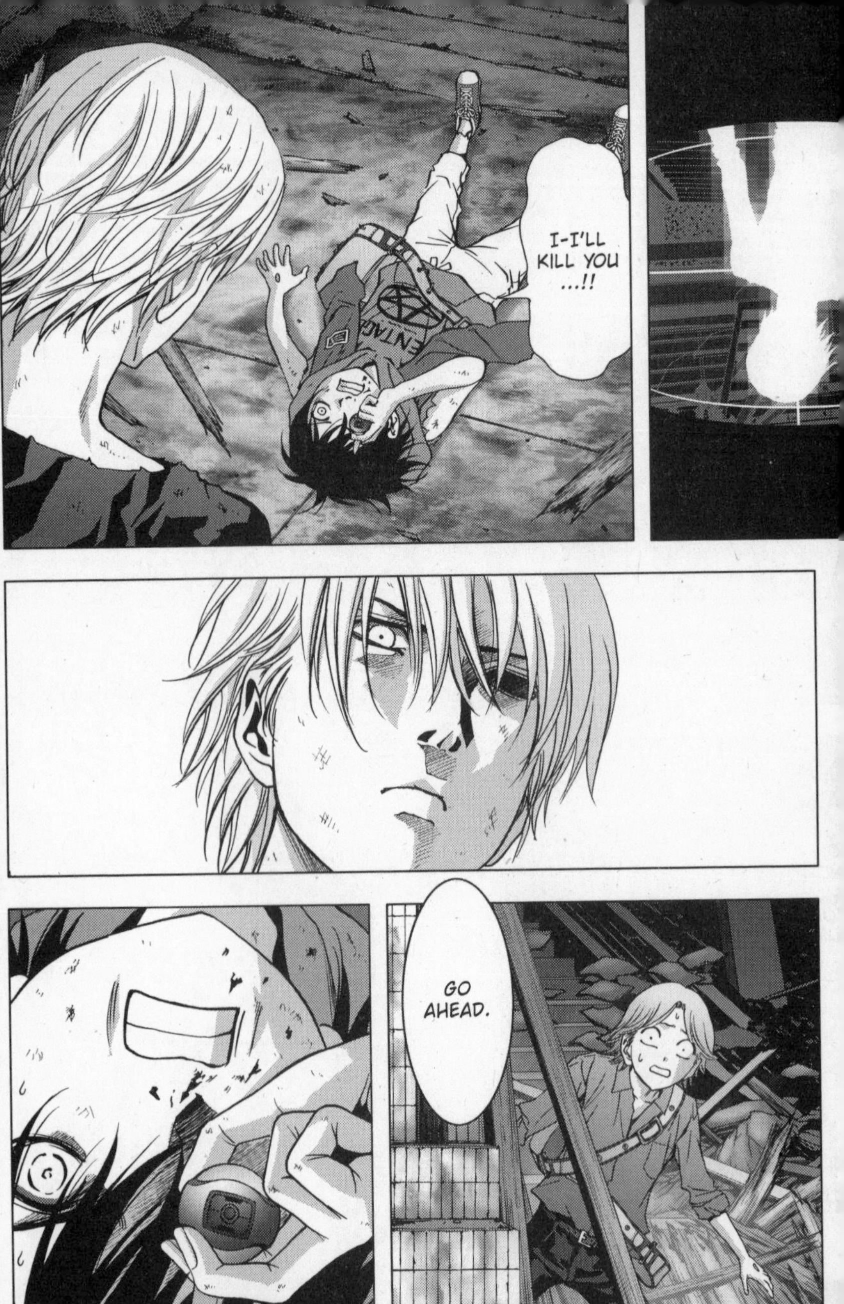
I-I'LL KILL YOU ...!!
GO AHEAD.

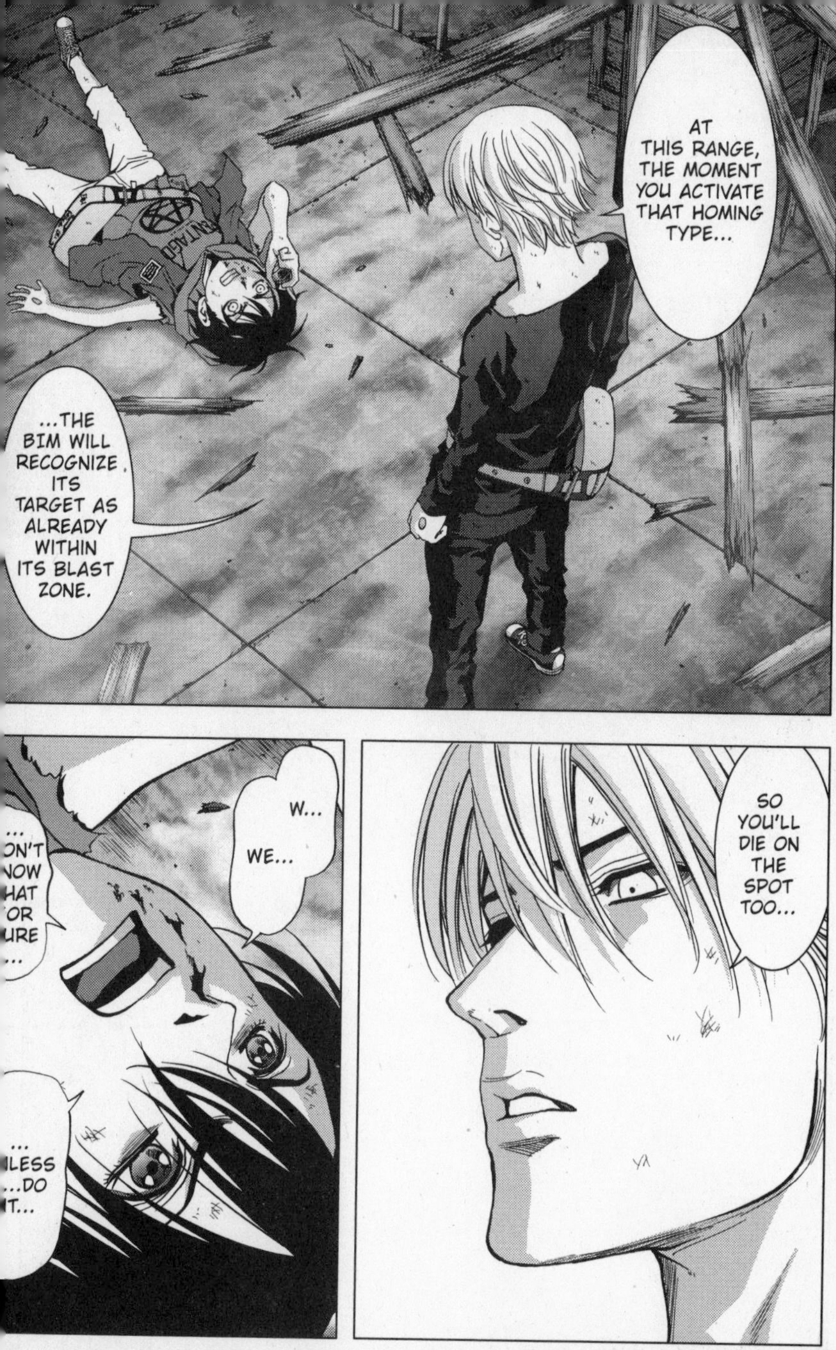
AT THIS RANGE, THE MOMENT YOU ACTIVATE THAT HOMING TYPE...
...THE BIM WILL RECOGNIZE ITS TARGET AS ALREADY WITHIN ITS BLAST ZONE.
SO YOU'LL DIE ON THE SPOT TOO...
W...
WE...
... ON'T NOW HAT OR URE ...
... ILESS ...DO T...

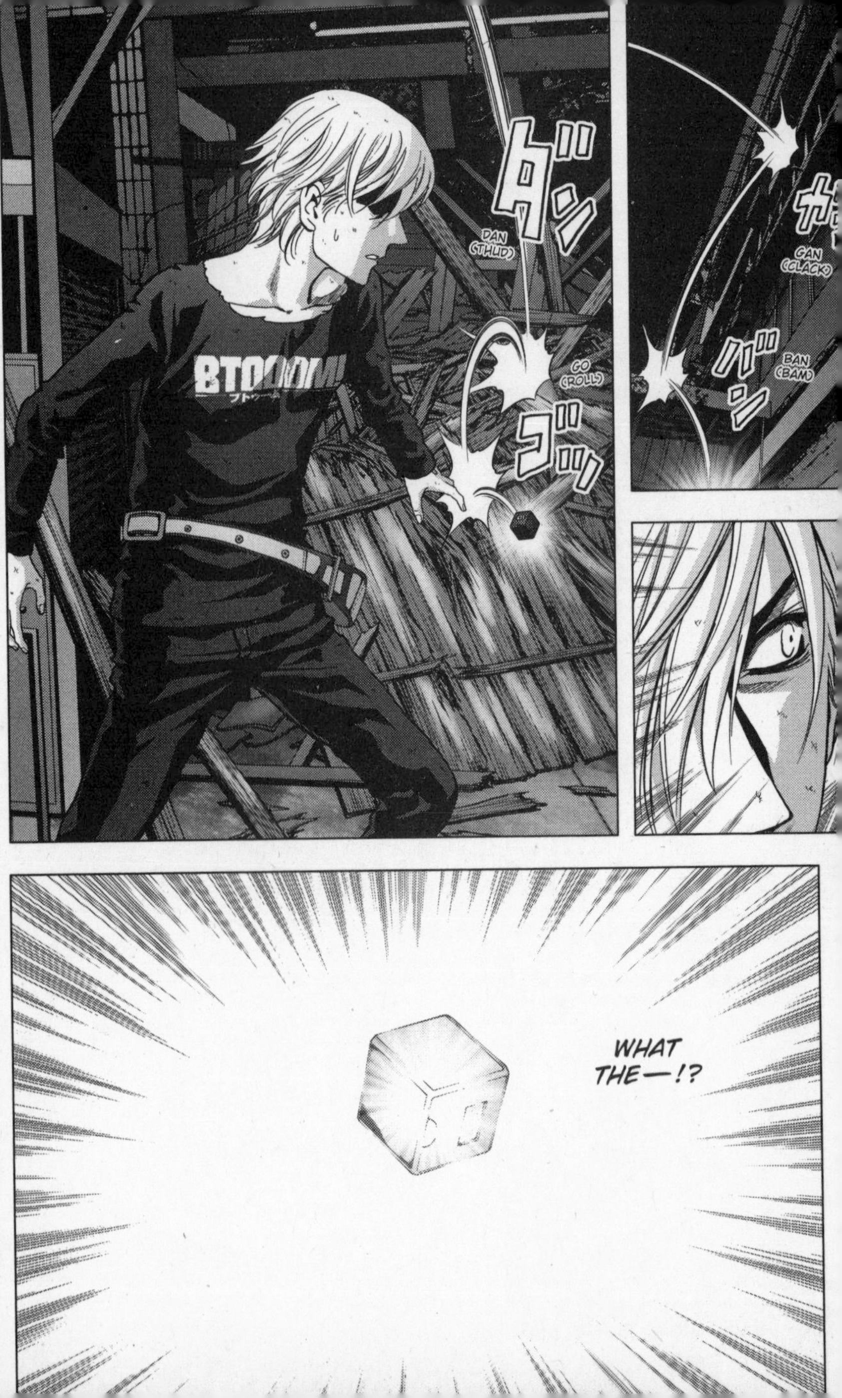
GAN (CLACK)
BAN (BAM)
DAN (THUD)
GO (ROLL)
WHAT THE—!?

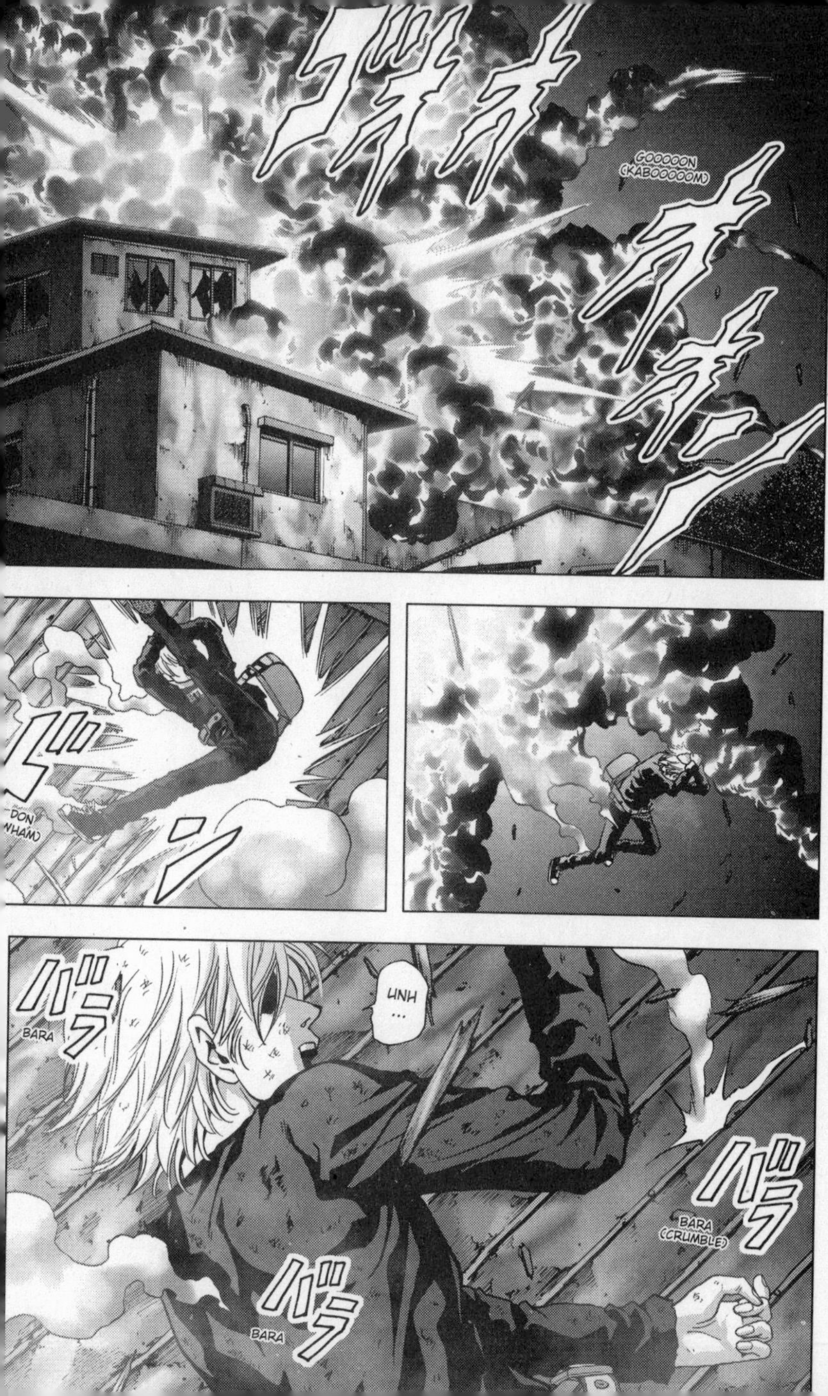
GOOOOON (KABOOOOOOM)
DON
WHAM)
UNH ...
BARA
BARA (CRUMBLE)
BARA

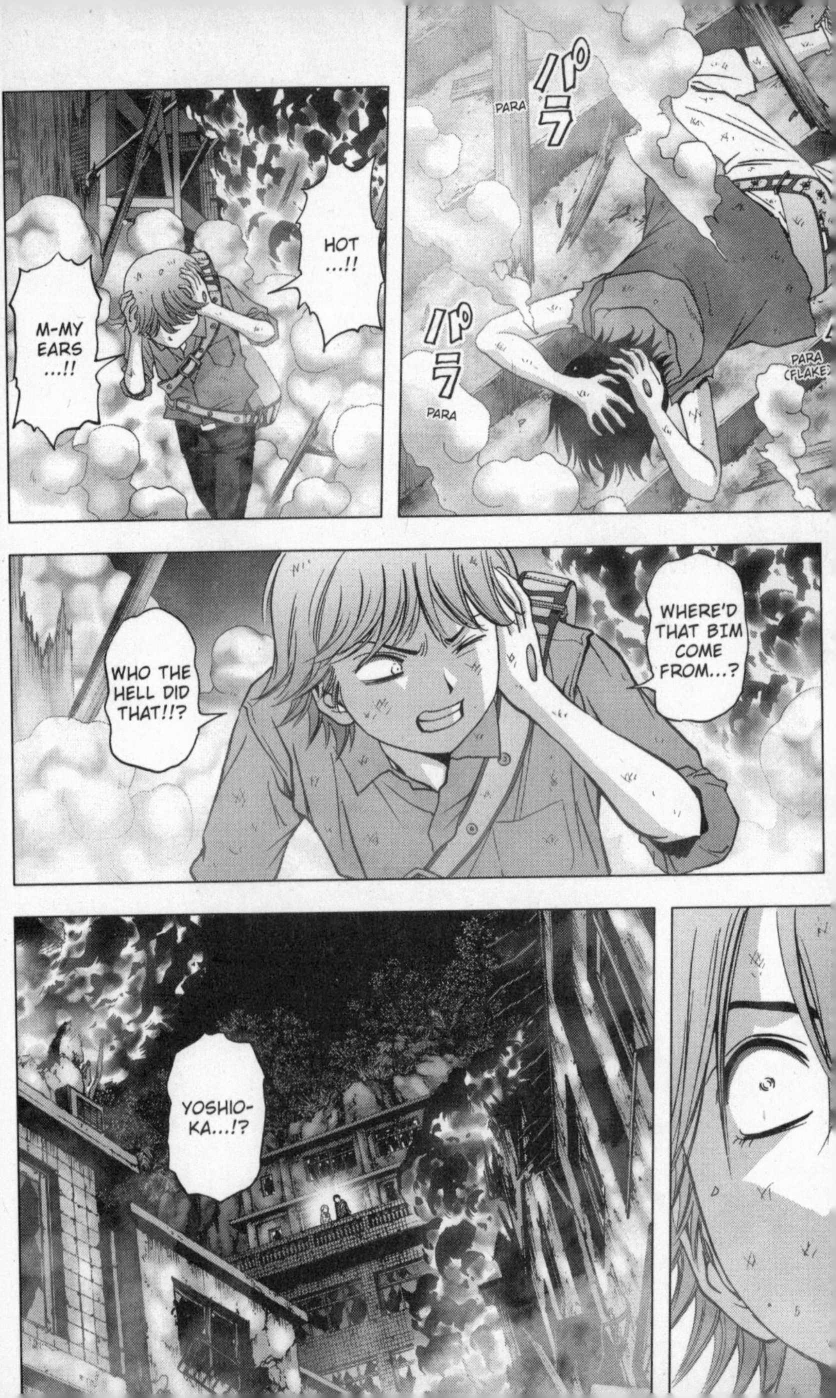
パラ
PARA
PARA (FLAKE)
パラ
PARA
HOT ...!!
M-MY EARS ...!!
WHERE'D THAT BIM COME FROM...?
WHO THE HELL DID THAT!!?
YOSHIO-KA...!?

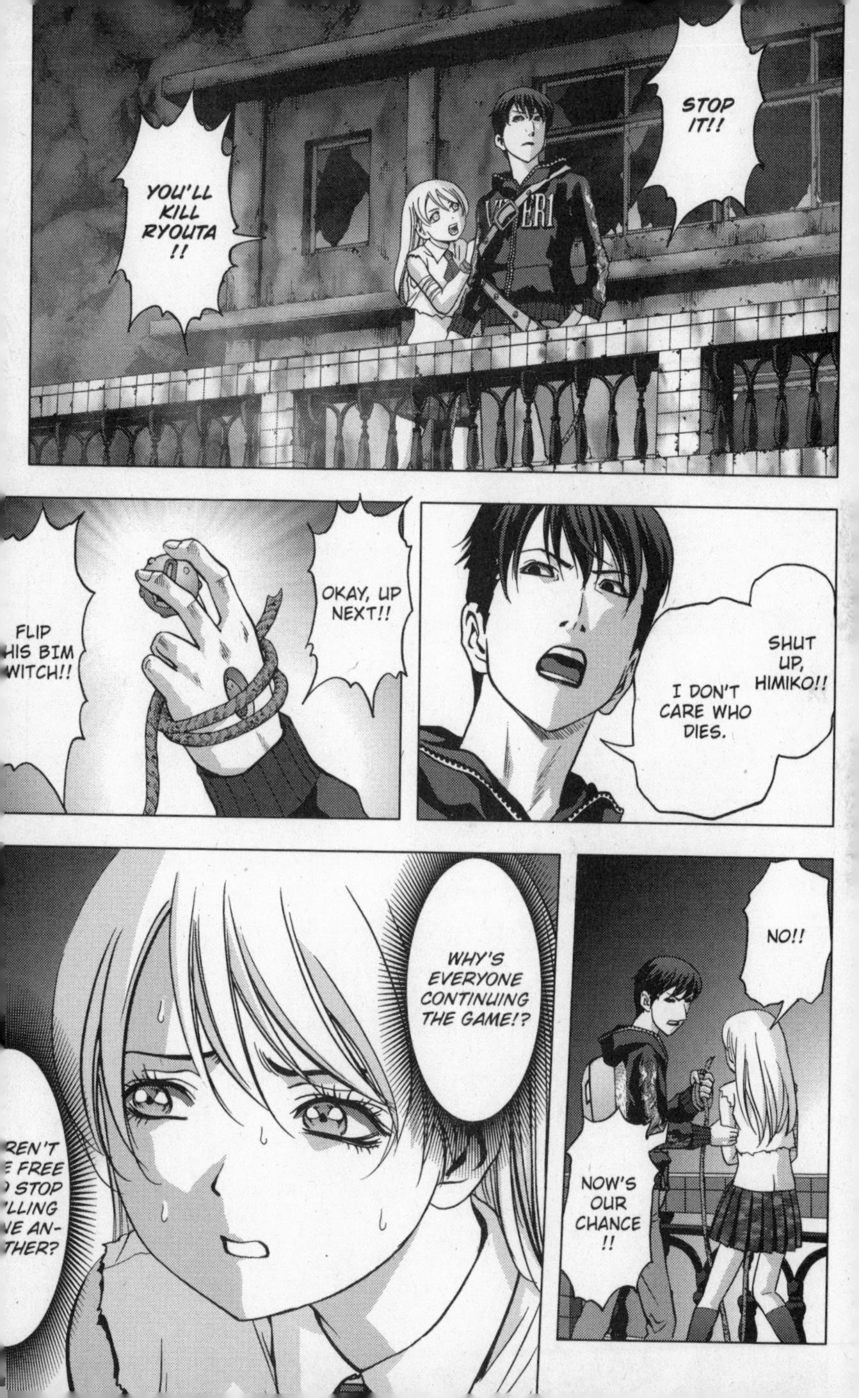
STOP IT!!
YOU'LL KILL RYOUTA !!
SHUT UP, HIMIKO!!
I DON'T CARE WHO DIES.
OKAY, UP NEXT!!
FLIP HIS BIM WITCH!!
NO!!
NOW'S OUR CHANCE !!
WHY'S EVERYONE CONTINUING THE GAME!?
REN'T E FREE STOP LLING NE AN- THER?

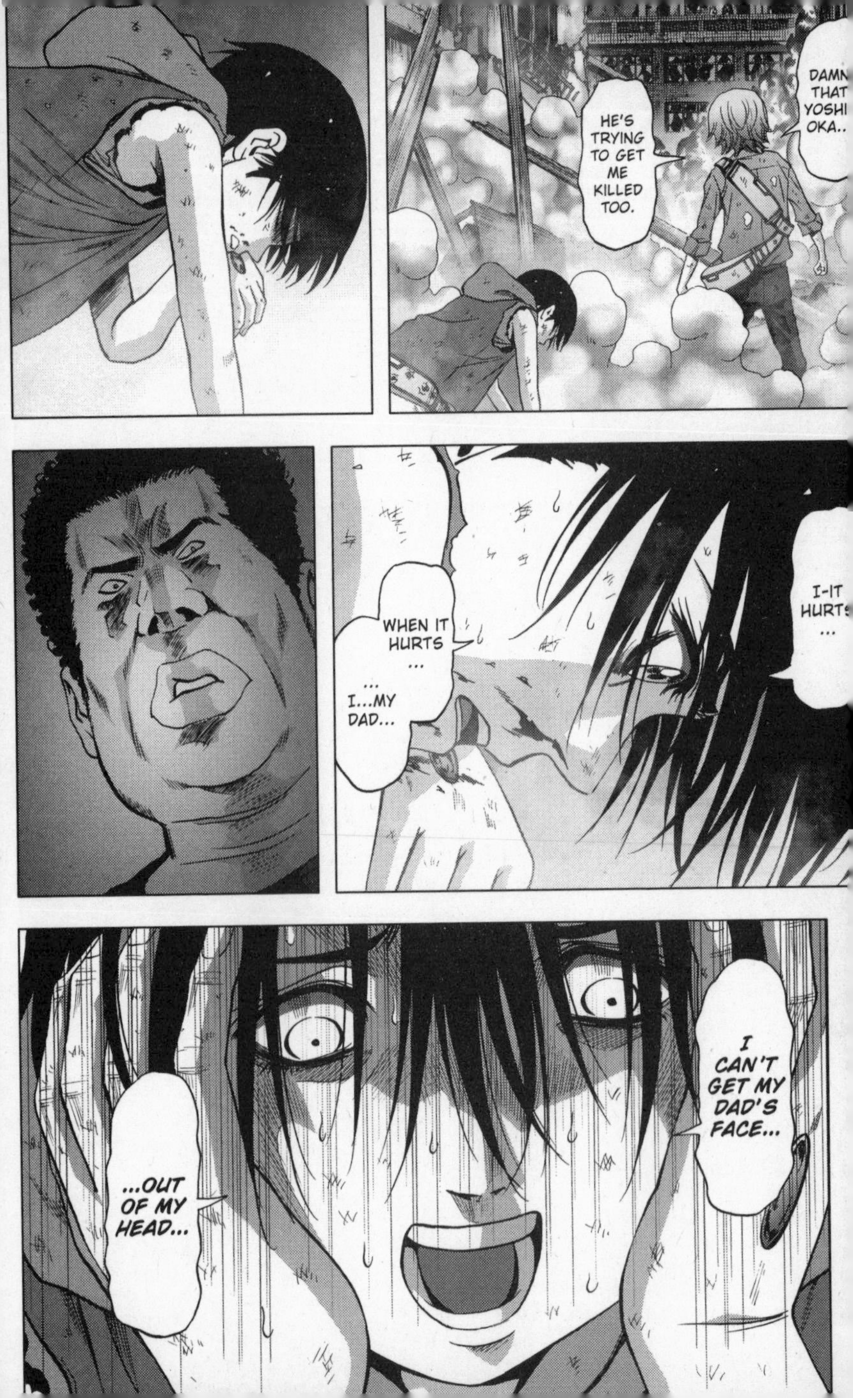
DAMN THAT YOSHIOKA..
HE'S TRYING TO GET ME KILLED TOO.
I-IT HURTS ...
WHEN IT HURTS ...
... I...MY DAD...
I CAN'T GET MY DAD'S FACE...
...OUT OF MY HEAD...

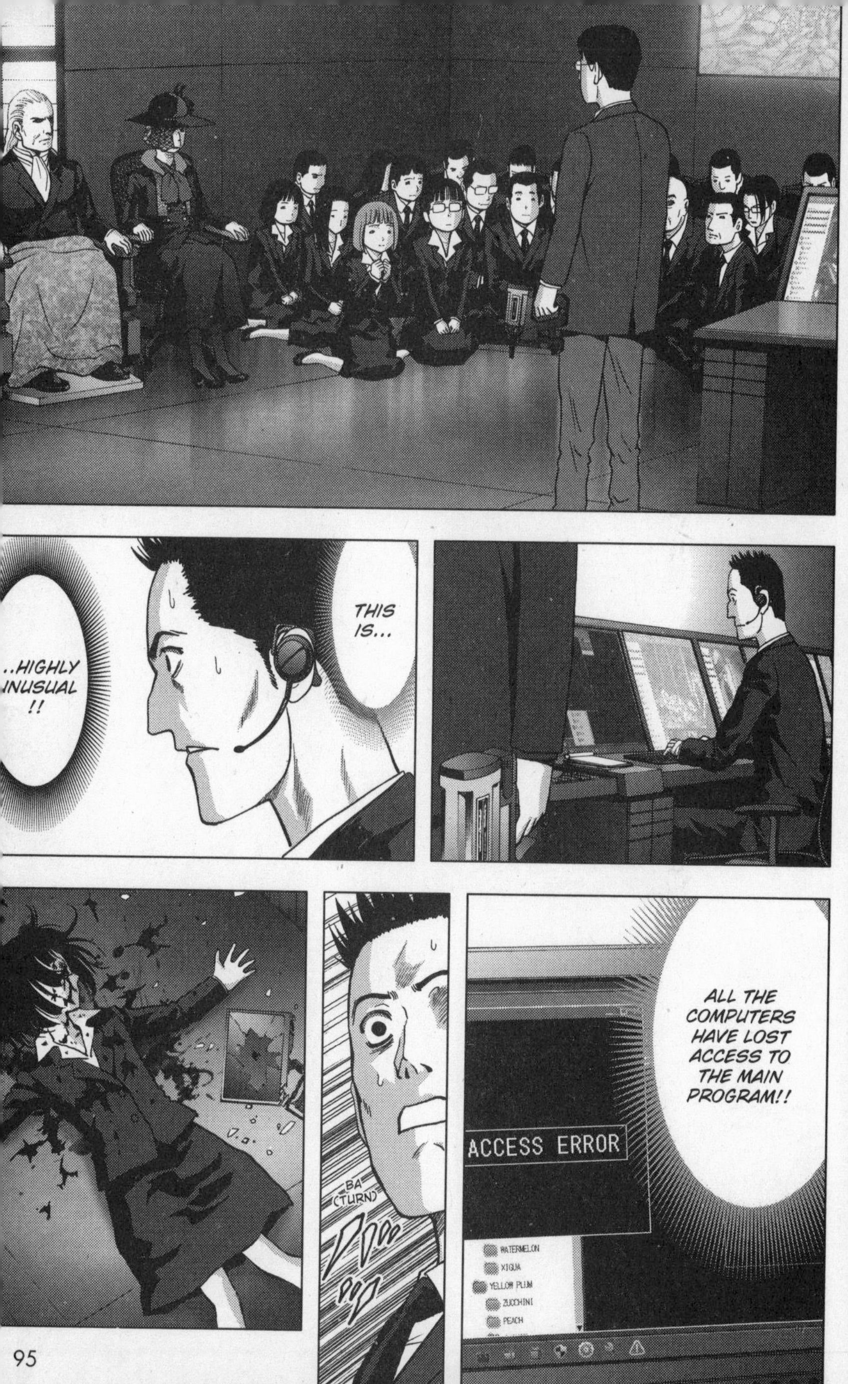
THIS IS...
..HIGHLY UNUSUAL!!
ALL THE COMPUTERS HAVE LOST ACCESS TO THE MAIN PROGRAM!!
ACCESS ERROR
WATERMELON
XIGUA
YELLOW PLUM
ZUCCHINI
PEACH
BA (TURN)

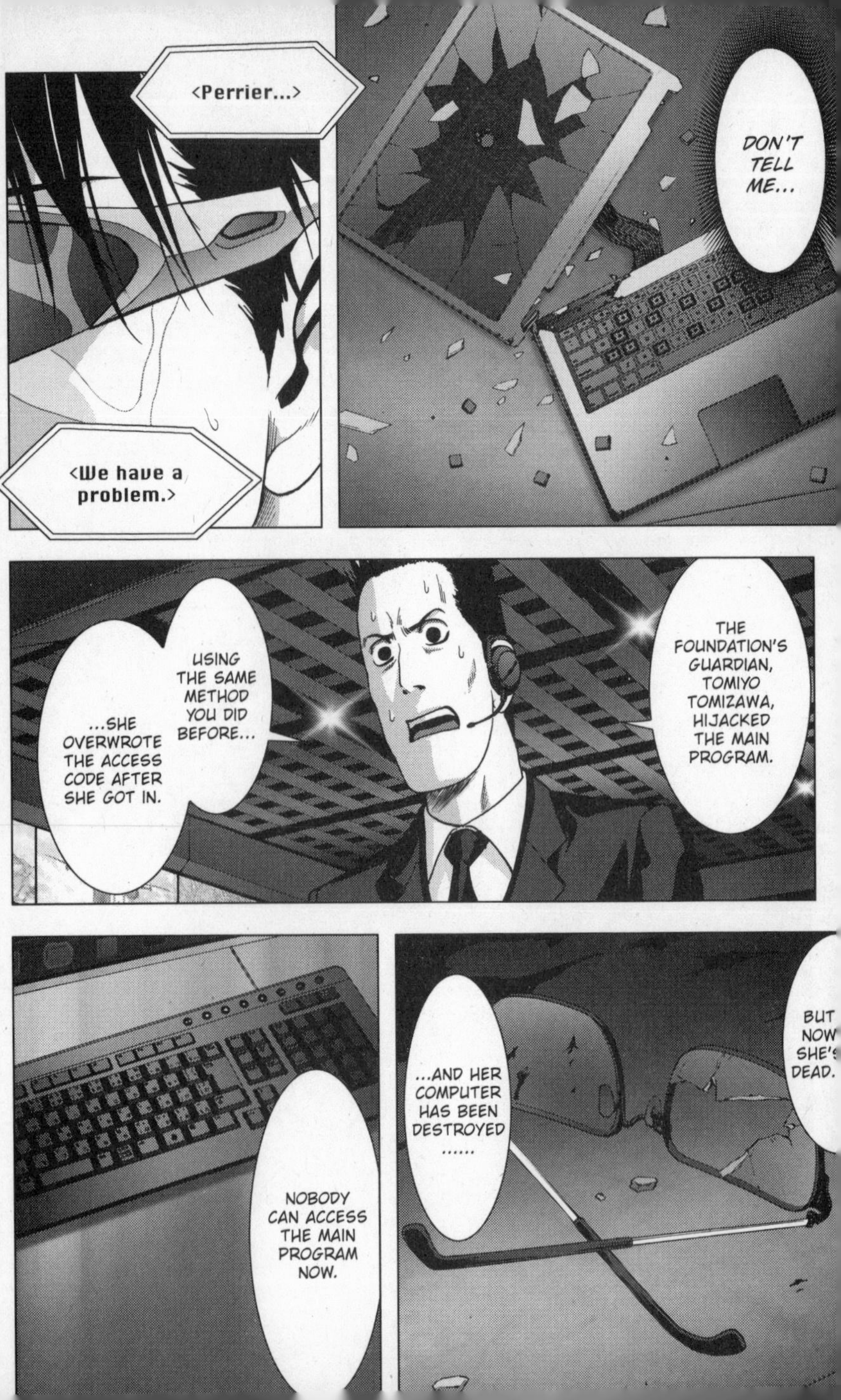
DON'T TELL ME...
<Perrier...>
<We have a problem.>
THE FOUNDATION'S GUARDIAN, TOMIYO TOMIZAWA, HIJACKED THE MAIN PROGRAM.
USING THE SAME METHOD YOU DID BEFORE...
...SHE OVERWROTE THE ACCESS CODE AFTER SHE GOT IN.
BUT NOW SHE'S DEAD.
...AND HER COMPUTER HAS BEEN DESTROYED ......
NOBODY CAN ACCESS THE MAIN PROGRAM NOW.

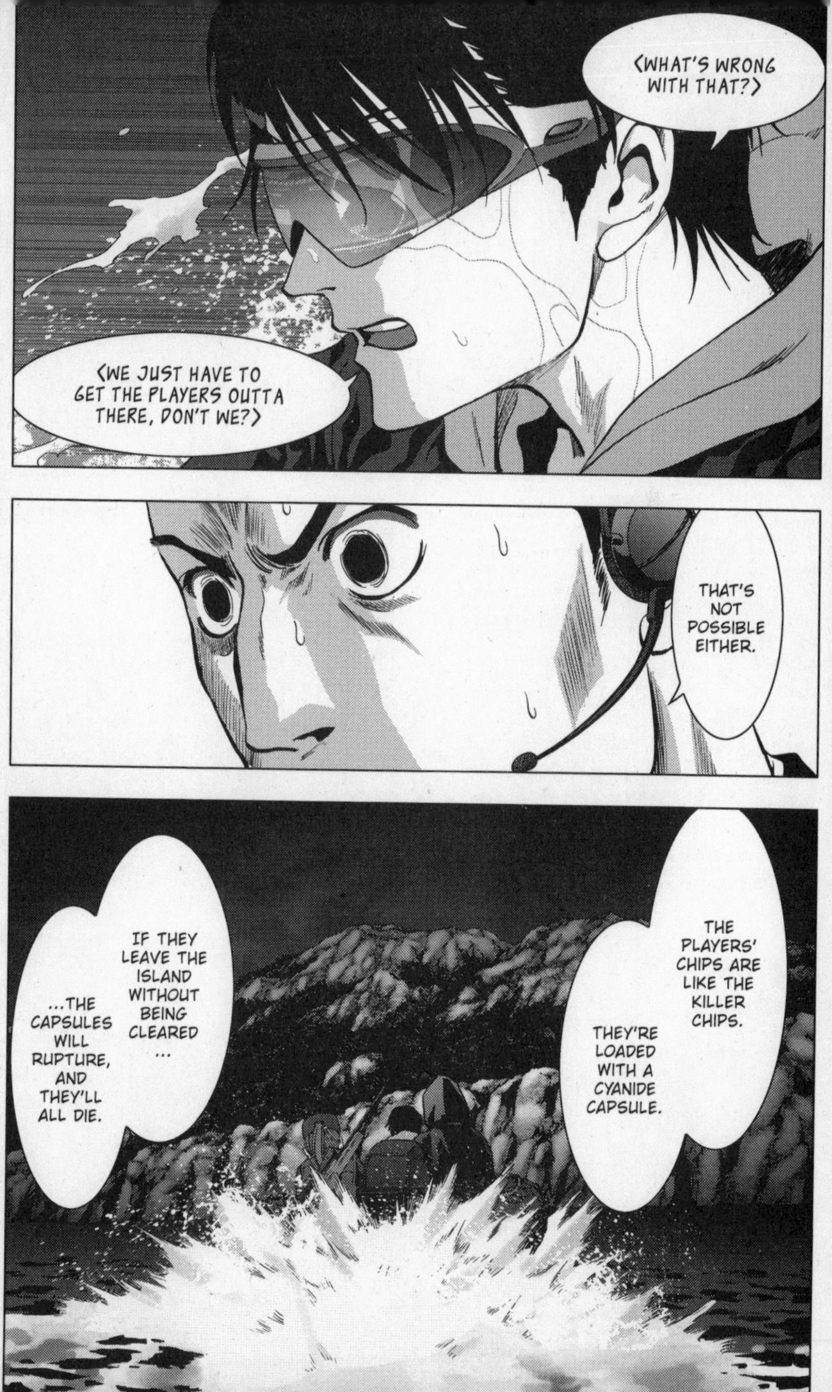

⟨WHAT'S WRONG WITH THAT?⟩
⟨WE JUST HAVE TO GET THE PLAYERS OUTTA THERE, DON'T WE?⟩
THAT'S NOT POSSIBLE EITHER.
THE PLAYERS' CHIPS ARE LIKE THE KILLER CHIPS.
THEY'RE LOADED WITH A CYANIDE CAPSULE.
IF THEY LEAVE THE ISLAND WITHOUT BEING CLEARED ...
...THE CAPSULES WILL RUPTURE, AND THEY'LL ALL DIE.

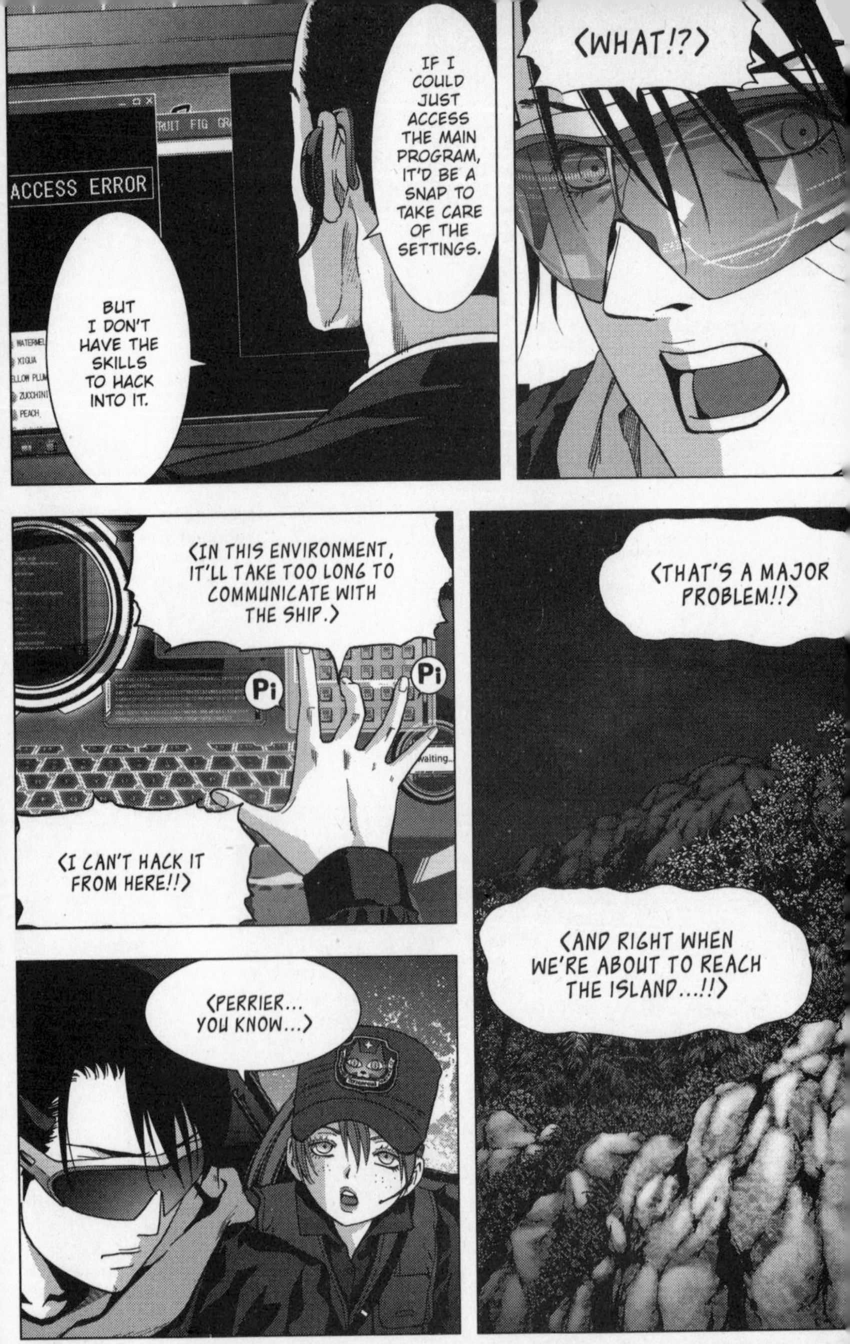

〈WHAT!?〉
IF I COULD JUST ACCESS THE MAIN PROGRAM, IT'D BE A SNAP TO TAKE CARE OF THE SETTINGS.
ACCESS ERROR
BUT I DON'T HAVE THE SKILLS TO HACK INTO IT.
〈THAT'S A MAJOR PROBLEM!!〉
〈AND RIGHT WHEN WE'RE ABOUT TO REACH THE ISLAND...!!〉
〈IN THIS ENVIRONMENT, IT'LL TAKE TOO LONG TO COMMUNICATE WITH THE SHIP.〉
Pi
Pi
waiting...
〈I CAN'T HACK IT FROM HERE!!〉
〈PERRIER... YOU KNOW...〉

‹...WE CAN'T GO BACK TO THE SHIP DURING THE OPERATION.›

‹I KNOW... YULIA GARLIN.›

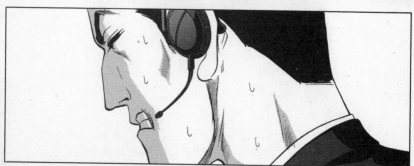

‹MR. IIDA.›

‹WASN'T THERE A BROADCASTING SATELLITE ON THE ISLAND?›

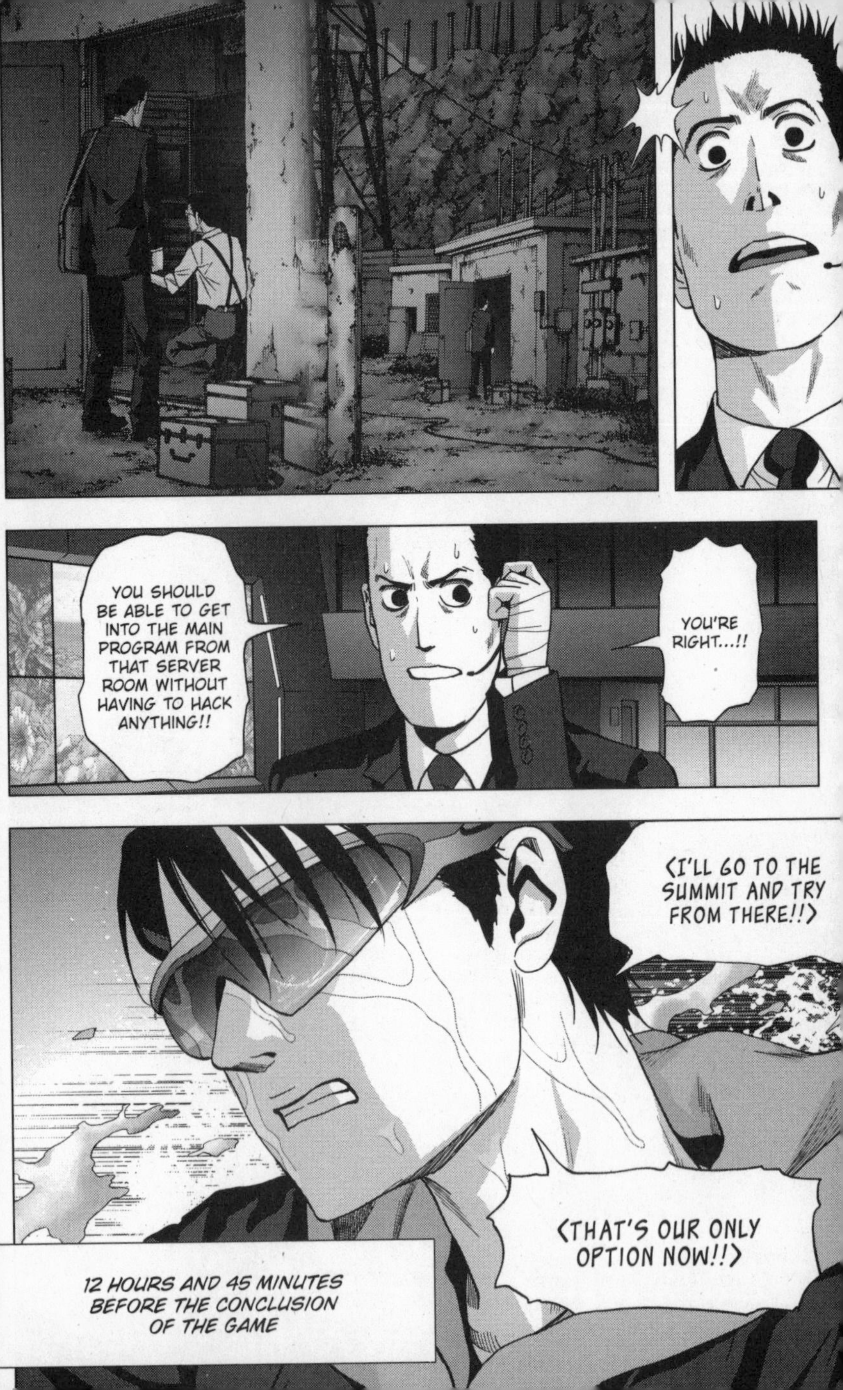
YOU'RE RIGHT...!!
YOU SHOULD BE ABLE TO GET INTO THE MAIN PROGRAM FROM THAT SERVER ROOM WITHOUT HAVING TO HACK ANYTHING!!
〈I'LL GO TO THE SUMMIT AND TRY FROM THERE!!〉
〈THAT'S OUR ONLY OPTION NOW!!〉
12 HOURS AND 45 MINUTES BEFORE THE CONCLUSION OF THE GAME

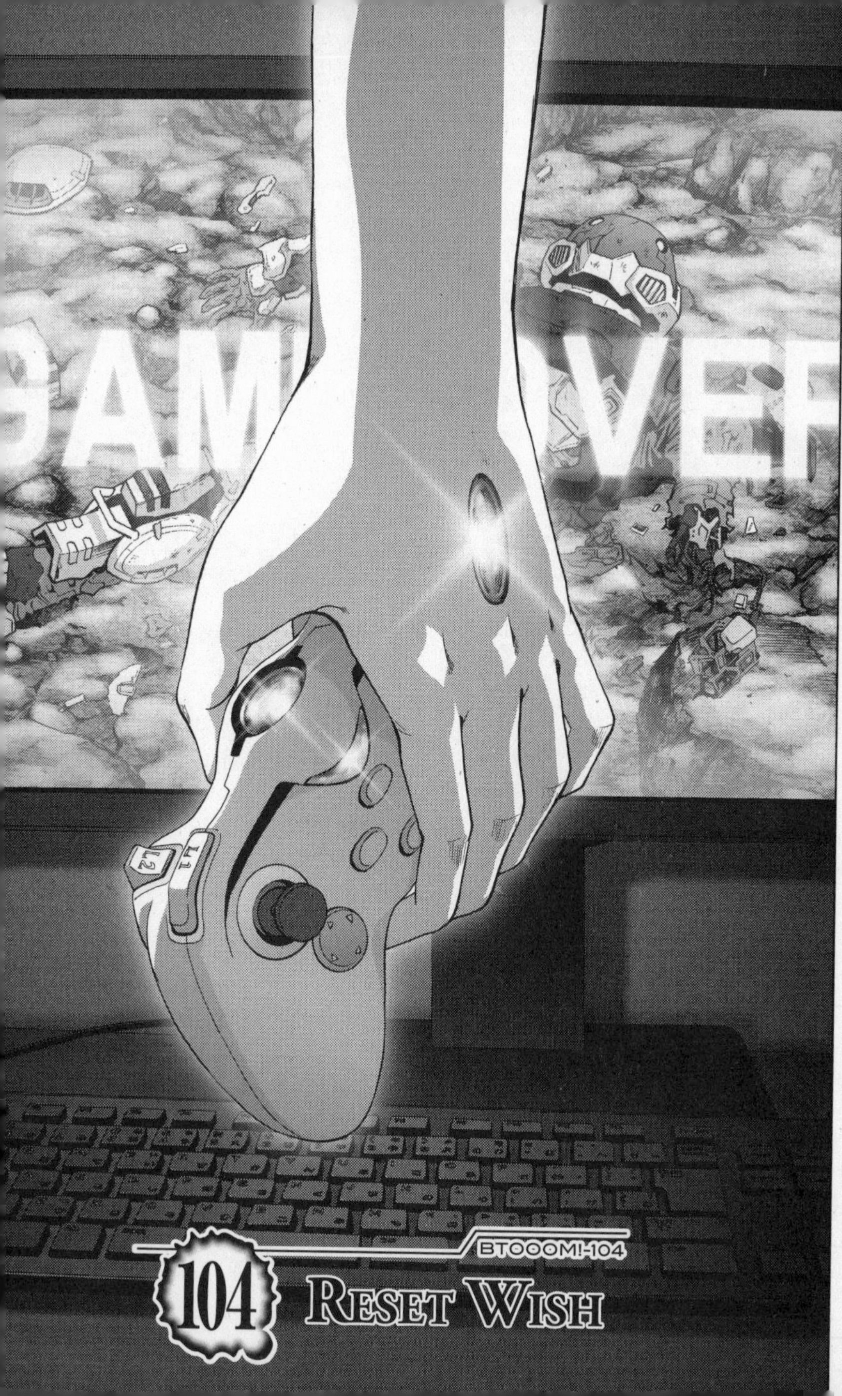
BTOOOM!-104

104 Reset Wish

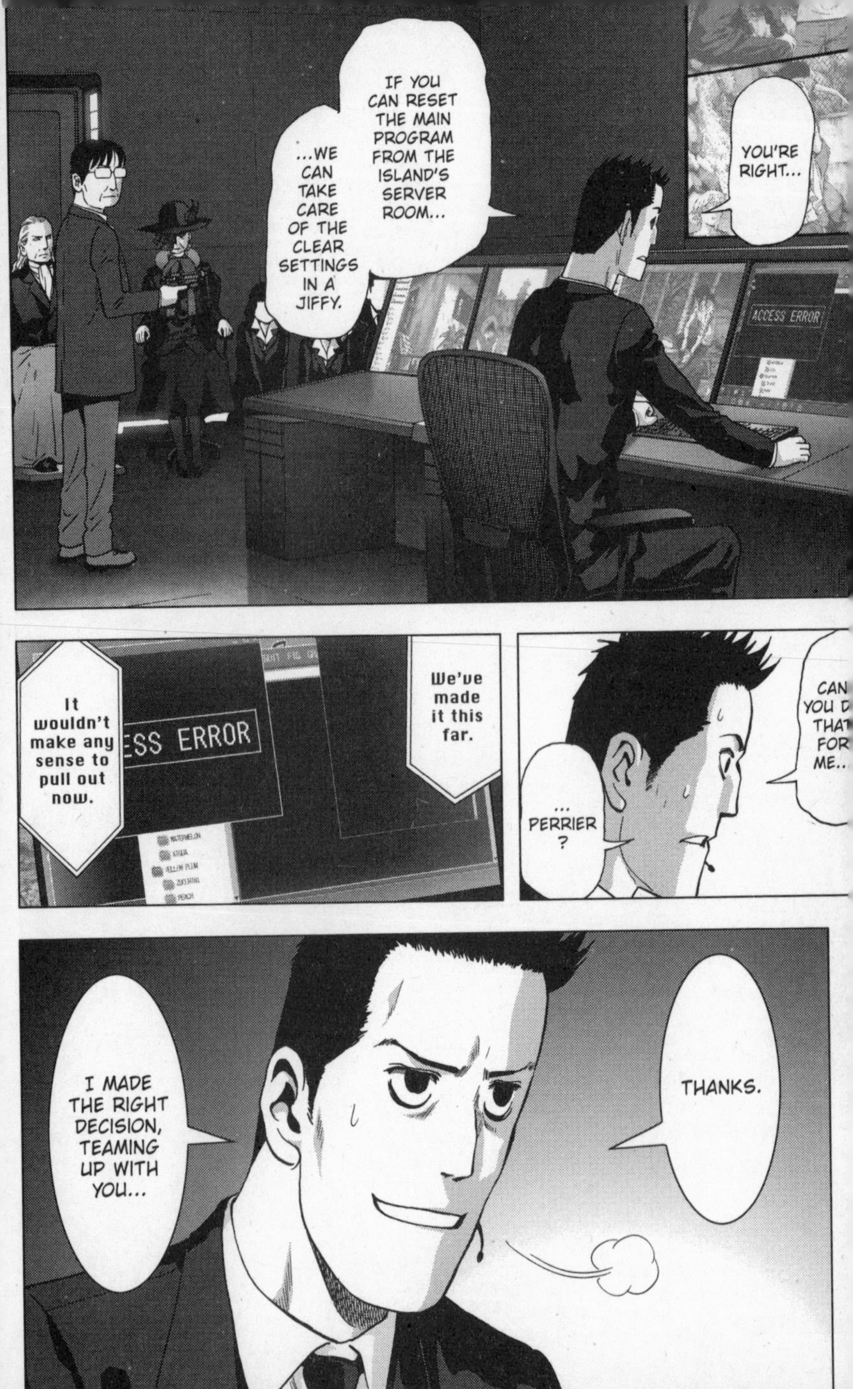
YOU'RE RIGHT...
IF YOU CAN RESET THE MAIN PROGRAM FROM THE ISLAND'S SERVER ROOM...
...WE CAN TAKE CARE OF THE CLEAR SETTINGS IN A JIFFY.
ACCESS ERROR
CAN YOU D THAT FOR ME..
...PERRIER?
We've made it this far.
It wouldn't make any sense to pull out now.
THANKS.
I MADE THE RIGHT DECISION, TEAMING UP WITH YOU...

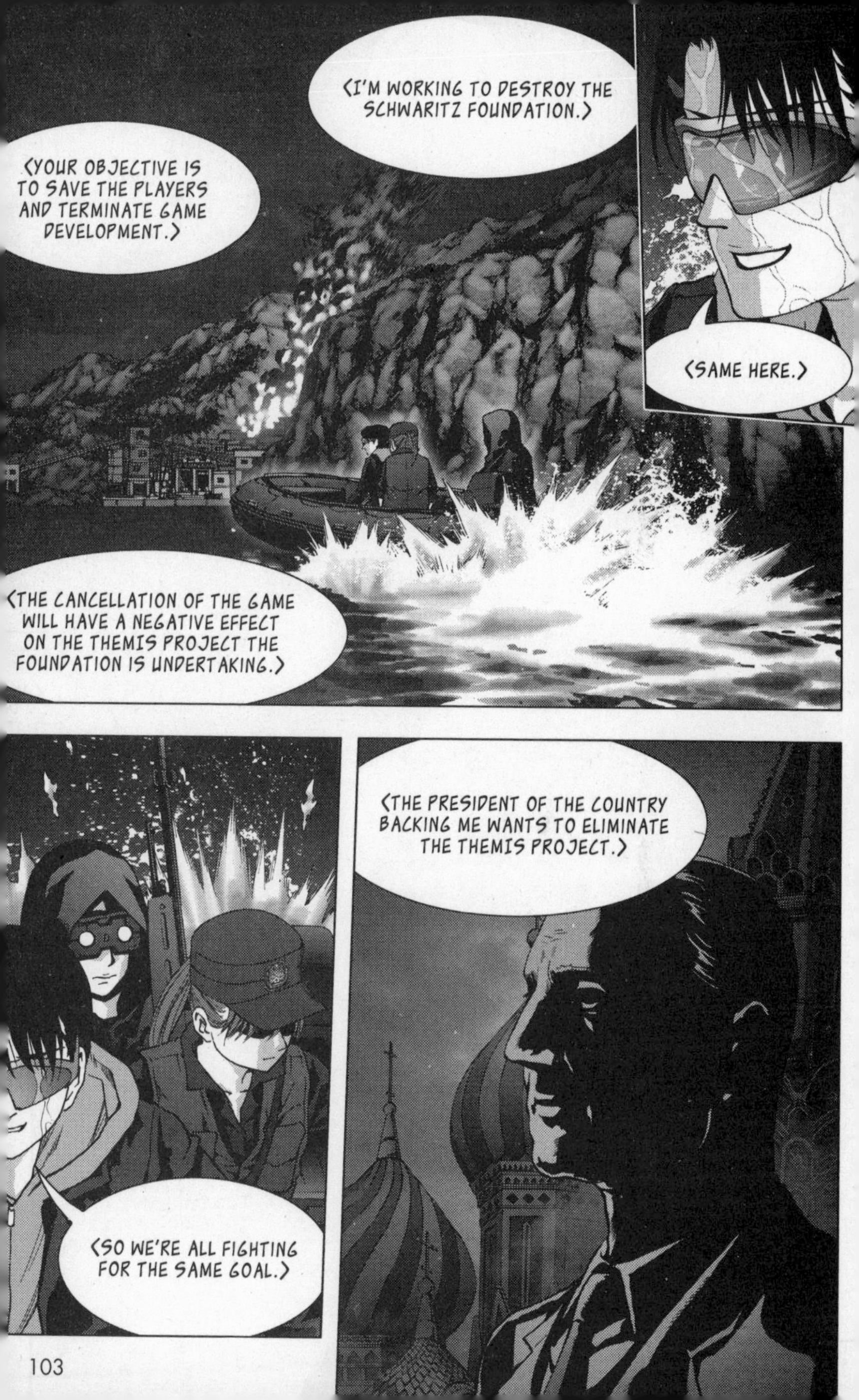
⟨I'M WORKING TO DESTROY THE SCHWARITZ FOUNDATION.⟩
⟨YOUR OBJECTIVE IS TO SAVE THE PLAYERS AND TERMINATE GAME DEVELOPMENT.⟩
⟨SAME HERE.⟩
⟨THE CANCELLATION OF THE GAME WILL HAVE A NEGATIVE EFFECT ON THE THEMIS PROJECT THE FOUNDATION IS UNDERTAKING.⟩
⟨THE PRESIDENT OF THE COUNTRY BACKING ME WANTS TO ELIMINATE THE THEMIS PROJECT.⟩
⟨SO WE'RE ALL FIGHTING FOR THE SAME GOAL.⟩

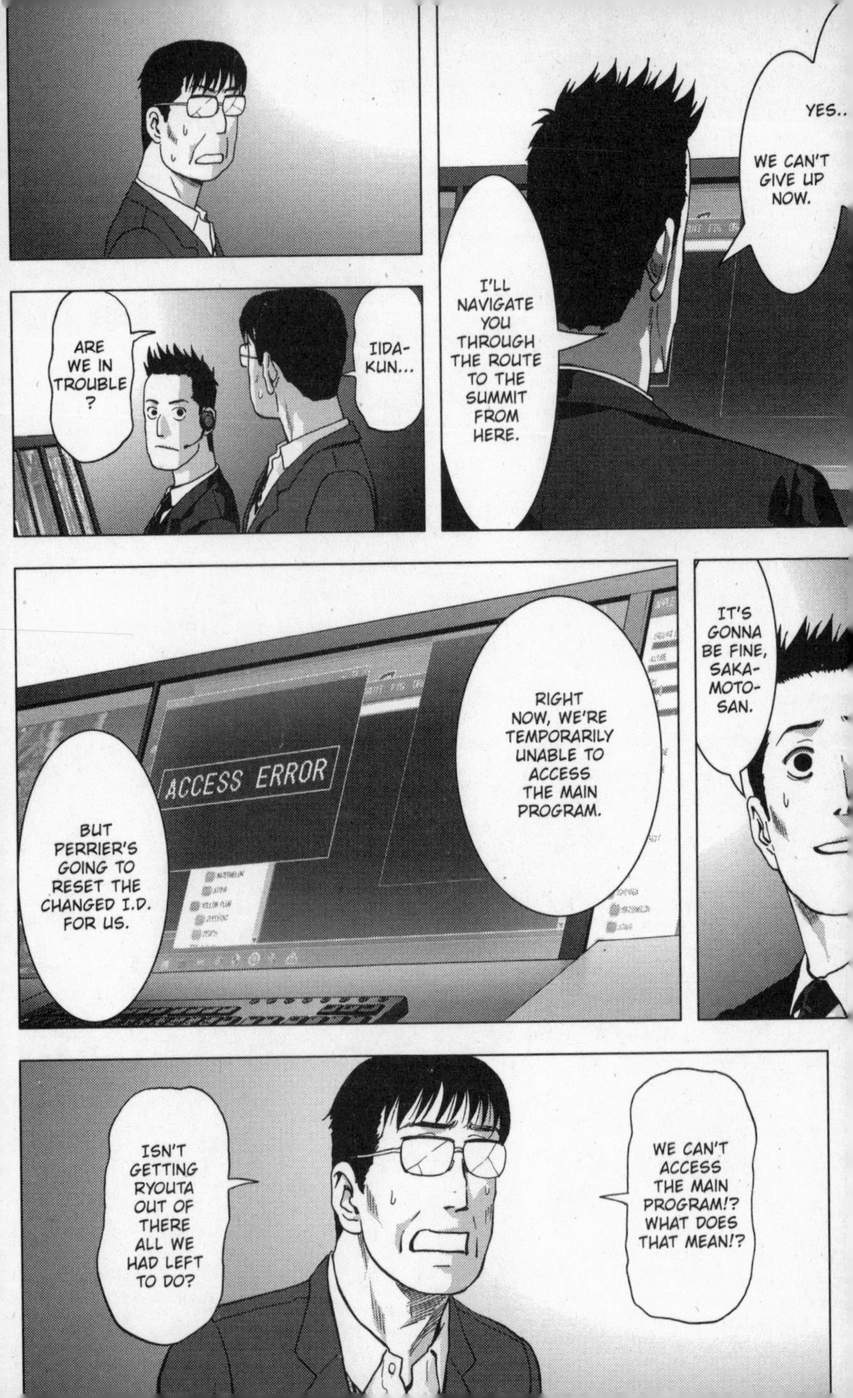
YES..
WE CAN'T GIVE UP NOW.
I'LL NAVIGATE YOU THROUGH THE ROUTE TO THE SUMMIT FROM HERE.
IIDA-KUN...
ARE WE IN TROUBLE?
IT'S GONNA BE FINE, SAKA-MOTO-SAN.
RIGHT NOW, WE'RE TEMPORARILY UNABLE TO ACCESS THE MAIN PROGRAM.
ACCESS ERROR
BUT PERRIER'S GOING TO RESET THE CHANGED I.D. FOR US.
WE CAN'T ACCESS THE MAIN PROGRAM!? WHAT DOES THAT MEAN!?
ISN'T GETTING RYOUTA OUT OF THERE ALL WE HAD LEFT TO DO?

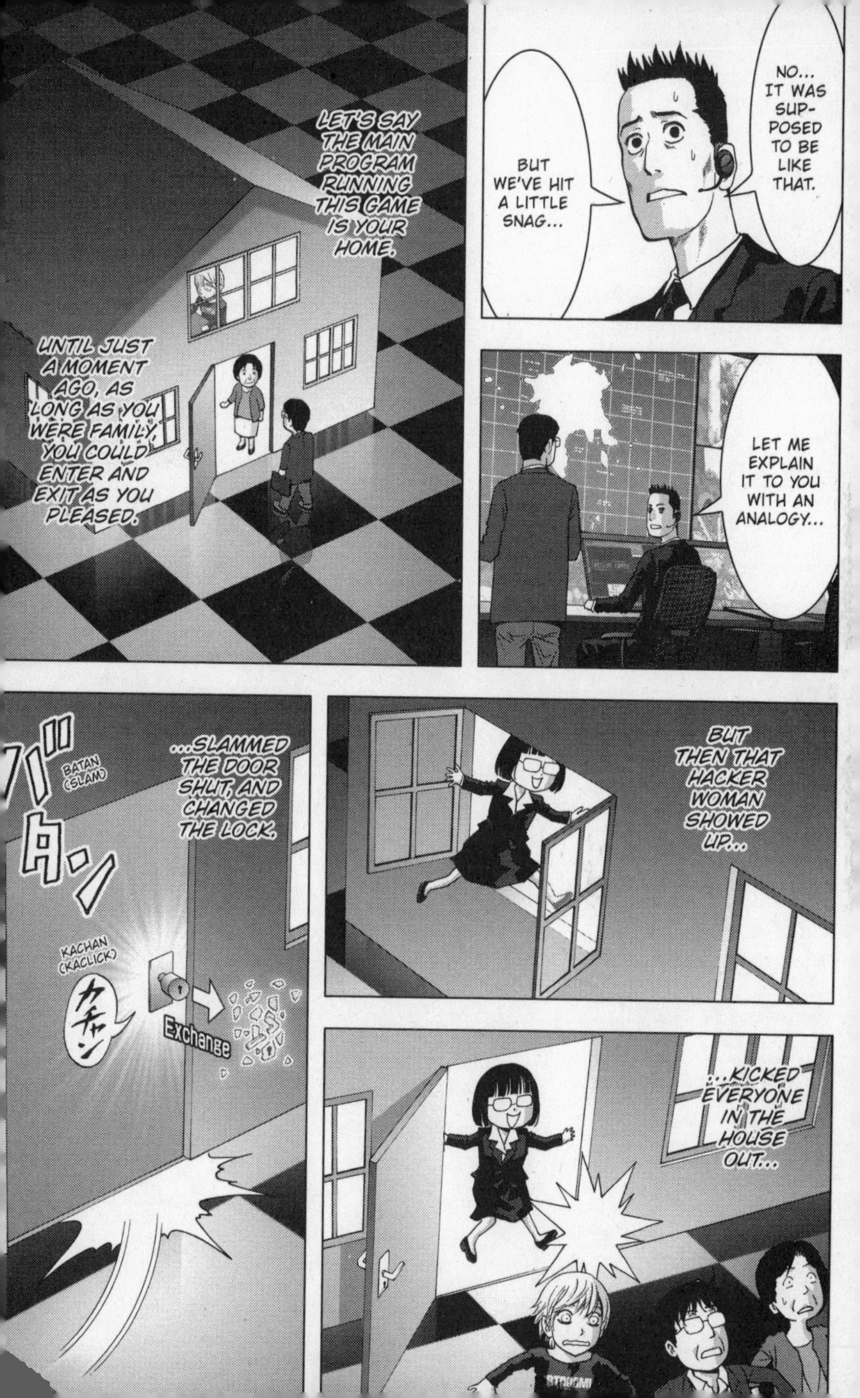
NO... IT WAS SUP-POSED TO BE LIKE THAT.
BUT WE'VE HIT A LITTLE SNAG...
LET ME EXPLAIN IT TO YOU WITH AN ANALOGY...
LET'S SAY THE MAIN PROGRAM RUNNING THIS GAME IS YOUR HOME.
UNTIL JUST A MOMENT AGO, AS LONG AS YOU WERE FAMILY, YOU COULD ENTER AND EXIT AS YOU PLEASED.
BUT THEN THAT HACKER WOMAN SHOWED UP...
...KICKED EVERYONE IN THE HOUSE OUT...
...SLAMMED THE DOOR SHUT, AND CHANGED THE LOCK.
バタン
BATAN (SLAM)
KACHAN (KACLICK)
カチャン
Exchange

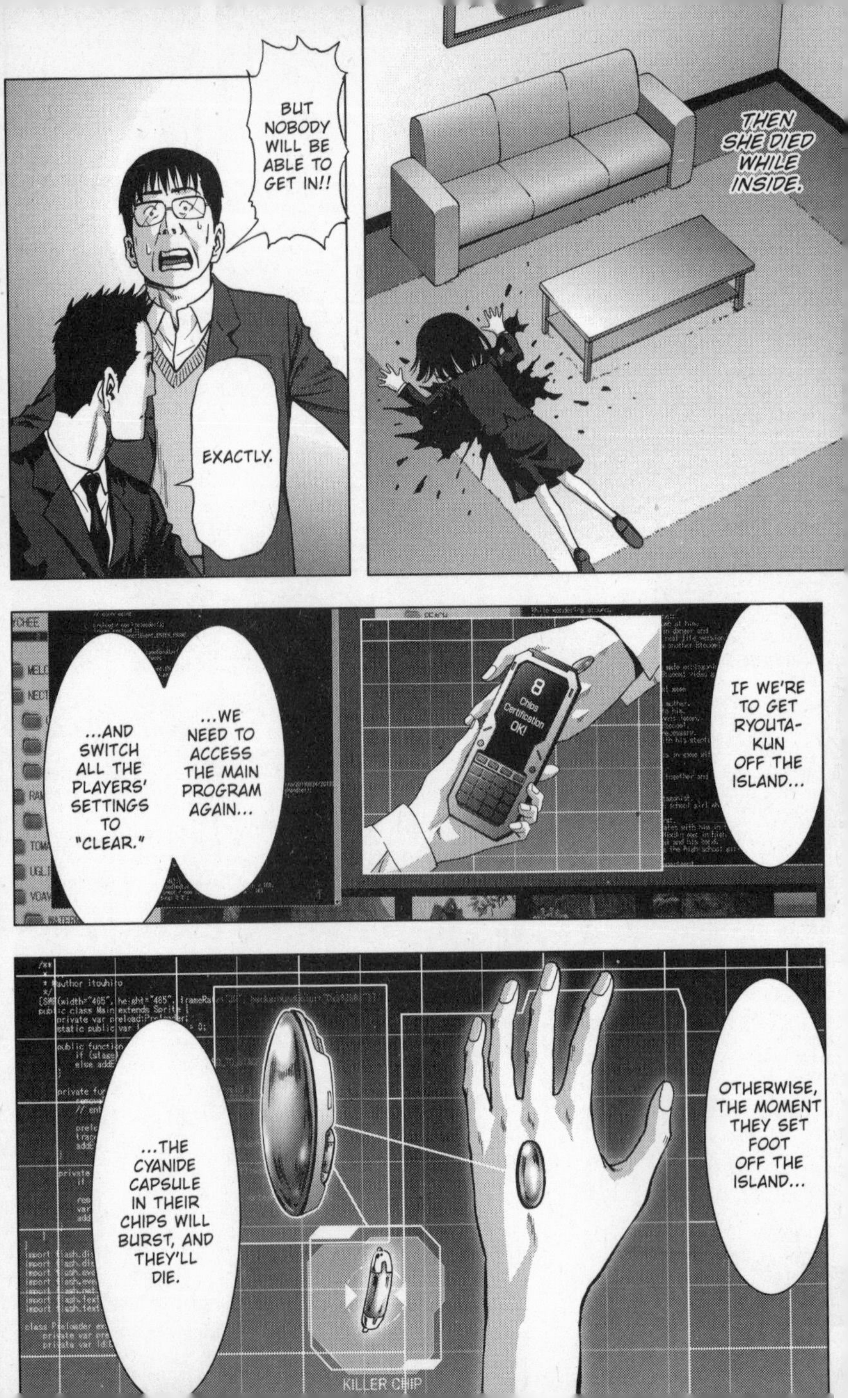
THEN SHE DIED WHILE INSIDE.
BUT NOBODY WILL BE ABLE TO GET IN!!
EXACTLY.
IF WE'RE TO GET RYOUTA-KUN OFF THE ISLAND...
...WE NEED TO ACCESS THE MAIN PROGRAM AGAIN...
...AND SWITCH ALL THE PLAYERS' SETTINGS TO "CLEAR."
8 Chips Certification OK!
OTHERWISE, THE MOMENT THEY SET FOOT OFF THE ISLAND...
...THE CYANIDE CAPSULE IN THEIR CHIPS WILL BURST, AND THEY'LL DIE.
KILLER CHIP

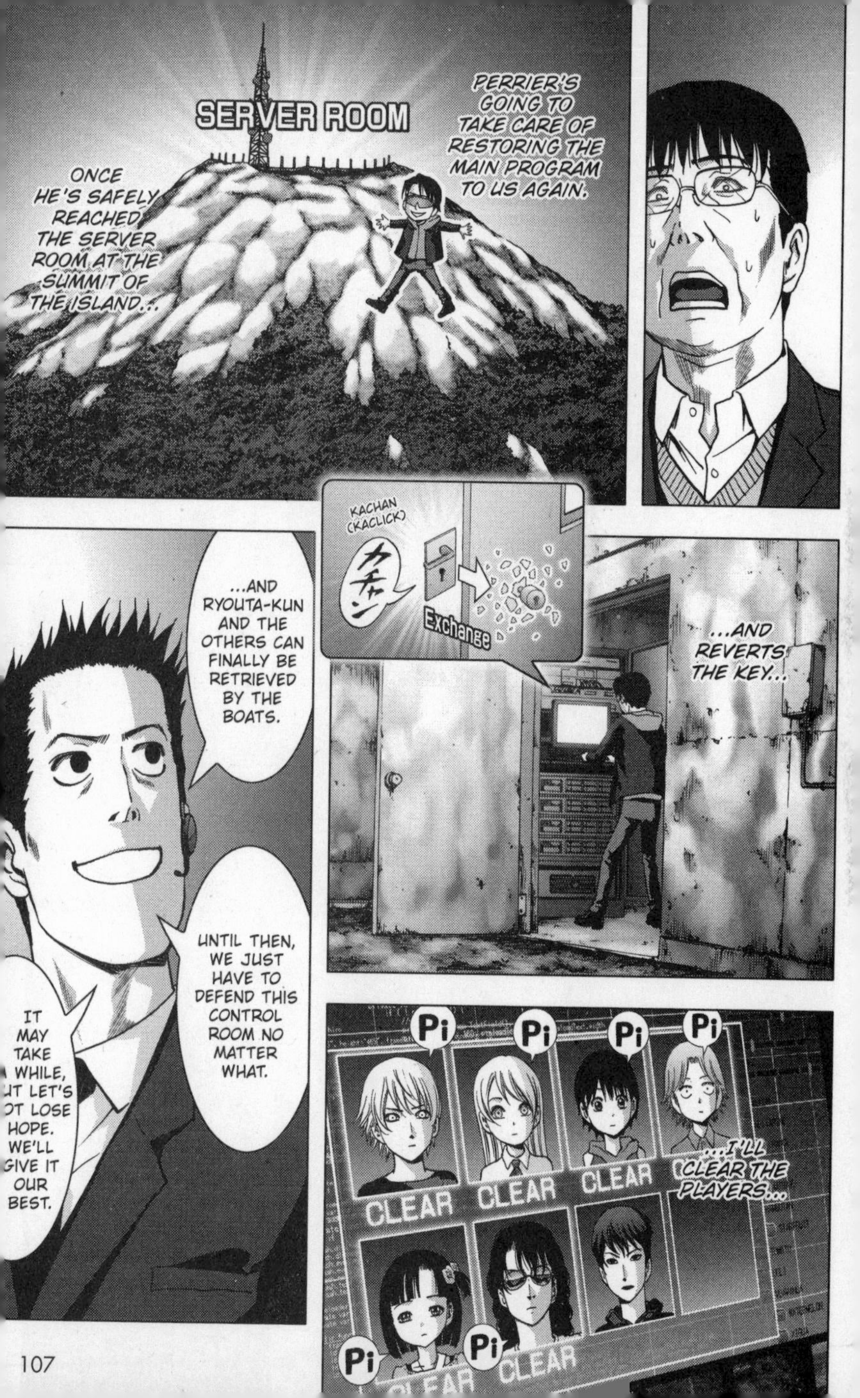

PERRIER'S GOING TO TAKE CARE OF RESTORING THE MAIN PROGRAM TO US AGAIN.
SERVER ROOM
ONCE HE'S SAFELY REACHED THE SERVER ROOM AT THE SUMMIT OF THE ISLAND...
KACHAN (KACLICK)
カチャン
Exchange
...AND REVERTS THE KEY...
Pi
Pi
Pi
Pi
...I'LL CLEAR THE PLAYERS...
CLEAR
CLEAR
CLEAR
CLEAR
Pi
Pi
CLEAR
CLEAR
...AND RYOUTA-KUN AND THE OTHERS CAN FINALLY BE RETRIEVED BY THE BOATS.
UNTIL THEN, WE JUST HAVE TO DEFEND THIS CONTROL ROOM NO MATTER WHAT.
IT MAY TAKE WHILE, UT LET'S OT LOSE HOPE. WE'LL GIVE IT OUR BEST.

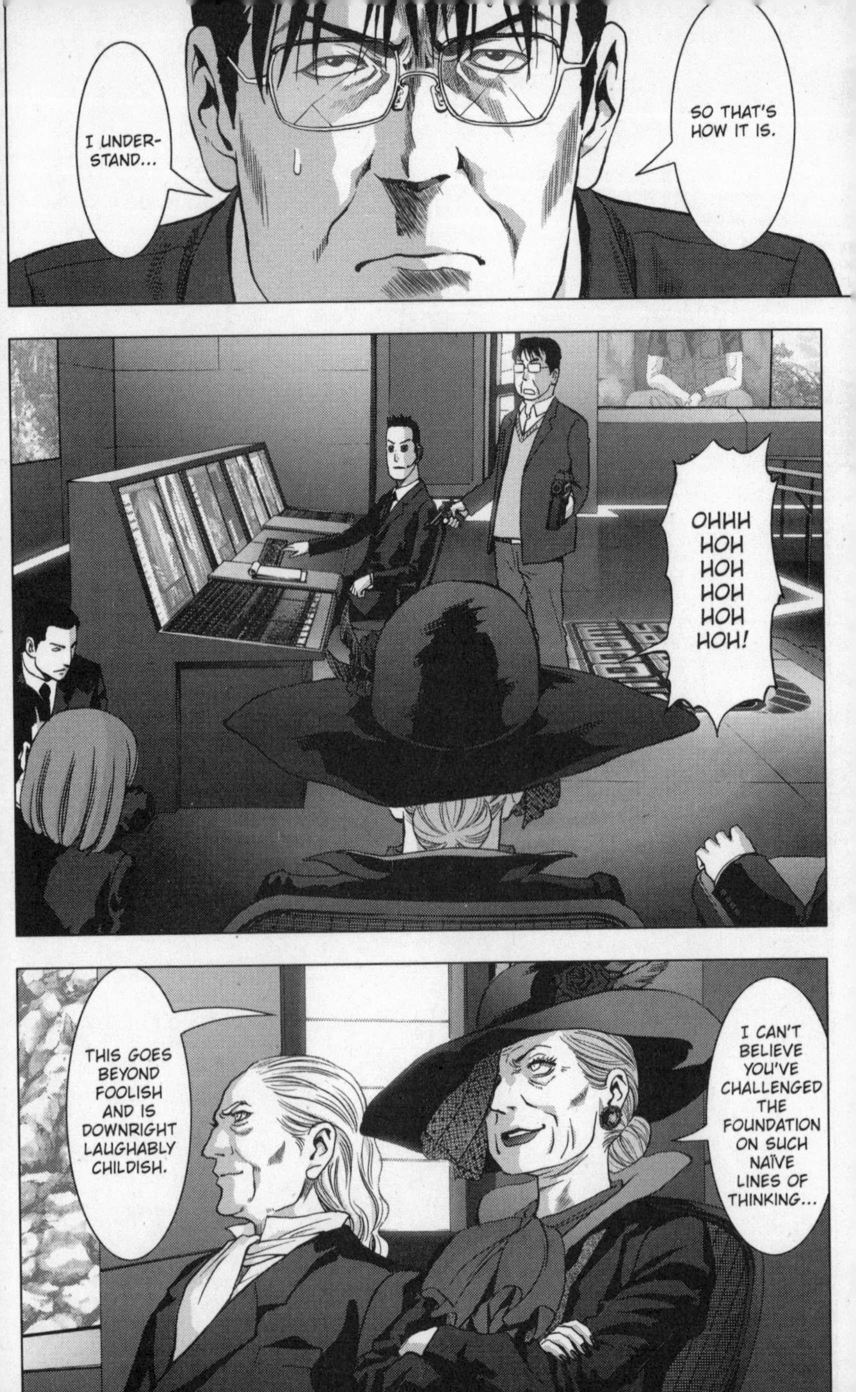
SO THAT'S HOW IT IS.
I UNDER-STAND...
OHHH HOH HOH HOH HOH HOH!
I CAN'T BELIEVE YOU'VE CHALLENGED THE FOUNDATION ON SUCH NAÏVE LINES OF THINKING...
THIS GOES BEYOND FOOLISH AND IS DOWNRIGHT LAUGHABLY CHILDISH.

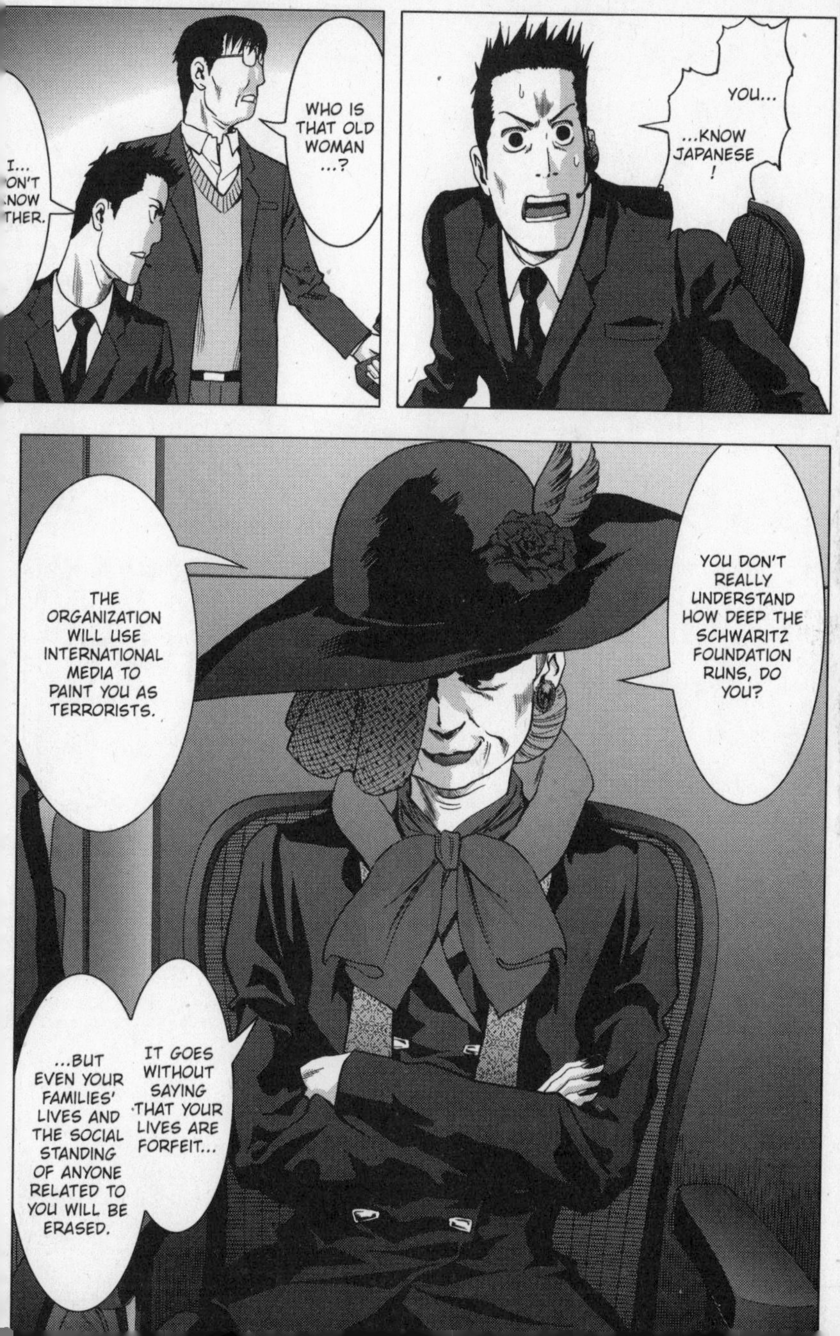
YOU... ...KNOW JAPANESE!
WHO IS THAT OLD WOMAN ...?
I... ON'T NOW THER.
YOU DON'T REALLY UNDERSTAND HOW DEEP THE SCHWARITZ FOUNDATION RUNS, DO YOU?
THE ORGANIZATION WILL USE INTERNATIONAL MEDIA TO PAINT YOU AS TERRORISTS.
IT GOES WITHOUT SAYING THAT YOUR LIVES ARE FORFEIT...
...BUT EVEN YOUR FAMILIES' LIVES AND THE SOCIAL STANDING OF ANYONE RELATED TO YOU WILL BE ERASED.

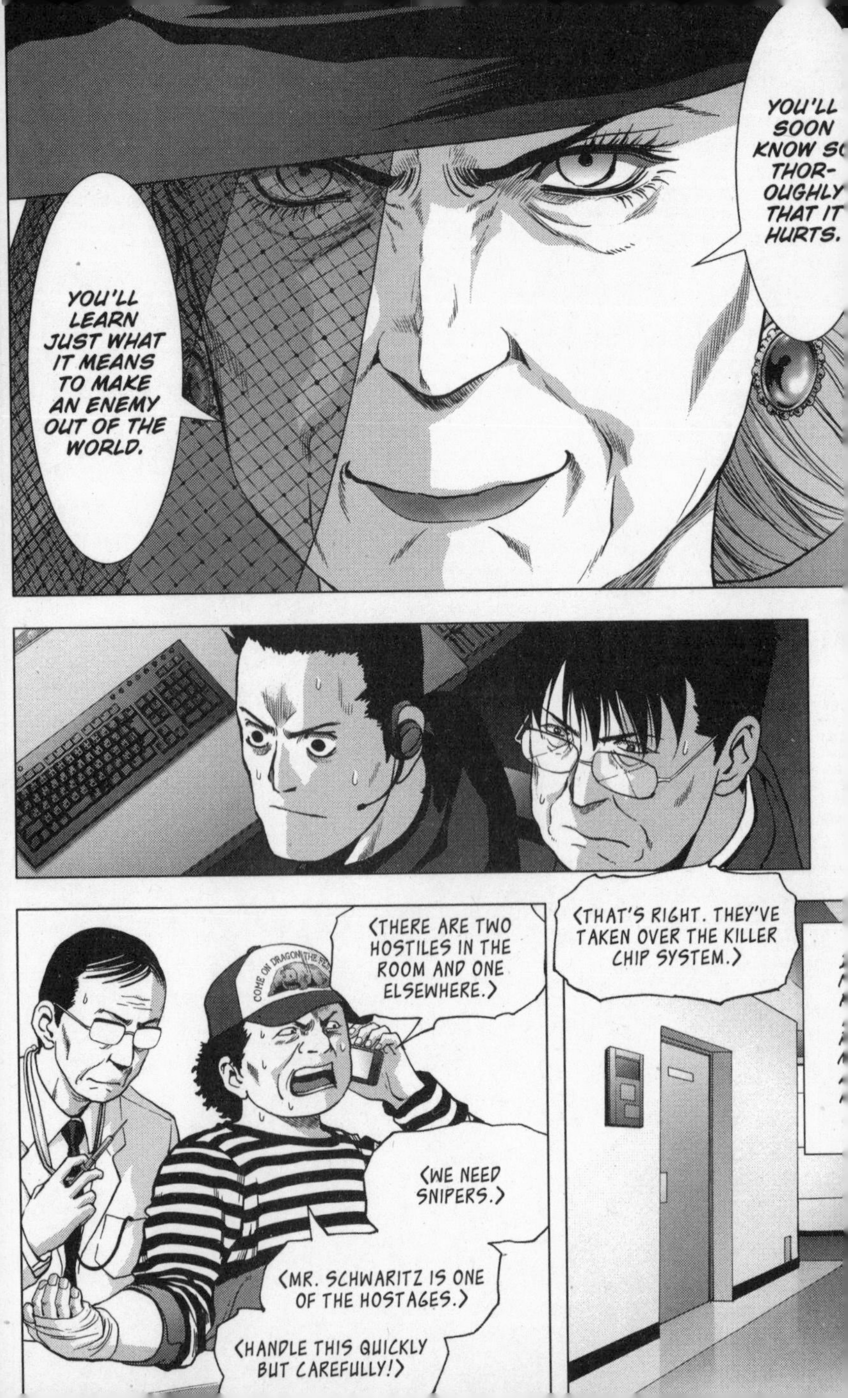

YOU'LL SOON KNOW S THOROUGHLY THAT IT HURTS.
YOU'LL LEARN JUST WHAT IT MEANS TO MAKE AN ENEMY OUT OF THE WORLD.
‹THAT'S RIGHT. THEY'VE TAKEN OVER THE KILLER CHIP SYSTEM.›
‹THERE ARE TWO HOSTILES IN THE ROOM AND ONE ELSEWHERE.›
‹WE NEED SNIPERS.›
‹MR. SCHWARITZ IS ONE OF THE HOSTAGES.›
‹HANDLE THIS QUICKLY BUT CAREFULLY!›

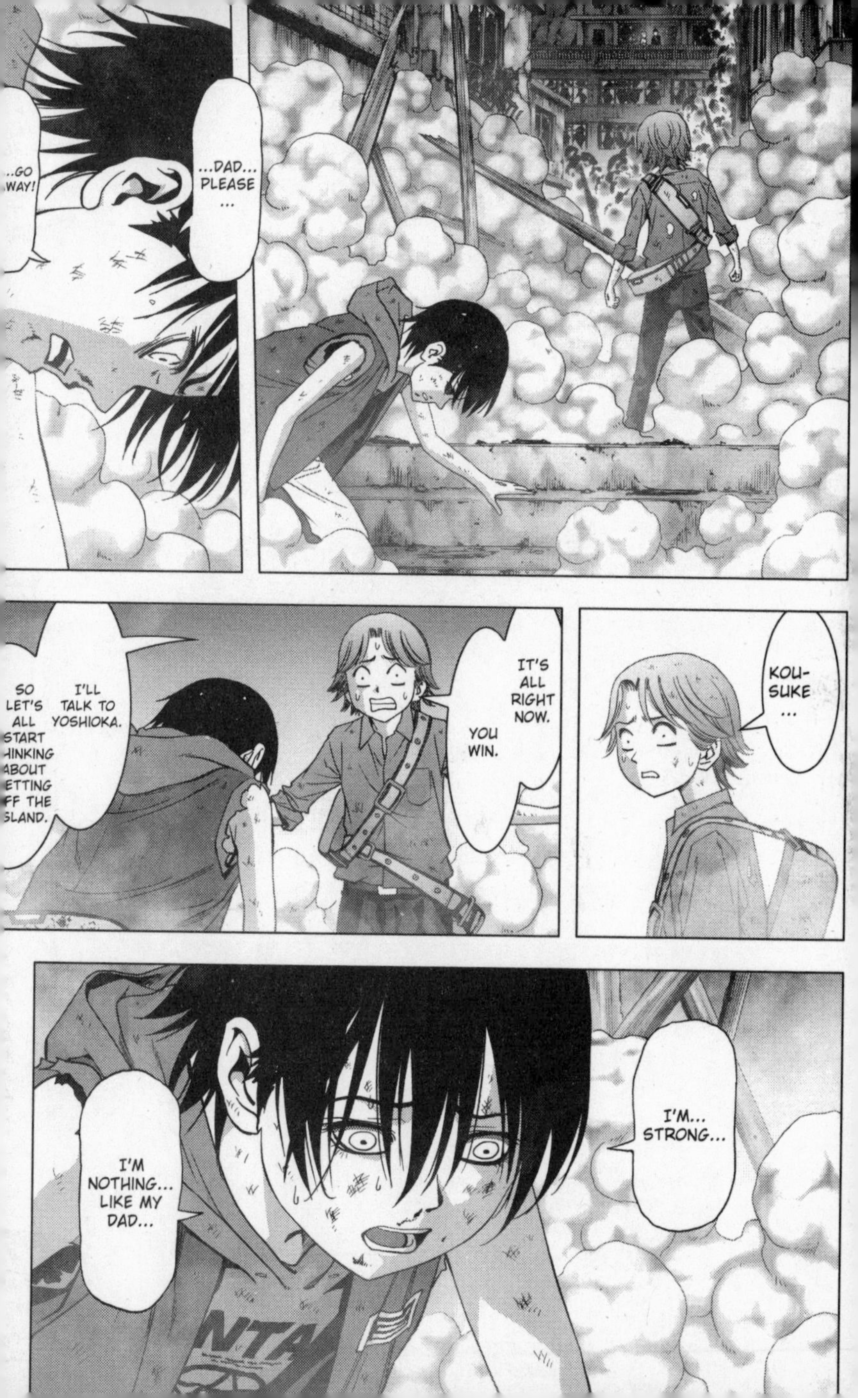
...DAD... PLEASE ...
..GO WAY!
KOU-SUKE ...
IT'S ALL RIGHT NOW.
YOU WIN.
I'LL TALK TO YOSHIOKA.
SO LET'S ALL START HINKING ABOUT ETTING FF THE SLAND.
I'M... STRONG...
I'M NOTHING... LIKE MY DAD...

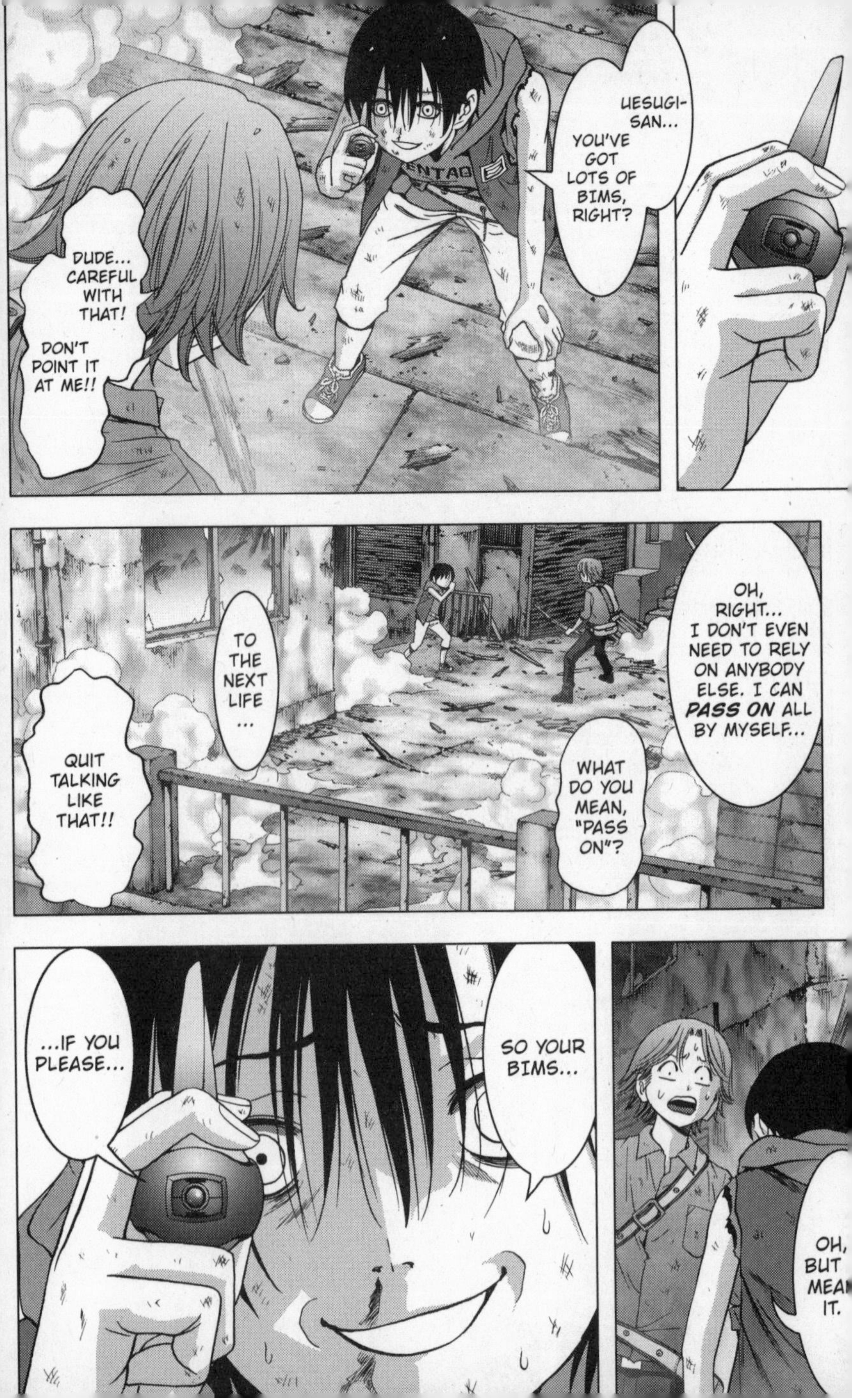
UESUGI-SAN... YOU'VE GOT LOTS OF BIMS, RIGHT?
DUDE... CAREFUL WITH THAT!
DON'T POINT IT AT ME!!
OH, RIGHT... I DON'T EVEN NEED TO RELY ON ANYBODY ELSE. I CAN PASS ON ALL BY MYSELF...
WHAT DO YOU MEAN, "PASS ON"?
TO THE NEXT LIFE...
QUIT TALKING LIKE THAT!!
OH, BUT MEA IT.
SO YOUR BIMS...
...IF YOU PLEASE...

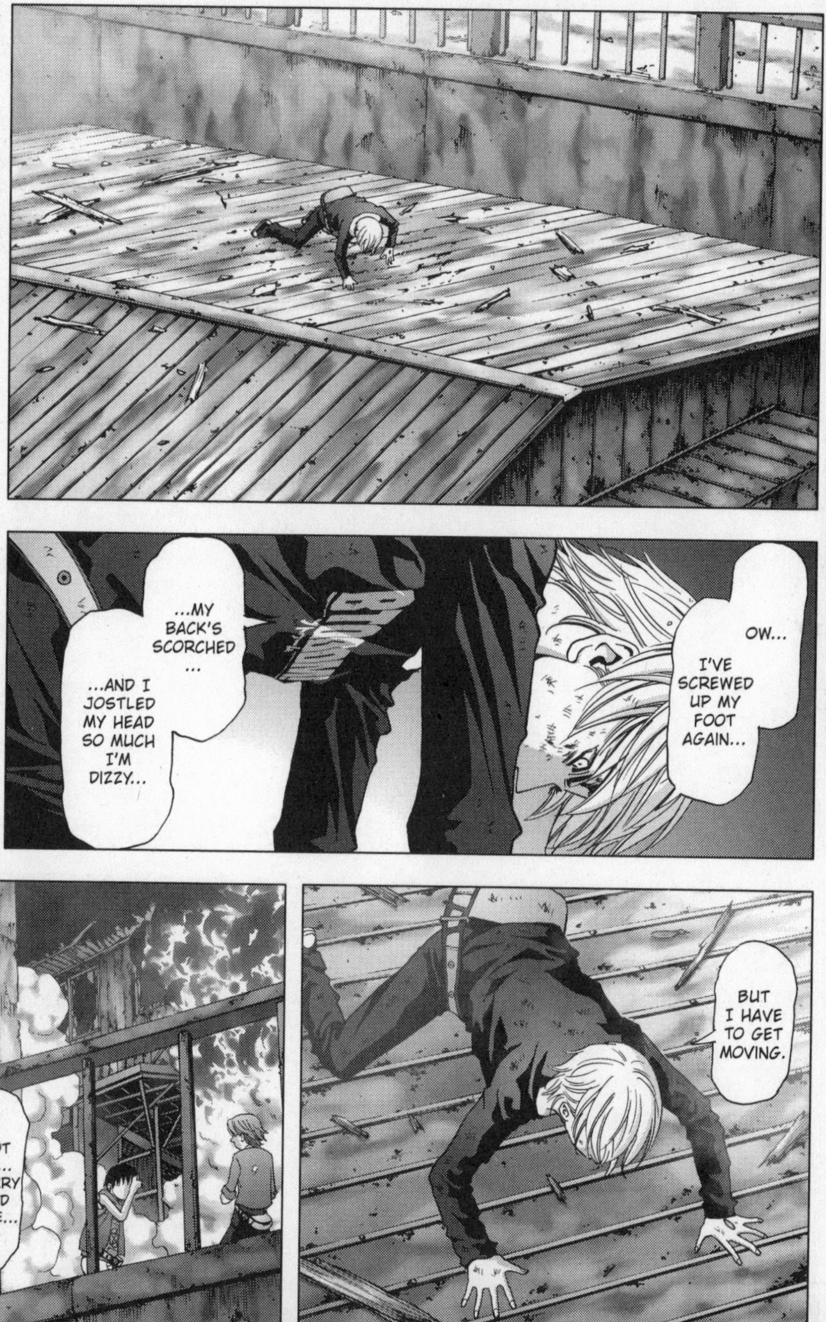
OW... I'VE SCREWED UP MY FOOT AGAIN...
...MY BACK'S SCORCHED...
...AND I JOSTLED MY HEAD SO MUCH I'M DIZZY...
BUT I HAVE TO GET MOVING.

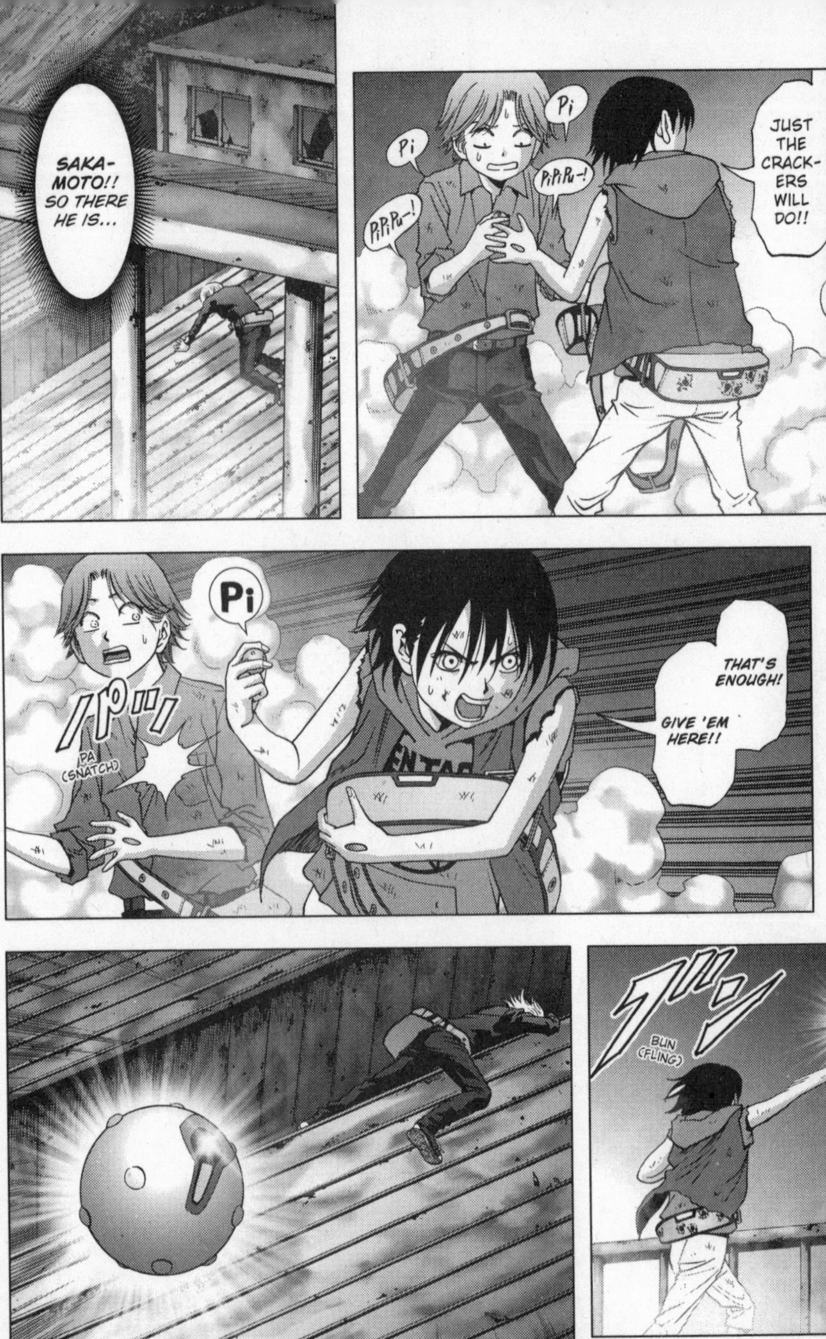
JUST THE CRACKERS WILL DO!!
Pi
PiPiPu-!
Pi
PiPiPu-!
SAKAMOTO!! SO THERE HE IS...
THAT'S ENOUGH!
GIVE 'EM HERE!!
Pi
PA (SNATCH)
BUN (FLING)

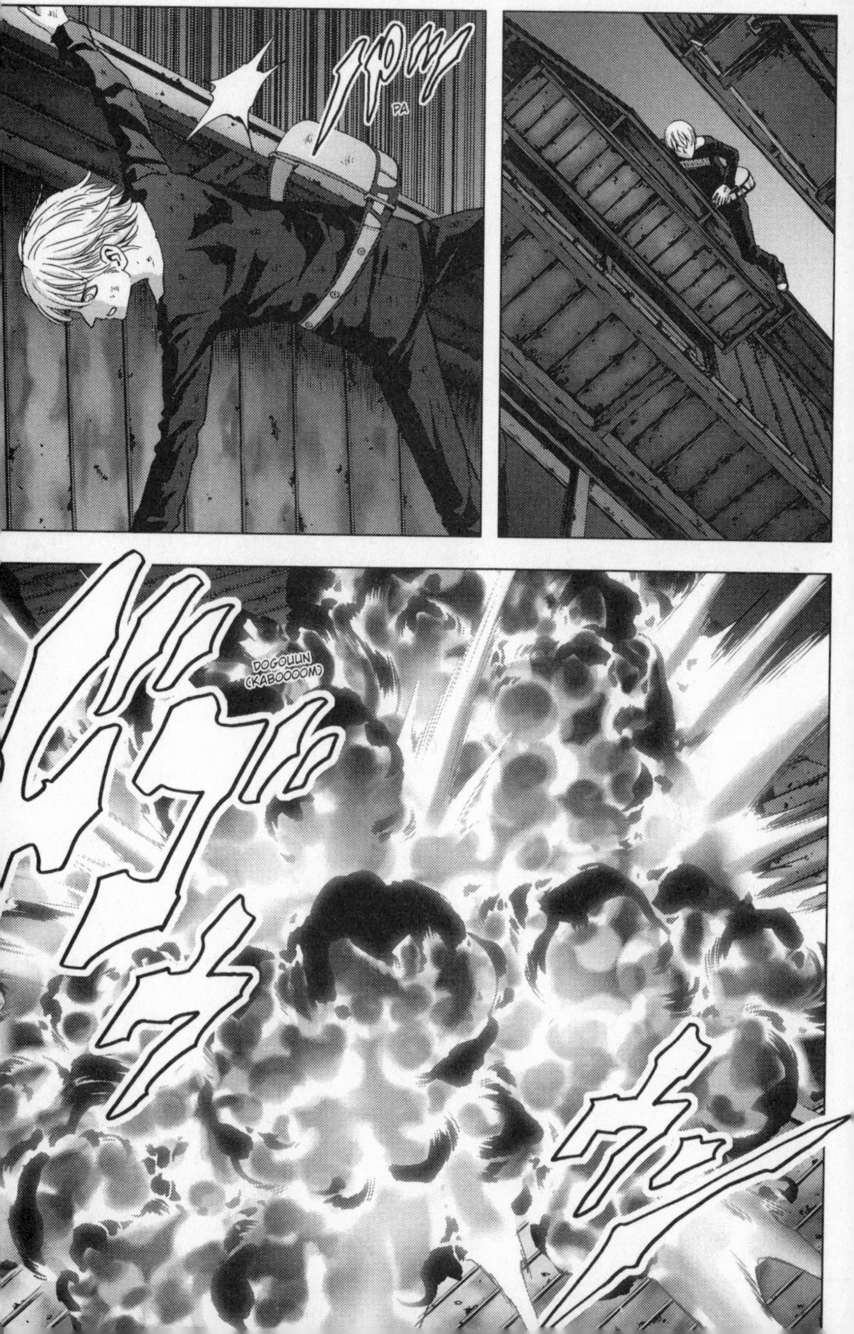
PA
DOGOUUN (KABOOOOM)

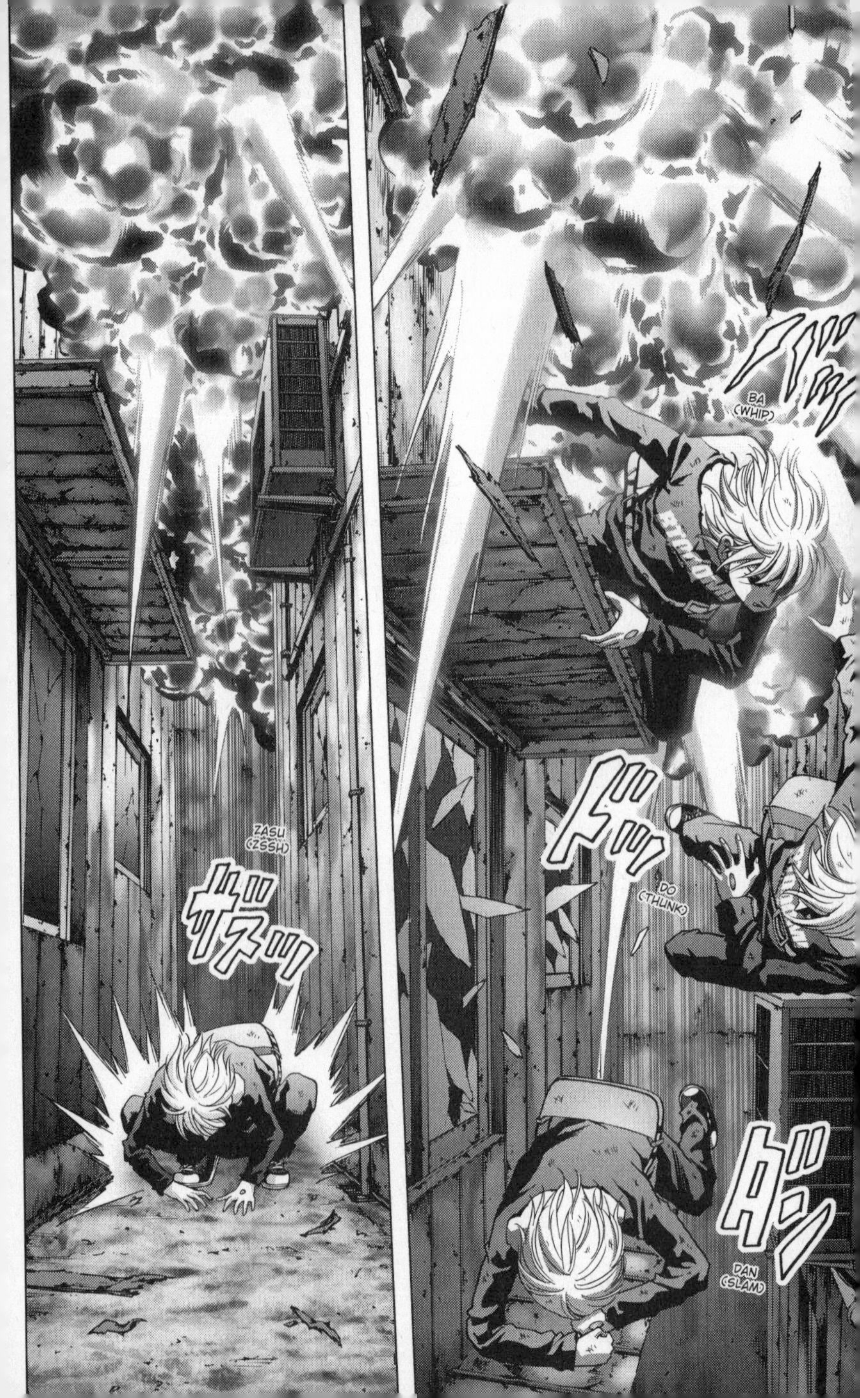
バッ
BA (WHIP)
ドッ
DO (THUNK)
ダン
DAN (SLAM)
ザスッ
ZASU (ZSSH)

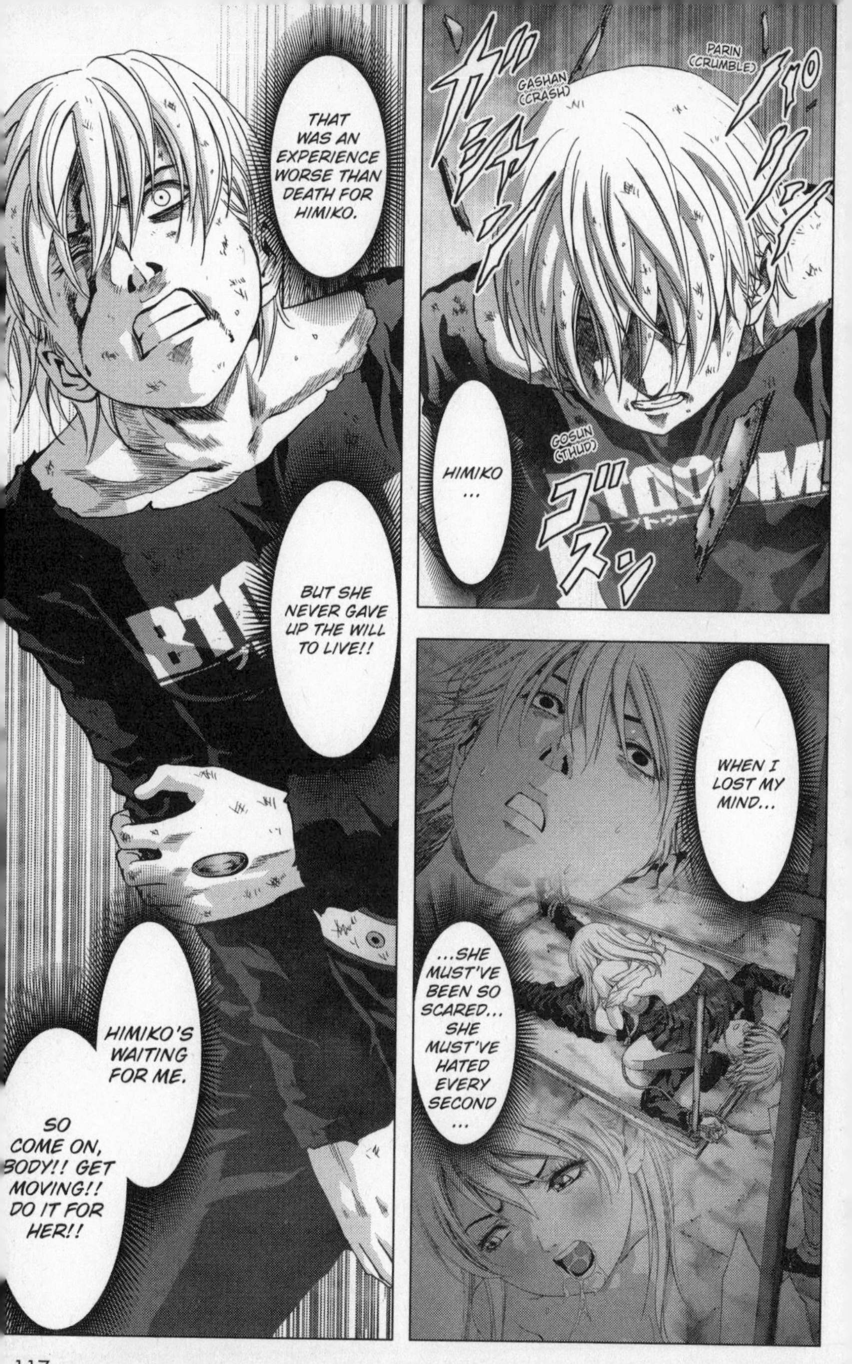
PARIN (CRUMBLE)
GASHAN (CRASH)
GOSUN (THUD)
HIMIKO...
WHEN I LOST MY MIND...
...SHE MUST'VE BEEN SO SCARED... SHE MUST'VE HATED EVERY SECOND...
THAT WAS AN EXPERIENCE WORSE THAN DEATH FOR HIMIKO.
BUT SHE NEVER GAVE UP THE WILL TO LIVE!!
HIMIKO'S WAITING FOR ME.
SO COME ON, BODY!! GET MOVING!! DO IT FOR HER!!

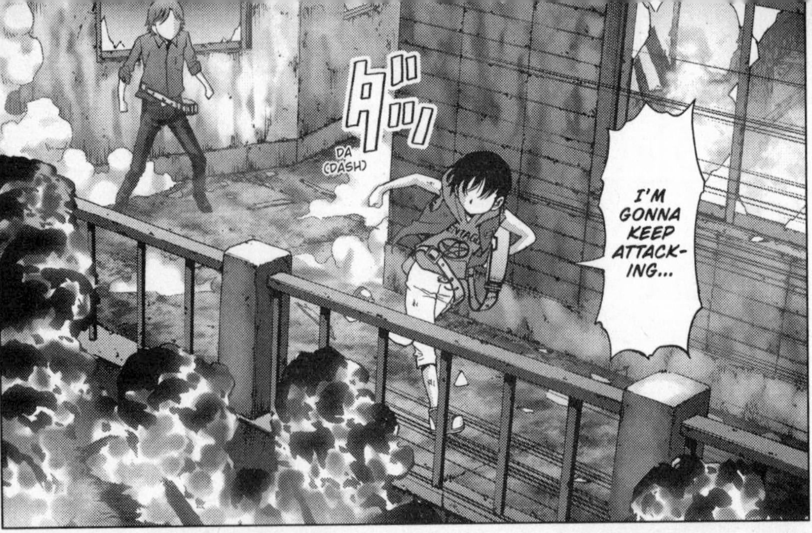
ダッ
DA (DASH)
I'M GONNA KEEP ATTACK-ING...
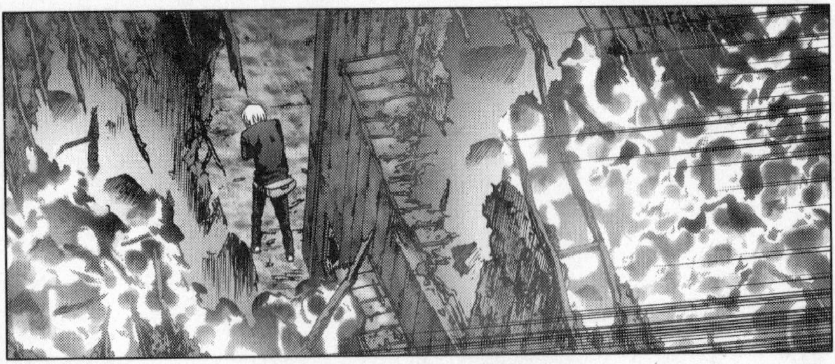
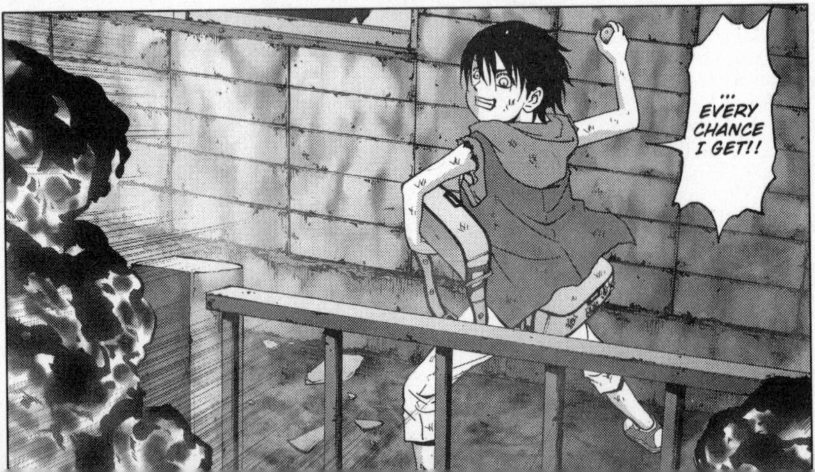
...EVERY CHANCE I GET!!

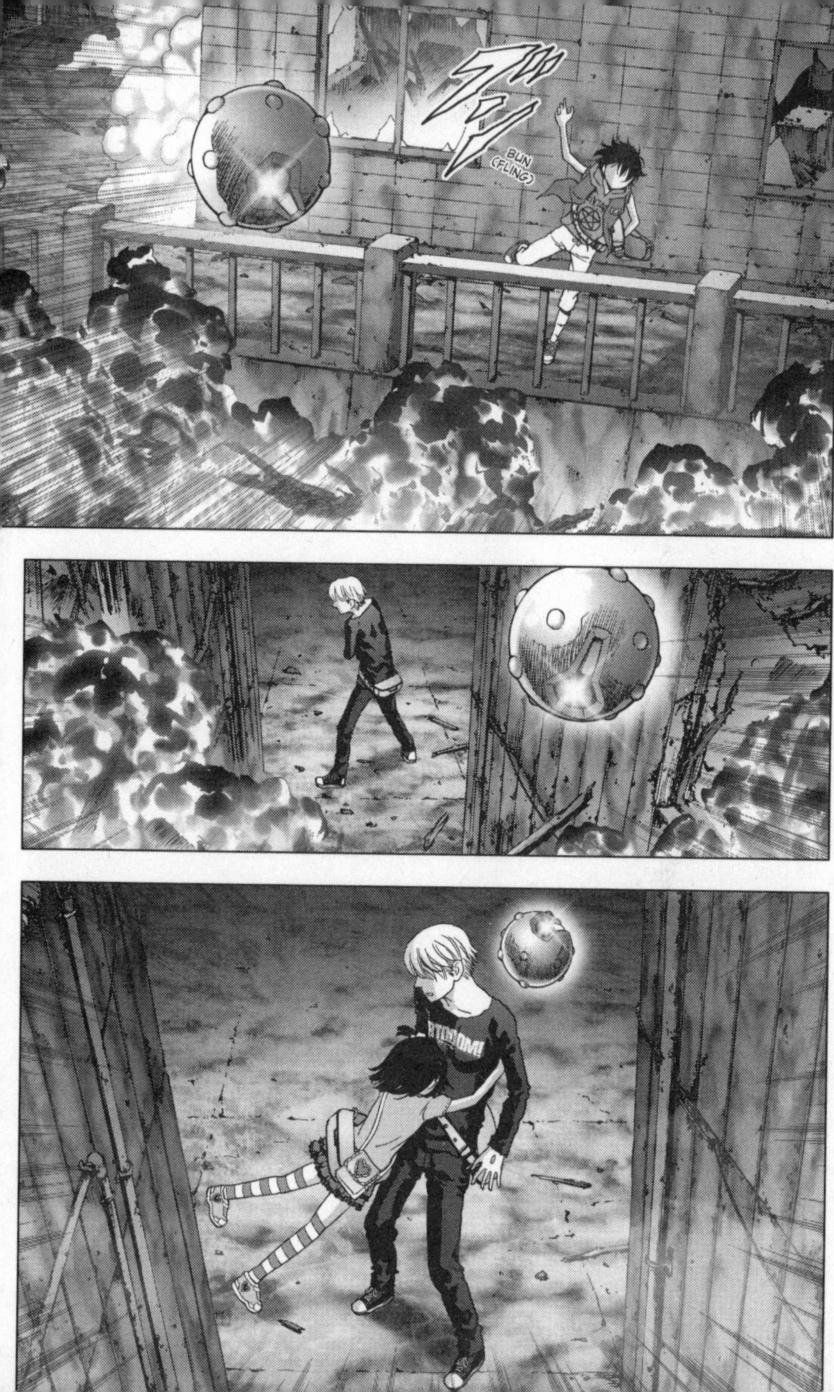
BUN
(FLING)

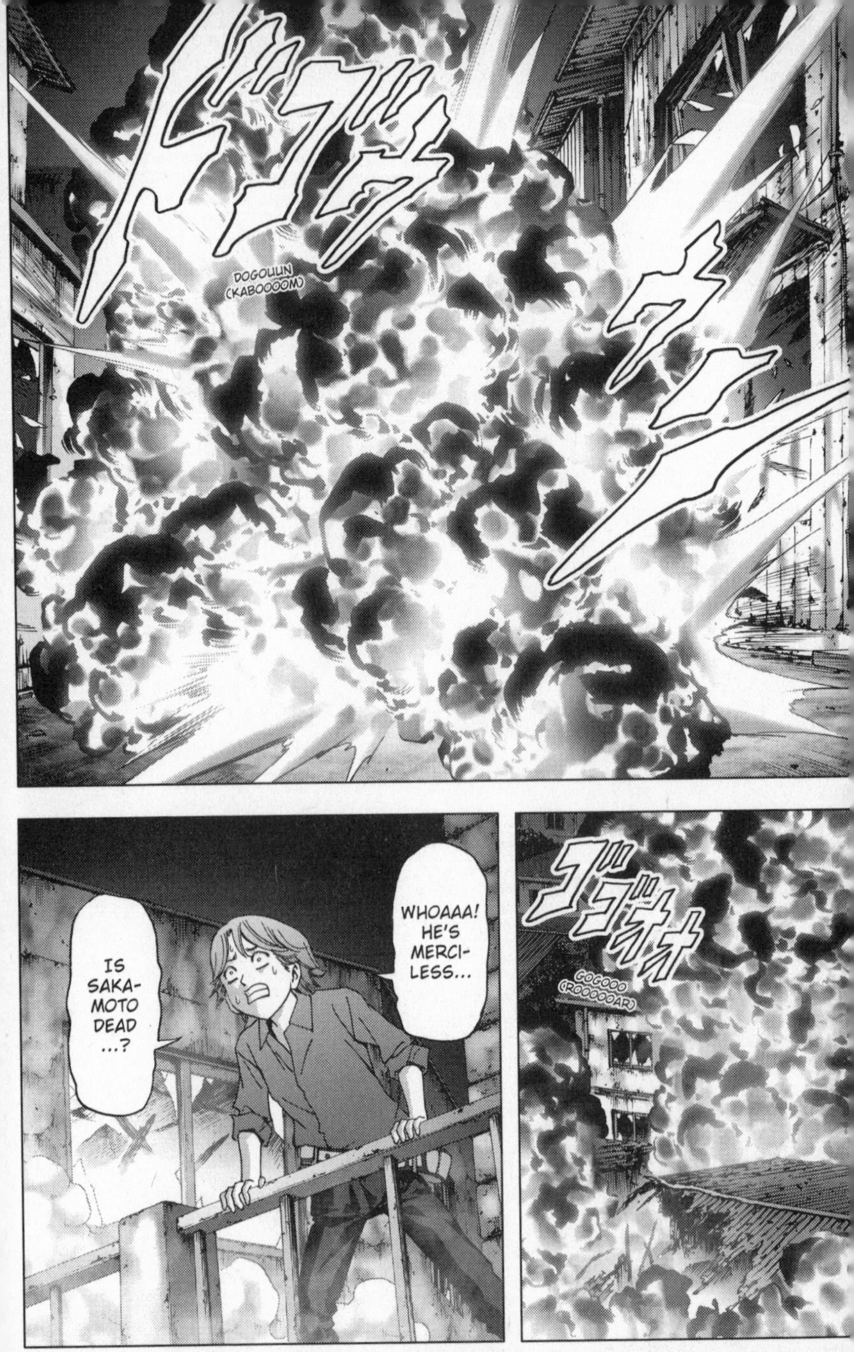
DOGOUUN (KABOOOOM)
GOGOOO (ROOOOOAR)
WHOAAA! HE'S MERCILESS...
IS SAKAMOTO DEAD ...?

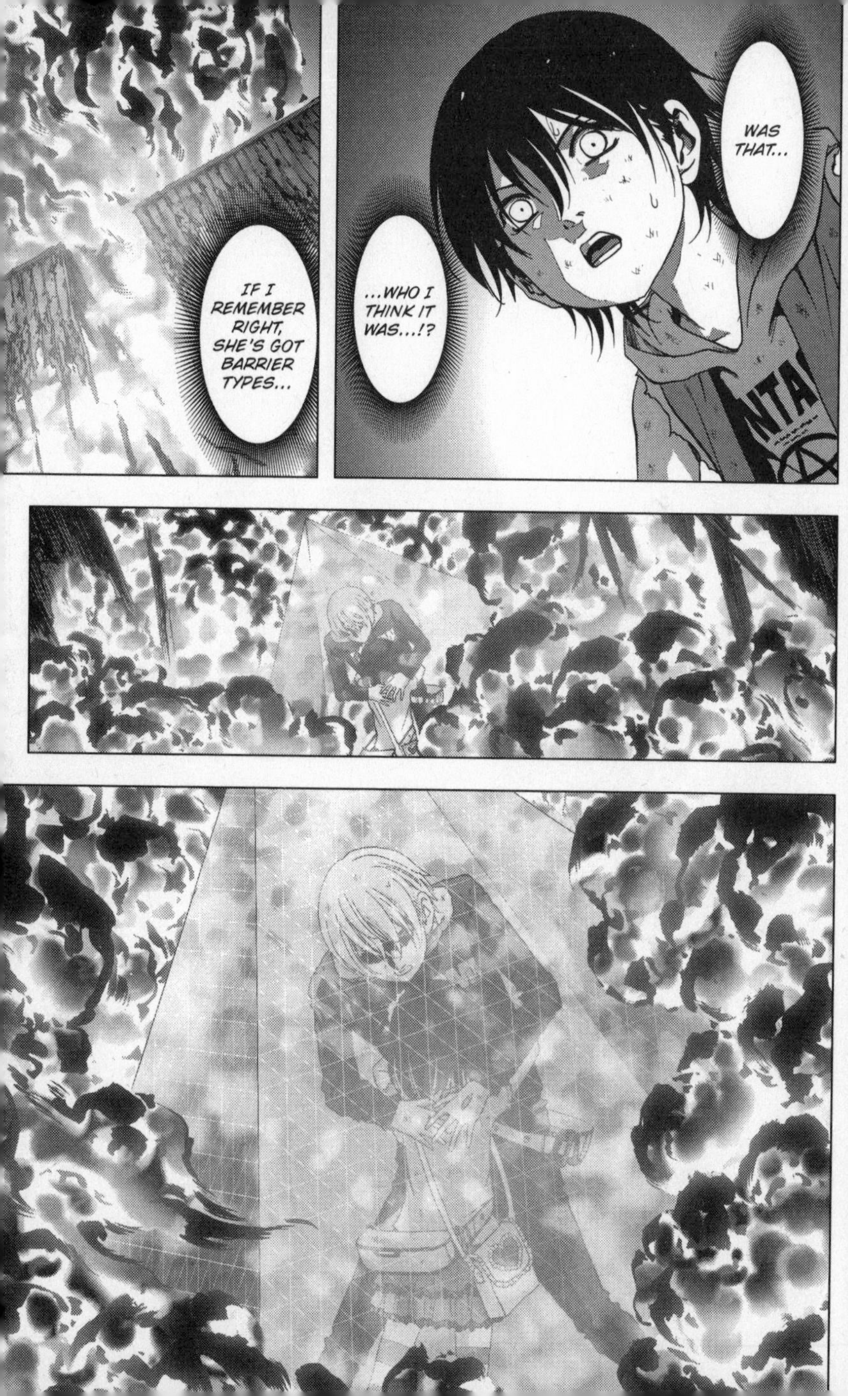
WAS THAT...
...WHO I THINK IT WAS...!?
IF I REMEMBER RIGHT, SHE'S GOT BARRIER TYPES...

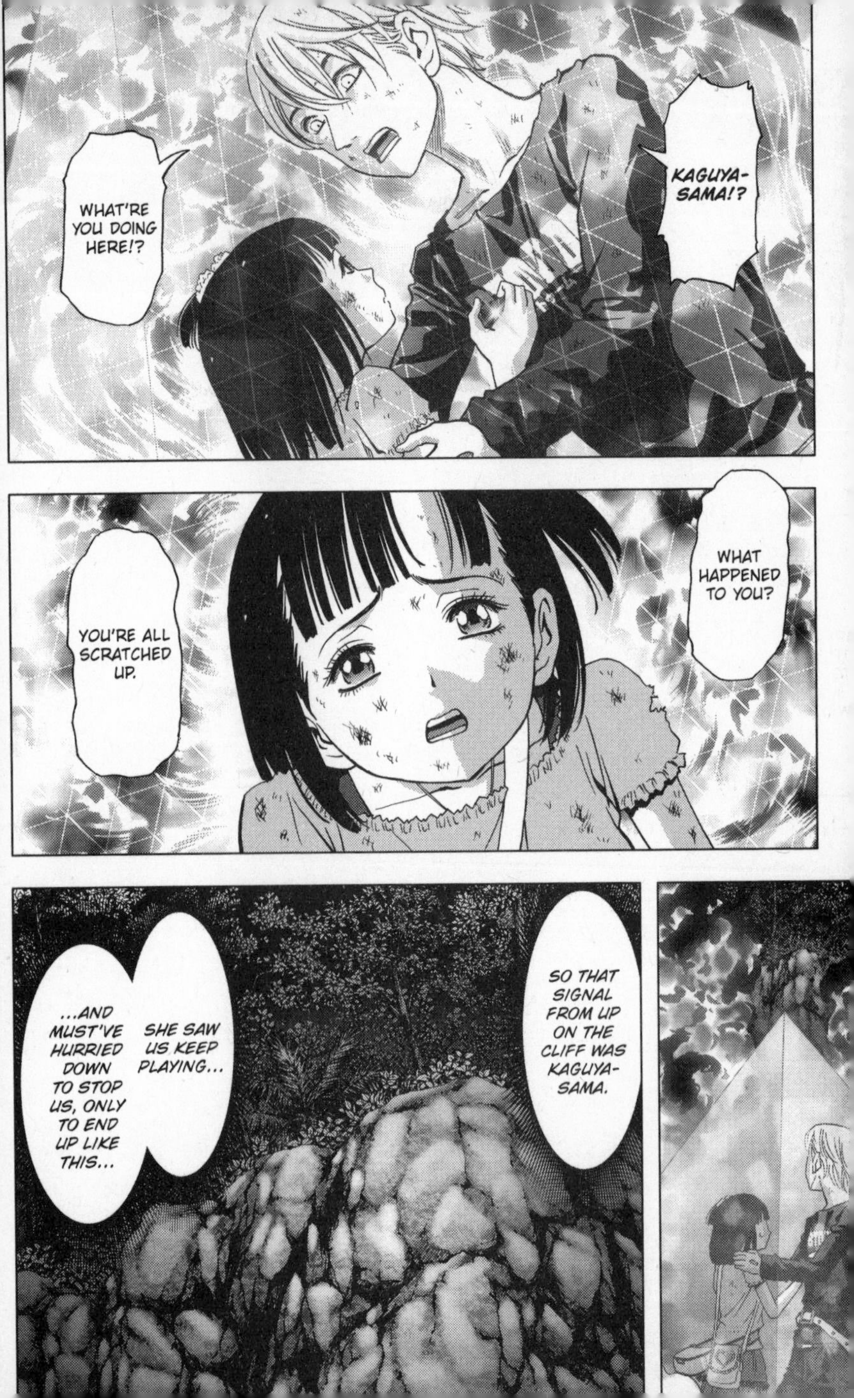
KAGUYA-SAMA!?
WHAT'RE YOU DOING HERE!?
WHAT HAPPENED TO YOU?
YOU'RE ALL SCRATCHED UP.
SO THAT SIGNAL FROM UP ON THE CLIFF WAS KAGUYA-SAMA.
SHE SAW US KEEP PLAYING...
...AND MUST'VE HURRIED DOWN TO STOP US, ONLY TO END UP LIKE THIS...

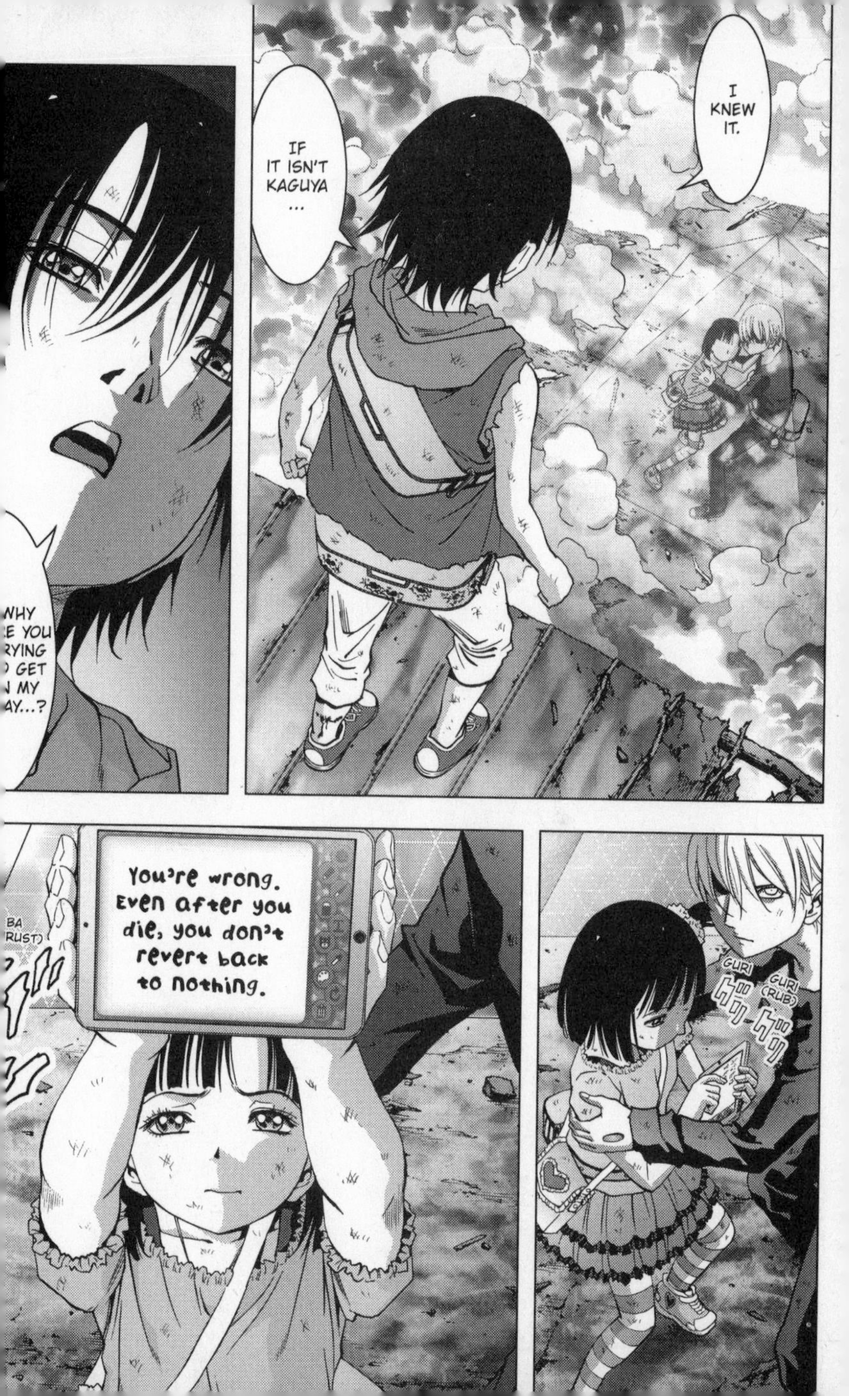
I KNEW IT.
IF IT ISN'T KAGUYA ...
NHY E YOU RYING GET N MY AY...?
GURI GURI (RUB)
You're wrong. Even after you die, you don't revert back to nothing.
BA RUST)

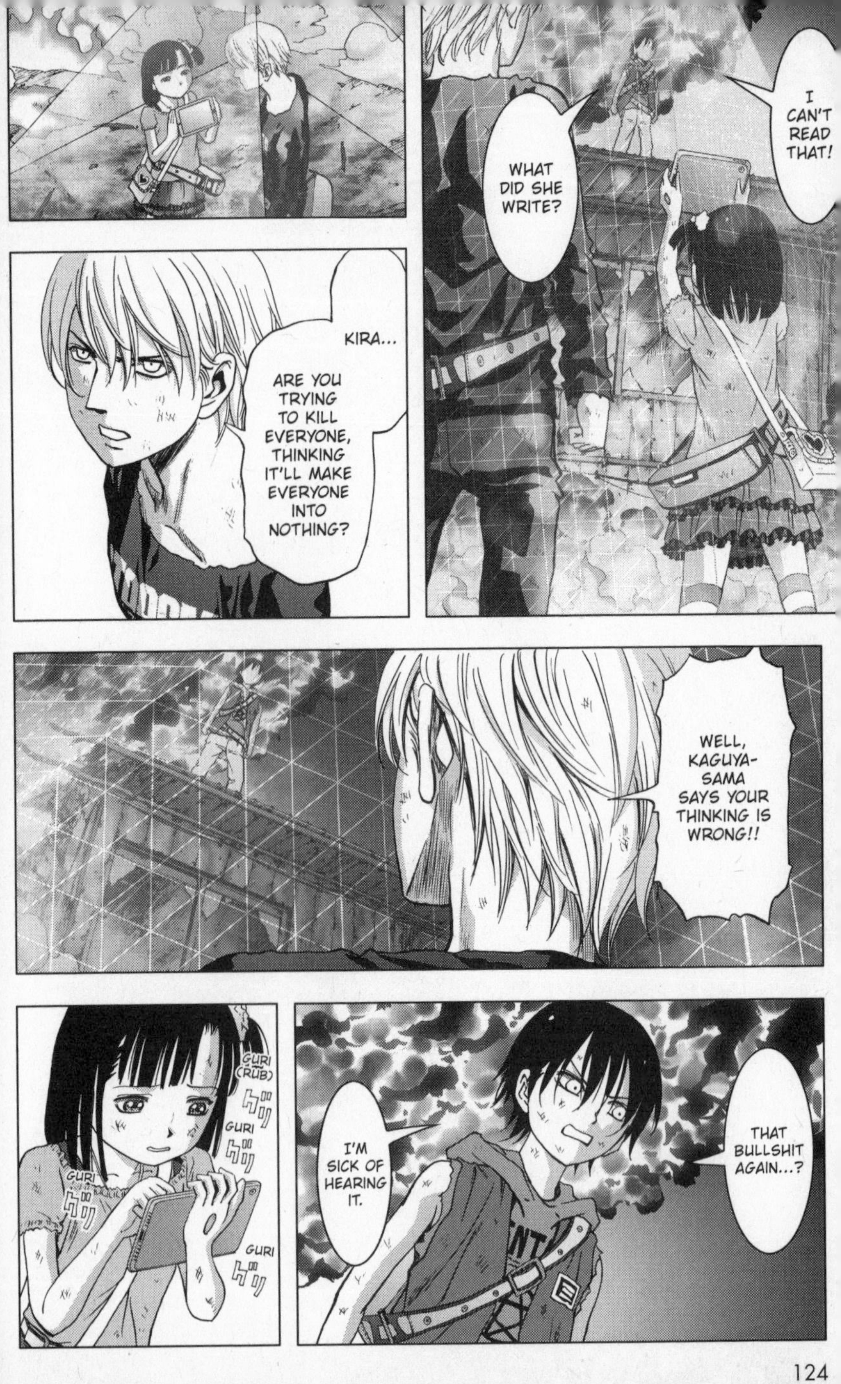
I CAN'T READ THAT!
WHAT DID SHE WRITE?
KIRA...
ARE YOU TRYING TO KILL EVERYONE, THINKING IT'LL MAKE EVERYONE INTO NOTHING?
WELL, KAGUYA-SAMA SAYS YOUR THINKING IS WRONG!!
THAT BULLSHIT AGAIN...?
I'M SICK OF HEARING IT.
GURI (RUB)
GURI
GURI
GURI

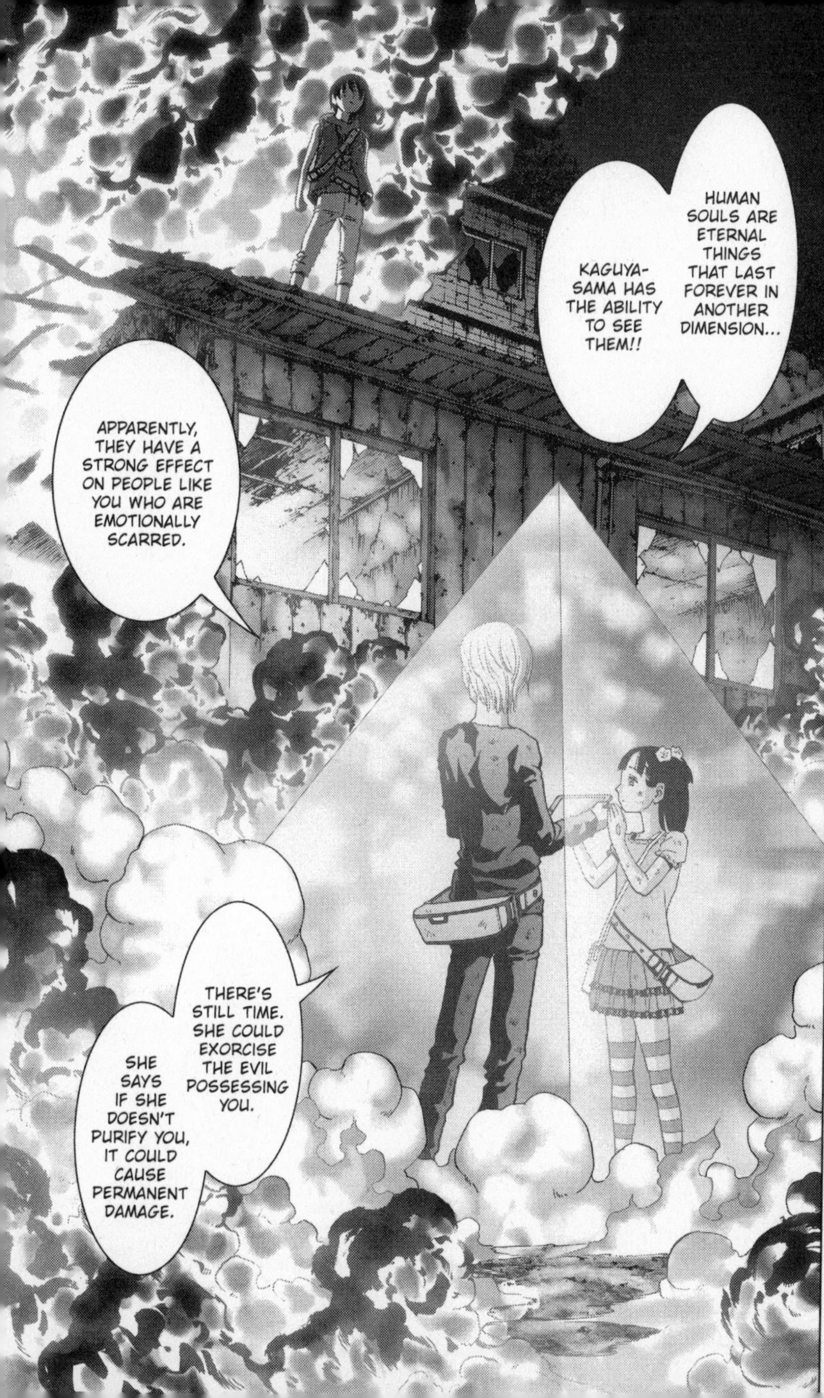
HUMAN SOULS ARE ETERNAL THINGS THAT LAST FOREVER IN ANOTHER DIMENSION...
KAGUYA-SAMA HAS THE ABILITY TO SEE THEM!!
APPARENTLY, THEY HAVE A STRONG EFFECT ON PEOPLE LIKE YOU WHO ARE EMOTIONALLY SCARRED.
THERE'S STILL TIME. SHE COULD EXORCISE THE EVIL POSSESSING YOU.
SHE SAYS IF SHE DOESN'T PURIFY YOU, IT COULD CAUSE PERMANENT DAMAGE.

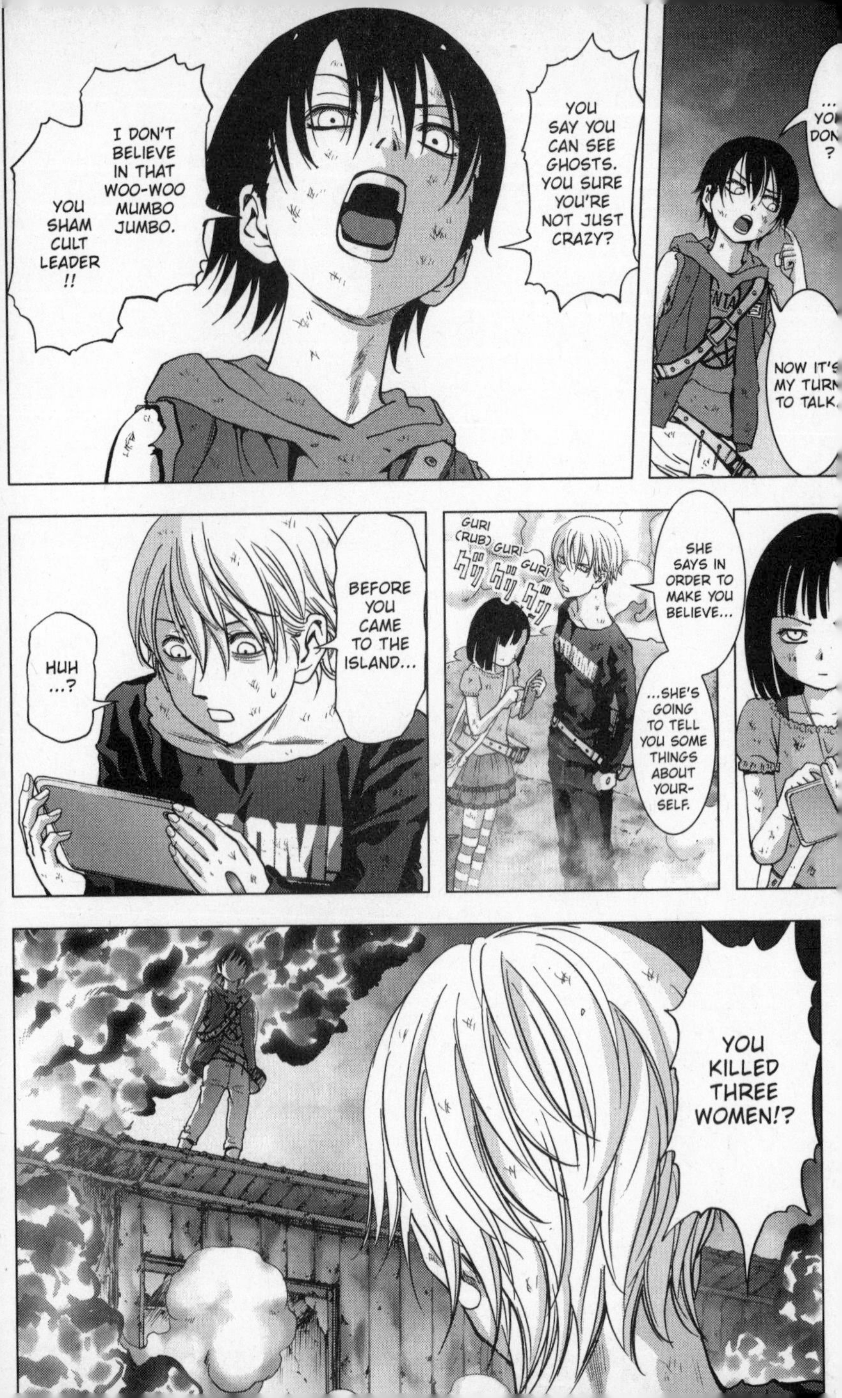

... YO DON ?
NOW IT'S MY TURN TO TALK.
YOU SAY YOU CAN SEE GHOSTS. YOU SURE YOU'RE NOT JUST CRAZY?
I DON'T BELIEVE IN THAT WOO-WOO MUMBO JUMBO.
YOU SHAM CULT LEADER !!
SHE SAYS IN ORDER TO MAKE YOU BELIEVE...
...SHE'S GOING TO TELL YOU SOME THINGS ABOUT YOUR-SELF.
GURI (RUB) GURI GURI
BEFORE YOU CAME TO THE ISLAND...
HUH ...?
YOU KILLED THREE WOMEN!?

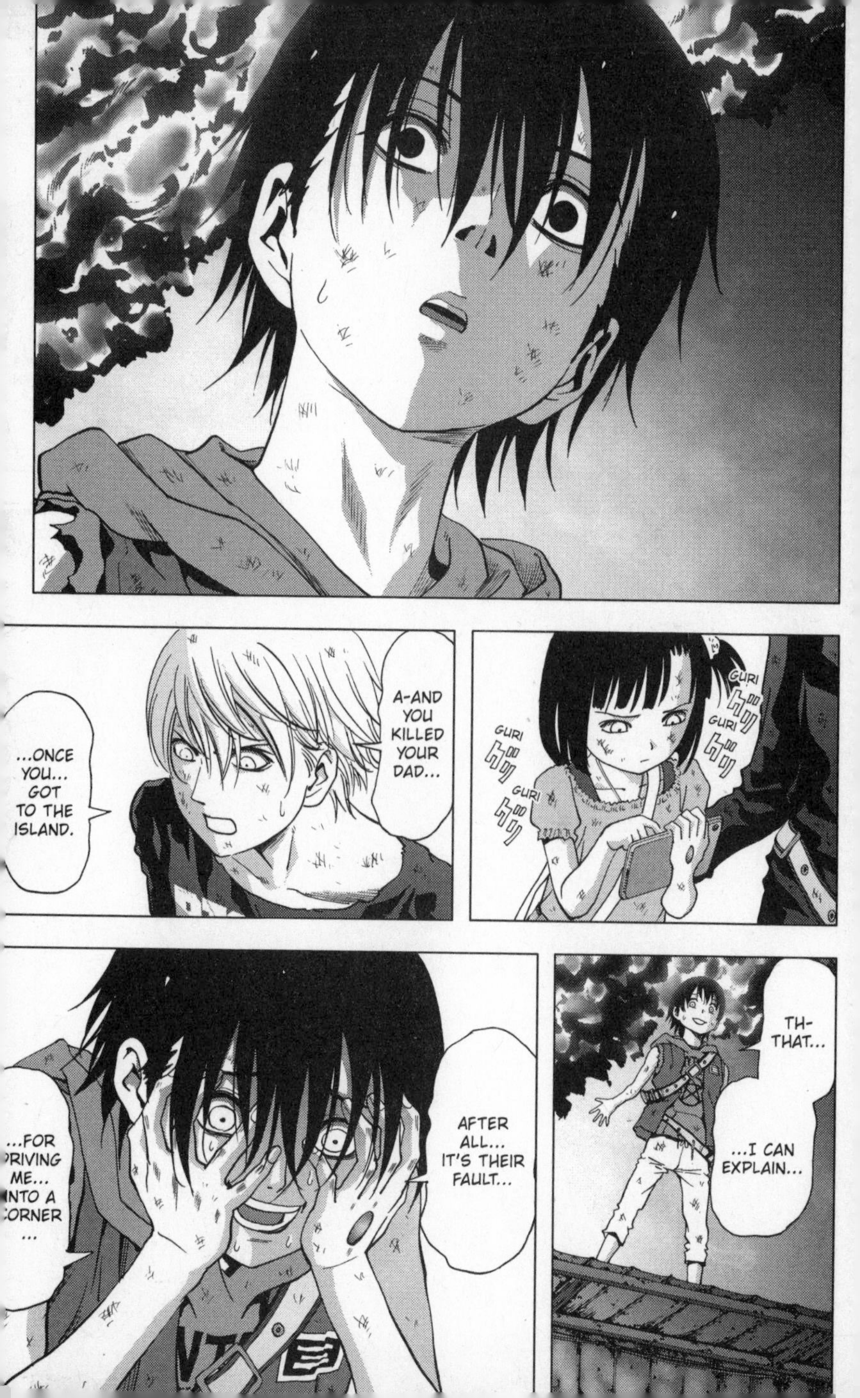
GURI
GURI
GURI
A-AND YOU KILLED YOUR DAD...
...ONCE YOU... GOT TO THE ISLAND.
TH-THAT...
...I CAN EXPLAIN...
AFTER ALL... IT'S THEIR FAULT...
...FOR DRIVING ME... INTO A CORNER ...

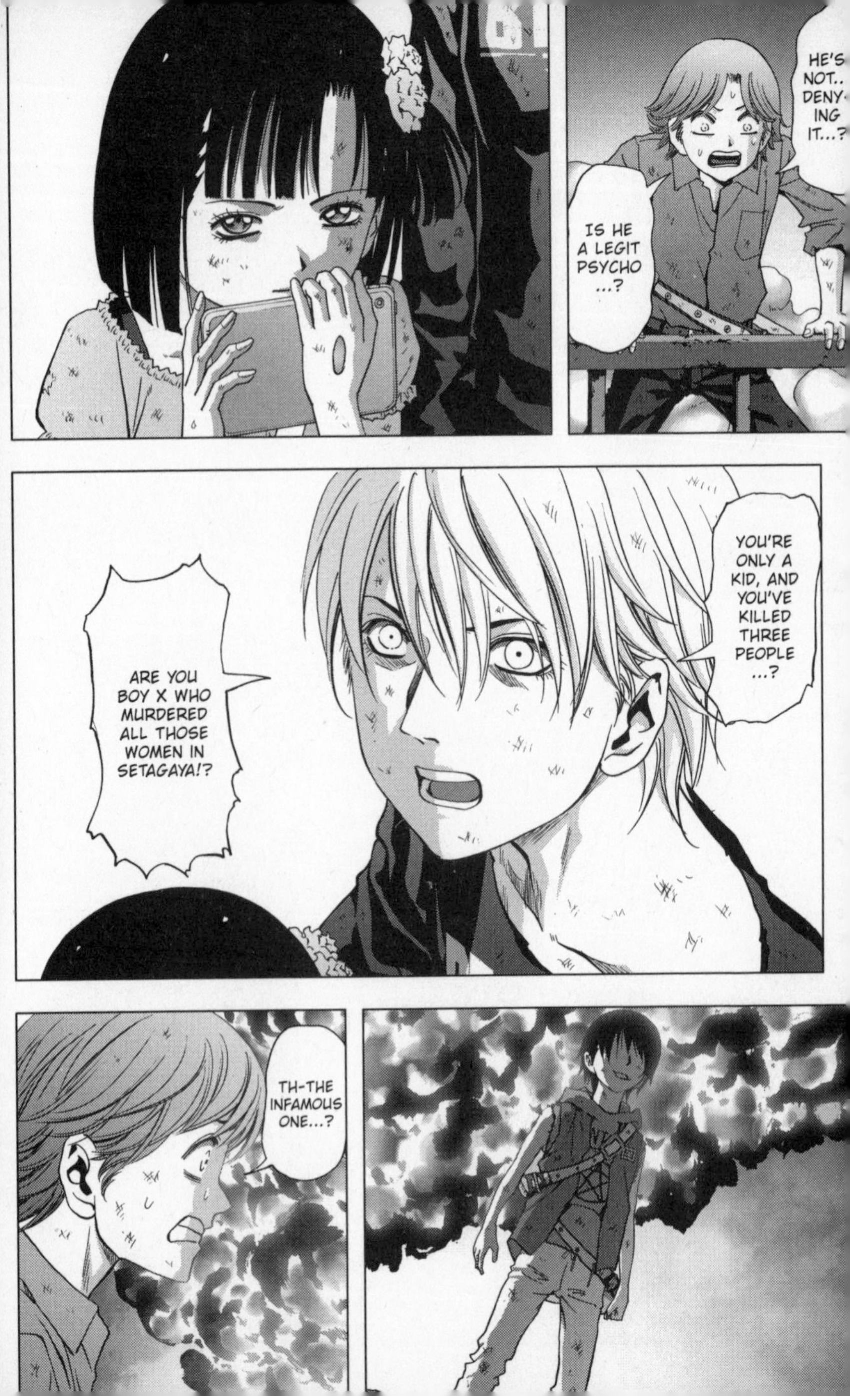
HE'S NOT.. DENYING IT...?
IS HE A LEGIT PSYCHO ...?
YOU'RE ONLY A KID, AND YOU'VE KILLED THREE PEOPLE ...?
ARE YOU BOY X WHO MURDERED ALL THOSE WOMEN IN SETAGAYA!?
TH-THE INFAMOUS ONE...?

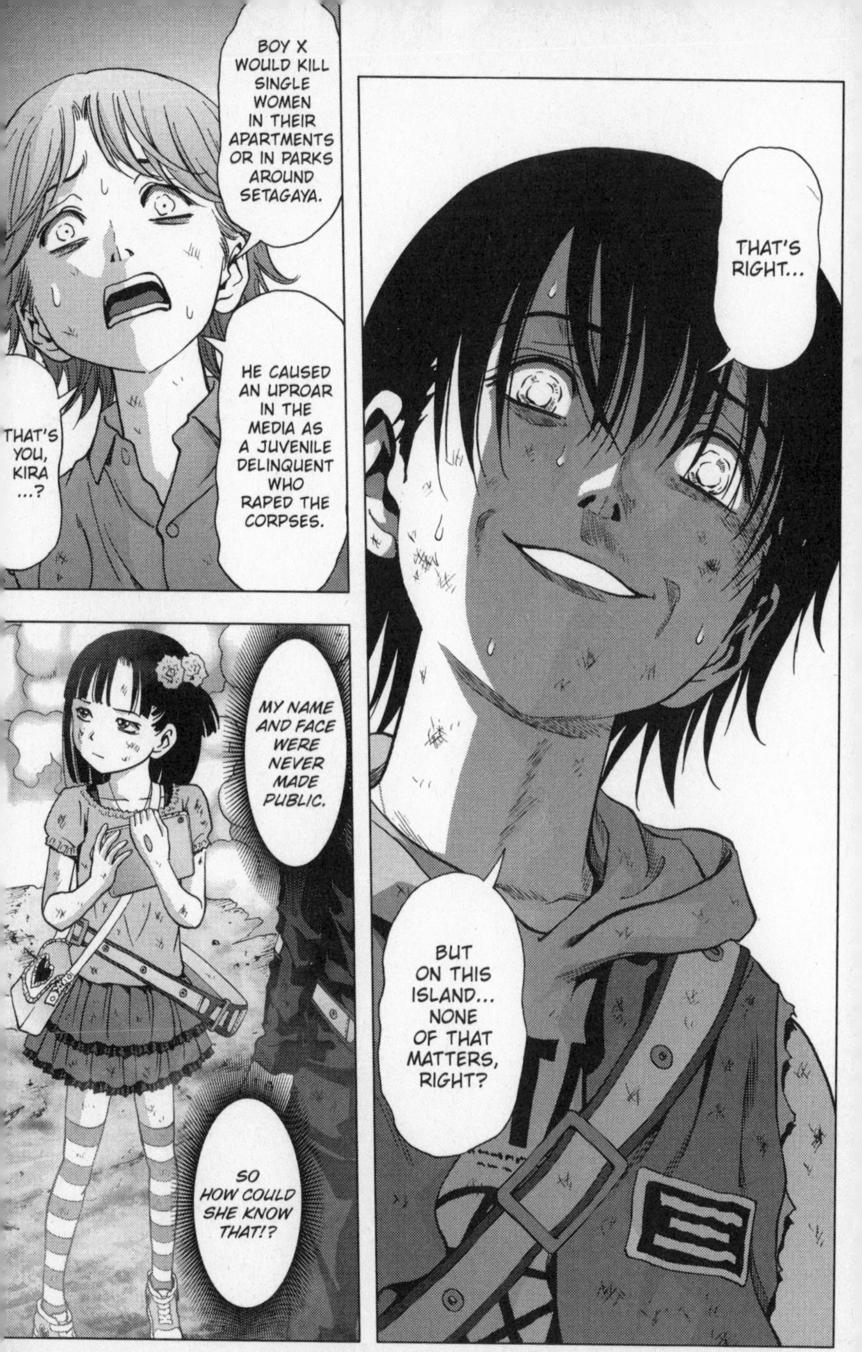
BOY X WOULD KILL SINGLE WOMEN IN THEIR APARTMENTS OR IN PARKS AROUND SETAGAYA.
HE CAUSED AN UPROAR IN THE MEDIA AS A JUVENILE DELINQUENT WHO RAPED THE CORPSES.
THAT'S YOU, KIRA ...?
THAT'S RIGHT...
BUT ON THIS ISLAND... NONE OF THAT MATTERS, RIGHT?
MY NAME AND FACE WERE NEVER MADE PUBLIC.
SO HOW COULD SHE KNOW THAT!?

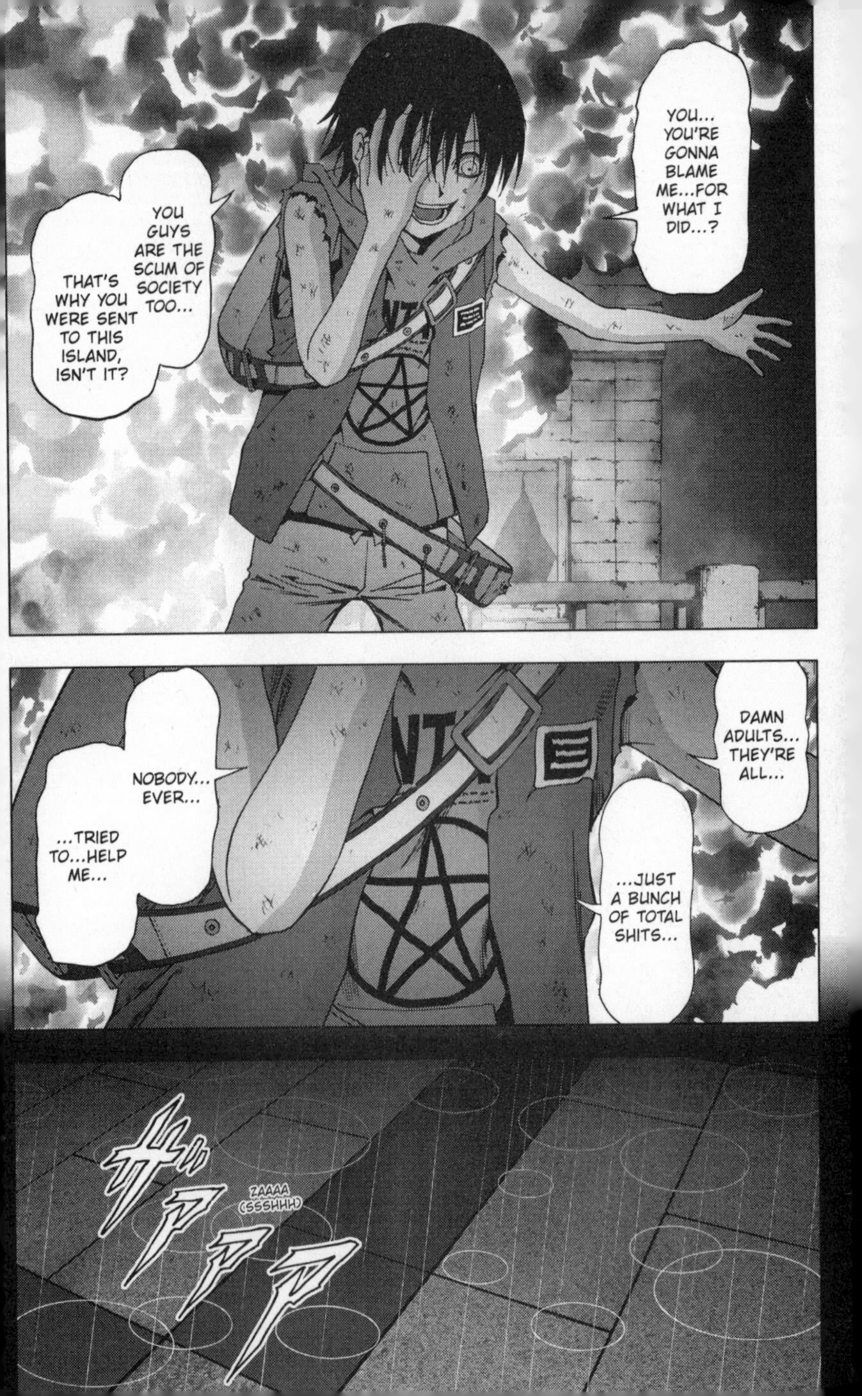

YOU... YOU'RE GONNA BLAME ME...FOR WHAT I DID...?
YOU GUYS ARE THE SCUM OF SOCIETY TOO...
THAT'S WHY YOU WERE SENT TO THIS ISLAND, ISN'T IT?
DAMN ADULTS... THEY'RE ALL...
...JUST A BUNCH OF TOTAL SHITS...
NOBODY... EVER...
...TRIED TO...HELP ME...
ZAAAA (SSSHHH)

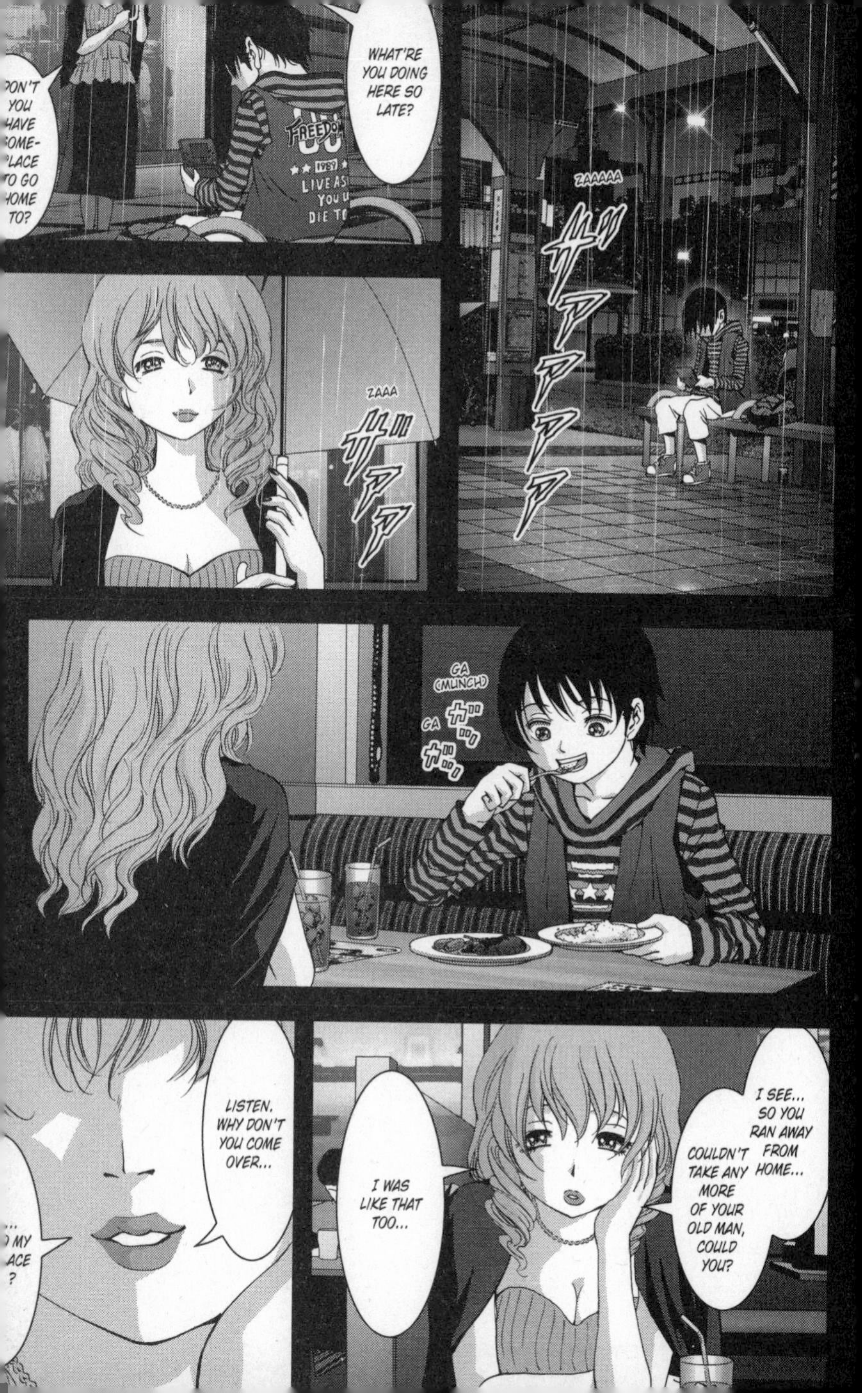
ZAAAAA
ザァァァァ
WHAT'RE YOU DOING HERE SO LATE?
DON'T YOU HAVE SOME-PLACE TO GO HOME TO?
ZAAA
ザァァ
GA (MUNCH) GA
ガッ ガッ
I SEE... SO YOU RAN AWAY FROM HOME...
COULDN'T TAKE ANY MORE OF YOUR OLD MAN, COULD YOU?
I WAS LIKE THAT TOO...
LISTEN. WHY DON'T YOU COME OVER...
...TO MY PLACE?

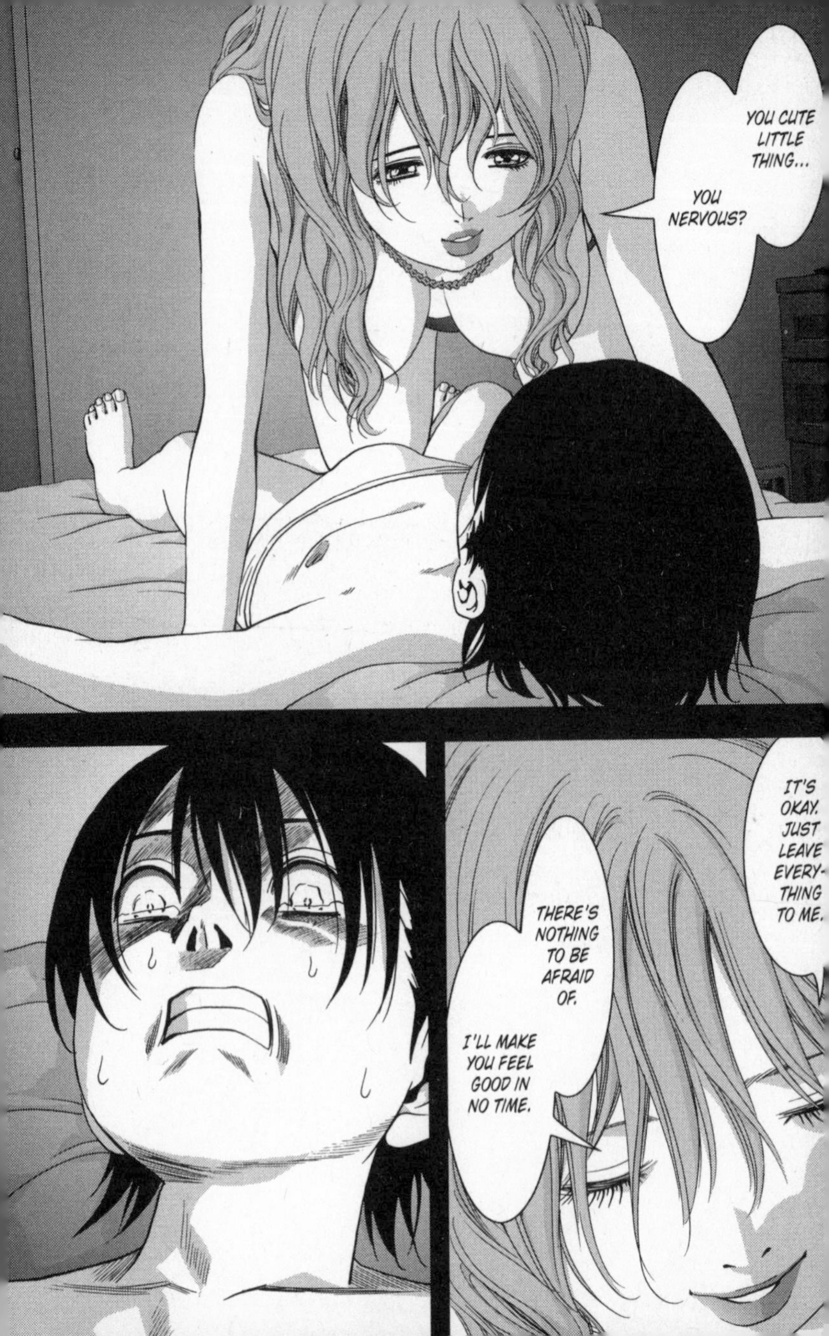
YOU CUTE LITTLE THING... YOU NERVOUS?
IT'S OKAY. JUST LEAVE EVERYTHING TO ME.
THERE'S NOTHING TO BE AFRAID OF. I'LL MAKE YOU FEEL GOOD IN NO TIME.

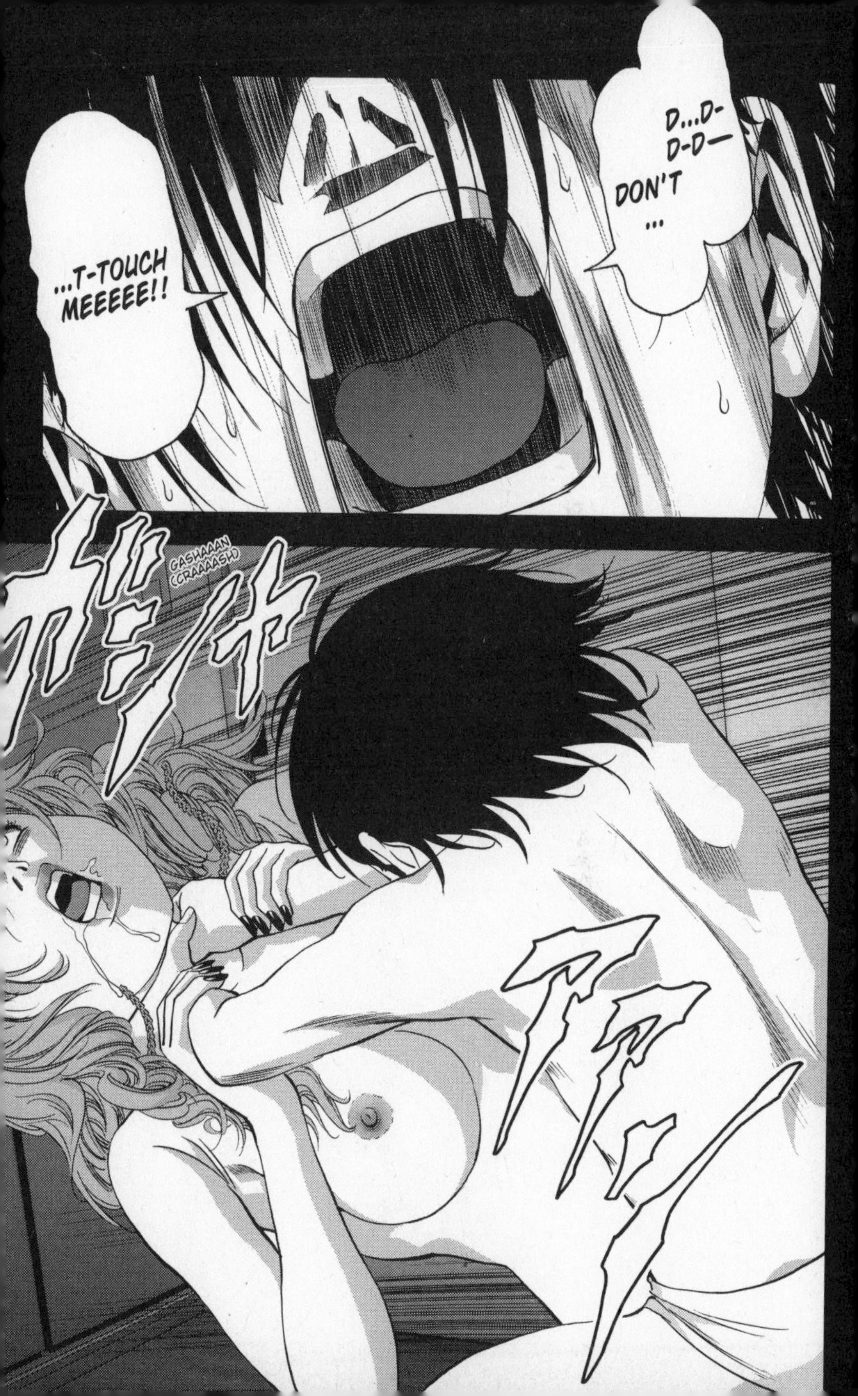
D...D- D-D— DON'T ...
...T-TOUCH MEEEEE!!
GASHAAAN (CRAAAASH)

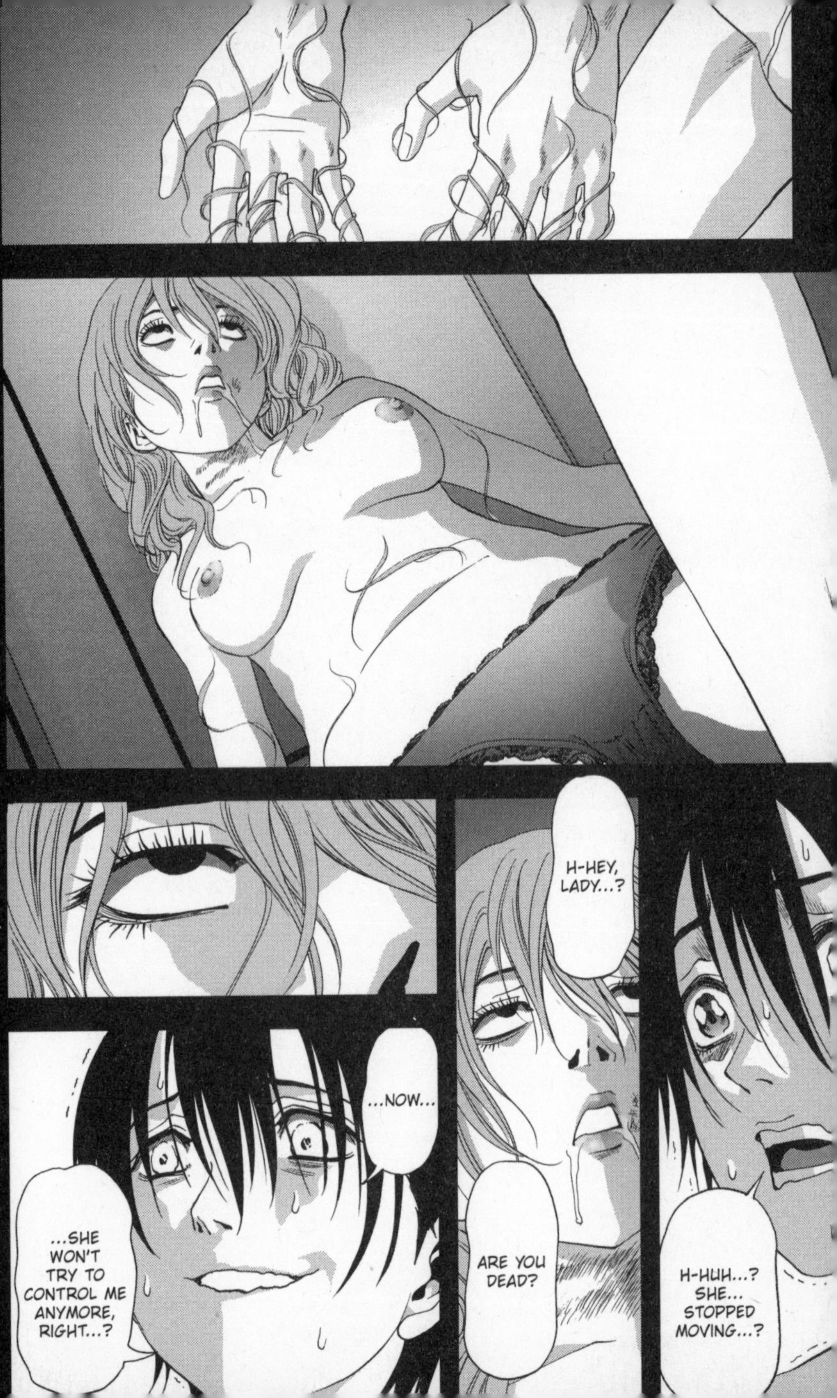
H-HEY, LADY...?
H-HUH...? SHE... STOPPED MOVING...?
ARE YOU DEAD?
...NOW...
...SHE WON'T TRY TO CONTROL ME ANYMORE, RIGHT...?

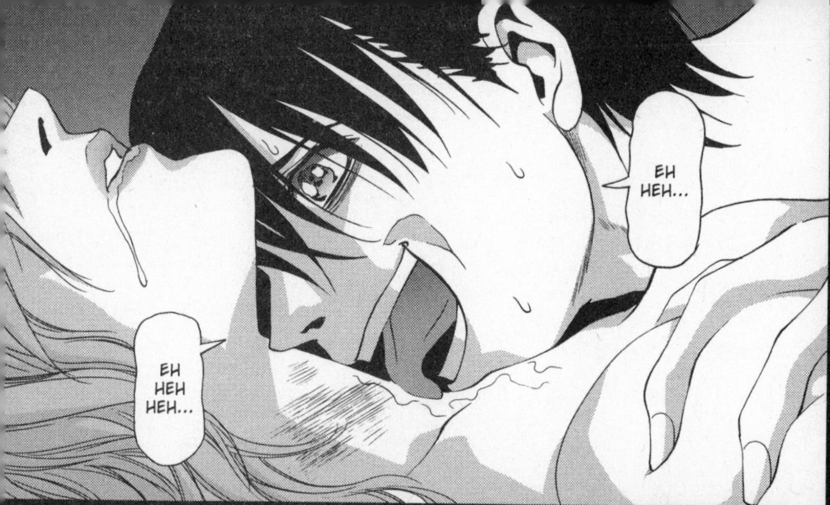
EH HEH...
EH HEH HEH...
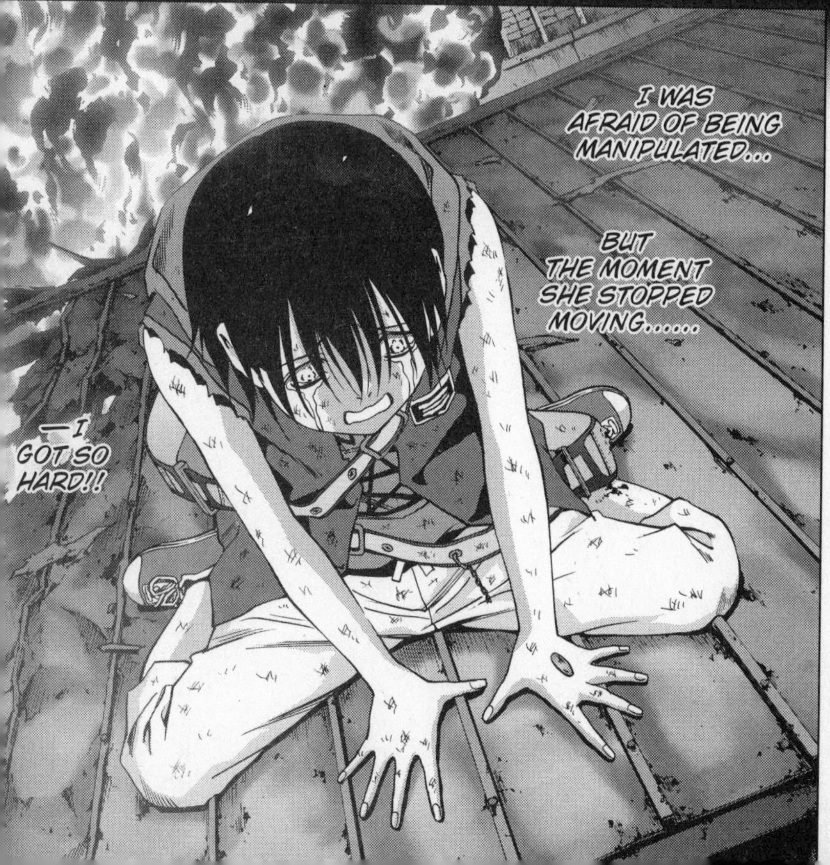
I WAS AFRAID OF BEING MANIPULATED...
BUT THE MOMENT SHE STOPPED MOVING......
—I GOT SO HARD!!

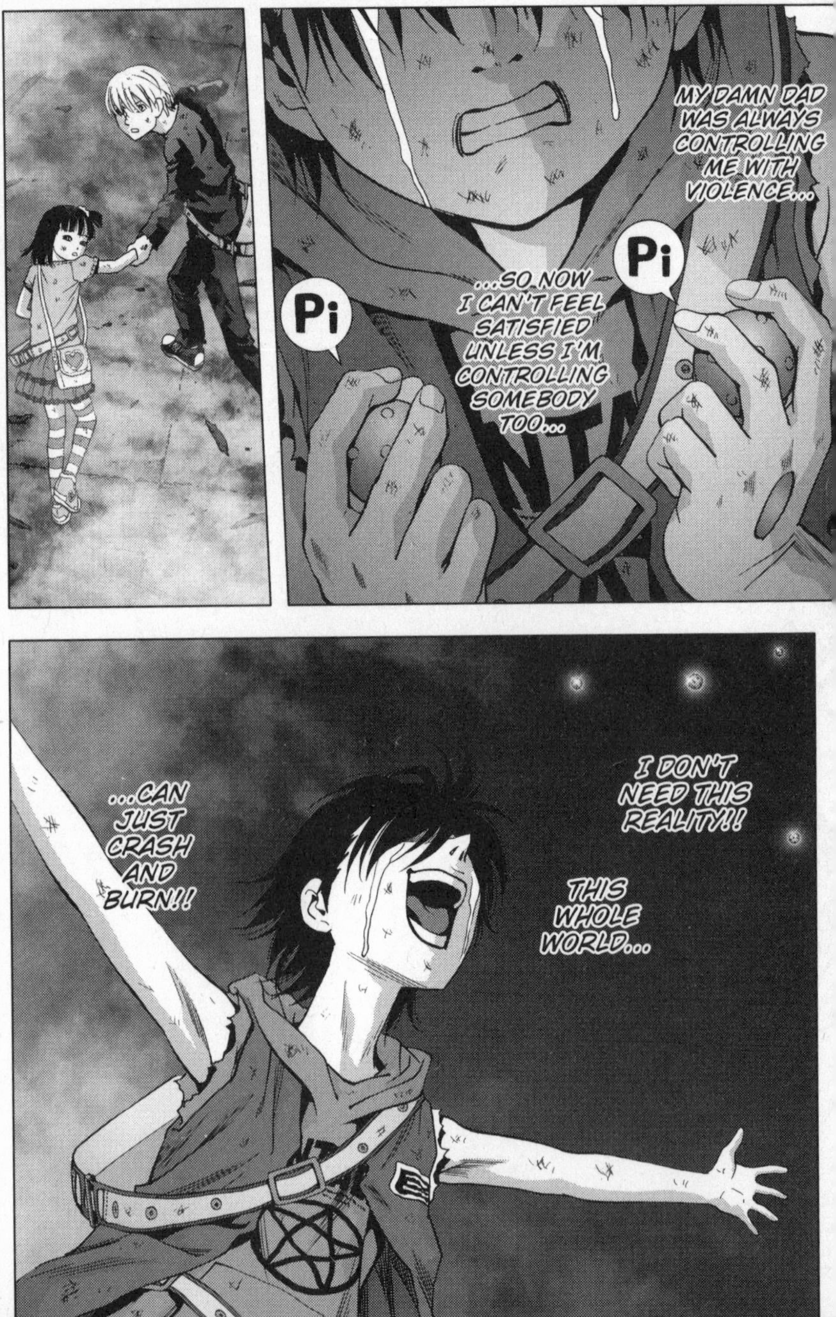
MY DAMN DAD WAS ALWAYS CONTROLLING ME WITH VIOLENCE...
Pi
...SO NOW I CAN'T FEEL SATISFIED UNLESS I'M CONTROLLING SOMEBODY TOO...
Pi
I DON'T NEED THIS REALITY!!
THIS WHOLE WORLD...
...CAN JUST CRASH AND BURN!!

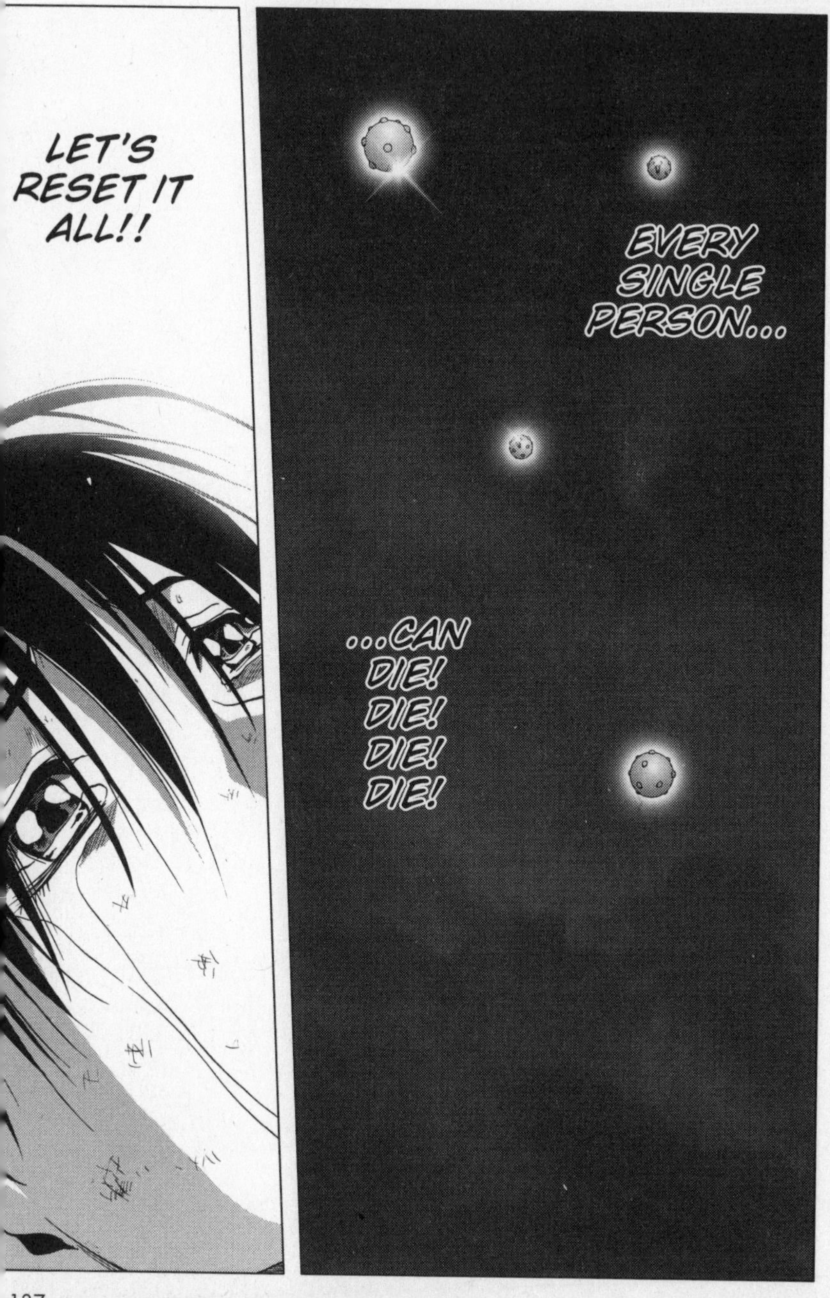
EVERY SINGLE PERSON...
...CAN DIE! DIE! DIE! DIE!
LET'S RESET IT ALL!!

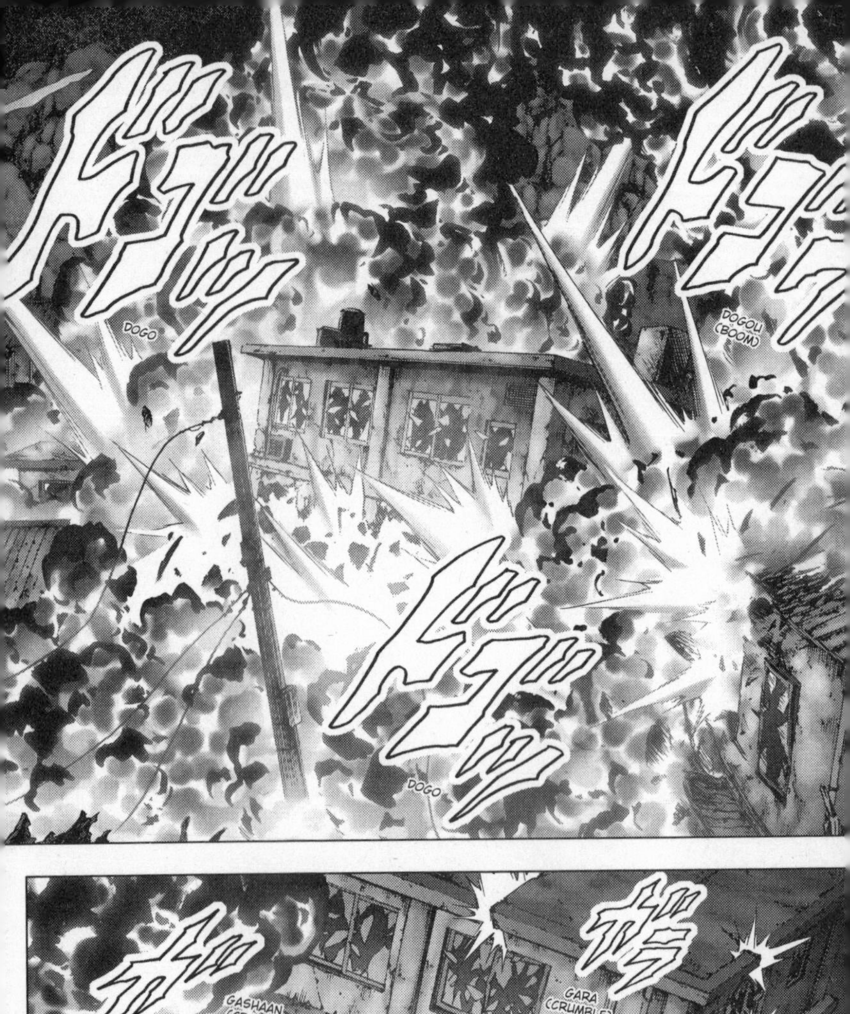
DOGOU
(BOOM)
DOGO
DOGO

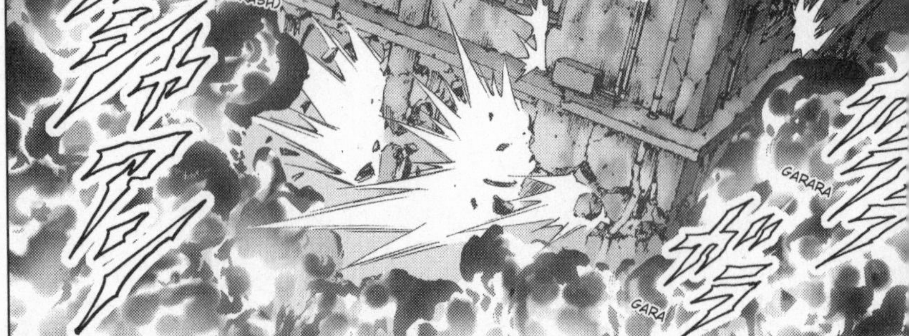
GARA
(CRUMBLE)
GARARA
GARA
GASHAAN
(CRASH)

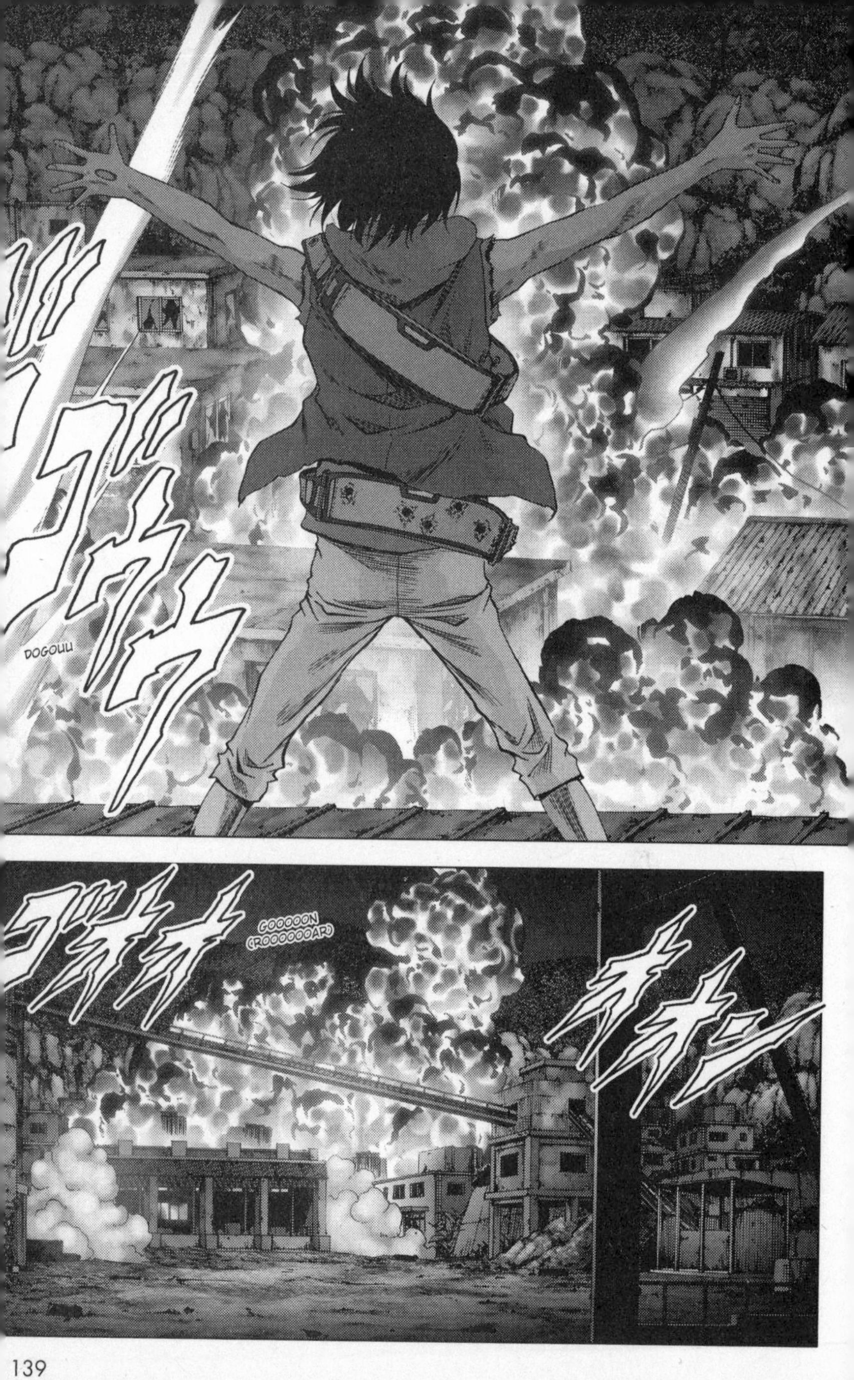
DOGOUU
GOOOOON
(ROOOOOOAR)

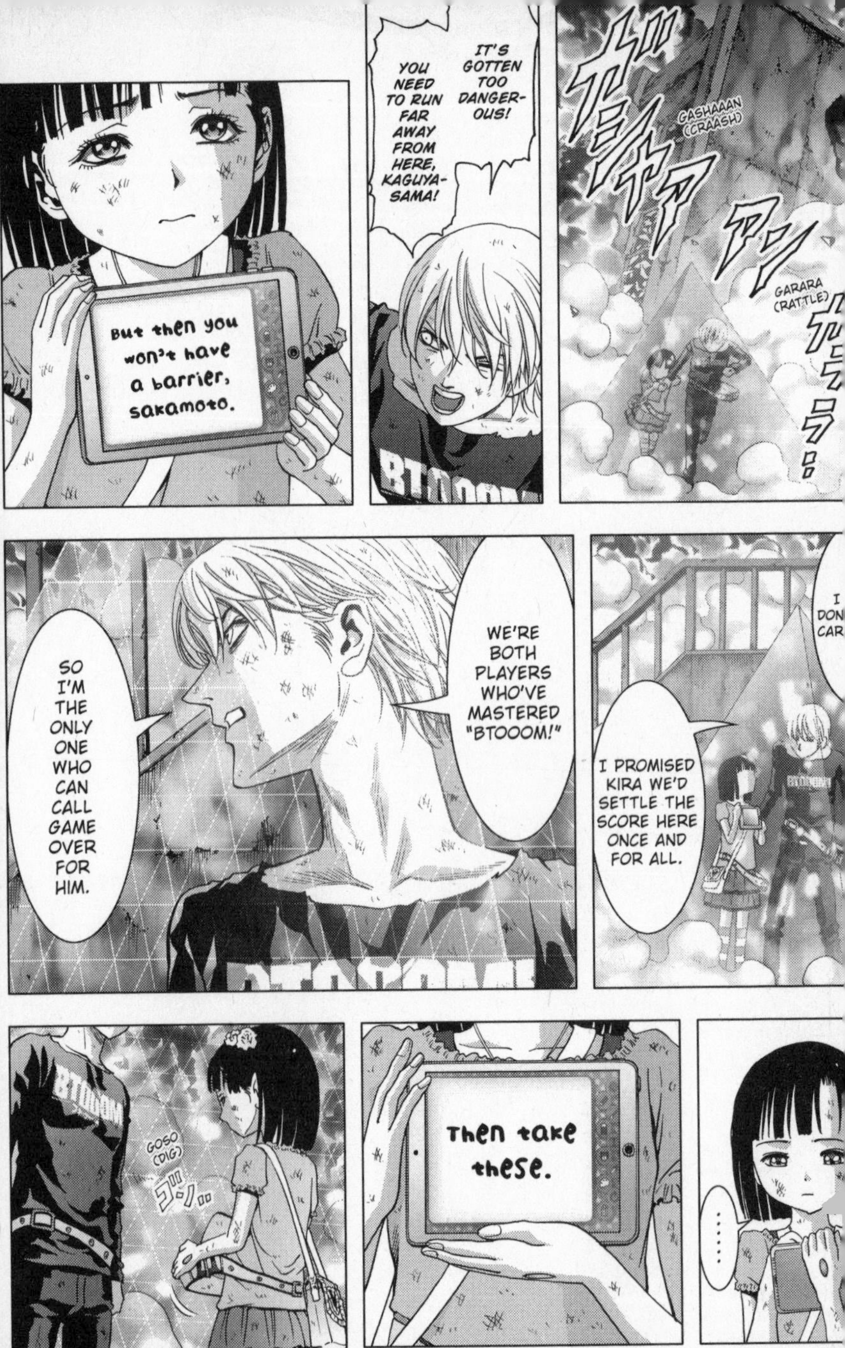
GASHAAAN (CRAASH)
GARARA (RATTLE)
IT'S GOTTEN TOO DANGER-OUS!
YOU NEED TO RUN FAR AWAY FROM HERE, KAGUYA-SAMA!
But then you won't have a barrier, sakamoto.
I PROMISED KIRA WE'D SETTLE THE SCORE HERE ONCE AND FOR ALL.
WE'RE BOTH PLAYERS WHO'VE MASTERED "BTOOOM!"
SO I'M THE ONLY ONE WHO CAN CALL GAME OVER FOR HIM.
......
Then take these.
GOSO (DIG)

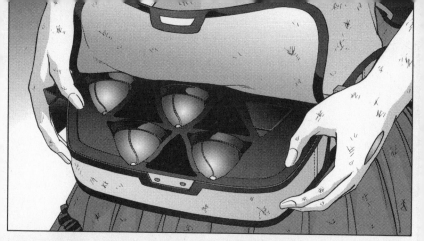

GOOOO (FOOOOOAP)
ゴォォォ

THANKS TO MY FUCKFACE DAD...

...MY LIFE WAS SHIT.

NOW ALL I CAN DO TO FIX IT...

...IS RESET EVERYTHING...

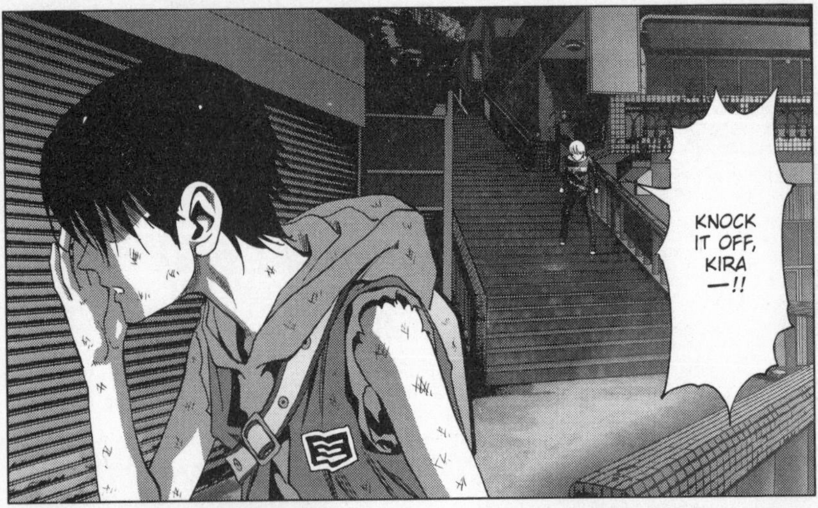
KNOCK IT OFF, KIRA—!!

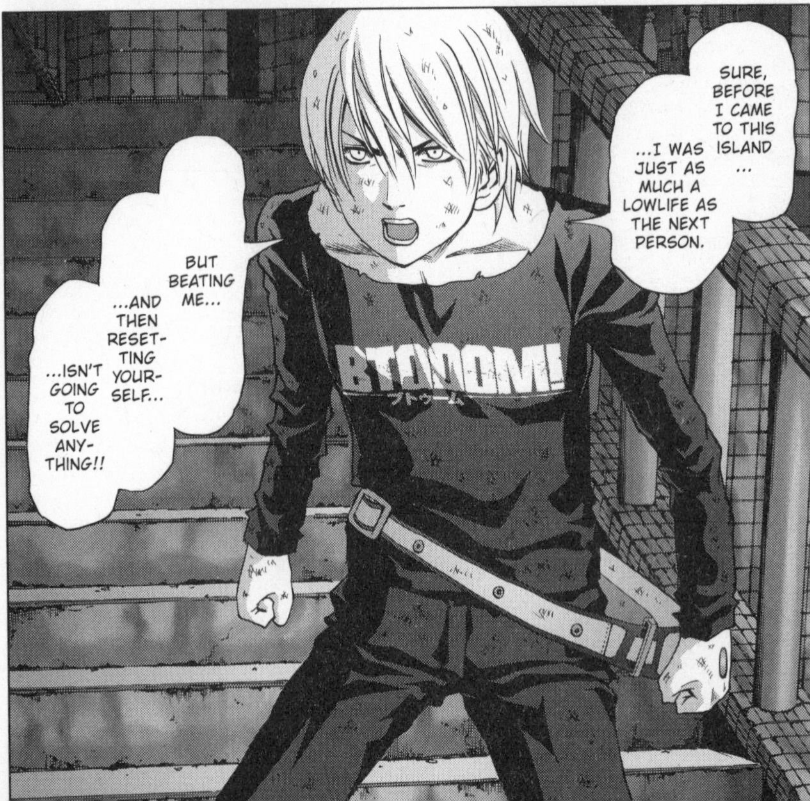
SURE, BEFORE I CAME TO THIS ISLAND ...
...I WAS JUST AS MUCH A LOWLIFE AS THE NEXT PERSON.
BUT BEATING ME...
...AND THEN RESET-TING YOUR-SELF...
...ISN'T GOING TO SOLVE ANY-THING!!
BTOOOM!
ブトゥーム

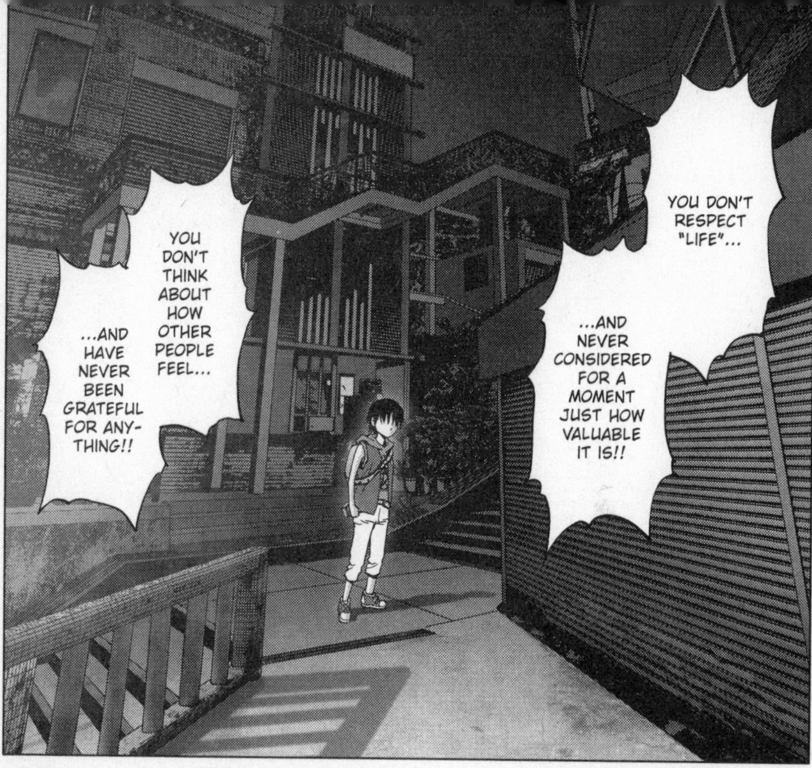
YOU DON'T RESPECT "LIFE"...
...AND NEVER CONSIDERED FOR A MOMENT JUST HOW VALUABLE IT IS!!
YOU DON'T THINK ABOUT HOW OTHER PEOPLE FEEL...
...AND HAVE NEVER BEEN GRATEFUL FOR ANY-THING!!

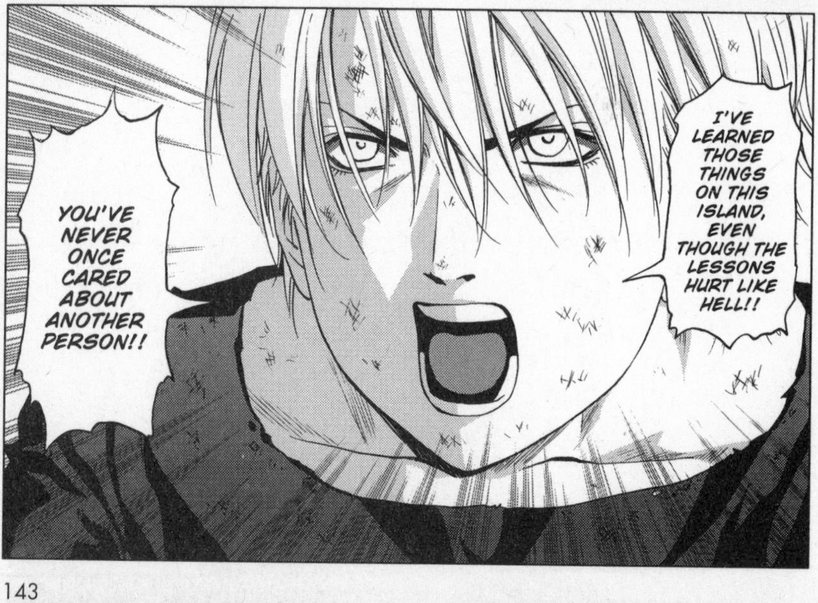
I'VE LEARNED THOSE THINGS ON THIS ISLAND, EVEN THOUGH THE LESSONS HURT LIKE HELL!!
YOU'VE NEVER ONCE CARED ABOUT ANOTHER PERSON!!

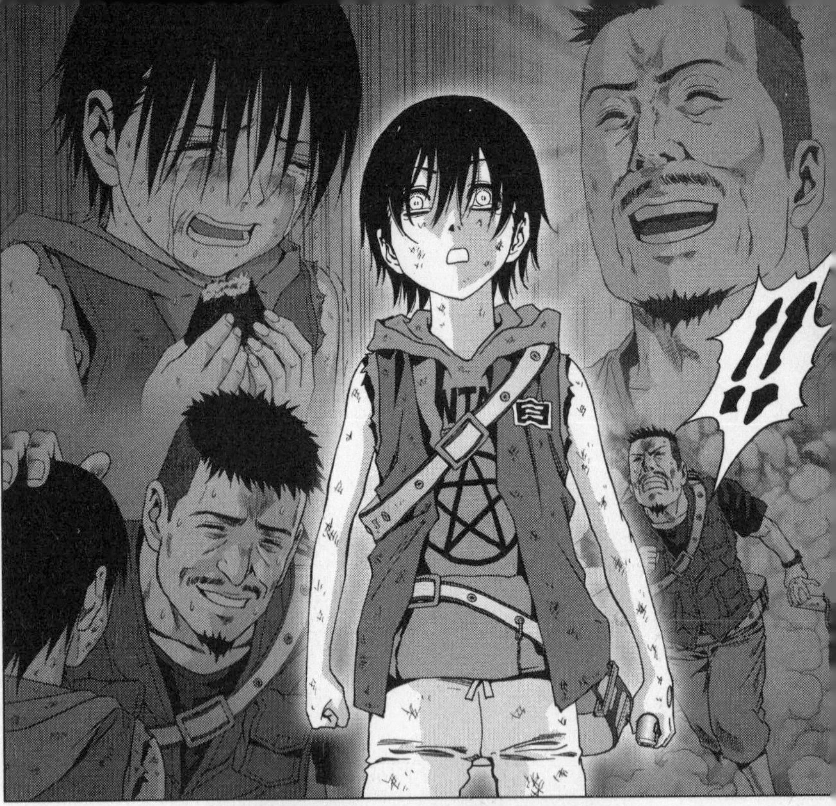
!!

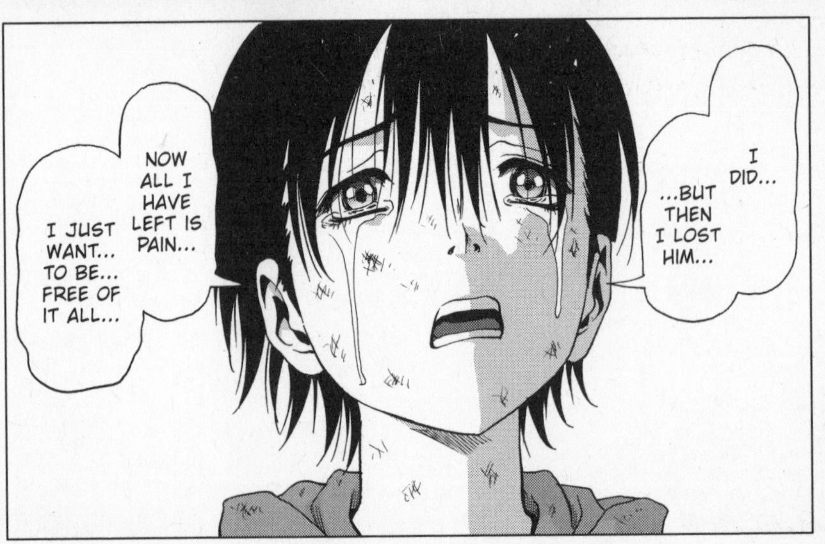
I DID...
...BUT THEN I LOST HIM...
NOW ALL I HAVE LEFT IS PAIN...
I JUST WANT... TO BE... FREE OF IT ALL...

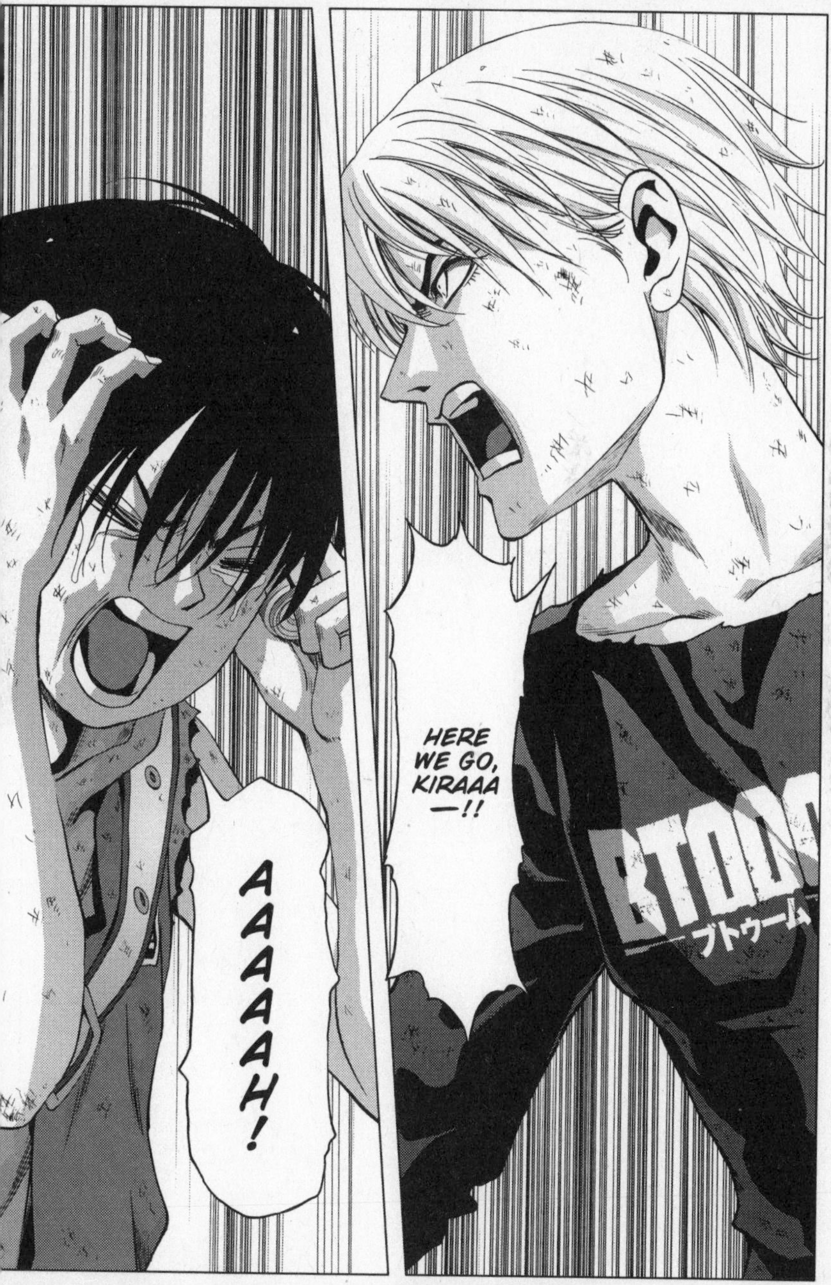
HERE WE GO, KIRAAA—!!
AAAAAAH!

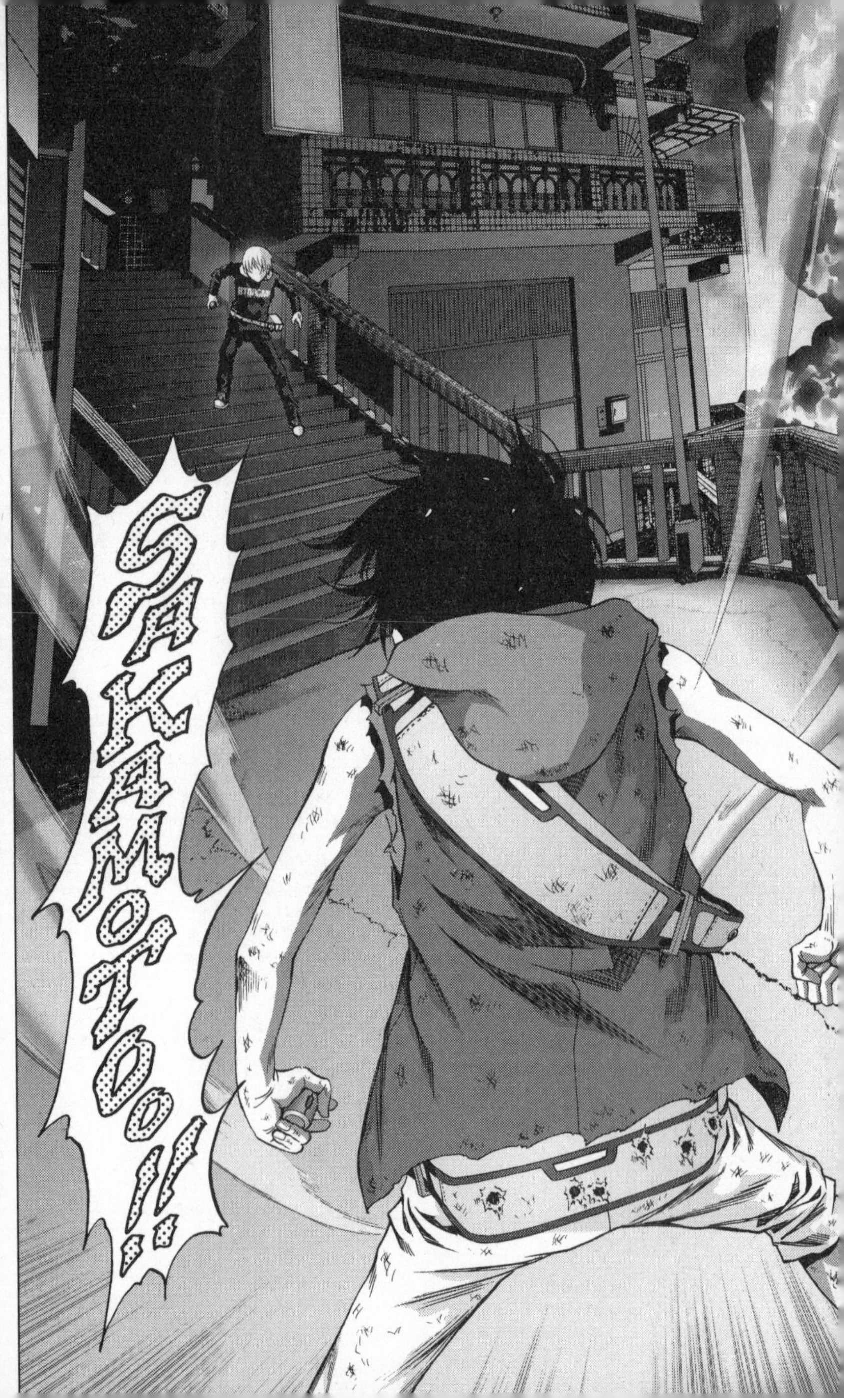
SAKAMOTO!!

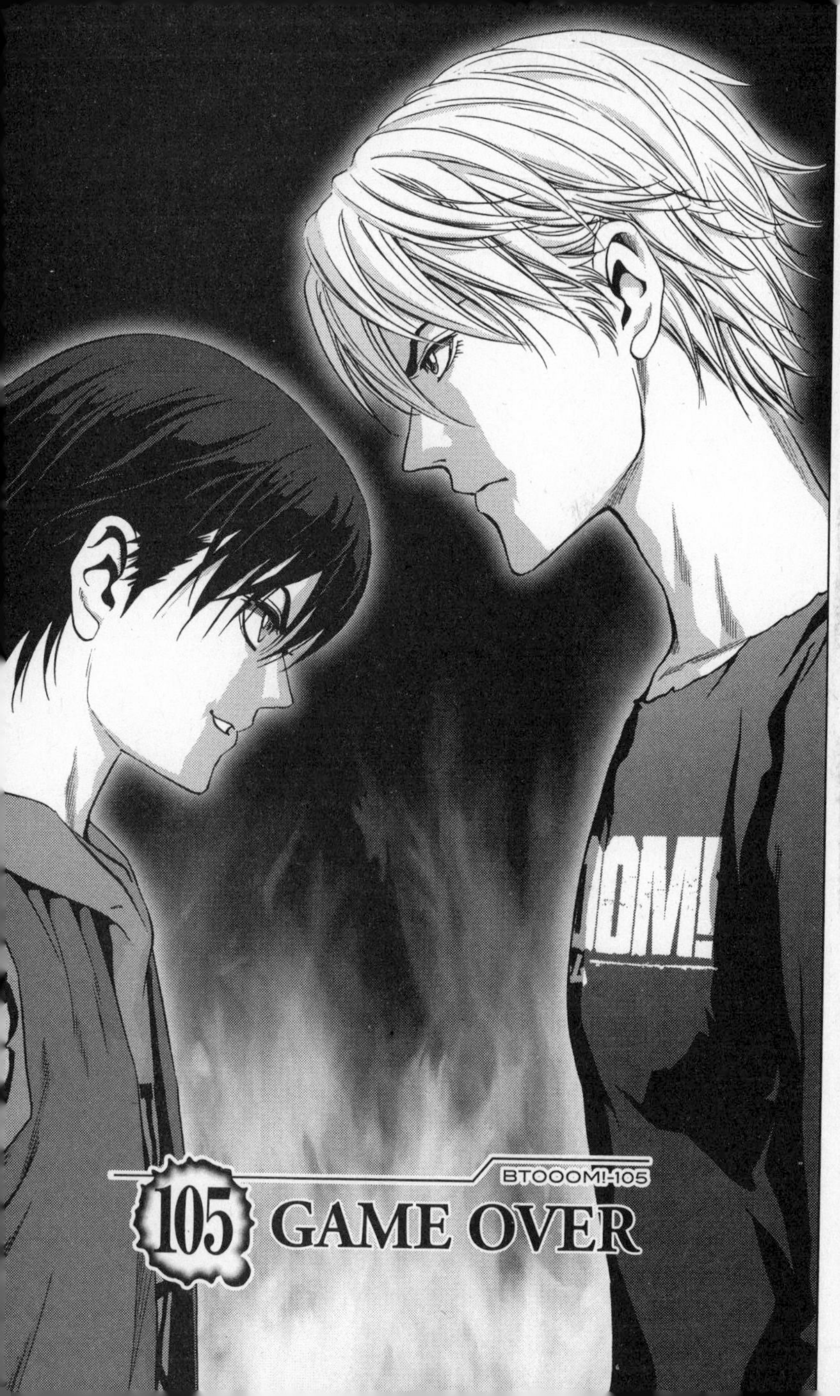
BTOOOM!-105
105 GAME OVER

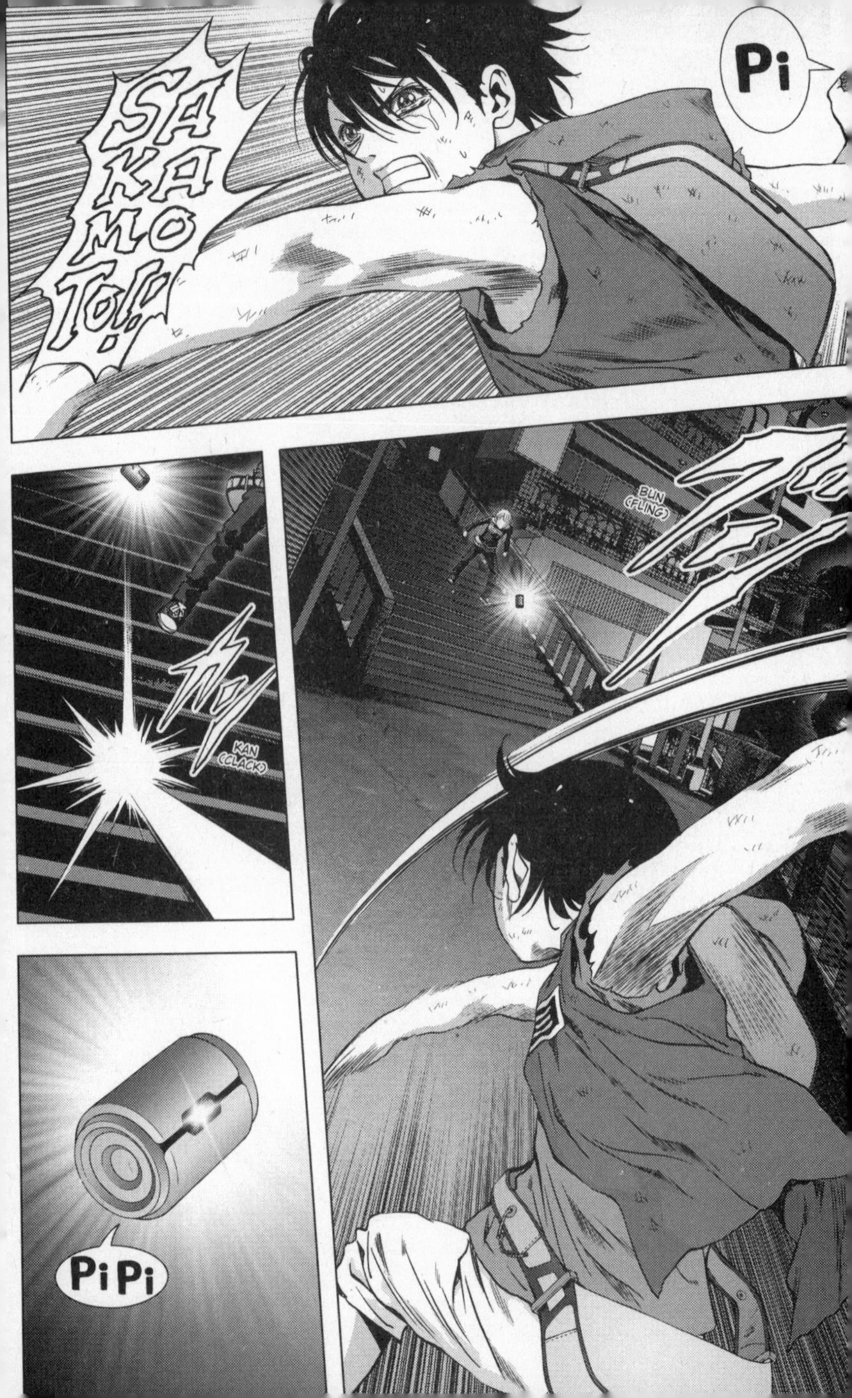
Pi
SAKAMOTO!!
BUN (FLING)
KAN (CLACK)
PiPi

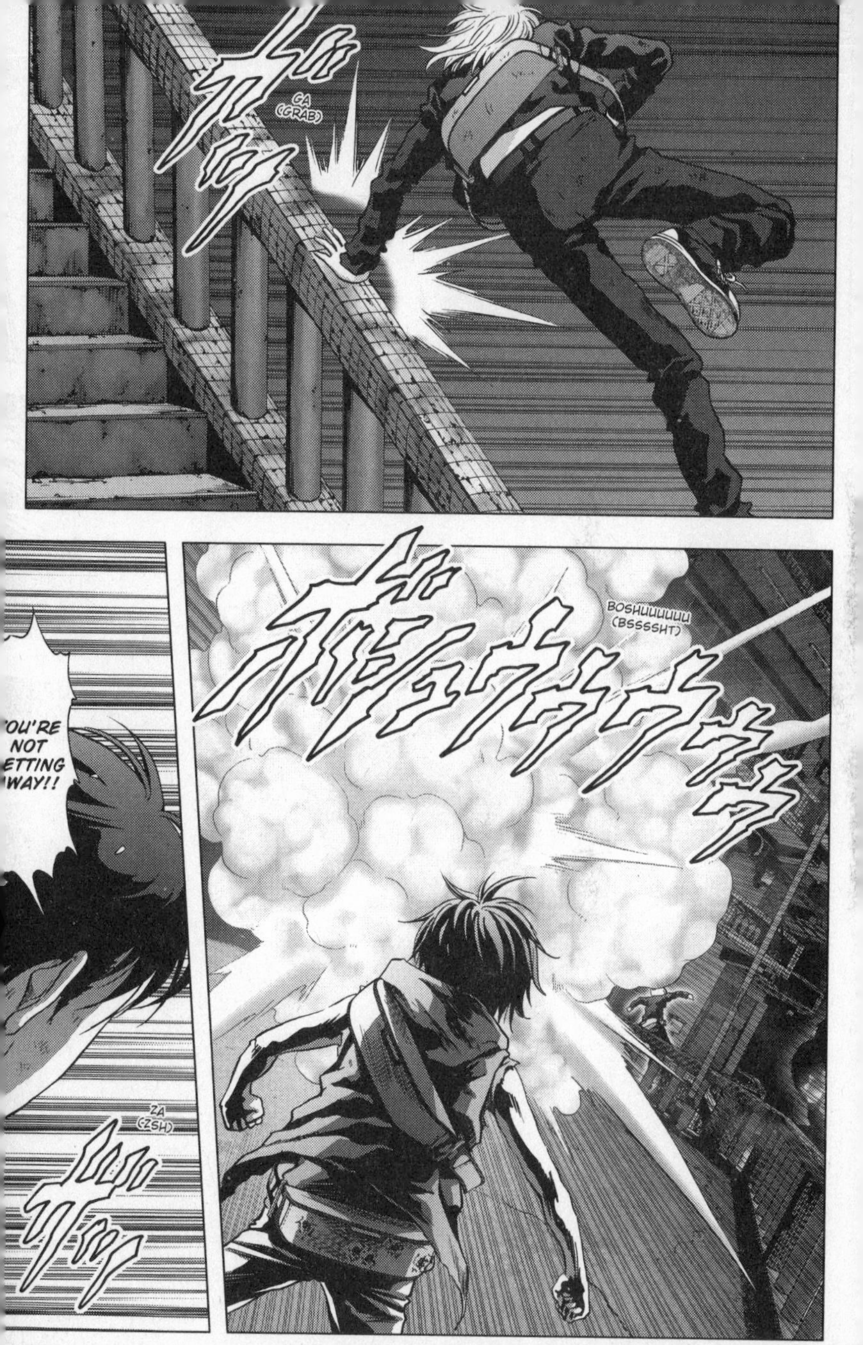
GA (GRAB)
BOSHUUUUUU (BSSSSHT)
OU'RE NOT ETTING WAY!!
ZA (ZSH)

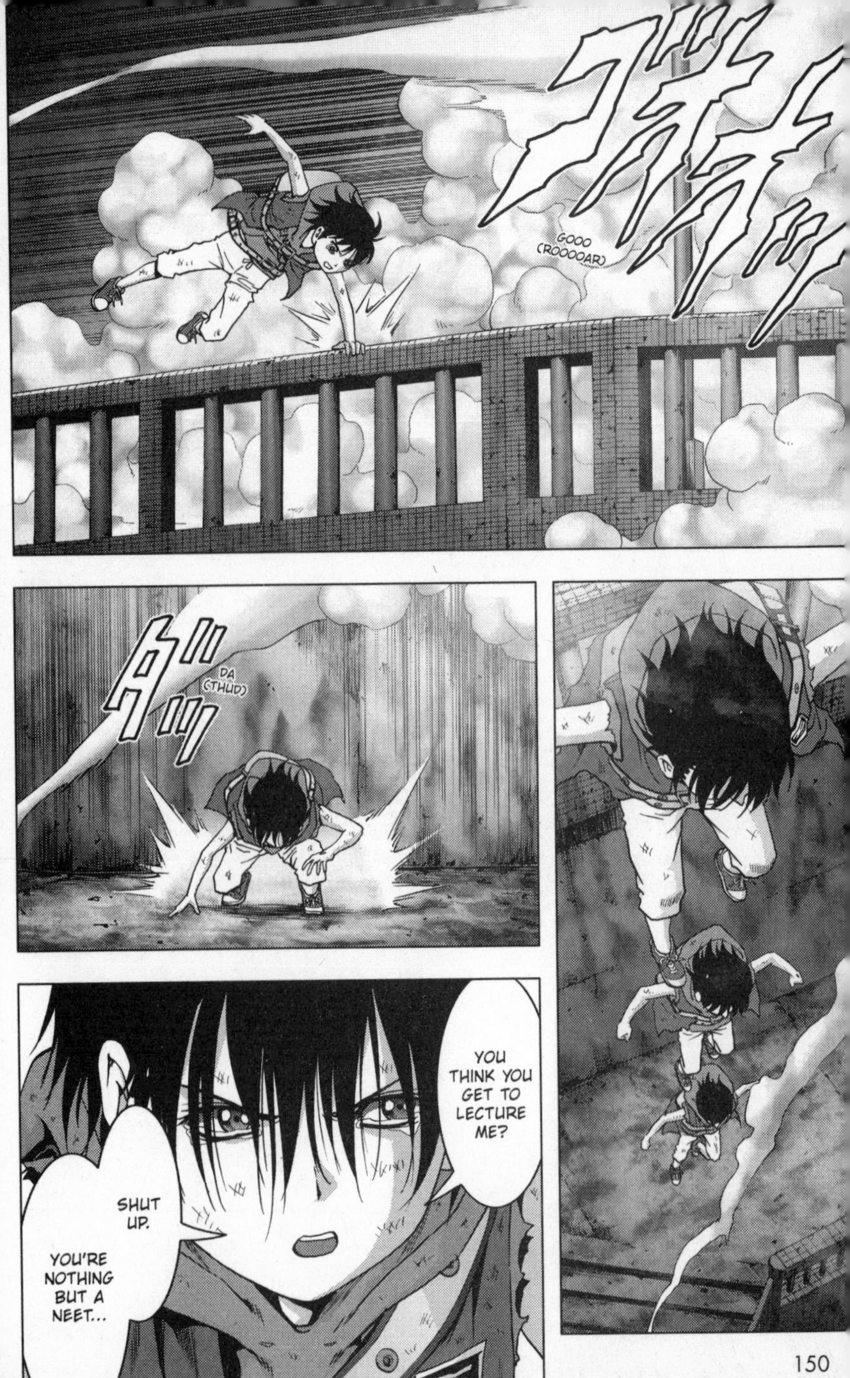
GOOO (ROOOOAR)
DA (THUD)
YOU THINK YOU GET TO LECTURE ME?
SHUT UP.
YOU'RE NOTHING BUT A NEET...

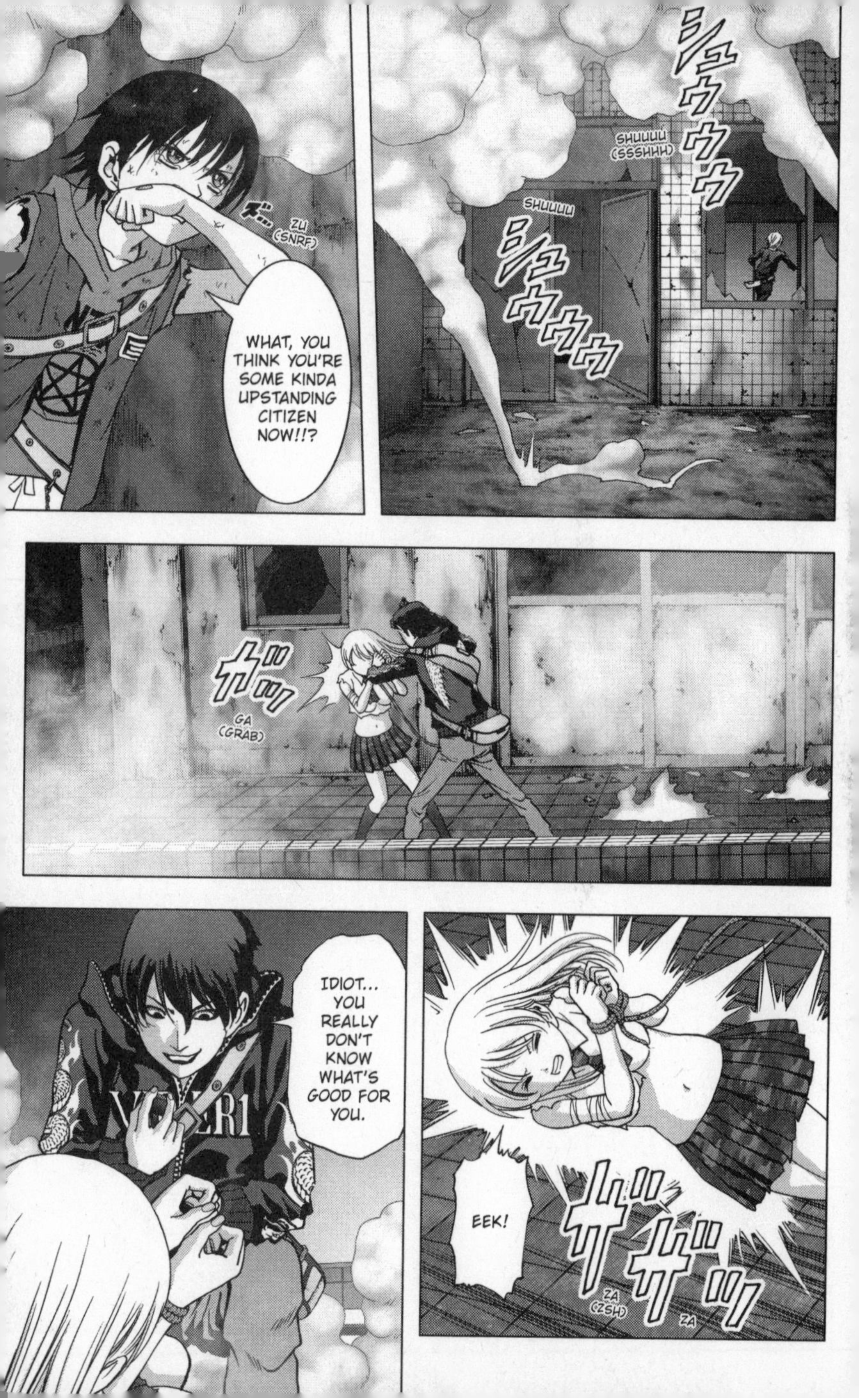
SHUUUU
(SSSHHH)
SHUUUU
ZU
(SNRF)
WHAT, YOU THINK YOU'RE SOME KINDA UPSTANDING CITIZEN NOW!!?
GA
(GRAB)
EEK!
ZA
(ZSH)
ZA
IDIOT... YOU REALLY DON'T KNOW WHAT'S GOOD FOR YOU.

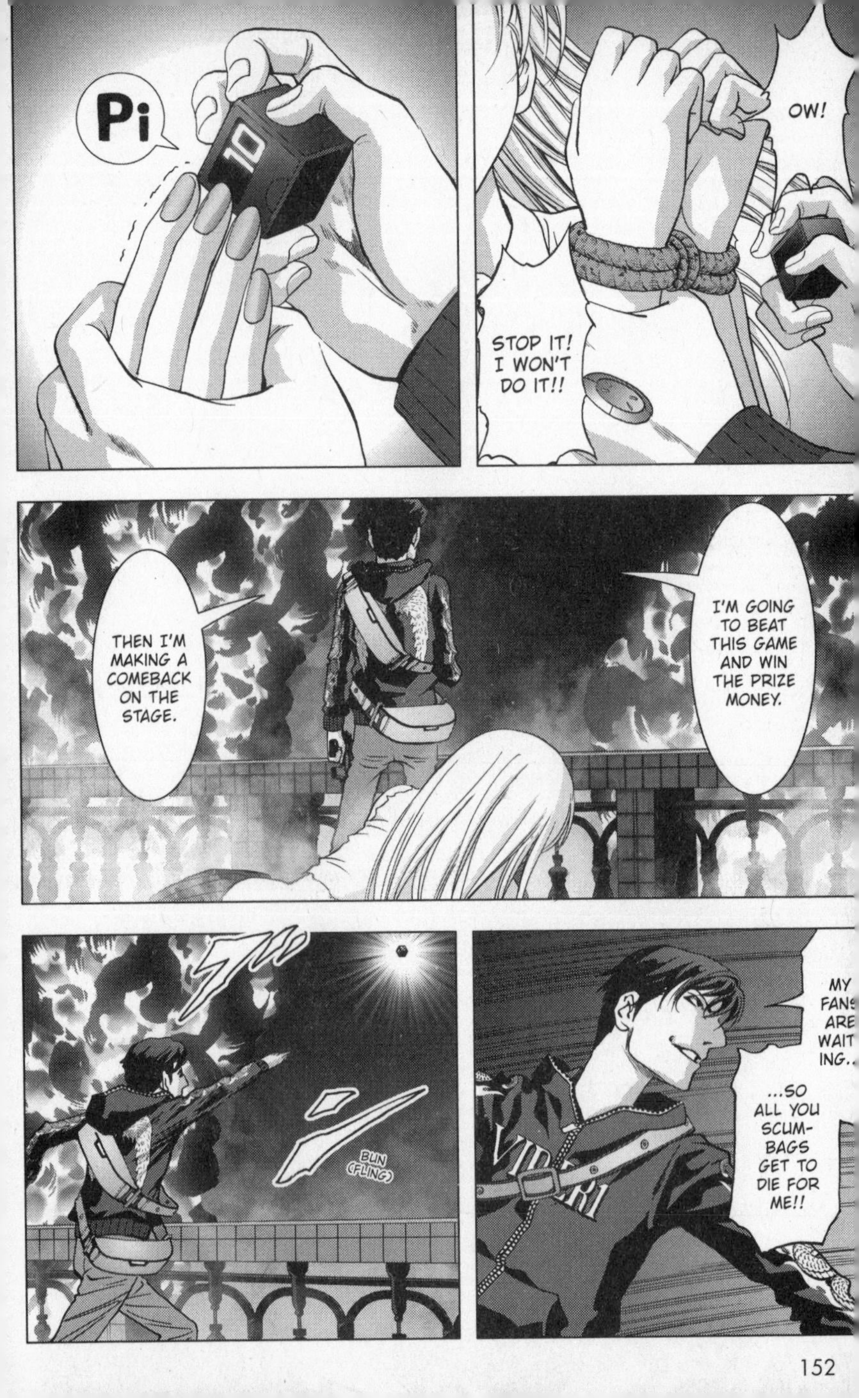
OW!
STOP IT! I WON'T DO IT!!
Pi
10
I'M GOING TO BEAT THIS GAME AND WIN THE PRIZE MONEY.
THEN I'M MAKING A COMEBACK ON THE STAGE.
MY FANS ARE WAITING..
...SO ALL YOU SCUMBAGS GET TO DIE FOR ME!!
BUN (FLING)

GASHAN
(SHATTER)

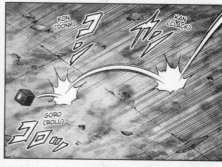

KON
(DONK)

KAN
(CLACK)

GORO
(ROLL)

DOGOLIIN
(KABOOOOM)

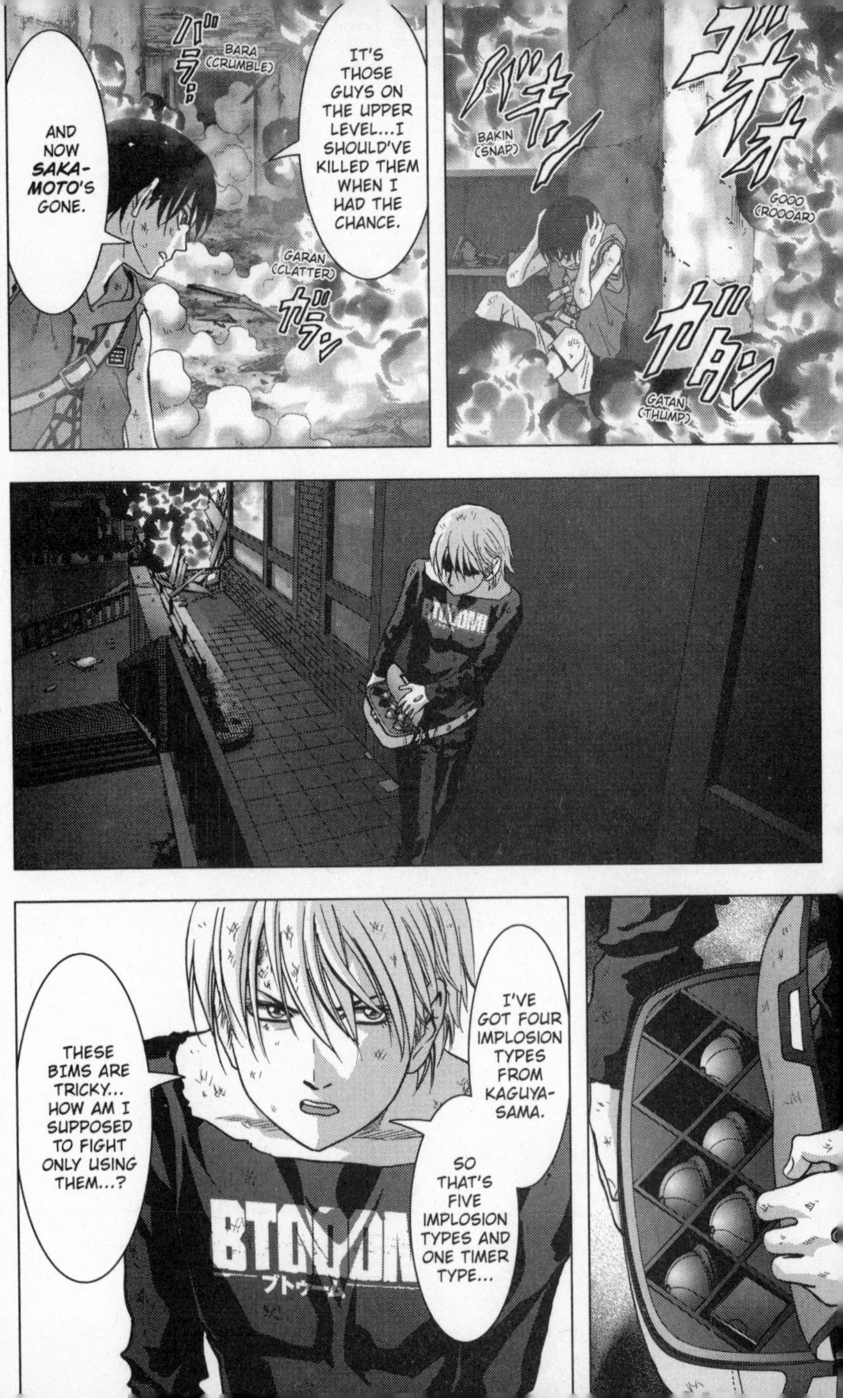
GOOO (ROOOAR)
BAKIN (SNAP)
GATAN (THUMP)
BARA (CRUMBLE)
IT'S THOSE GUYS ON THE UPPER LEVEL...I SHOULD'VE KILLED THEM WHEN I HAD THE CHANCE.
AND NOW SAKA-MOTO'S GONE.
GARAN (CLATTER)
I'VE GOT FOUR IMPLOSION TYPES FROM KAGUYA-SAMA.
SO THAT'S FIVE IMPLOSION TYPES AND ONE TIMER TYPE...
THESE BIMS ARE TRICKY... HOW AM I SUPPOSED TO FIGHT ONLY USING THEM...?

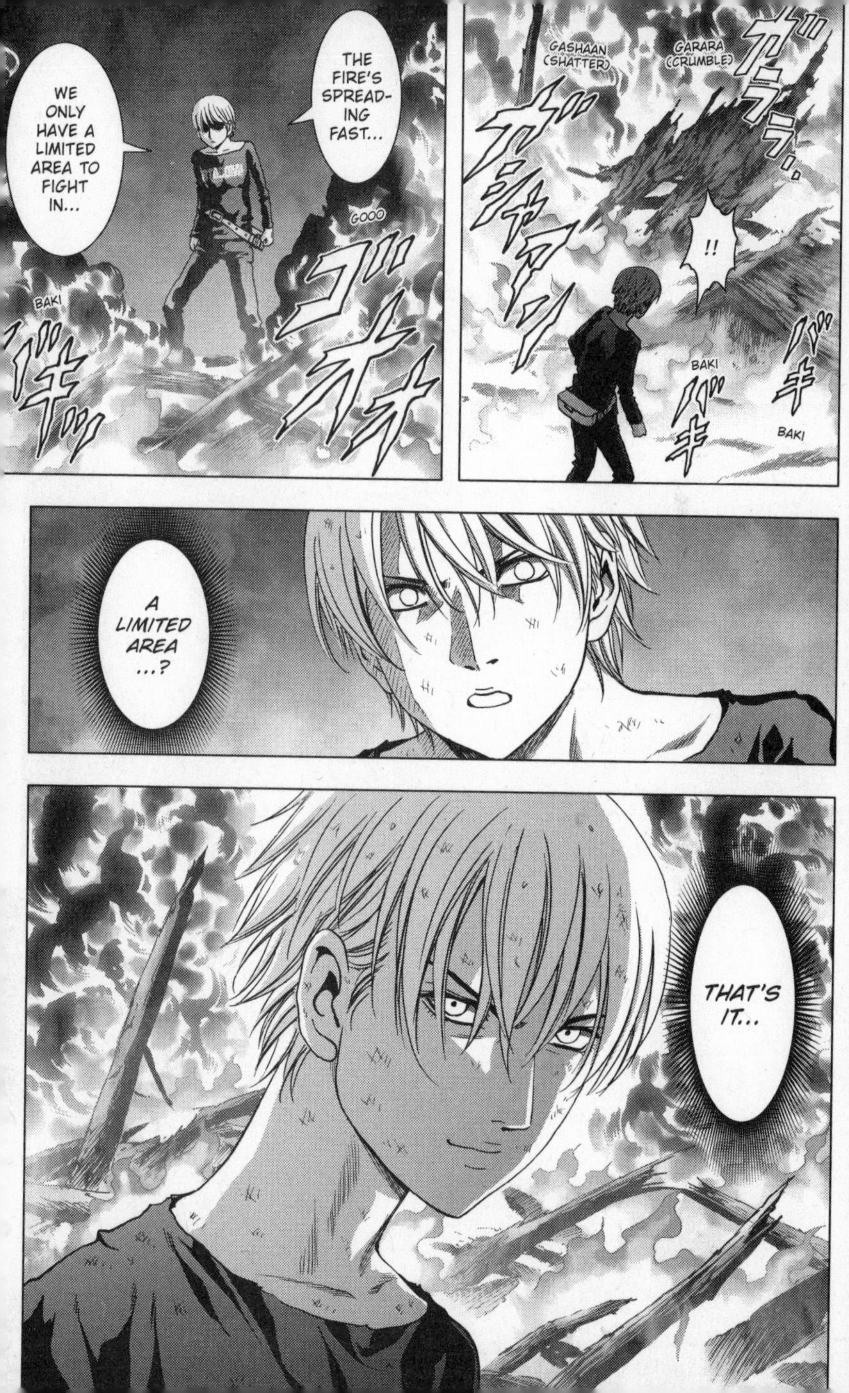
GARARA (CRUMBLE)
GASHAAN (SHATTER)
!!
BAKI
BAKI
THE FIRE'S SPREADING FAST...
WE ONLY HAVE A LIMITED AREA TO FIGHT IN...
GOOO
BAKI
A LIMITED AREA ...?
THAT'S IT...

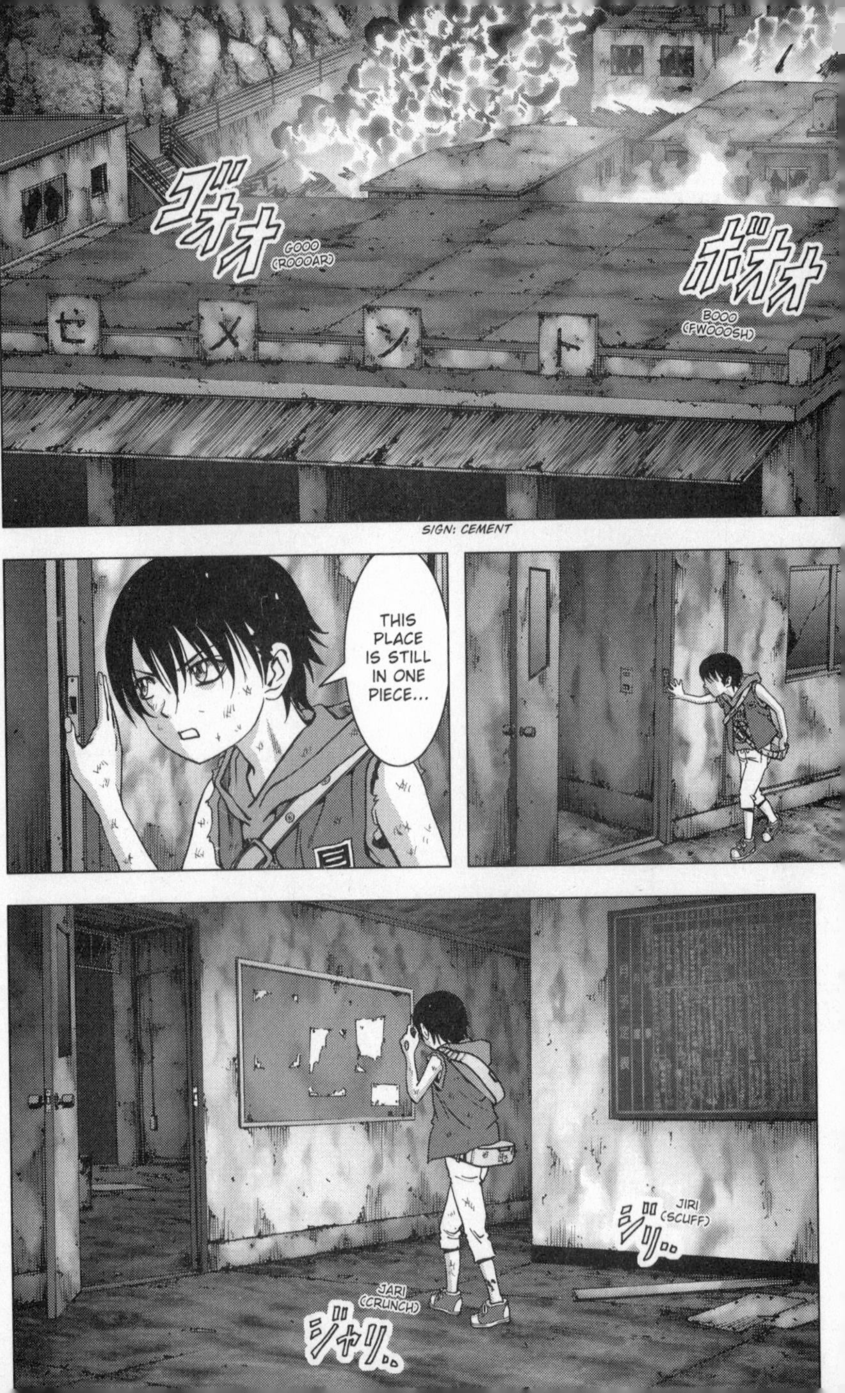
ボオオ
BOOO (FWOOOSH)
ゴオオ
GOOO (ROOOAR)
セメント
SIGN: CEMENT
THIS PLACE IS STILL IN ONE PIECE...
ジリ..
JIRI (SCUFF)
ジャリ..
JARI (CRUNCH)

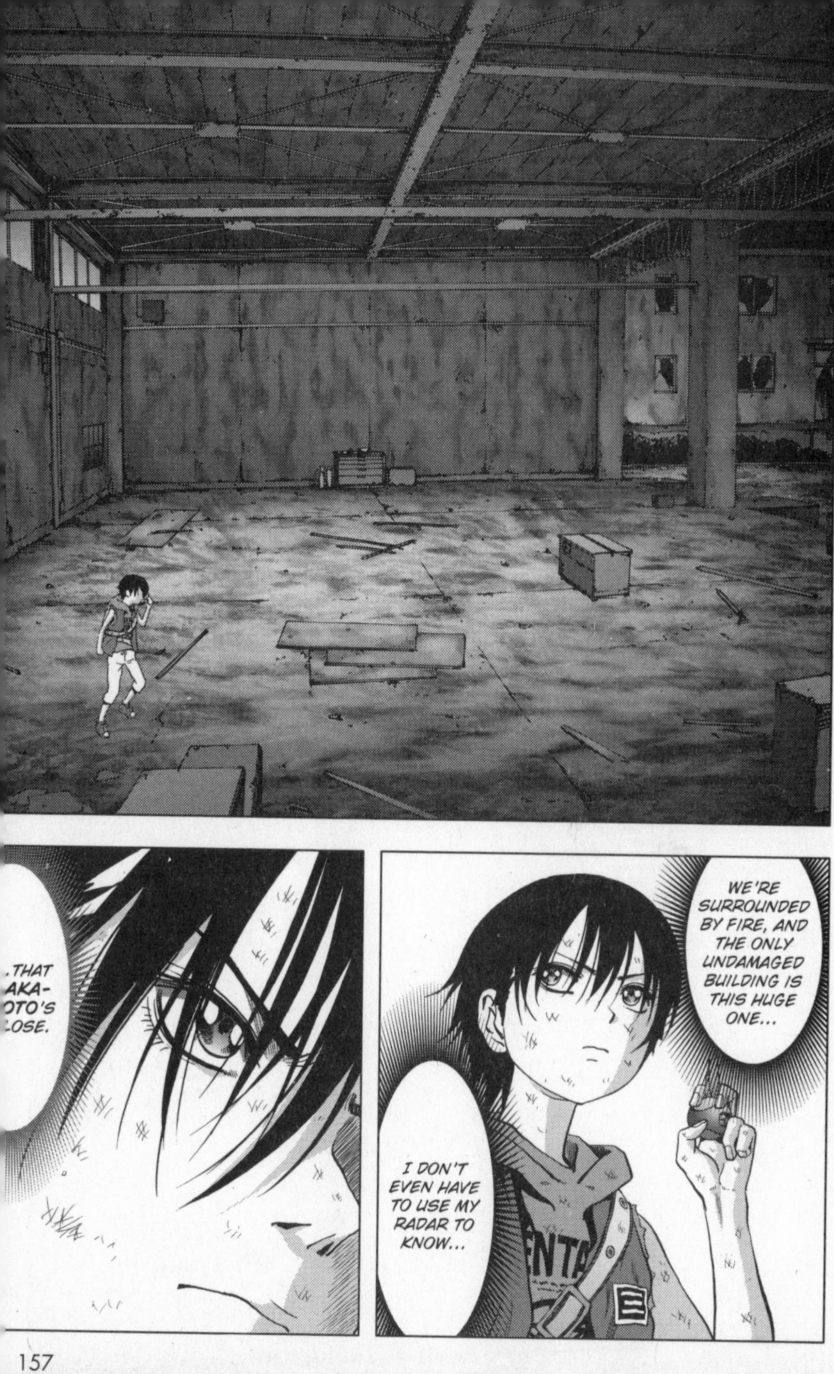
WE'RE SURROUNDED BY FIRE, AND THE ONLY UNDAMAGED BUILDING IS THIS HUGE ONE...
I DON'T EVEN HAVE TO USE MY RADAR TO KNOW...
.THAT AKA- OTO'S LOSE.

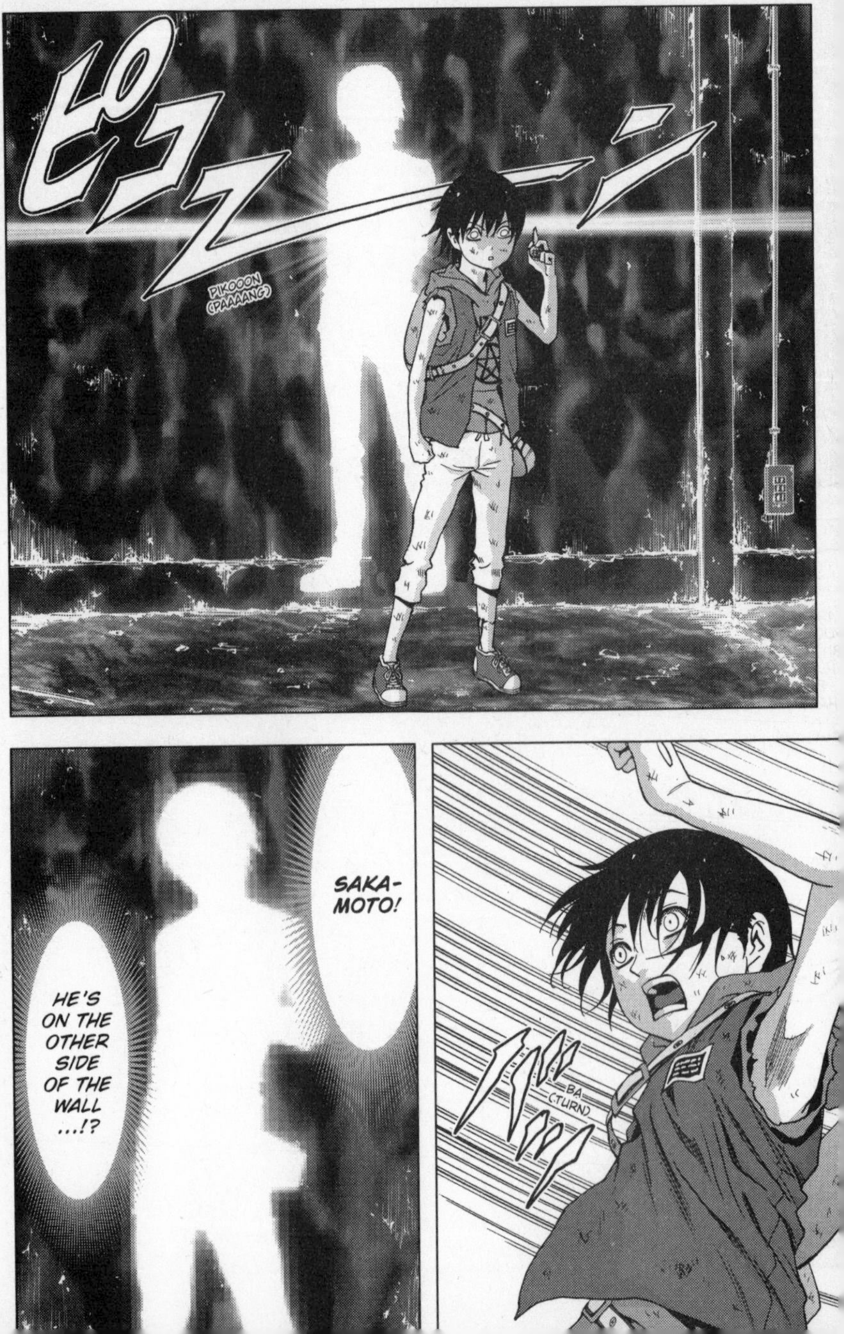
PIKOOON (PAAAANG)
BA (TURN)
SAKA-MOTO!
HE'S ON THE OTHER SIDE OF THE WALL ...!?

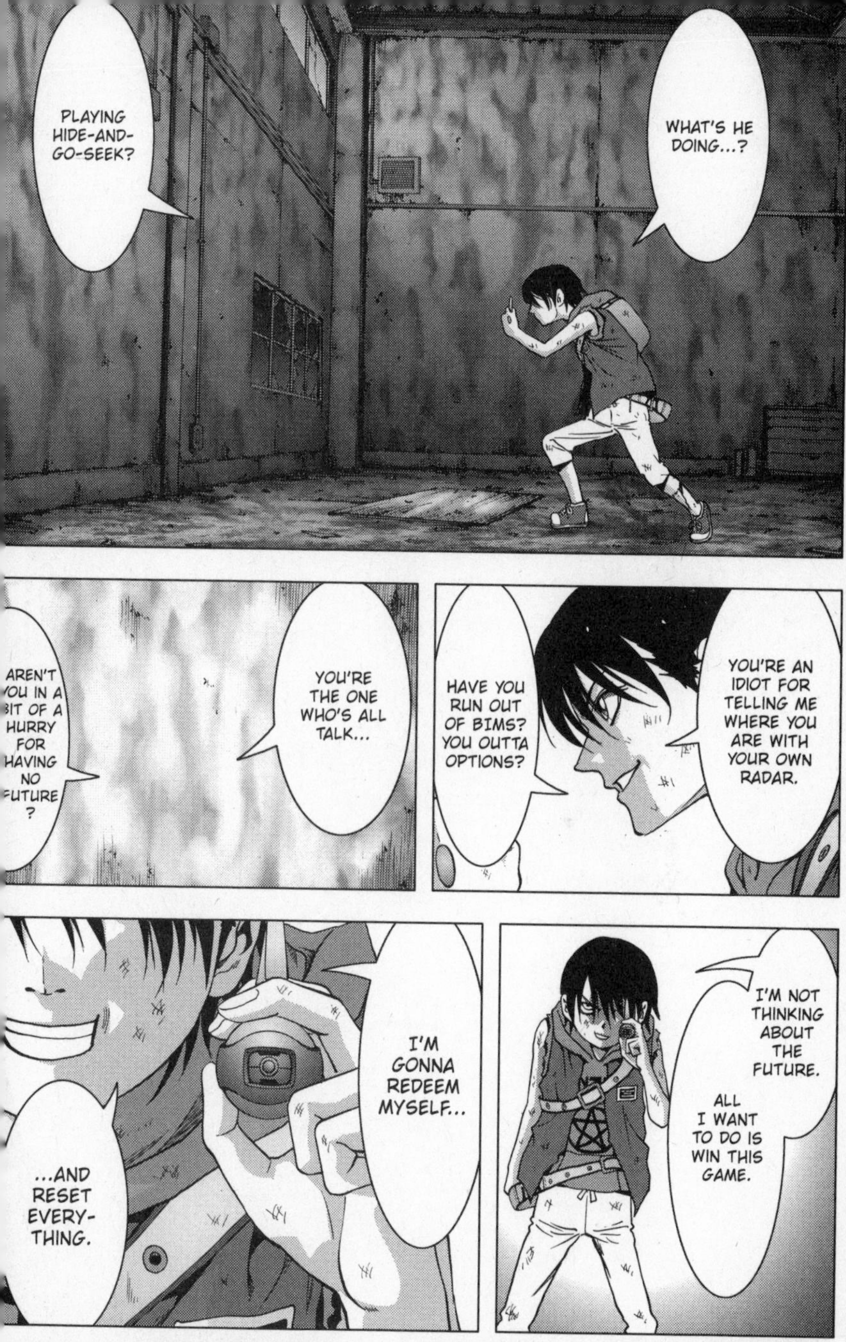
WHAT'S HE DOING...?
PLAYING HIDE-AND-GO-SEEK?
YOU'RE AN IDIOT FOR TELLING ME WHERE YOU ARE WITH YOUR OWN RADAR.
HAVE YOU RUN OUT OF BIMS? YOU OUTTA OPTIONS?
YOU'RE THE ONE WHO'S ALL TALK...
AREN'T YOU IN A BIT OF A HURRY FOR HAVING NO FUTURE?
I'M NOT THINKING ABOUT THE FUTURE.
ALL I WANT TO DO IS WIN THIS GAME.
I'M GONNA REDEEM MYSELF...
...AND RESET EVERYTHING.

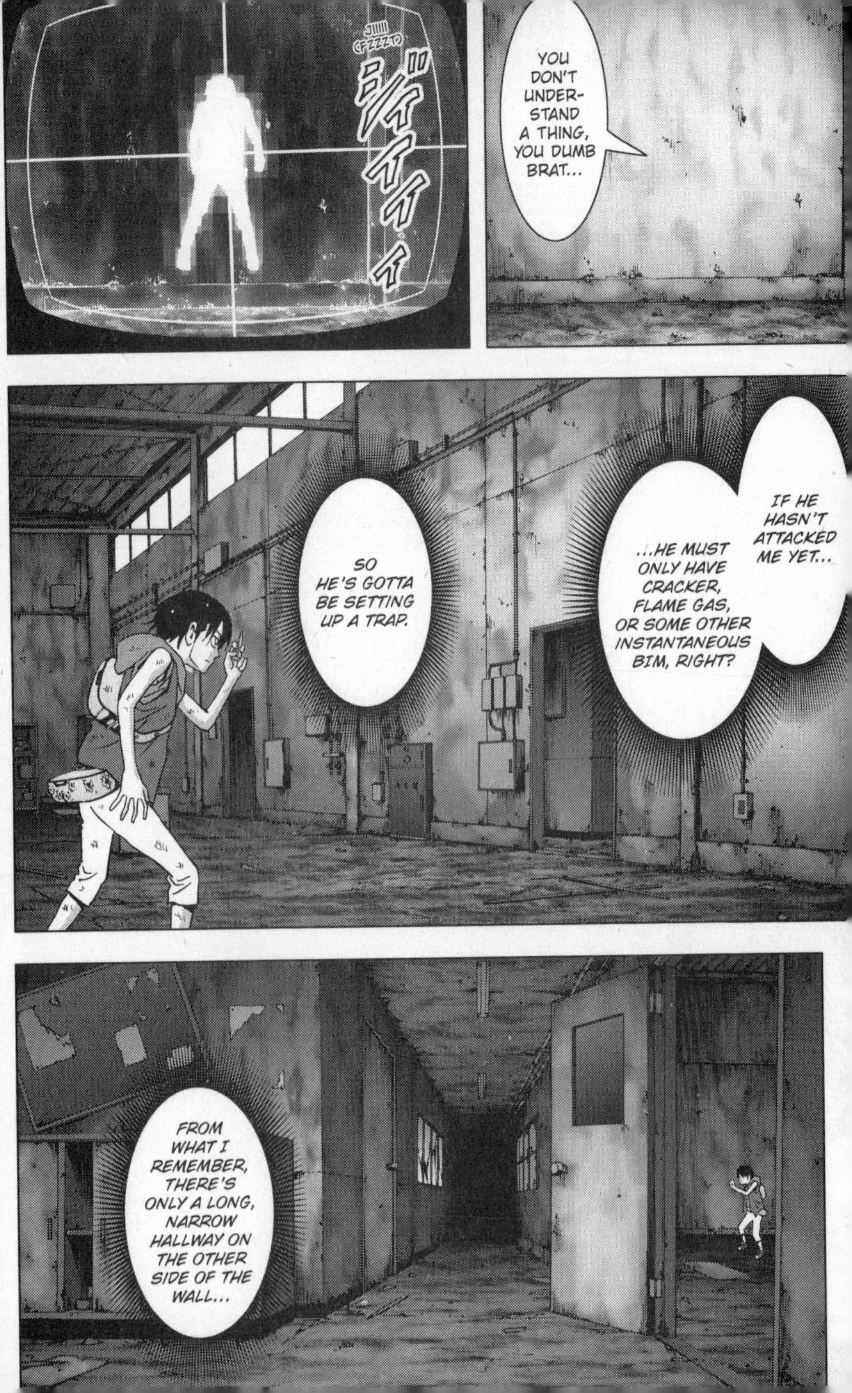
YOU DON'T UNDER-STAND A THING, YOU DUMB BRAT...
JIIIII (FZZZT)
IF HE HASN'T ATTACKED ME YET...
...HE MUST ONLY HAVE CRACKER, FLAME GAS, OR SOME OTHER INSTANTANEOUS BIM, RIGHT?
SO HE'S GOTTA BE SETTING UP A TRAP.
FROM WHAT I REMEMBER, THERE'S ONLY A LONG, NARROW HALLWAY ON THE OTHER SIDE OF THE WALL...

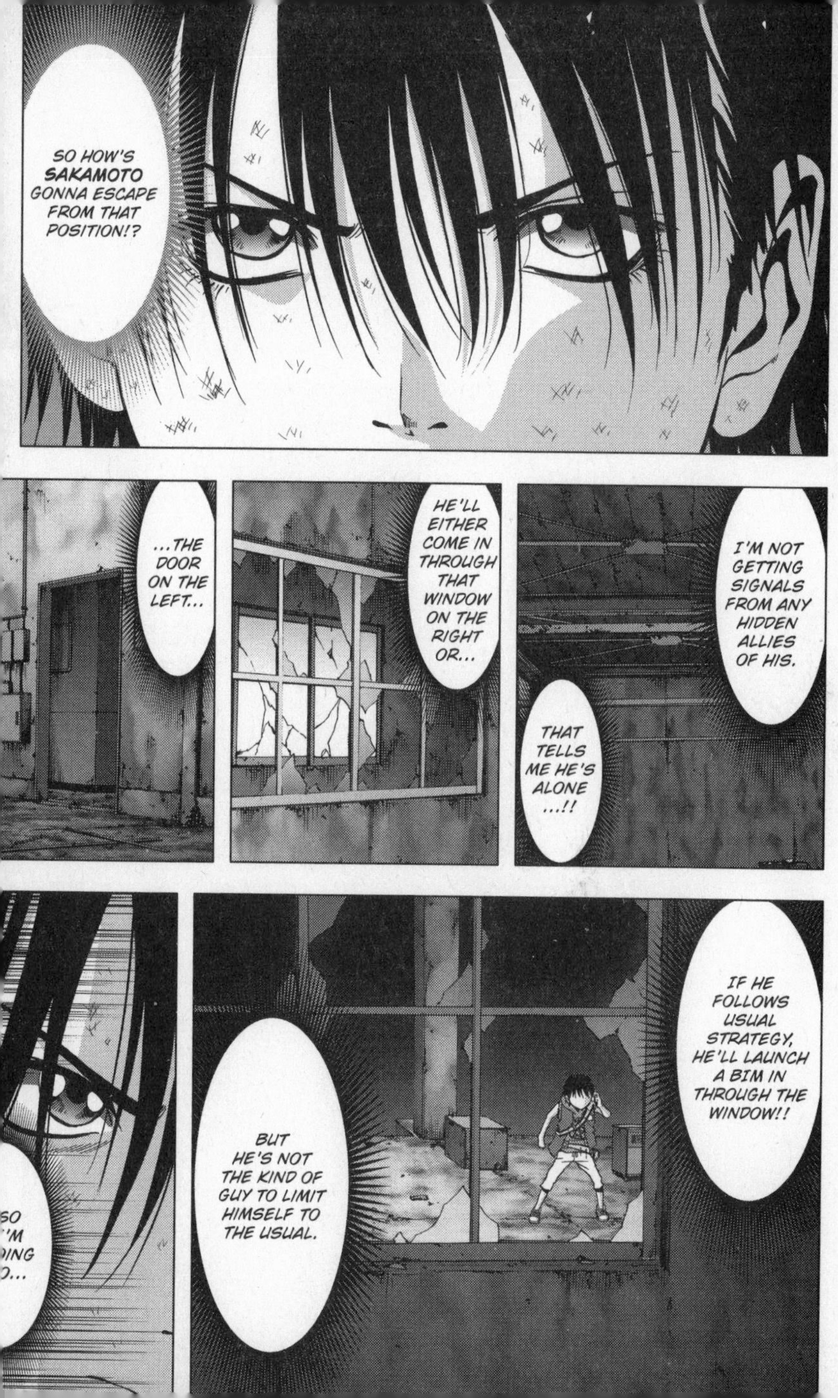
SO HOW'S **SAKAMOTO** GONNA ESCAPE FROM THAT POSITION!?
I'M NOT GETTING SIGNALS FROM ANY HIDDEN ALLIES OF HIS.
THAT TELLS ME HE'S ALONE ...!!
HE'LL EITHER COME IN THROUGH THAT WINDOW ON THE RIGHT OR...
...THE DOOR ON THE LEFT...
IF HE FOLLOWS USUAL STRATEGY, HE'LL LAUNCH A BIM IN THROUGH THE WINDOW!!
BUT HE'S NOT THE KIND OF GUY TO LIMIT HIMSELF TO THE USUAL.
SO

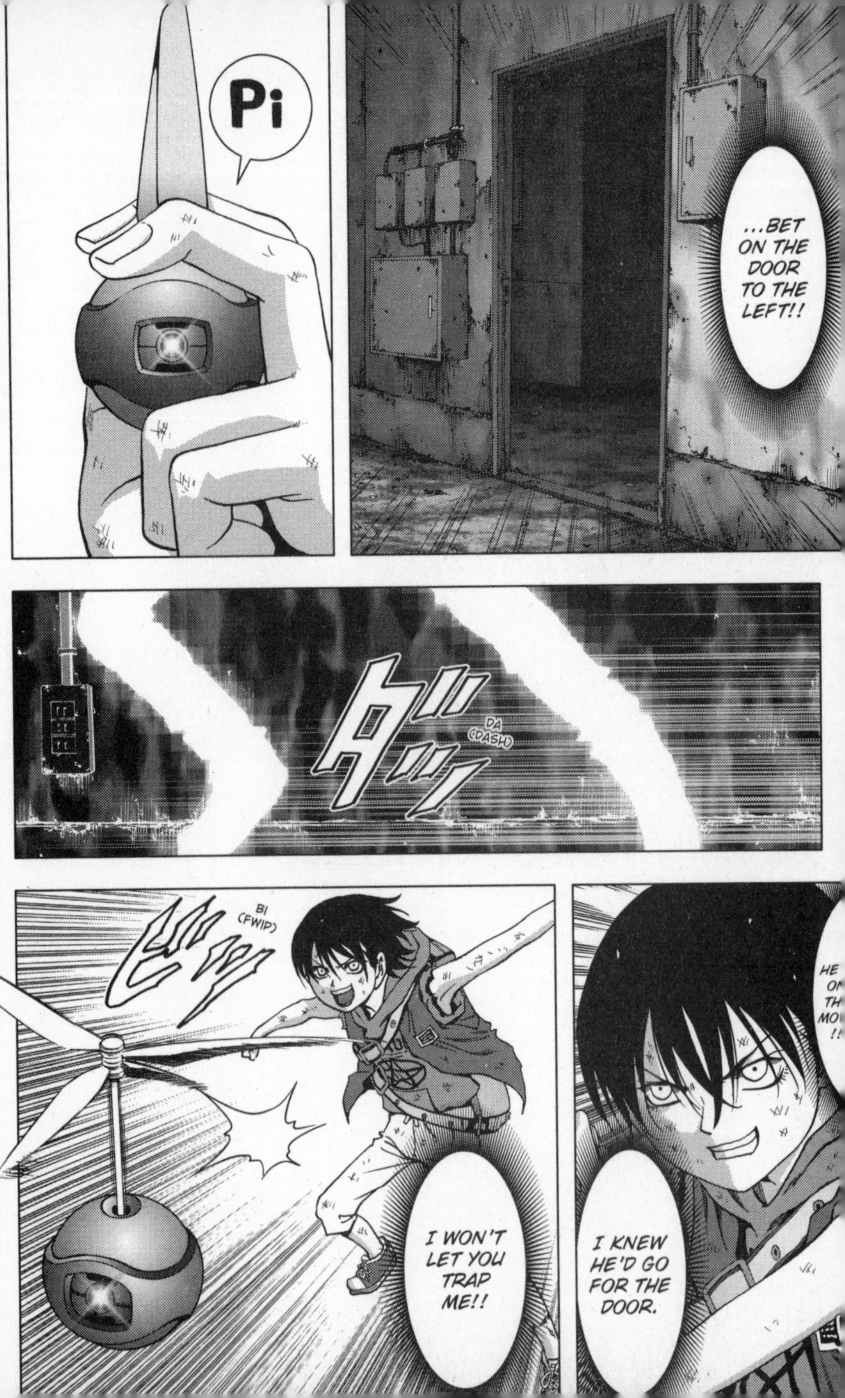
...BET ON THE DOOR TO THE LEFT!!
Pi
DA (DASH)
I KNEW HE'D GO FOR THE DOOR.
BI (FWIP)
I WON'T LET YOU TRAP ME!!

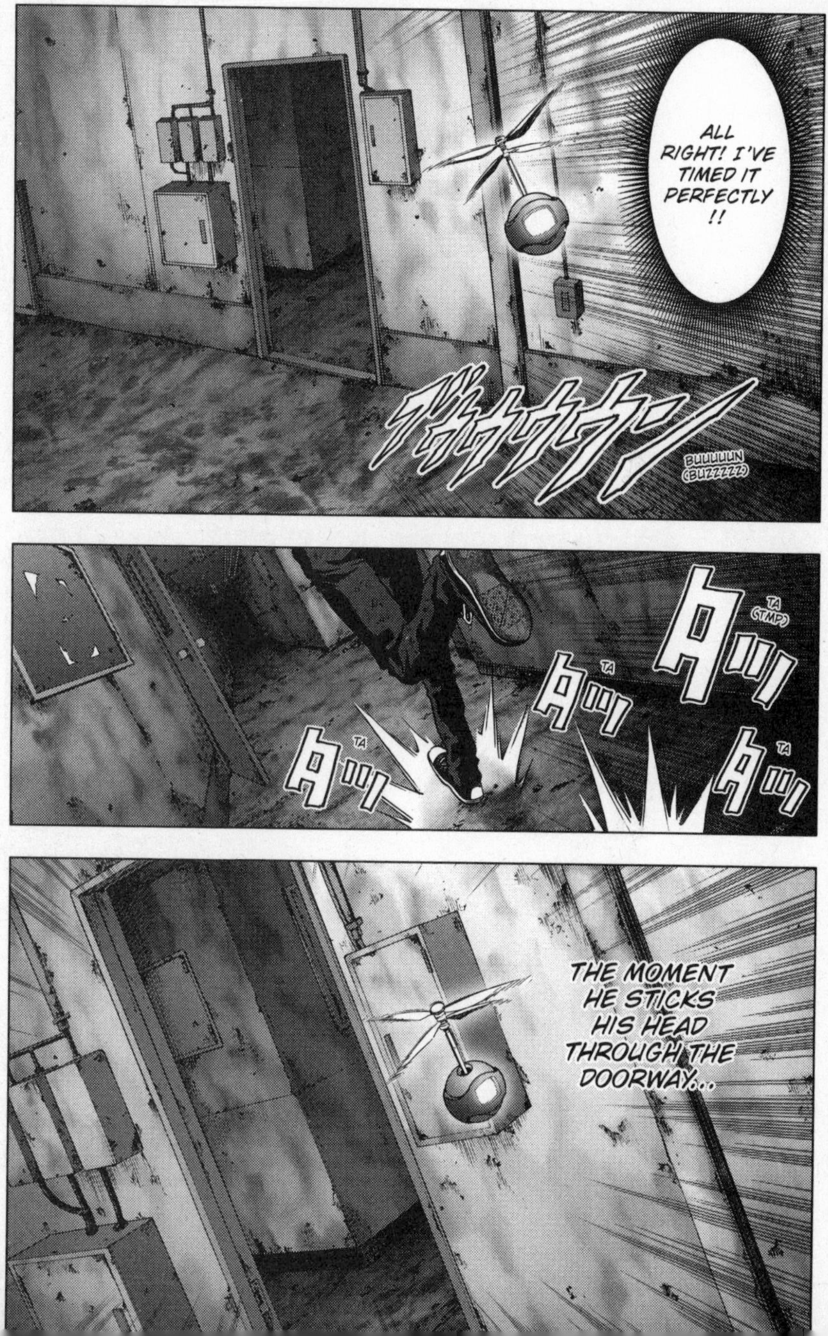
ALL RIGHT! I'VE TIMED IT PERFECTLY !!
ブゥゥゥウウン
BUUUUUN (BUZZZZZ)
タッ
TA (TMP)
タッ
TA
タッ
TA
タッ
TA
THE MOMENT HE STICKS HIS HEAD THROUGH THE DOORWAY...

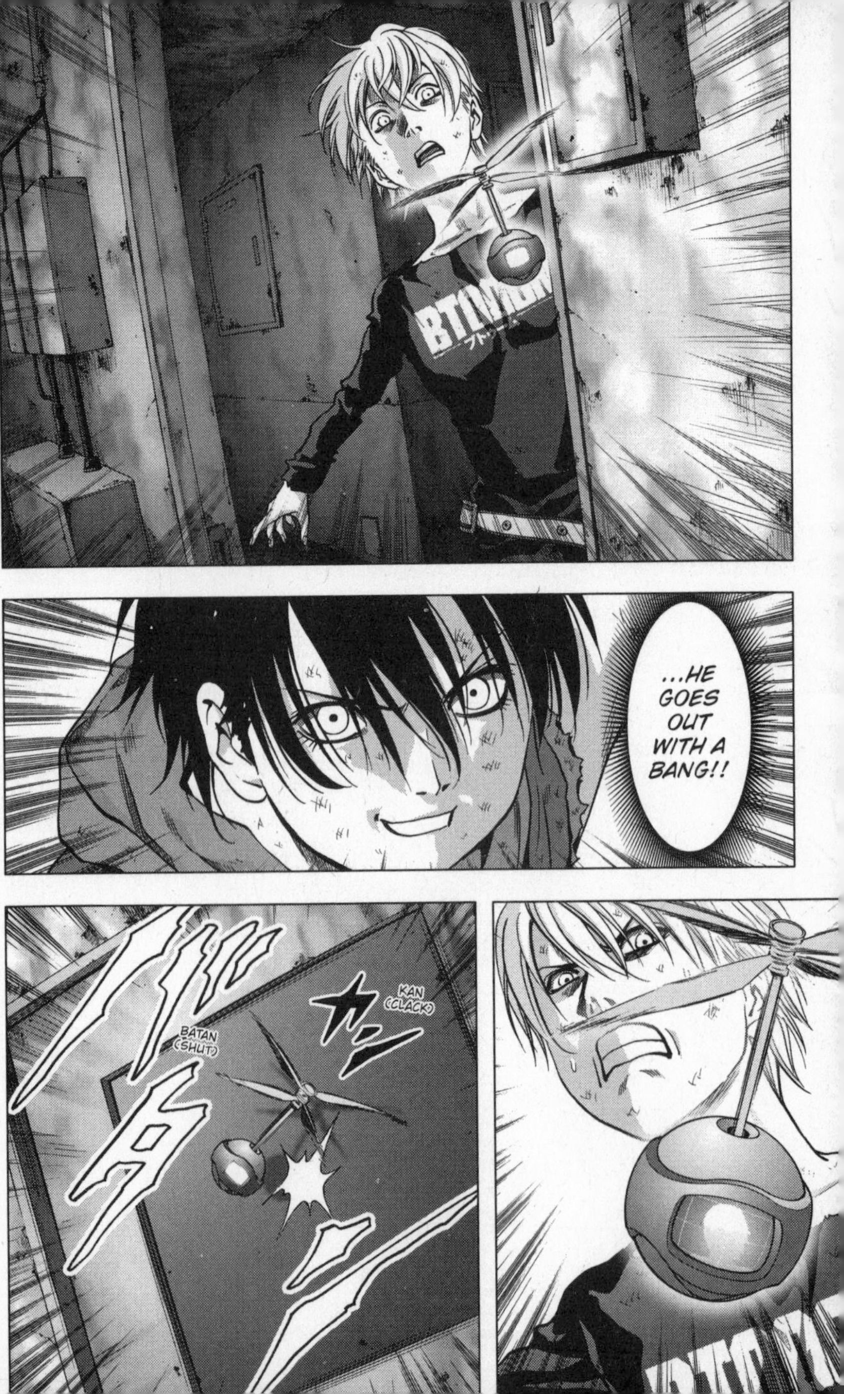
...HE GOES OUT WITH A BANG!!
KAN (CLACK)
BATAN (SHUT)

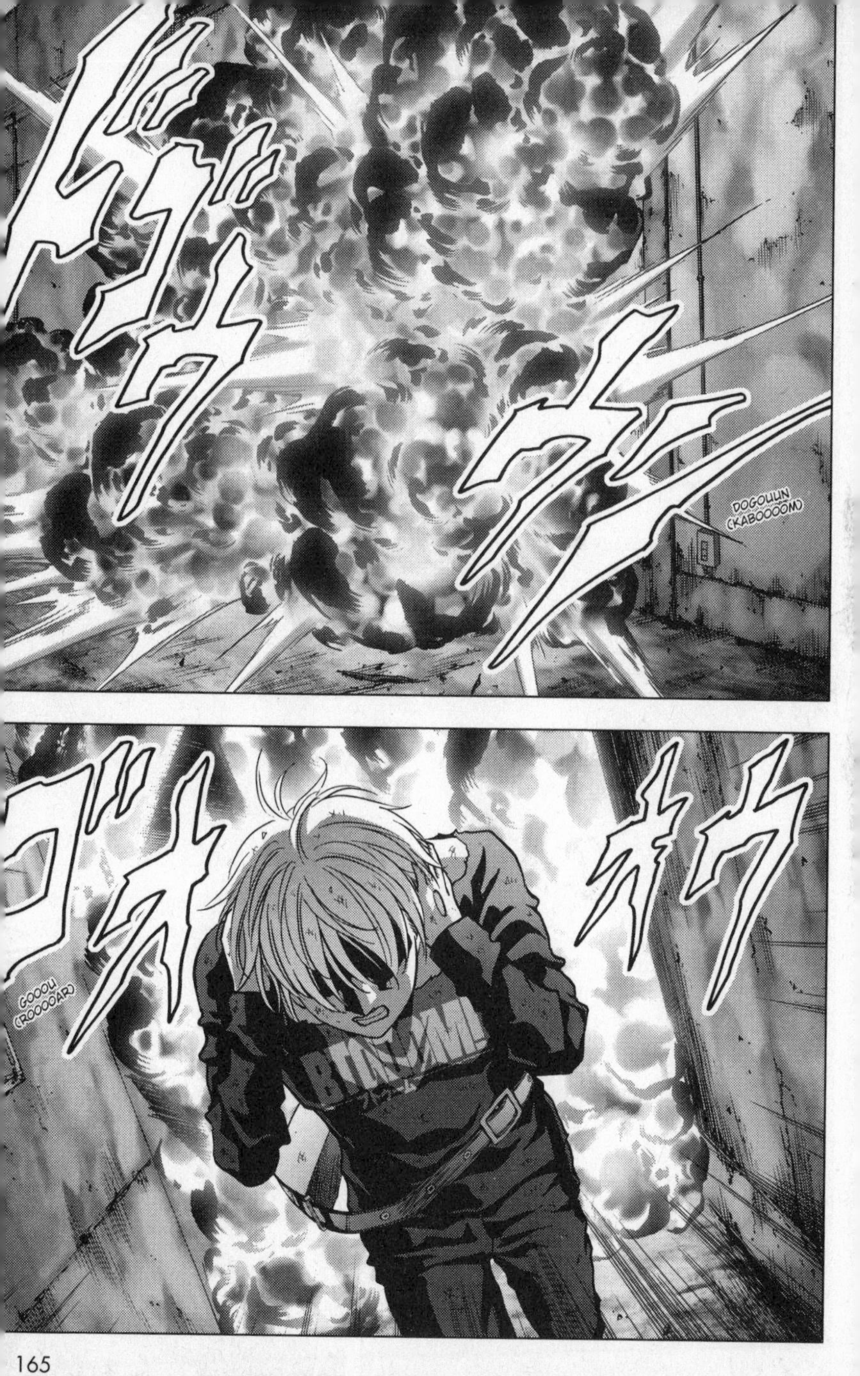
DOGOUUN
(KABOOOOM)
GOOOU
(ROOOOAR)

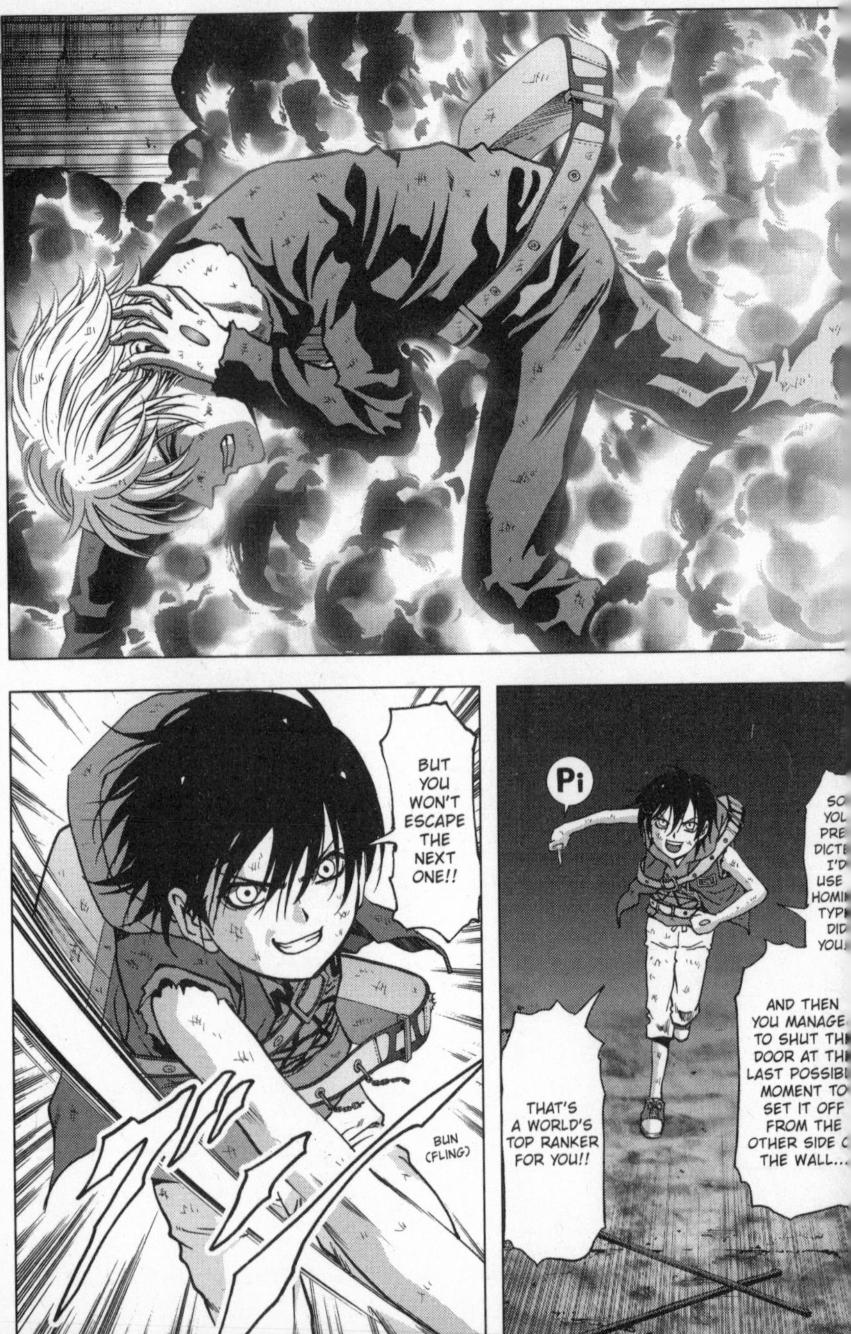
SO YOU PRE DICTE I'D USE HOMI TYP DID YOU!
Pi
AND THEN YOU MANAGE TO SHUT TH DOOR AT TH LAST POSSIBL MOMENT TO SET IT OFF FROM THE OTHER SIDE O THE WALL...
THAT'S A WORLD'S TOP RANKER FOR YOU!!
BUT YOU WON'T ESCAPE THE NEXT ONE!!
BUN (FLING)

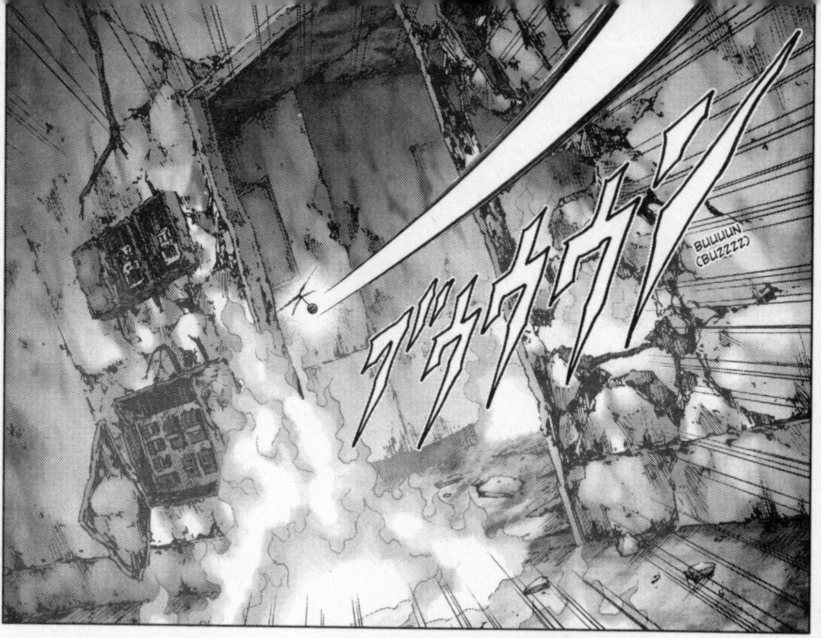
BUUUUN
(BUZZZZ)

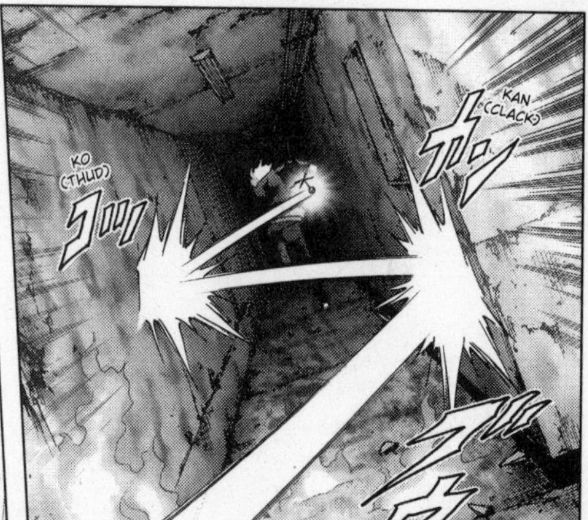
KAN
(CLACK)
KO
(THUD)
BUUUU

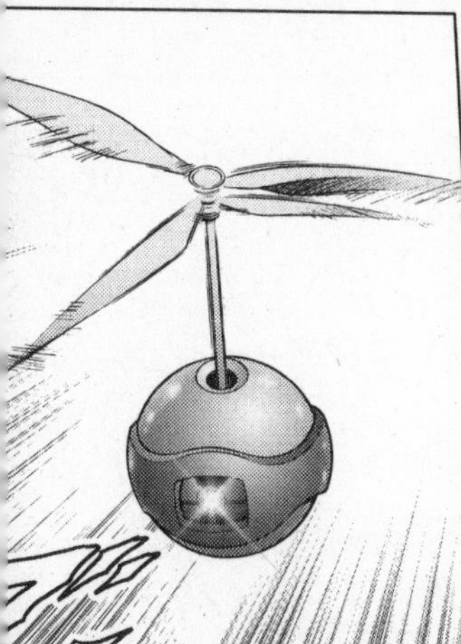
BUUUU

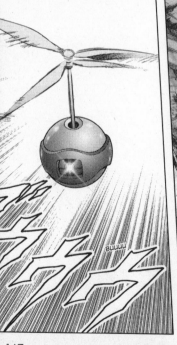

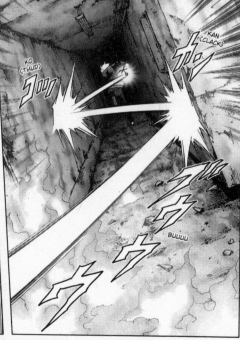

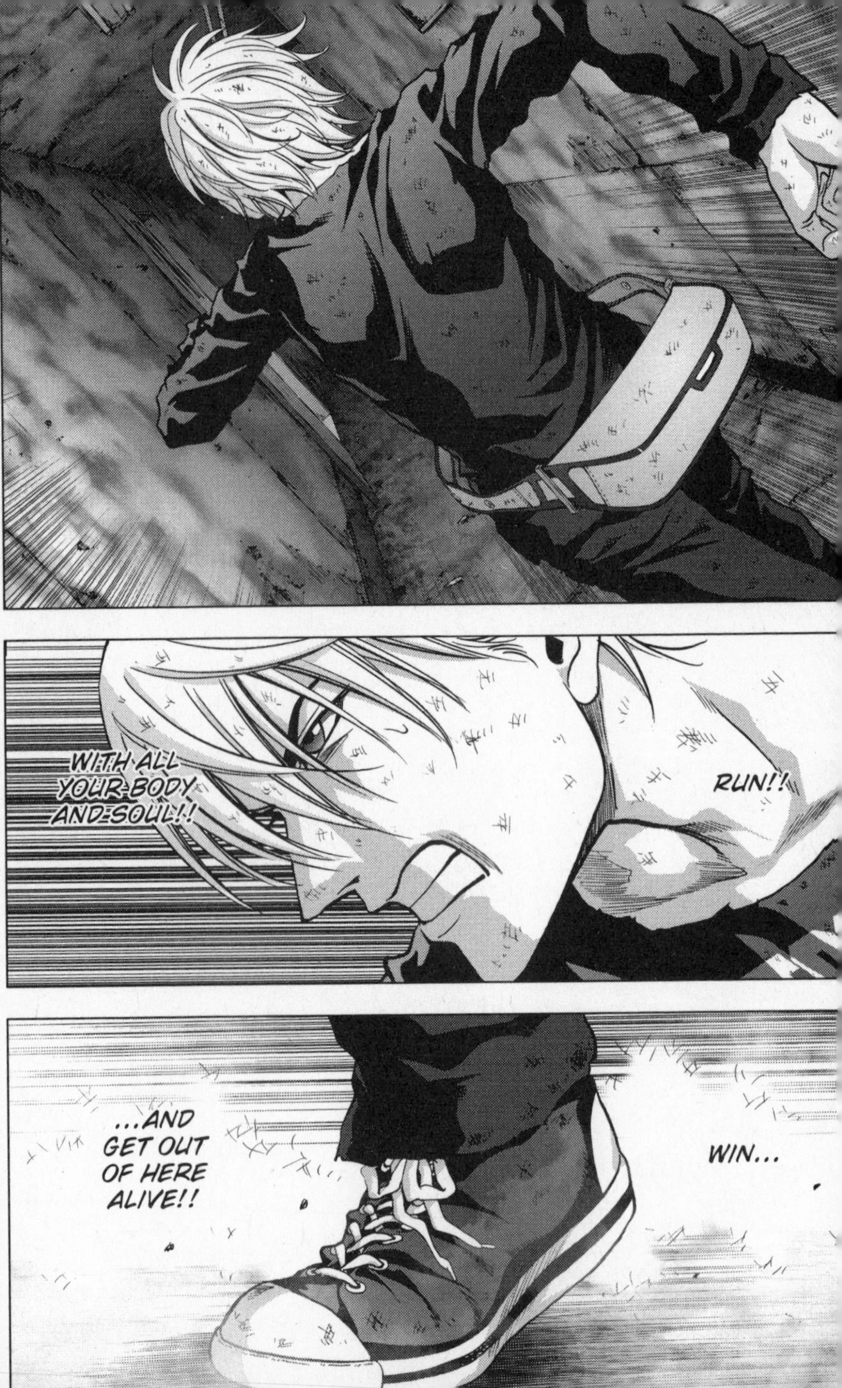
RUN!!
WITH ALL YOUR BODY AND SOUL!!
WIN...
...AND GET OUT OF HERE ALIVE!!

YOU PROMISED YOU'D MAKE IT BACK NO MATTER WHAT.

YOU CAN'T DIE AND LEAVE HIMIKO BEHIND!!

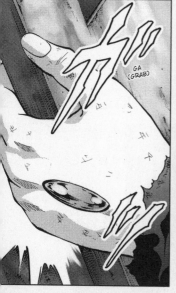

GA
(GRAB)

BUUUU
(BUZZZZ)

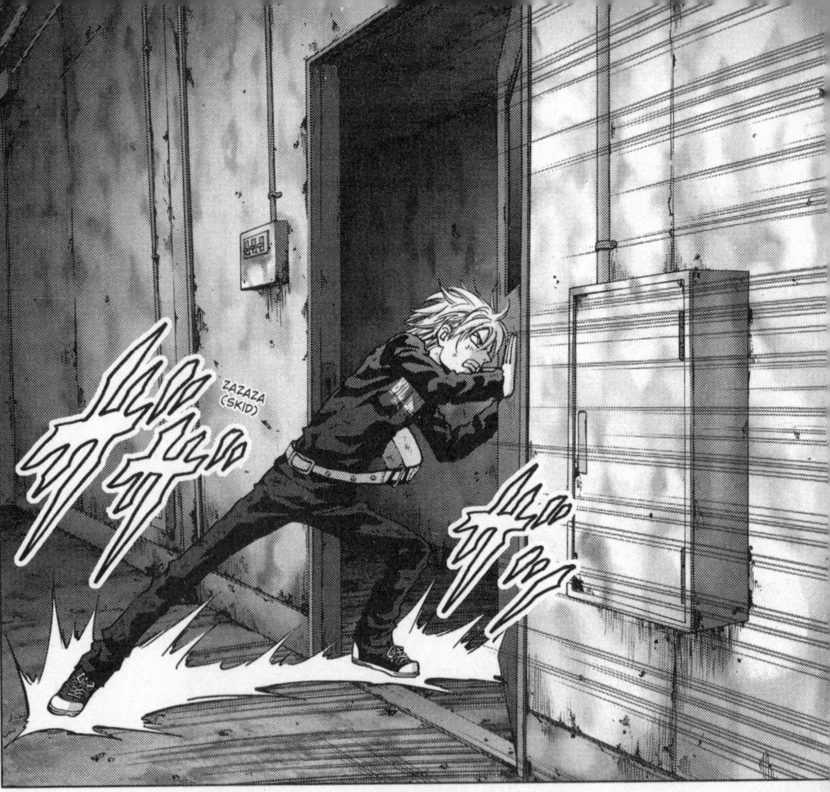
ZAZAZA
(SKID)

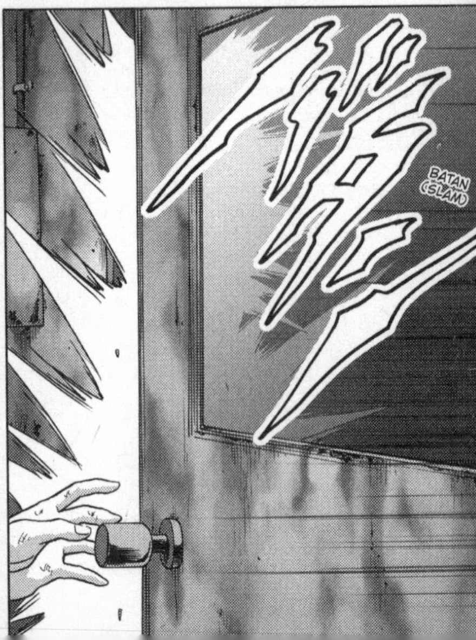
BATAN
(SLAM)

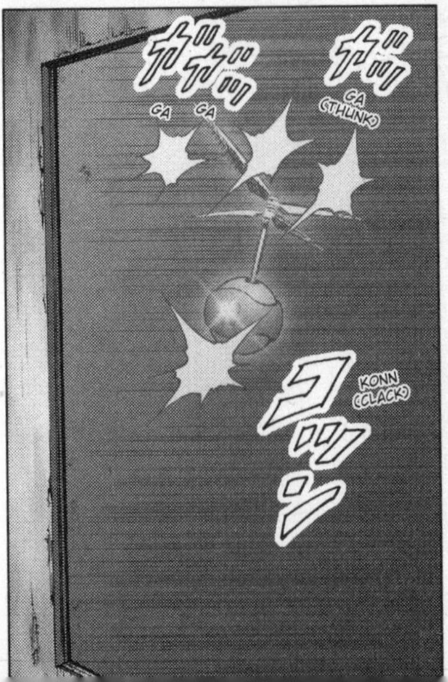
GA
(THUNK)
GA
GA
KONN
(CLACK)

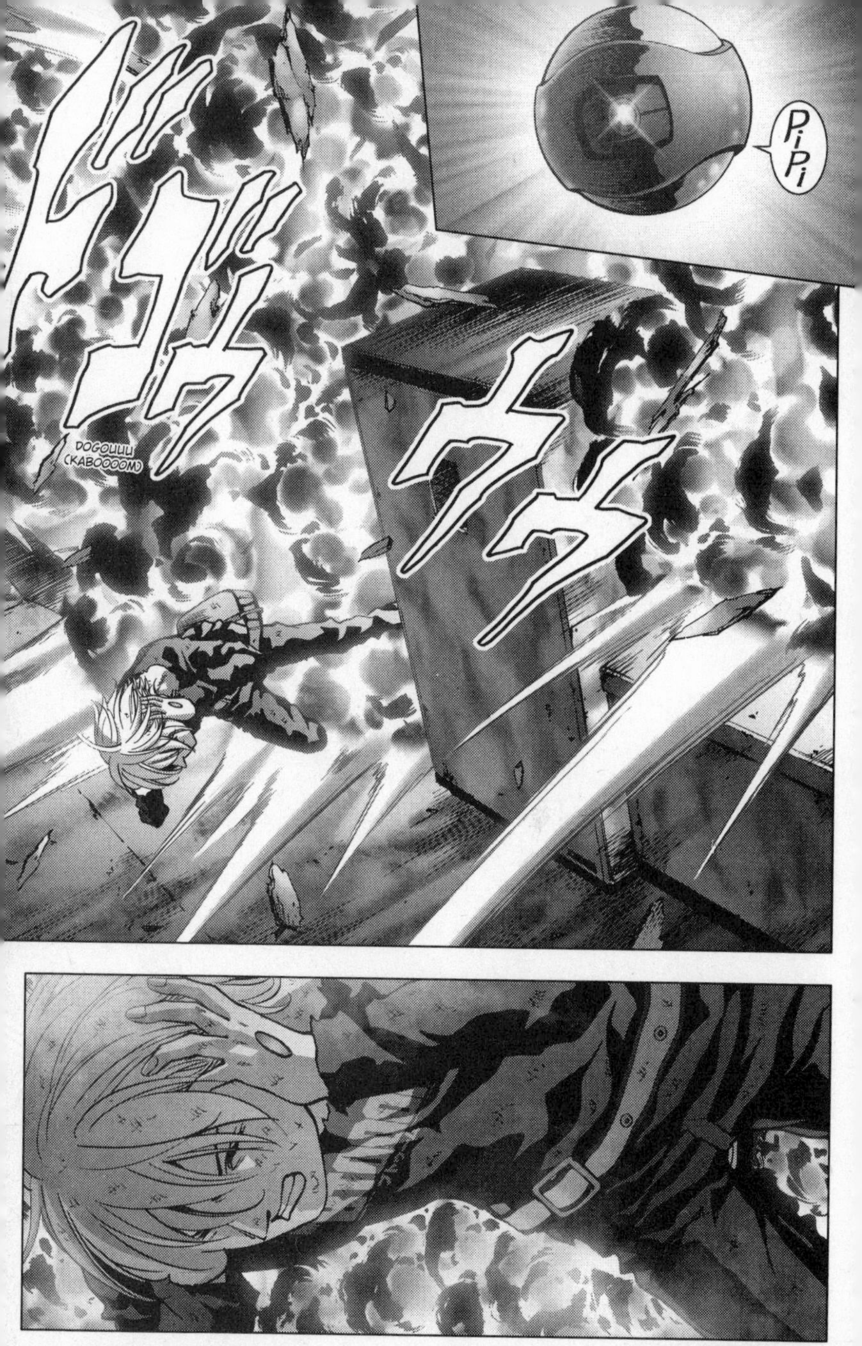
PiPi
DOGOUUU
(KABOOOOM)

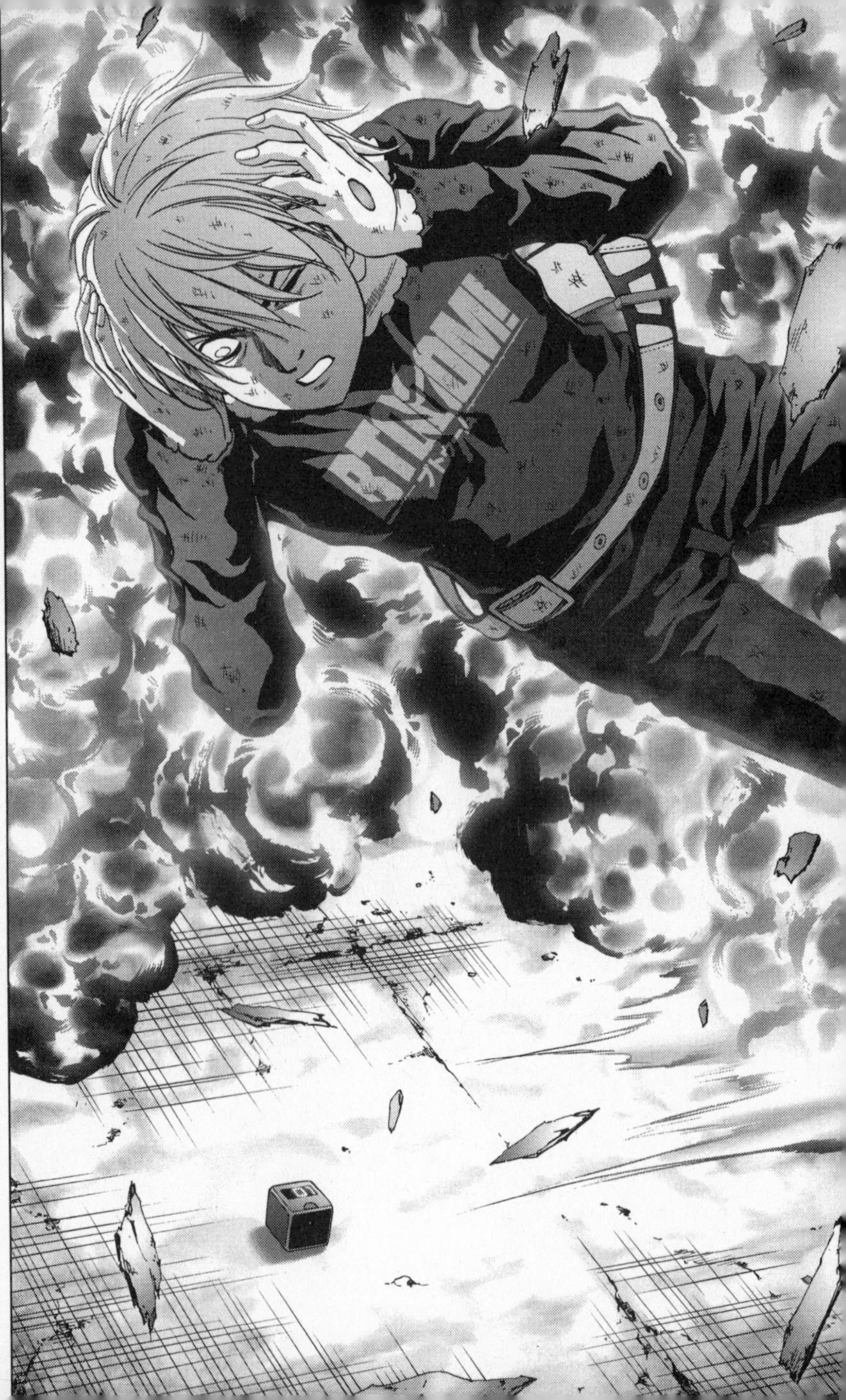

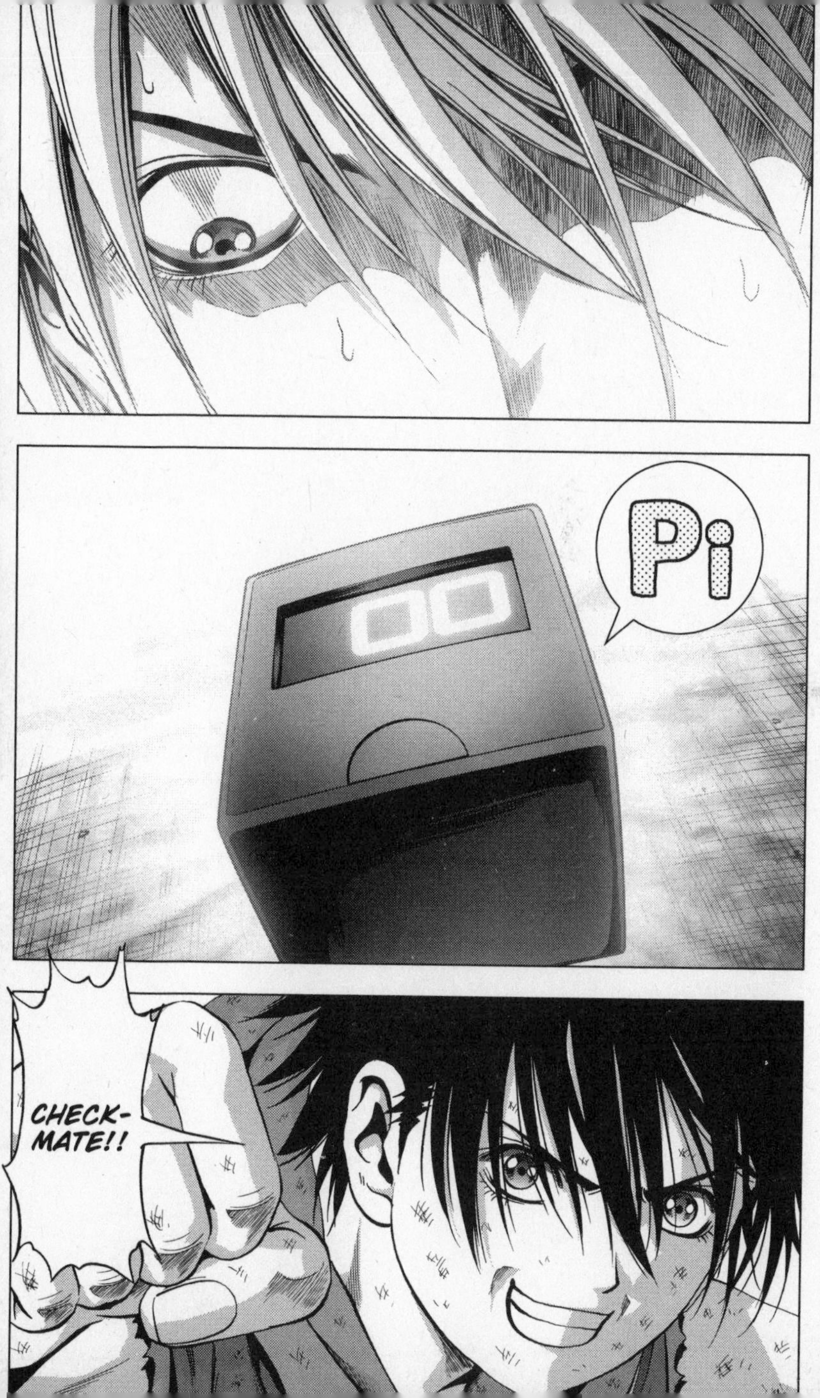
Pi
CHECK-MATE!!

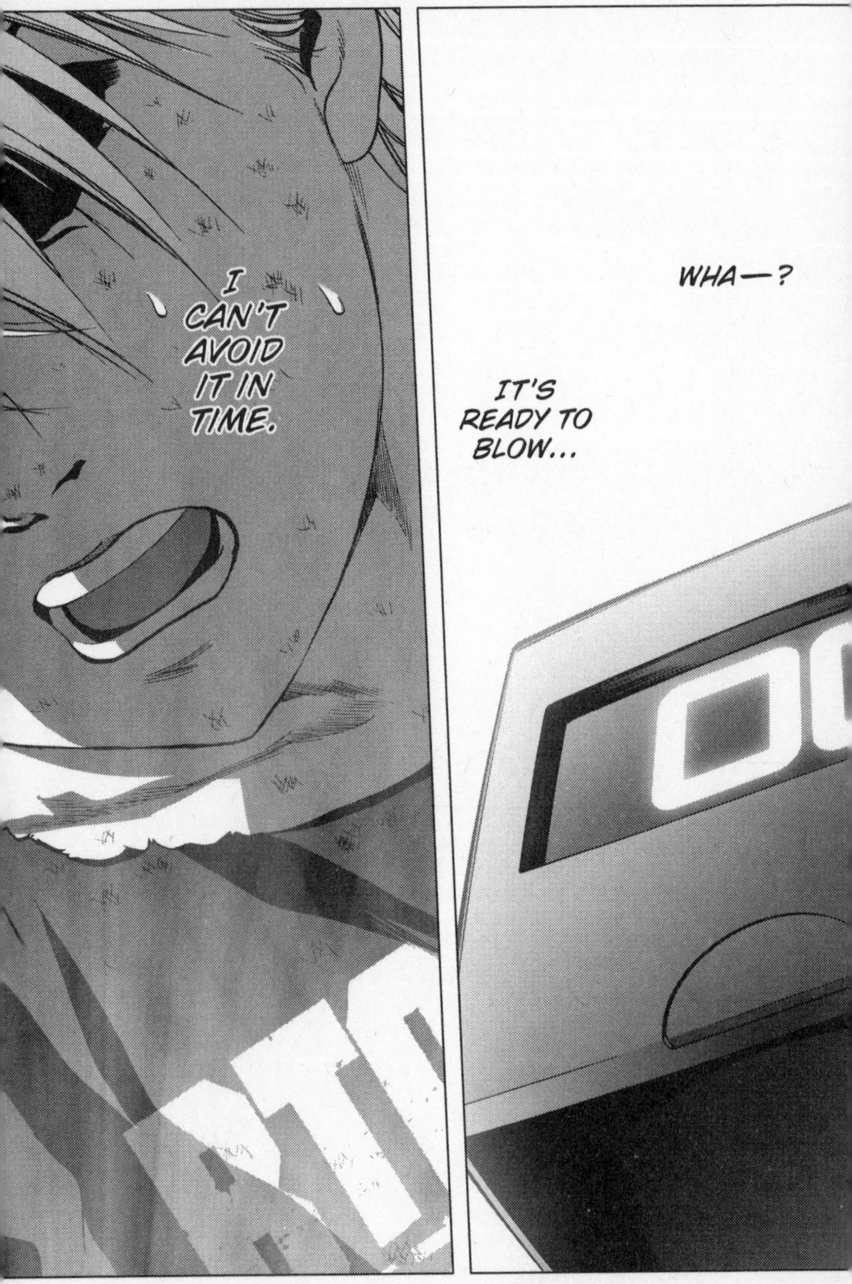
WHA—?
IT'S READY TO BLOW...
I CAN'T AVOID IT IN TIME.

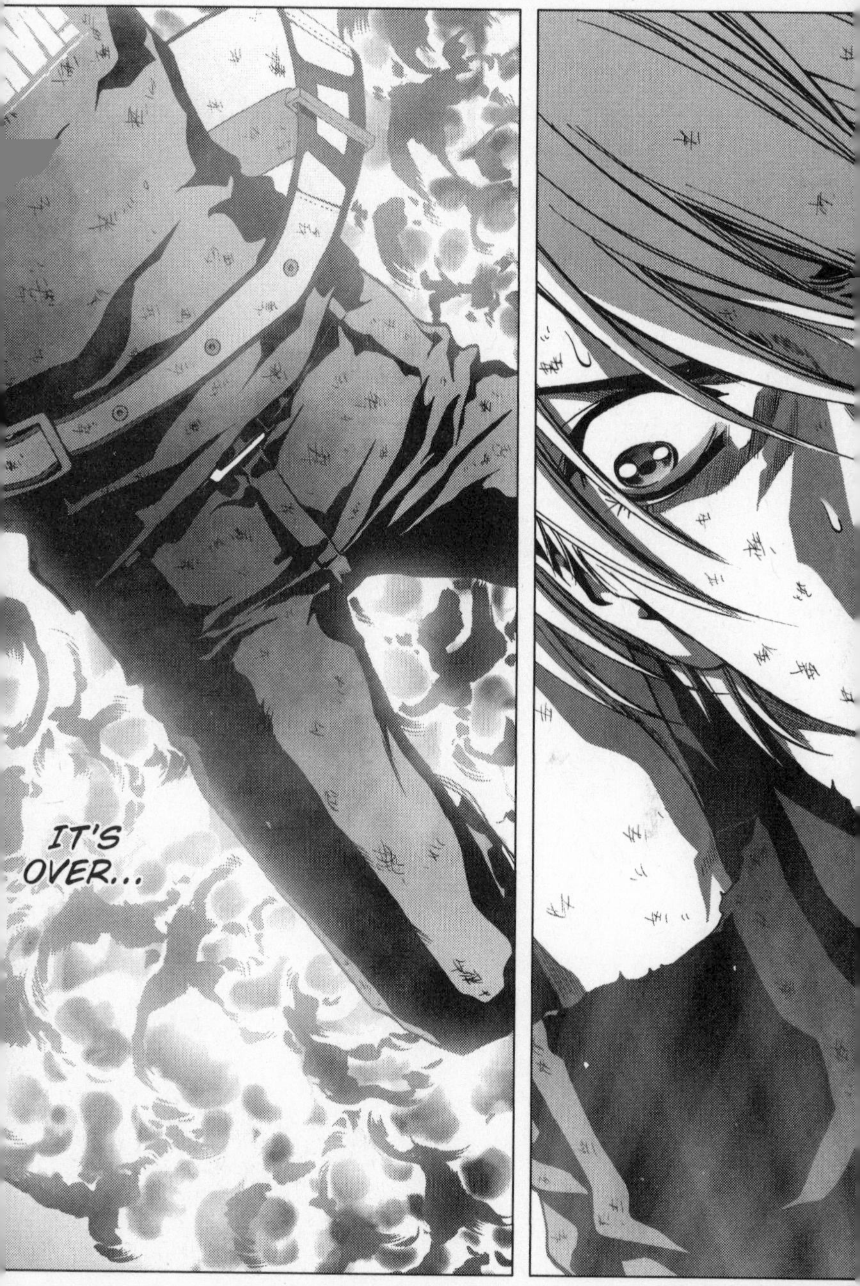
IT'S OVER...

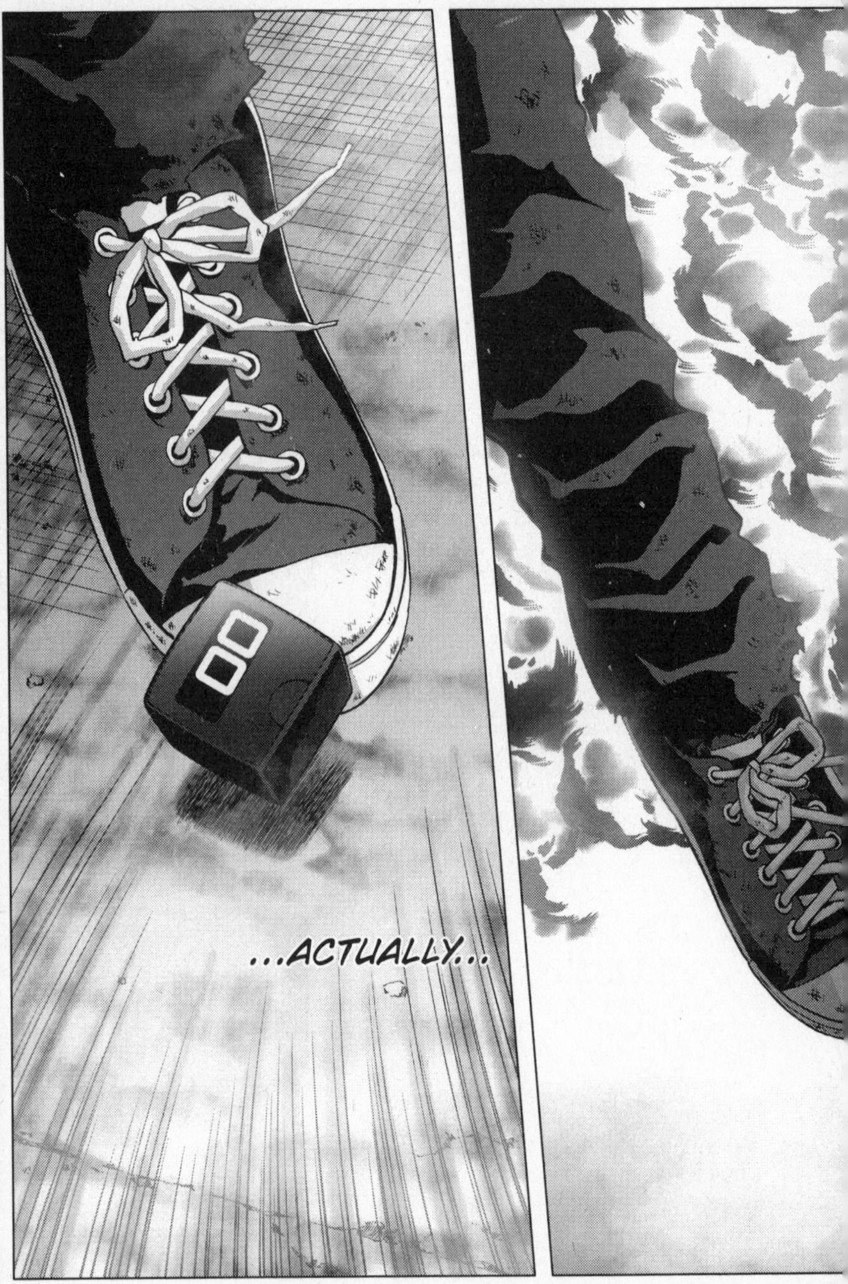
...ACTUALLY...

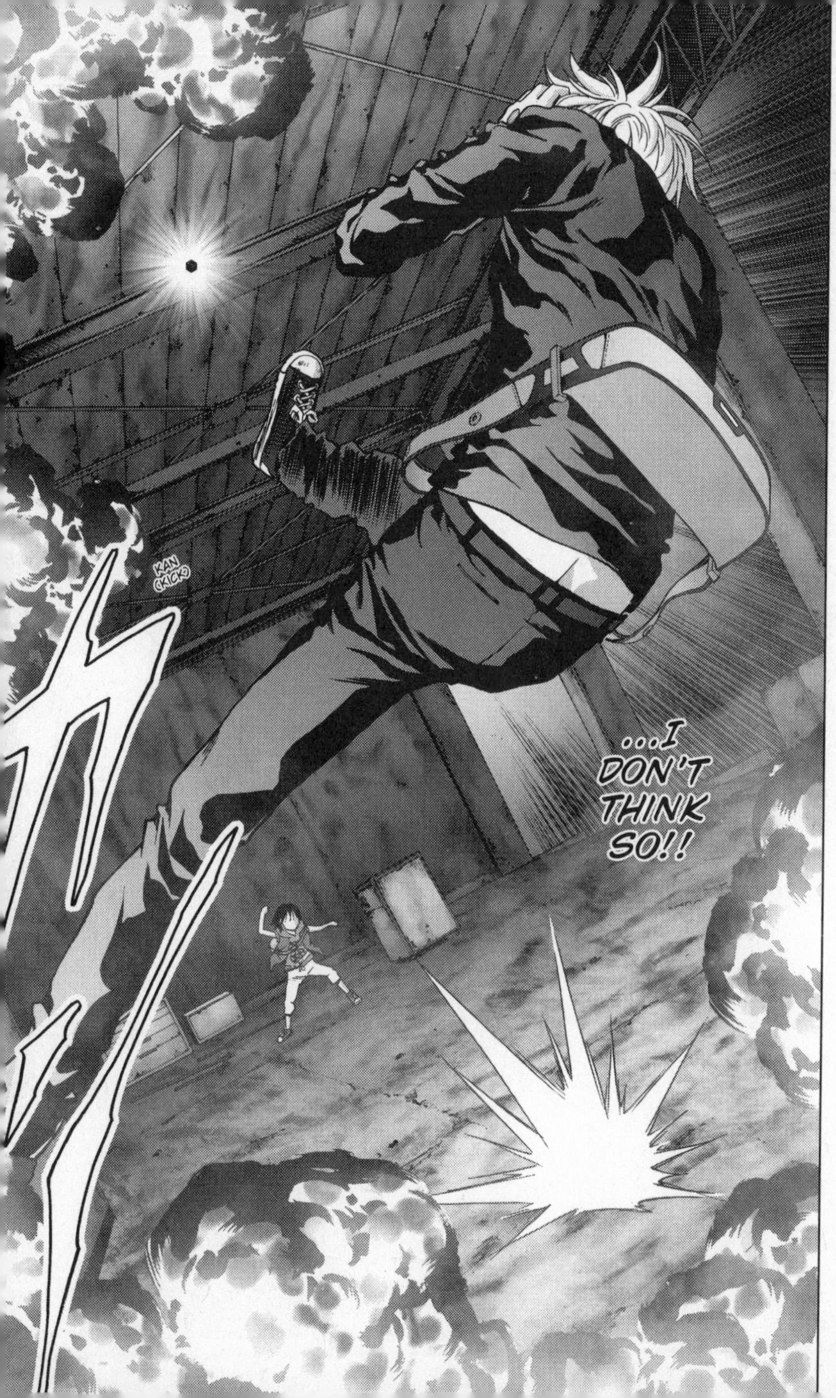
...I DON'T THINK SO!!
KAN (KICK)

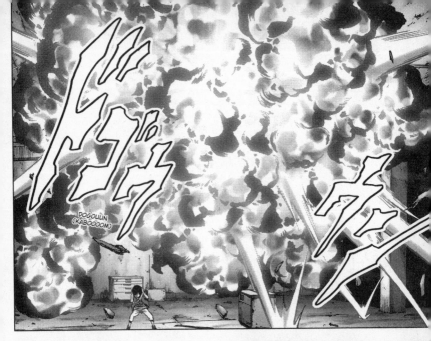

DOGOUUN (KABOOOOM)
GASHAN (CRASH)
GASHA
PARIN (SHATTER)
BARA
BARA (CRUMBLE)
OOF!!
KASHAN (CLATTER)
GARAN (CLANG)

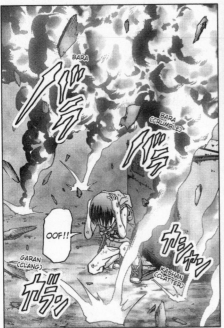

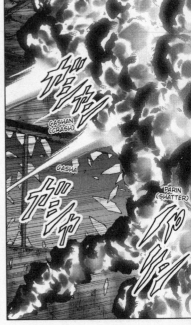

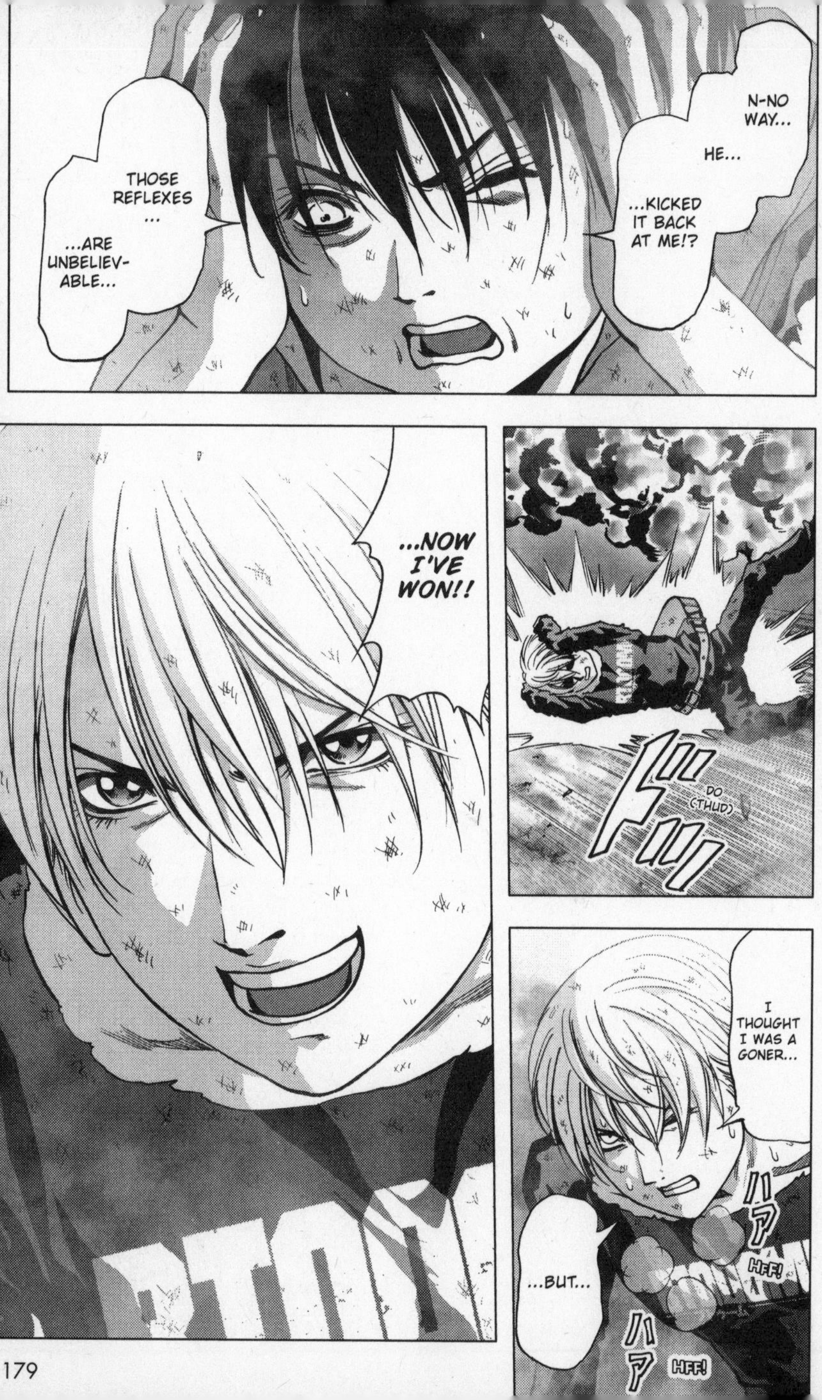
N-NO WAY...
HE...
...KICKED IT BACK AT ME!?
THOSE REFLEXES ...
...ARE UNBELIEV-ABLE...
DO (THUD)
I THOUGHT I WAS A GONER...
...BUT...
HFF!
HFF!
...NOW I'VE WON!!

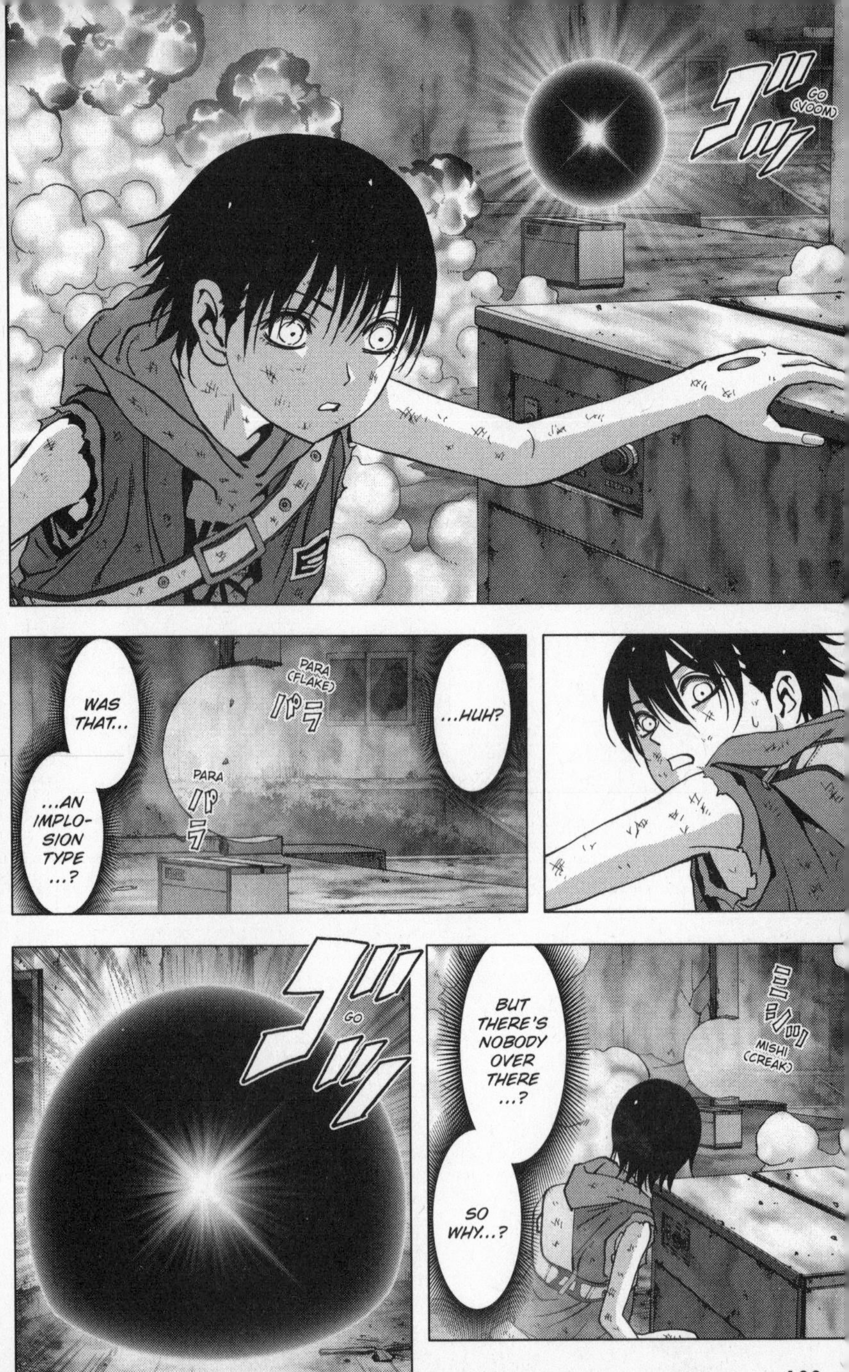
GO (VOOM)
...HUH?
PARA (FLAKE)
WAS THAT...
PARA
...AN IMPLOSION TYPE ...?
MISHI (CREAK)
BUT THERE'S NOBODY OVER THERE ...?
SO WHY...?
GO

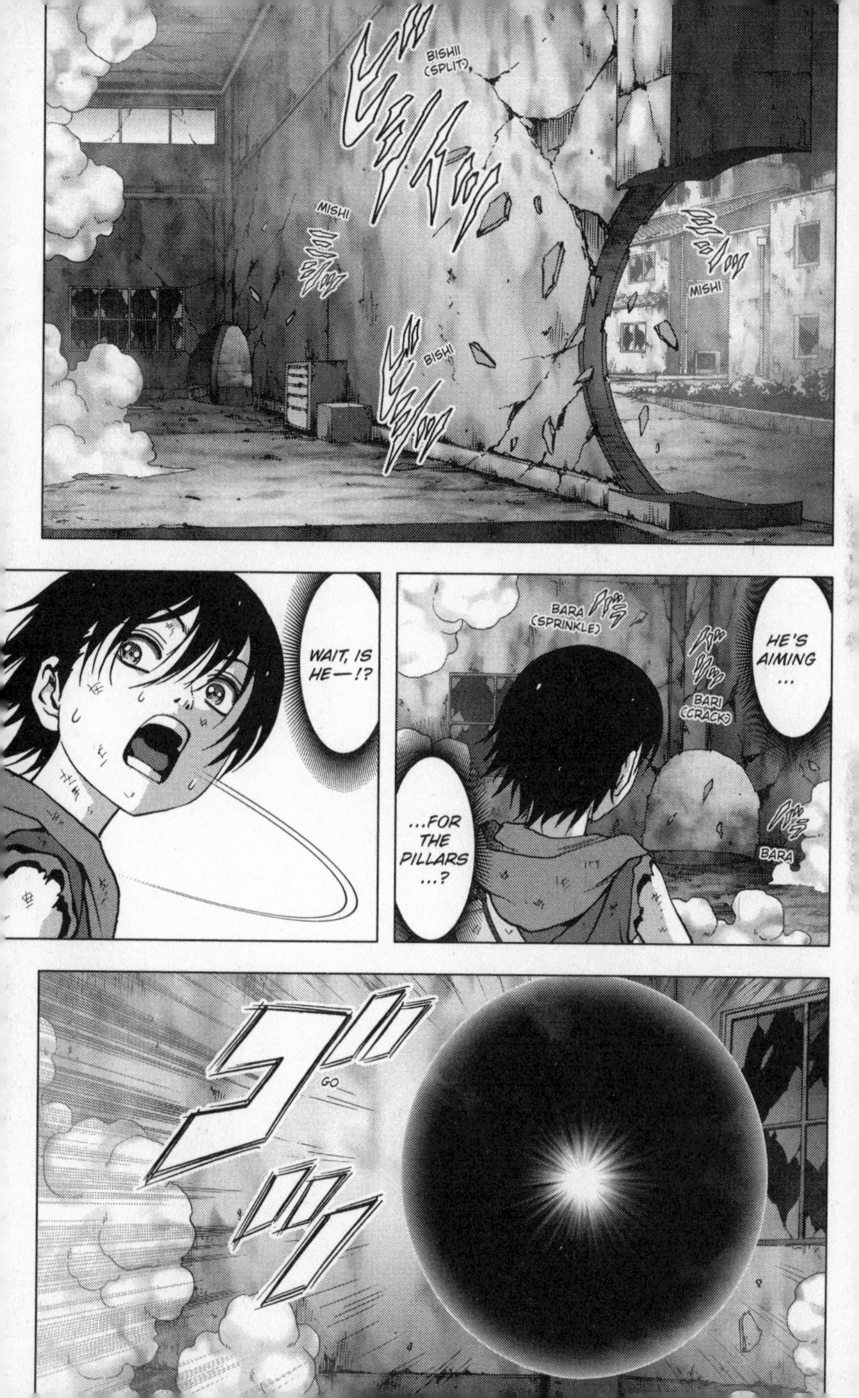
BISHII (SPLIT)
MISHI
MISHI
BISHI
HE'S AIMING ...
BARA (SPRINKLE)
BARI (CRACK)
BARA
...FOR THE PILLARS ...?
WAIT, IS HE—!?
GO

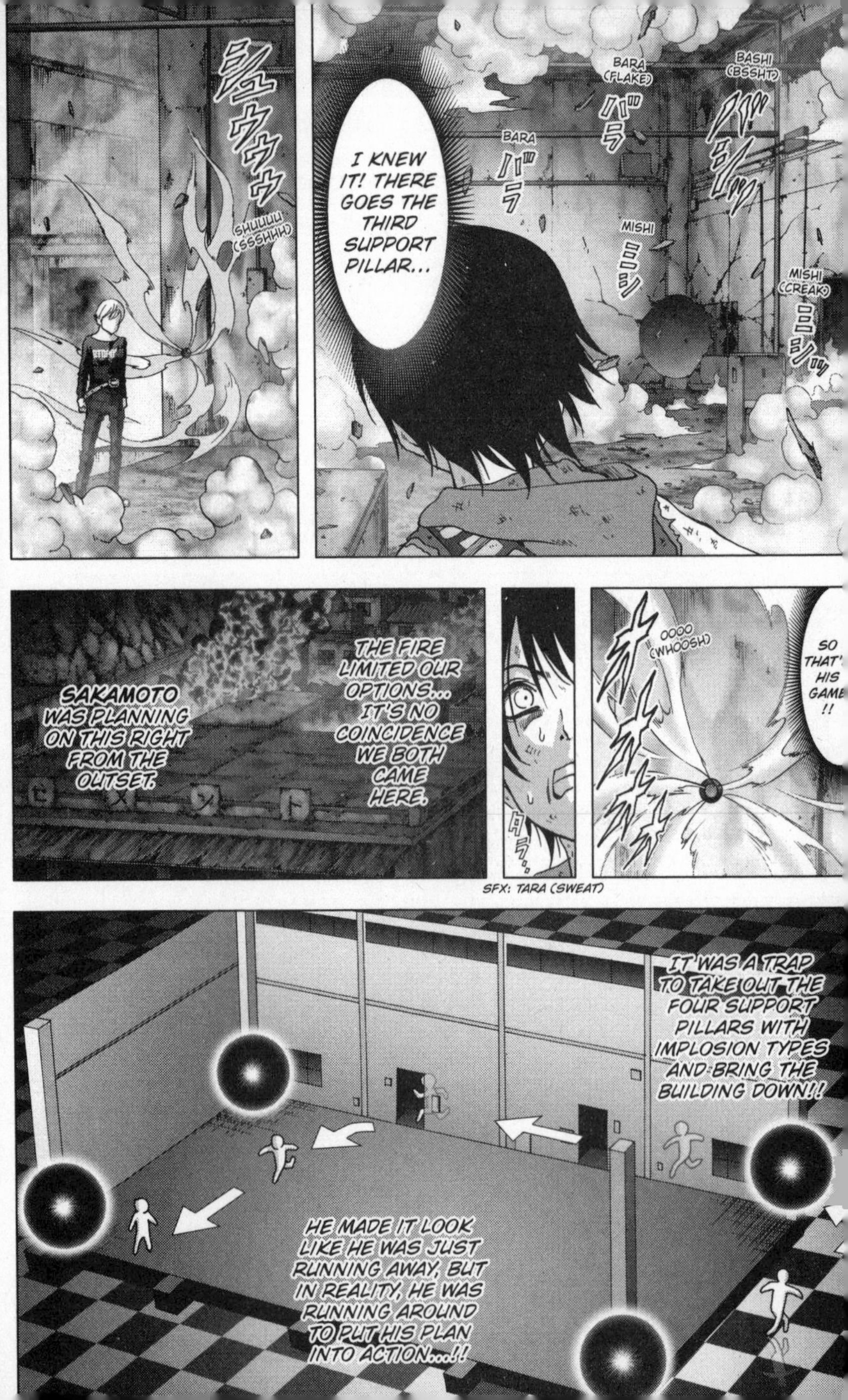
BASHI (BSSHT)
BARA (FLAKE)
BARA
MISHI
MISHI (CREAK)
I KNEW IT! THERE GOES THE THIRD SUPPORT PILLAR...
SHUUUU (SSSHHH)
SO THAT' HIS GAME !!
OOOO (WHOOSH)
SFX: TARA (SWEAT)
THE FIRE LIMITED OUR OPTIONS... IT'S NO COINCIDENCE WE BOTH CAME HERE.
SAKAMOTO WAS PLANNING ON THIS RIGHT FROM THE OUTSET.
IT WAS A TRAP TO TAKE OUT THE FOUR SUPPORT PILLARS WITH IMPLOSION TYPES AND BRING THE BUILDING DOWN!!
HE MADE IT LOOK LIKE HE WAS JUST RUNNING AWAY, BUT IN REALITY, HE WAS RUNNING AROUND TO PUT HIS PLAN INTO ACTION...!!

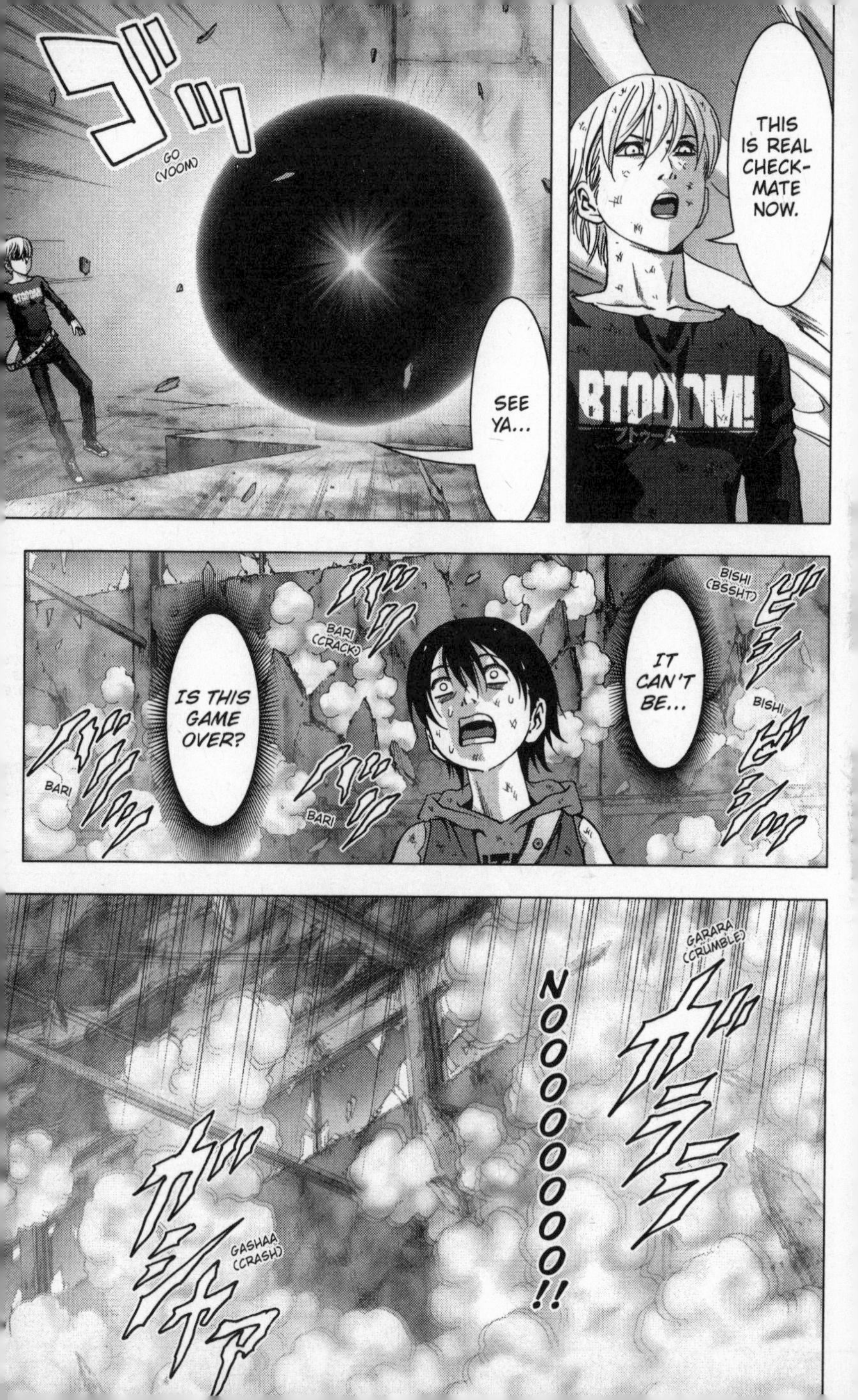
THIS IS REAL CHECKMATE NOW.
GO (VOOM)
SEE YA...
BISHI (BSSHT)
IT CAN'T BE...
BISHI
BARI (CRACK)
IS THIS GAME OVER?
BARI
BARI
GARARA (CRUMBLE)
NOOOOOOOOOOOO!!
GASHAA (CRASH)

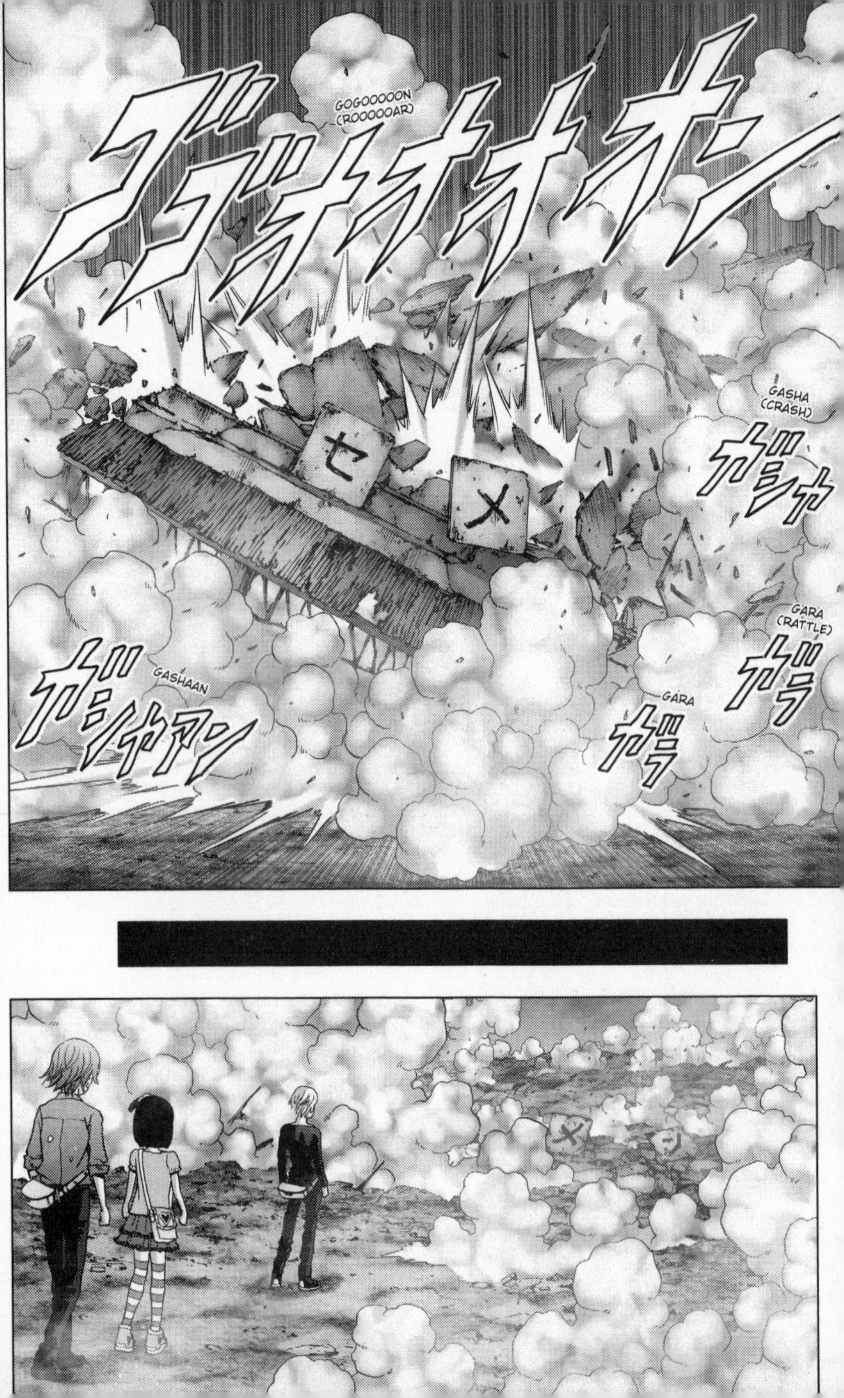
GOGOOOOON (ROOOOOAR)
GASHA (CRASH)
GARA (RATTLE)
GARA
GASHAAN

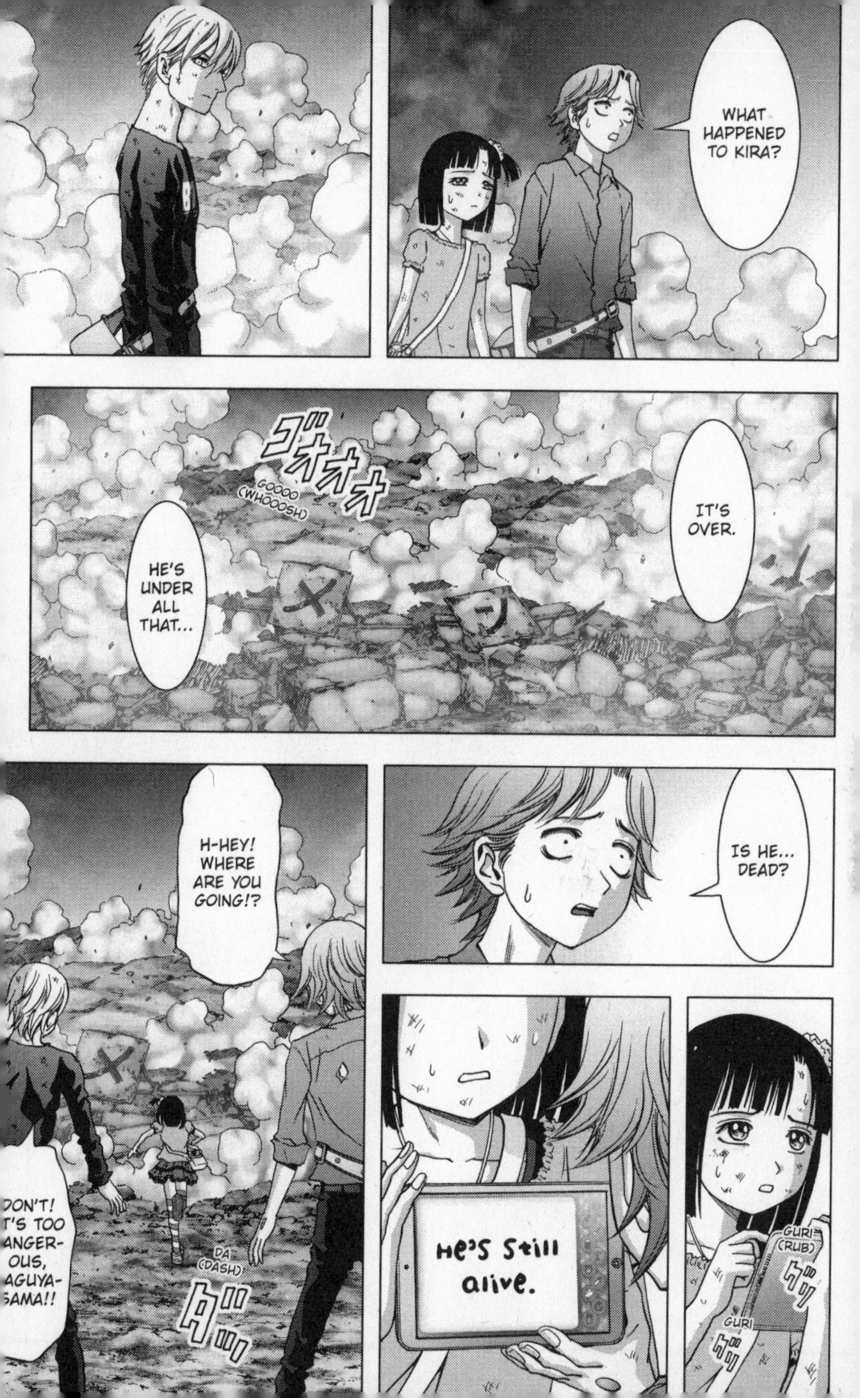
WHAT HAPPENED TO KIRA?
IT'S OVER.
ゴオオ
GOOOO (WHOOOSH)
HE'S UNDER ALL THAT...
IS HE... DEAD?
GURI (RUB)
グリ
GURI
グリ
He's still alive.
H-HEY! WHERE ARE YOU GOING!?
DA (DASH)
ダッ
DON'T! T'S TOO ANGER-OUS, AGUYA-SAMA!!

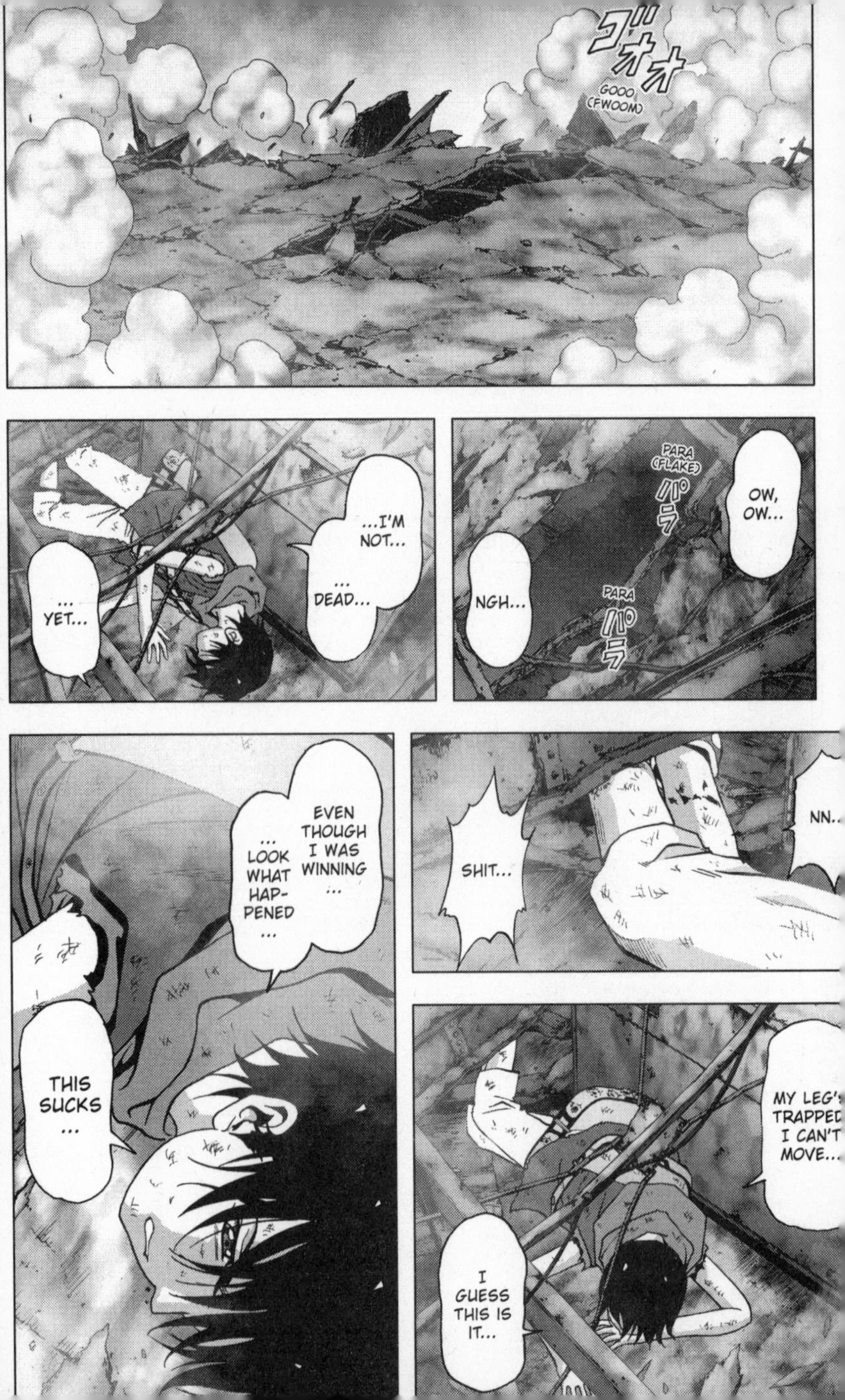

ゴォォ
GOOO (FWOOM)
OW, OW...
PARA (FLAKE) パラ
PARA パラ
NGH...
...I'M NOT...
... DEAD...
... YET...
NN..
SHIT...
MY LEG'S TRAPPED I CAN'T MOVE...
I GUESS THIS IS IT...
EVEN THOUGH I WAS WINNING ...
... LOOK WHAT HAP-PENED ...
THIS SUCKS ...

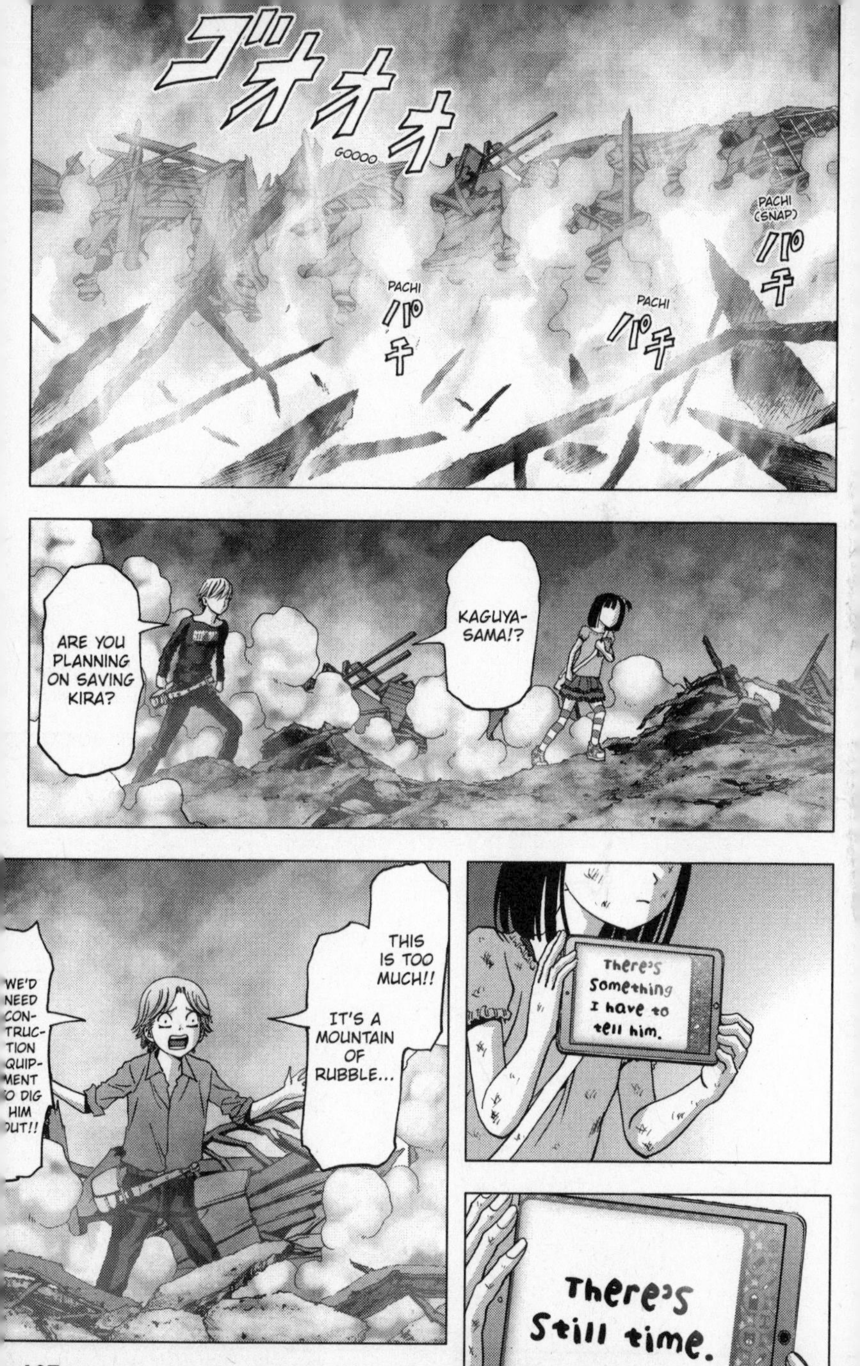
ゴオオオ
GOOOO
PACHI (SNAP)
パチ
PACHI
パチ
PACHI
パチ
KAGUYA-SAMA!?
ARE YOU PLANNING ON SAVING KIRA?
There's something I have to tell him.
There's still time.
THIS IS TOO MUCH!!
IT'S A MOUNTAIN OF RUBBLE...
WE'D NEED CON-TRUC-TION QUIP-MENT O DIG HIM UT!!

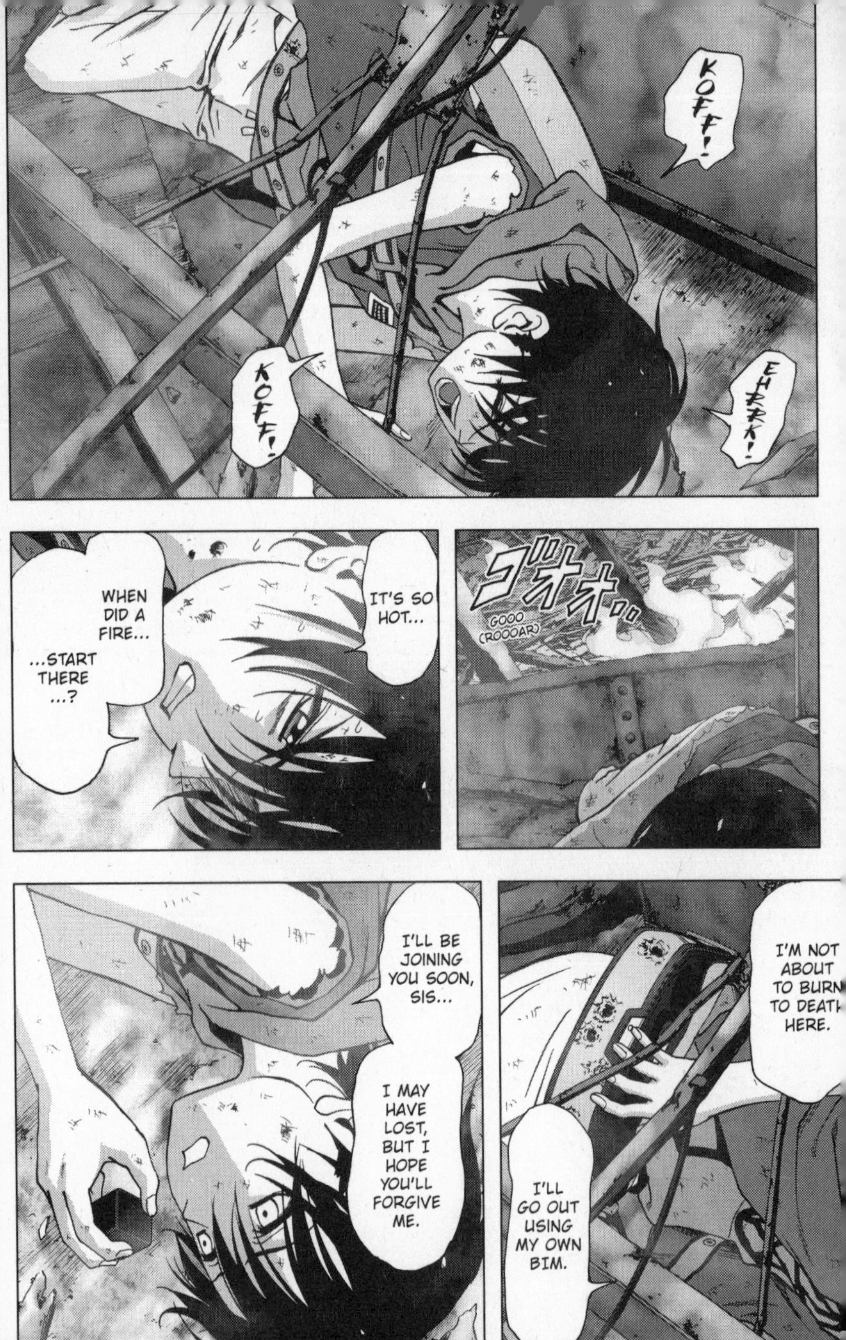
KOFF!
EHRRK!
KOFF!
ゴオオ
GOOO (ROOOAR)
IT'S SO HOT...
WHEN DID A FIRE...
...START THERE ...?
I'M NOT ABOUT TO BURN TO DEATH HERE.
I'LL GO OUT USING MY OWN BIM.
I'LL BE JOINING YOU SOON, SIS...
I MAY HAVE LOST, BUT I HOPE YOU'LL FORGIVE ME.

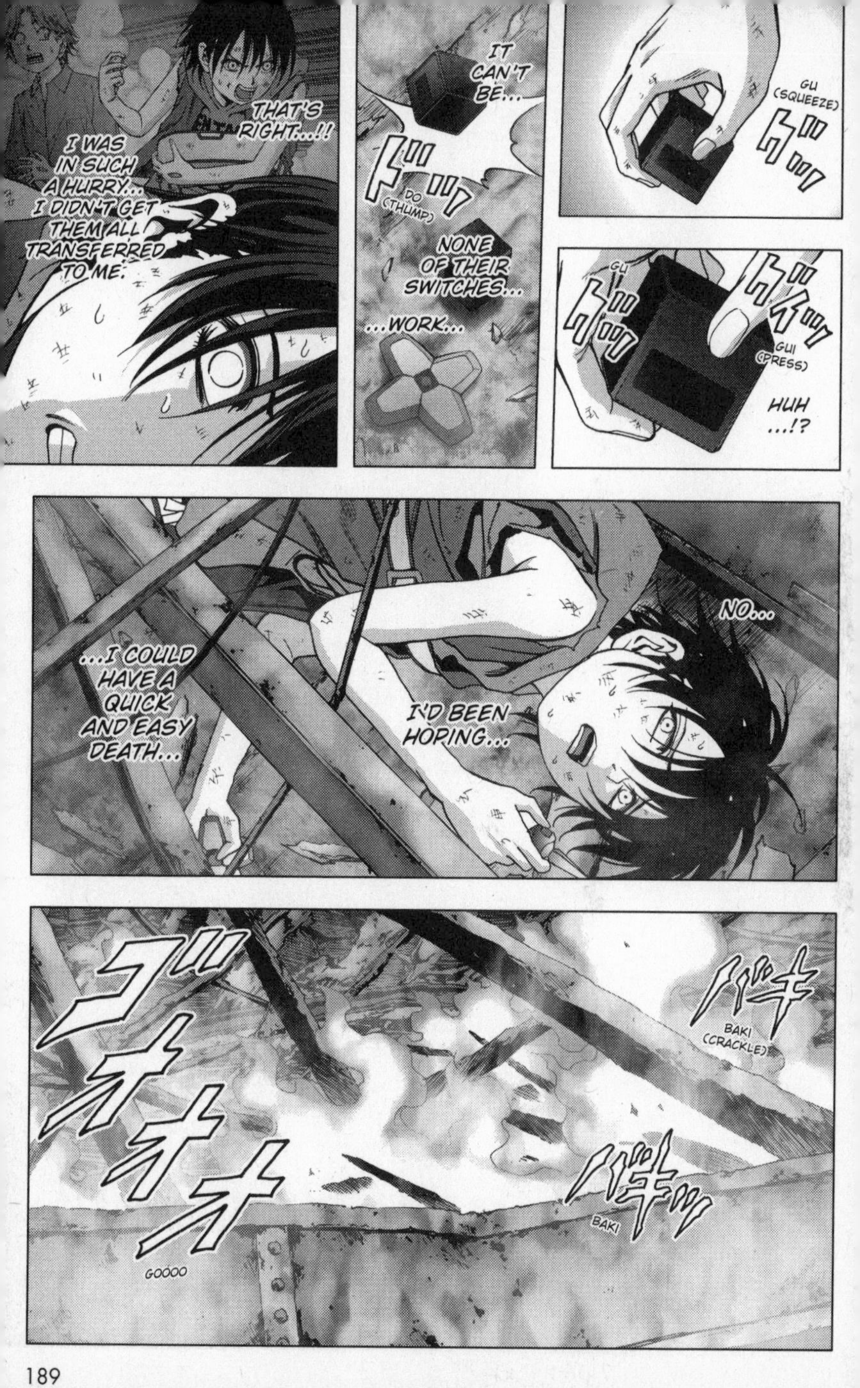
GU (SQUEEZE)
GU
GUI (PRESS)
HUH ...!?
IT CAN'T BE...
DO (THUMP)
NONE OF THEIR SWITCHES...
...WORK...
THAT'S RIGHT...!!
I WAS IN SUCH A HURRY... I DIDN'T GET THEM ALL TRANSFERRED TO ME.
NO...
I'D BEEN HOPING...
...I COULD HAVE A QUICK AND EASY DEATH...
BAKI (CRACKLE)
BAKI
GOOOO

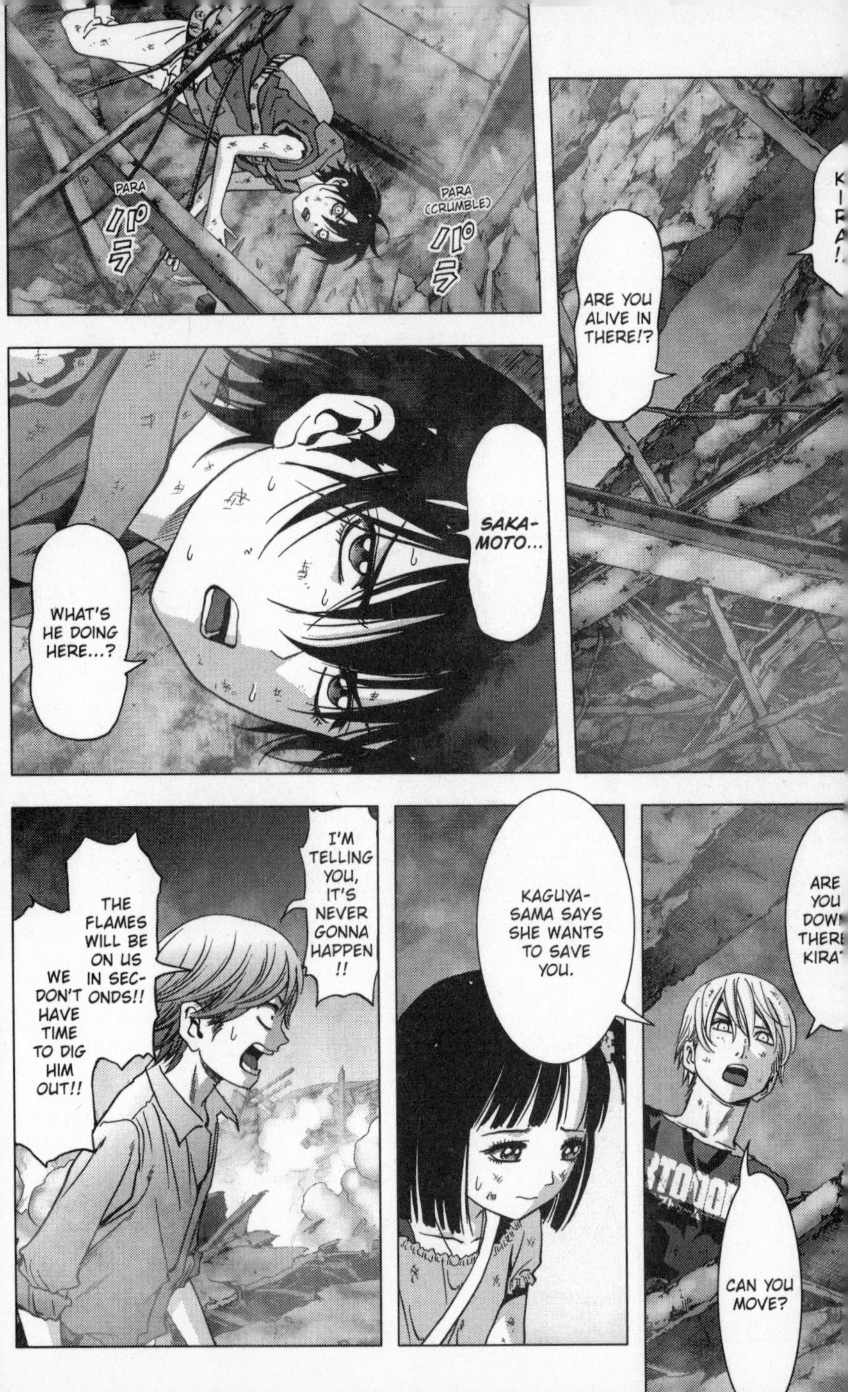

KIRA!
ARE YOU ALIVE IN THERE!?
PARA (CRUMBLE)
パラ
PARA
パラ
SAKA-MOTO...
WHAT'S HE DOING HERE...?
ARE YOU DOW THERE KIRA
CAN YOU MOVE?
KAGUYA-SAMA SAYS SHE WANTS TO SAVE YOU.
I'M TELLING YOU, IT'S NEVER GONNA HAPPEN!!
THE FLAMES WILL BE ON US IN SECONDS!!
WE DON'T HAVE TIME TO DIG HIM OUT!!

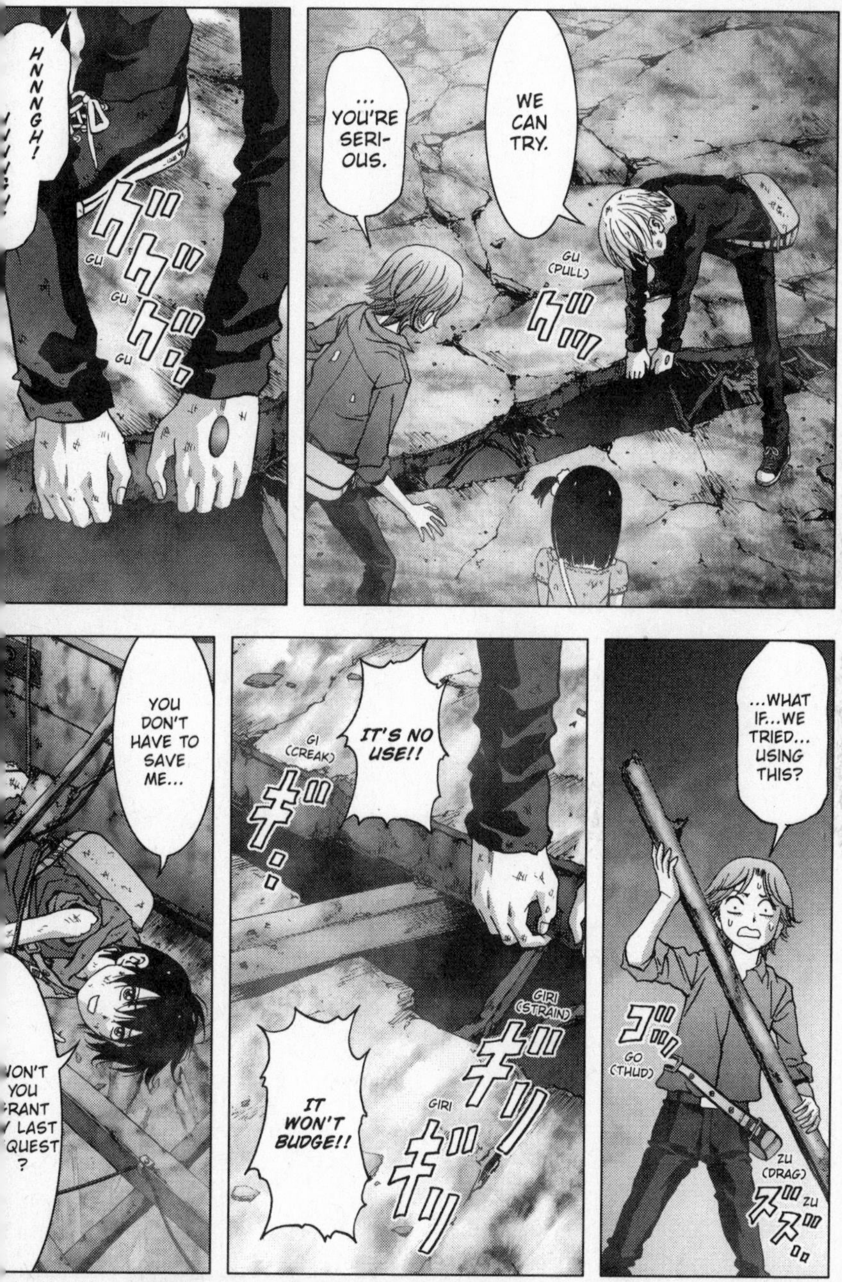

WE CAN TRY.
...YOU'RE SERIOUS.
GU (PULL)
HNNNGH!
GU
GU
GU
...WHAT IF...WE TRIED...USING THIS?
GO (THUD)
ZU (DRAG)
ZU
IT'S NO USE!!
GI (CREAK)
GIRI (STRAIN)
IT WON'T BUDGE!!
GIRI
YOU DON'T HAVE TO SAVE ME...
ON'T YOU RANT LAST QUEST ?

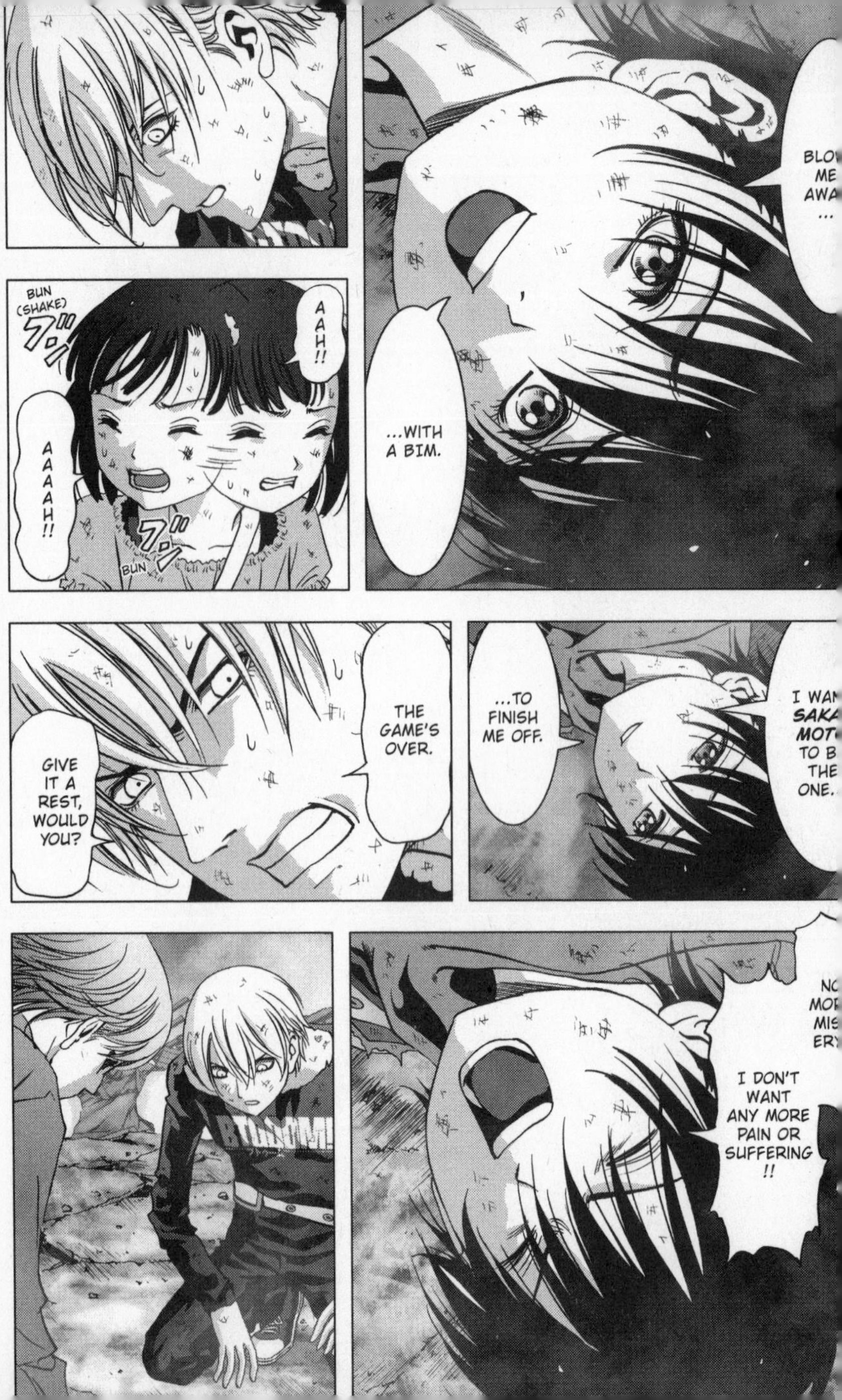
BLO ME AWA ...
...WITH A BIM.
AAH!!
BUN (SHAKE)
AAAAAH!!
BUN
I WAN SAKA MOT TO B THE ONE.
...TO FINISH ME OFF.
THE GAME'S OVER.
GIVE IT A REST, WOULD YOU?
NO MOR MIS ERY
I DON'T WANT ANY MORE PAIN OR SUFFERING !!

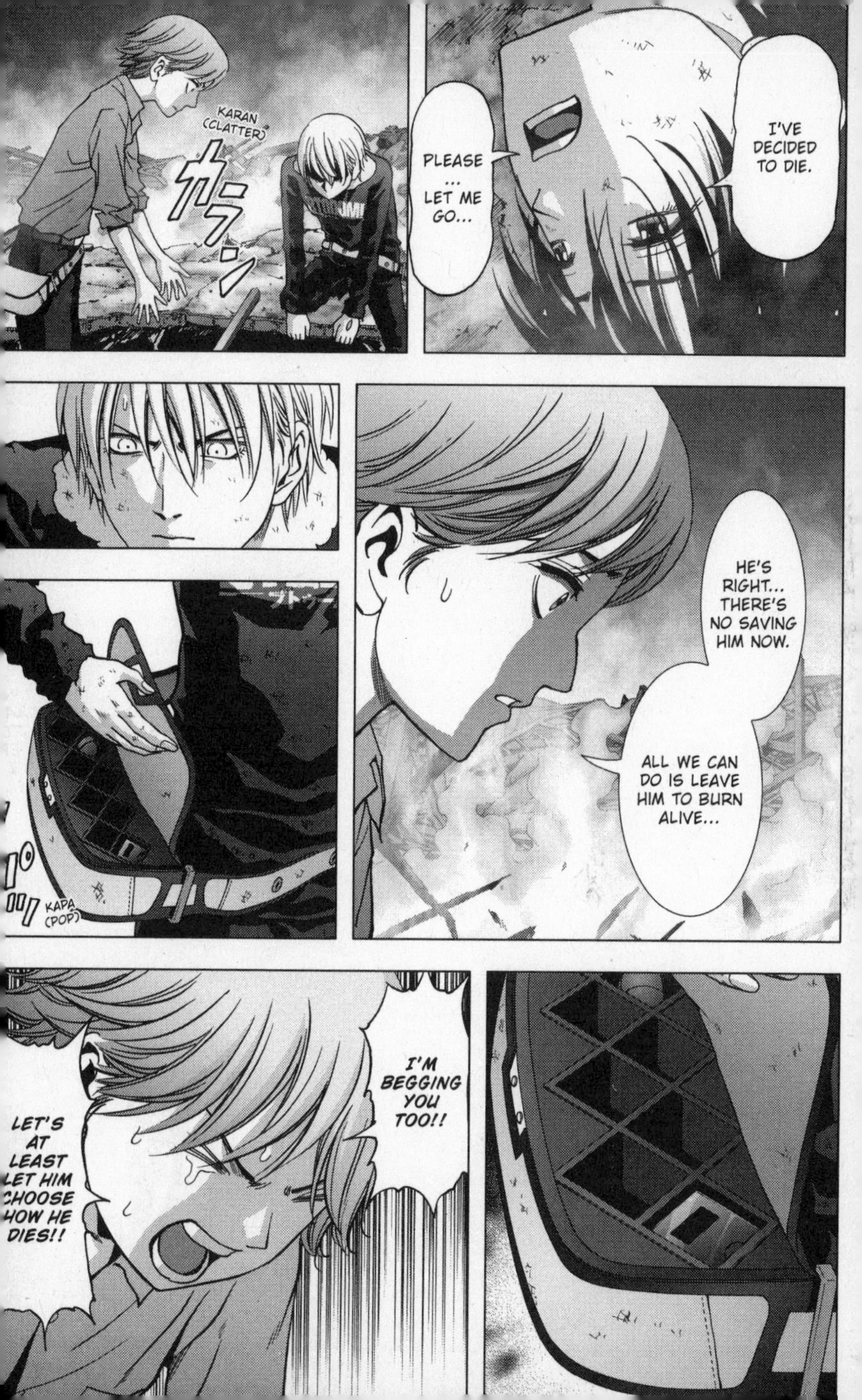
I'VE DECIDED TO DIE.
PLEASE ... LET ME GO...
KARAN (CLATTER)
カラン
HE'S RIGHT... THERE'S NO SAVING HIM NOW.
ALL WE CAN DO IS LEAVE HIM TO BURN ALIVE...
KAPA (POP)
I'M BEGGING YOU TOO!!
LET'S AT LEAST LET HIM CHOOSE HOW HE DIES!!

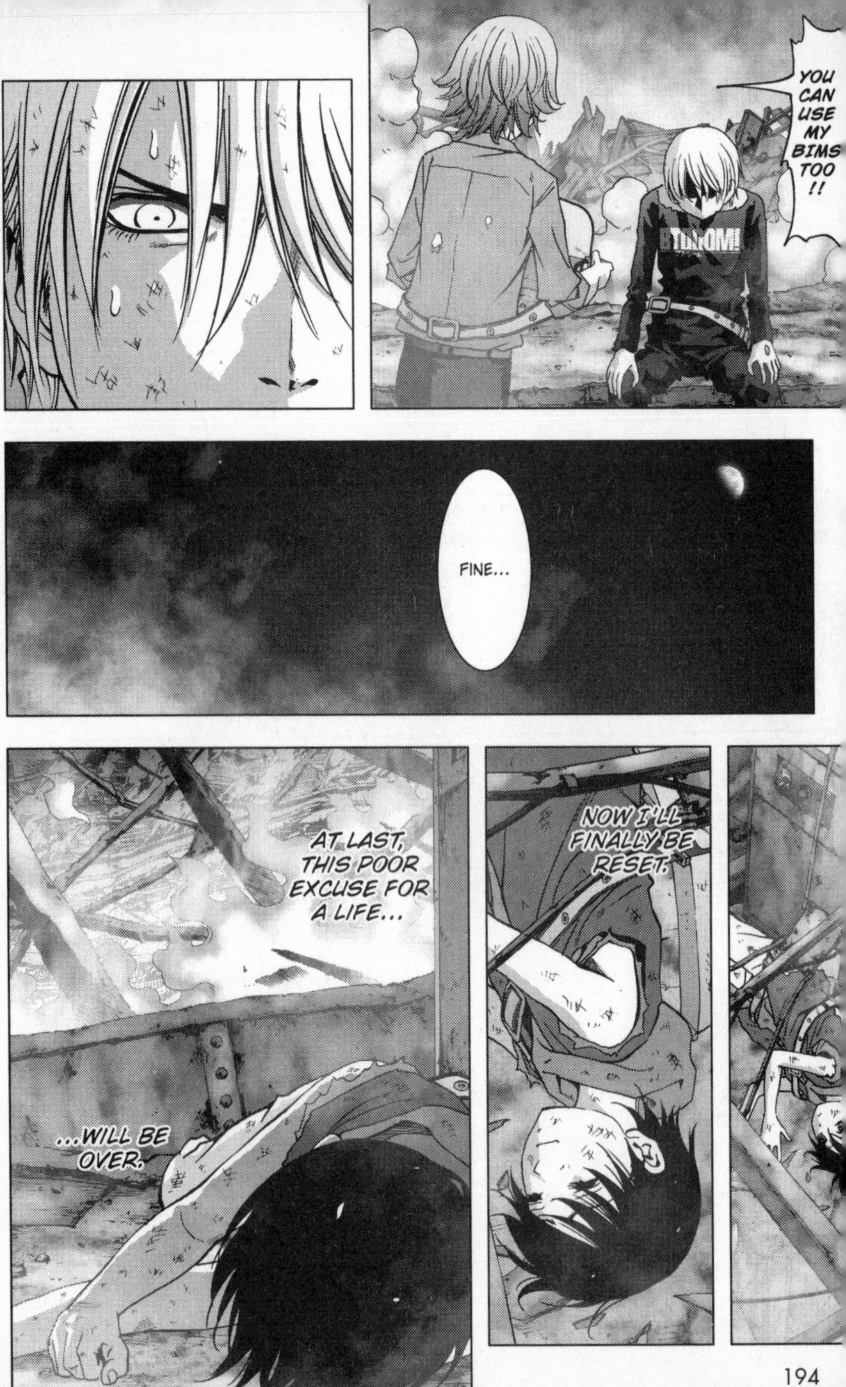
YOU CAN USE MY BIMS TOO!!
FINE...
NOW I'LL FINALLY BE RESET.
AT LAST, THIS POOR EXCUSE FOR A LIFE...
...WILL BE OVER.

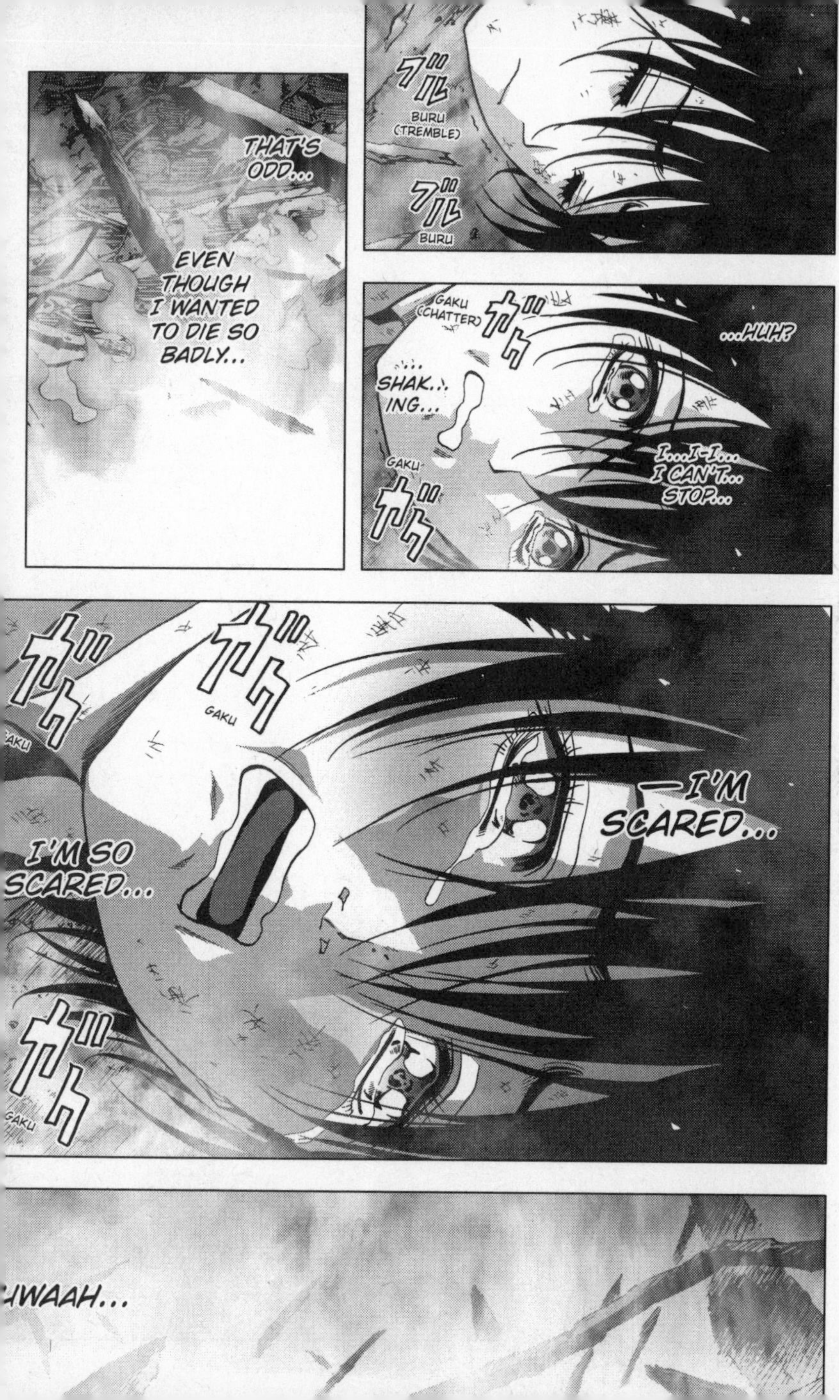
BURU (TREMBLE)
BURU
...HUH?
GAKU (CHATTER)
I...I-I... I CAN'T... STOP...
SHAK... ING...
GAKU
THAT'S ODD...
EVEN THOUGH I WANTED TO DIE SO BADLY...
—I'M SCARED...
GAKU
I'M SO SCARED...
GAKU
GAKU
HWAAH...

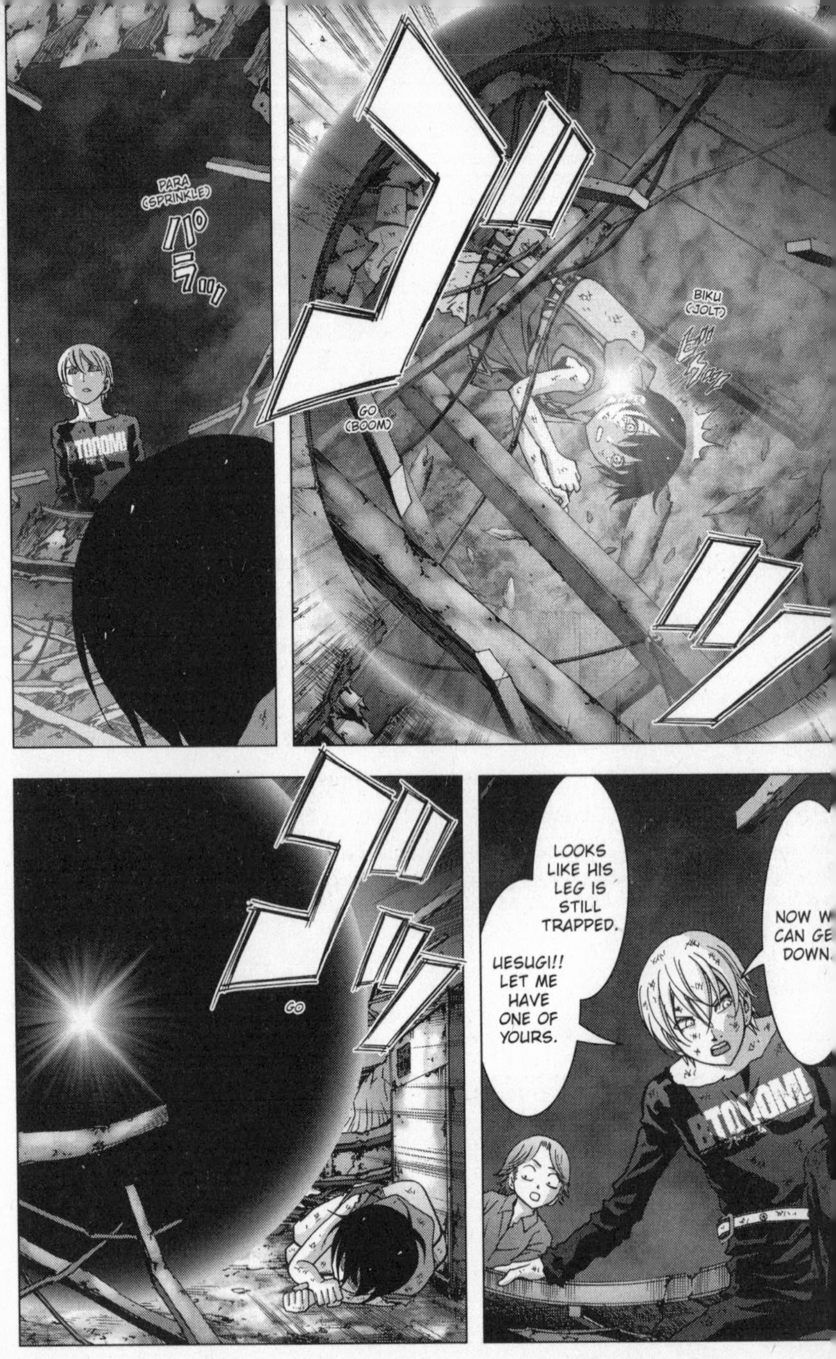
BIKU (JOLT)
GO (BOOM)
PARA (SPRINKLE)
NOW W CAN GE DOWN.
LOOKS LIKE HIS LEG IS STILL TRAPPED.
UESUGI!! LET ME HAVE ONE OF YOURS.
GO

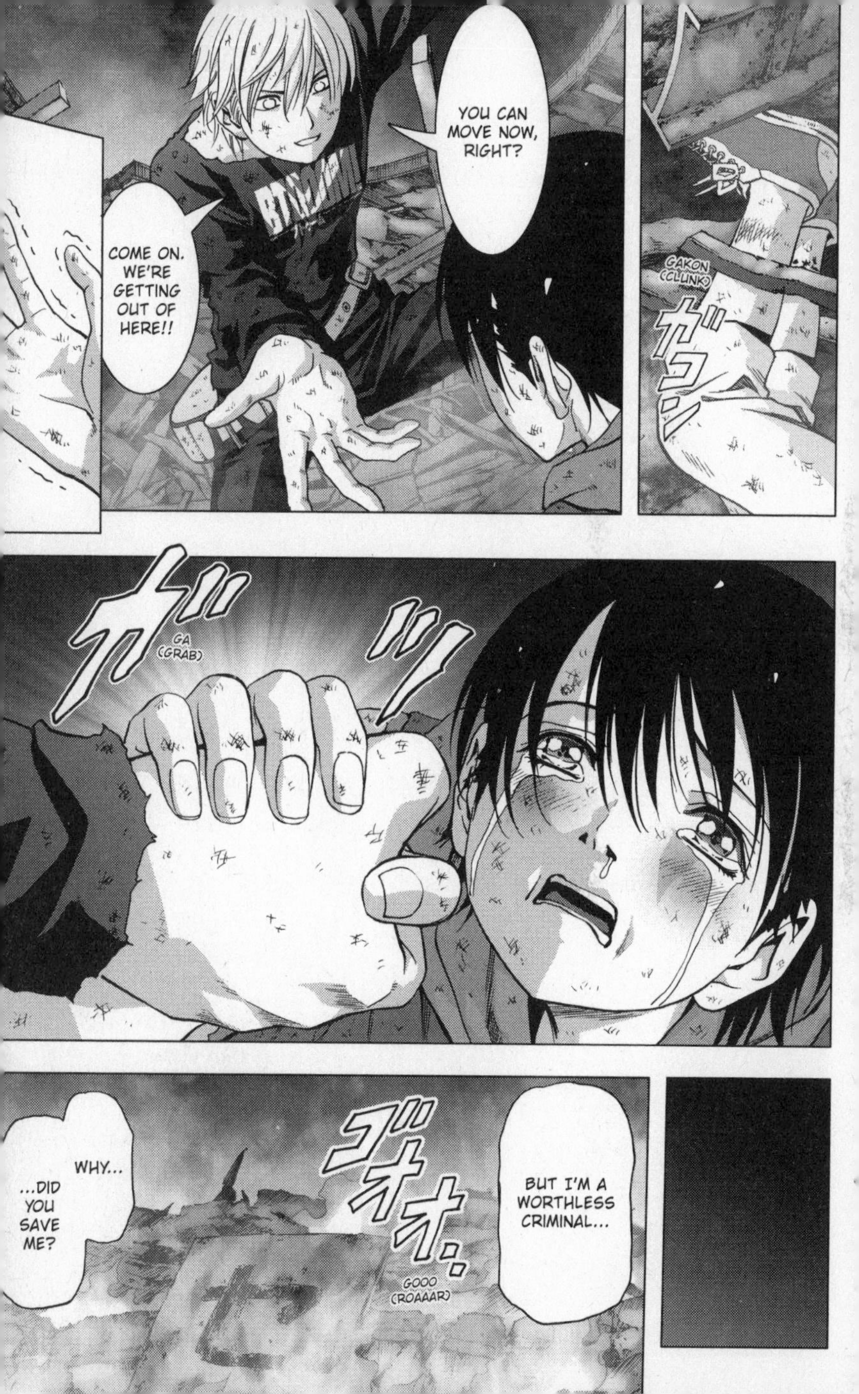
GAKON (CLUNK)
YOU CAN MOVE NOW, RIGHT?
COME ON. WE'RE GETTING OUT OF HERE!!
GA (GRAB)
BUT I'M A WORTHLESS CRIMINAL...
GOOO (ROAAAR)
WHY...
...DID YOU SAVE ME?

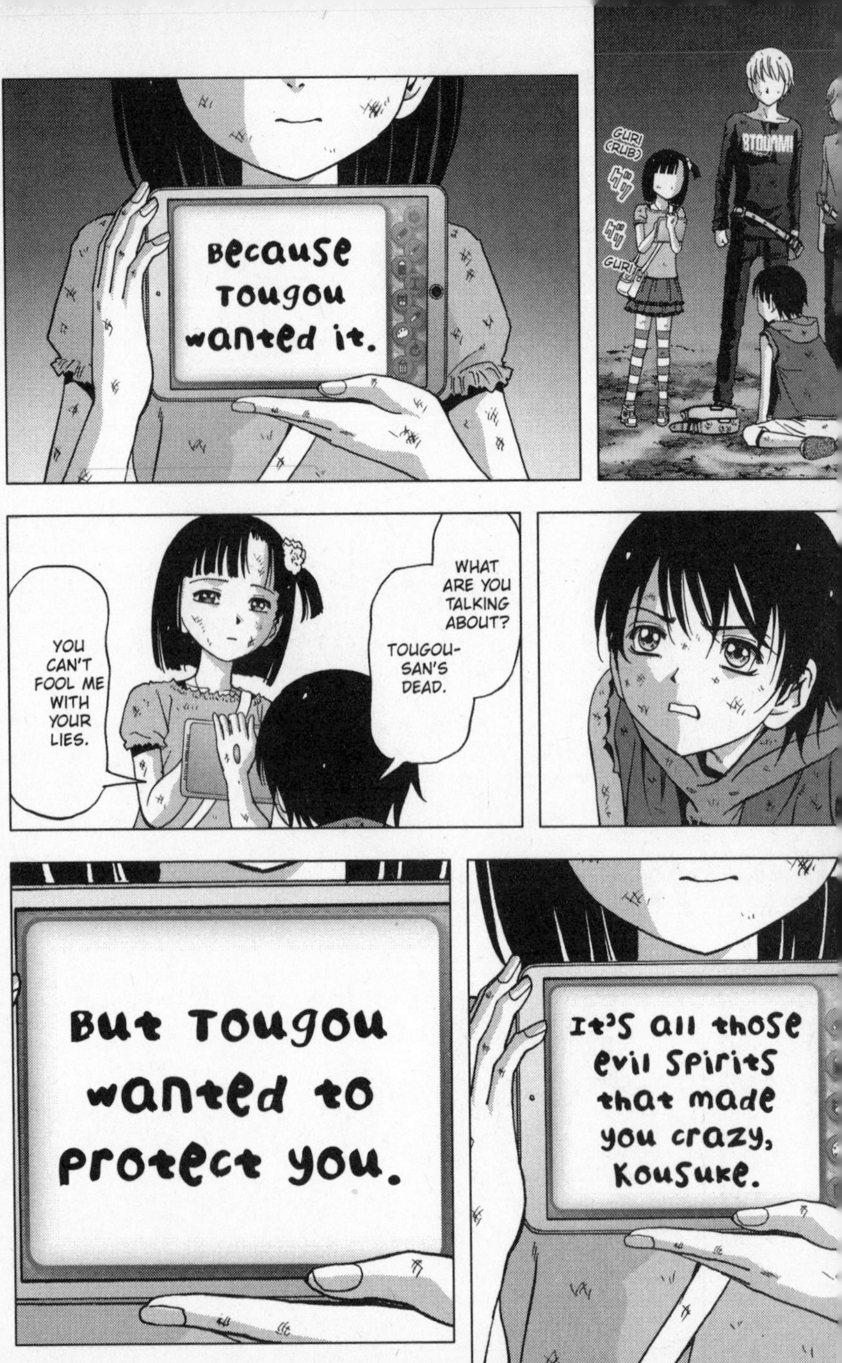
GURI (RUB)
グリ
グリ
GURI
Because Tougou wanted it.
WHAT ARE YOU TALKING ABOUT?
TOUGOU-SAN'S DEAD.
YOU CAN'T FOOL ME WITH YOUR LIES.
It's all those evil spirits that made you crazy, Kousuke.
But Tougou wanted to protect you.

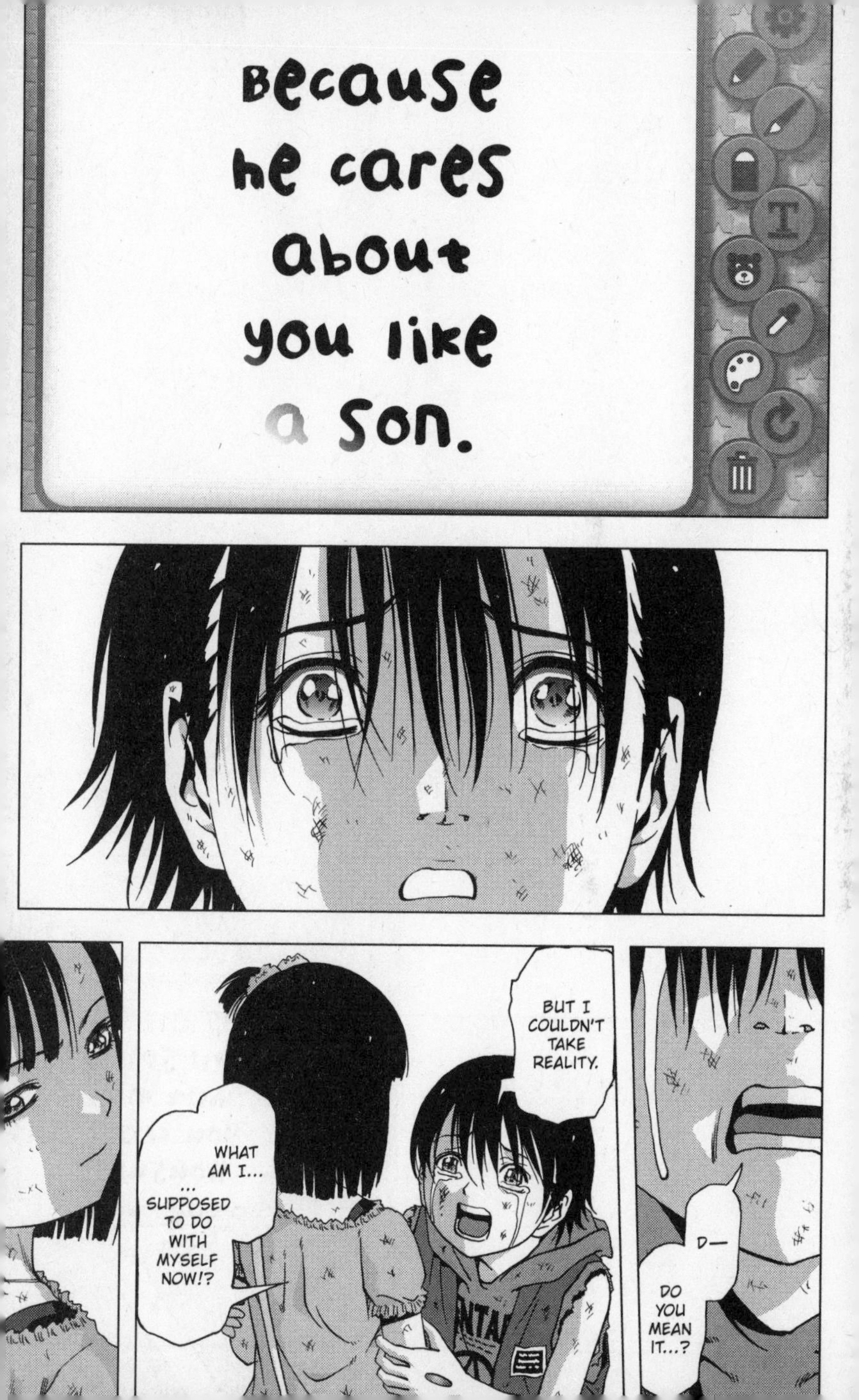
Because he cares about you like a son.
D—
DO YOU MEAN IT...?
BUT I COULDN'T TAKE REALITY.
WHAT AM I... ...SUPPOSED TO DO WITH MYSELF NOW!?

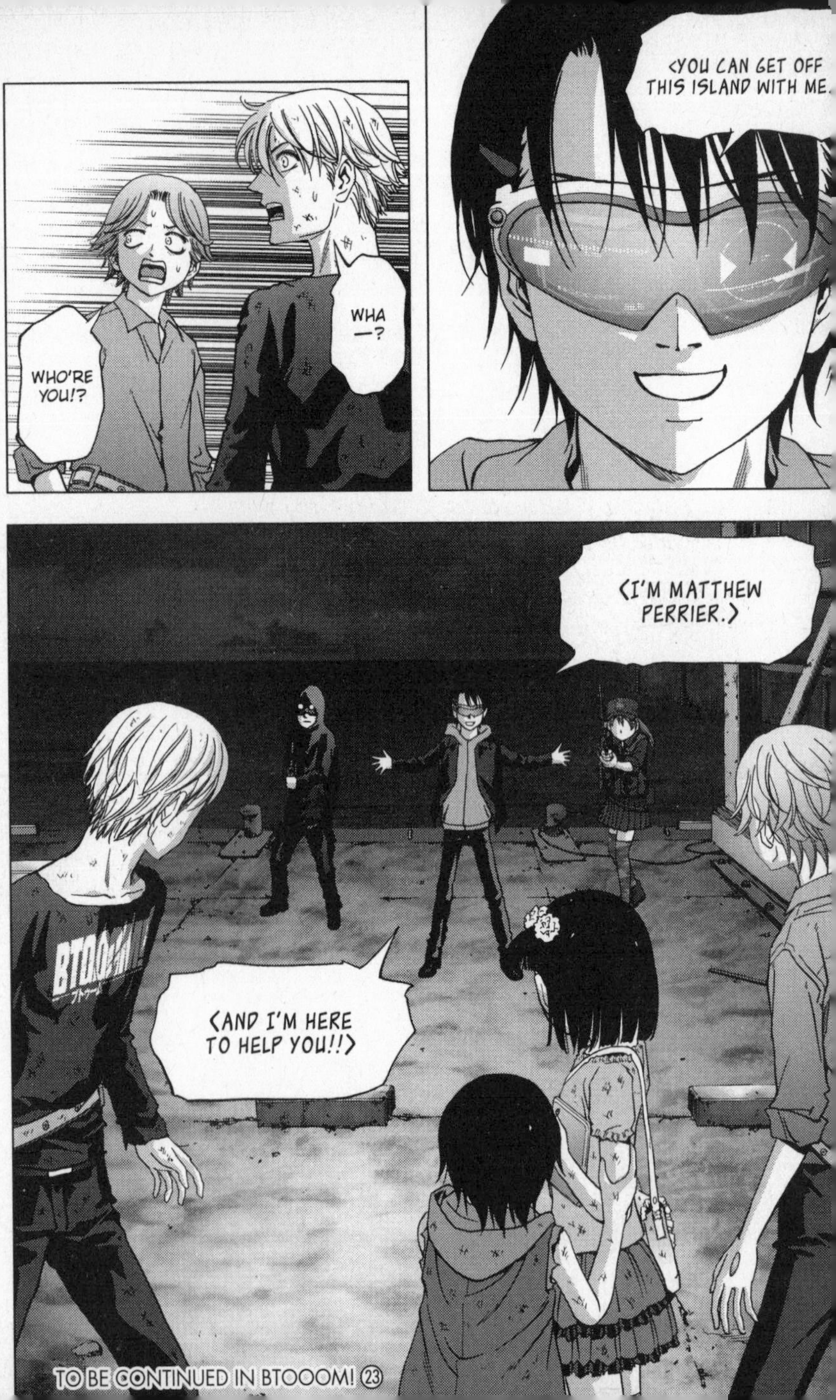
<YOU CAN GET OFF THIS ISLAND WITH ME.
WHA—?
WHO'RE YOU!?
<I'M MATTHEW PERRIER.>
<AND I'M HERE TO HELP YOU!!>
TO BE CONTINUED IN BTOOOM! 23

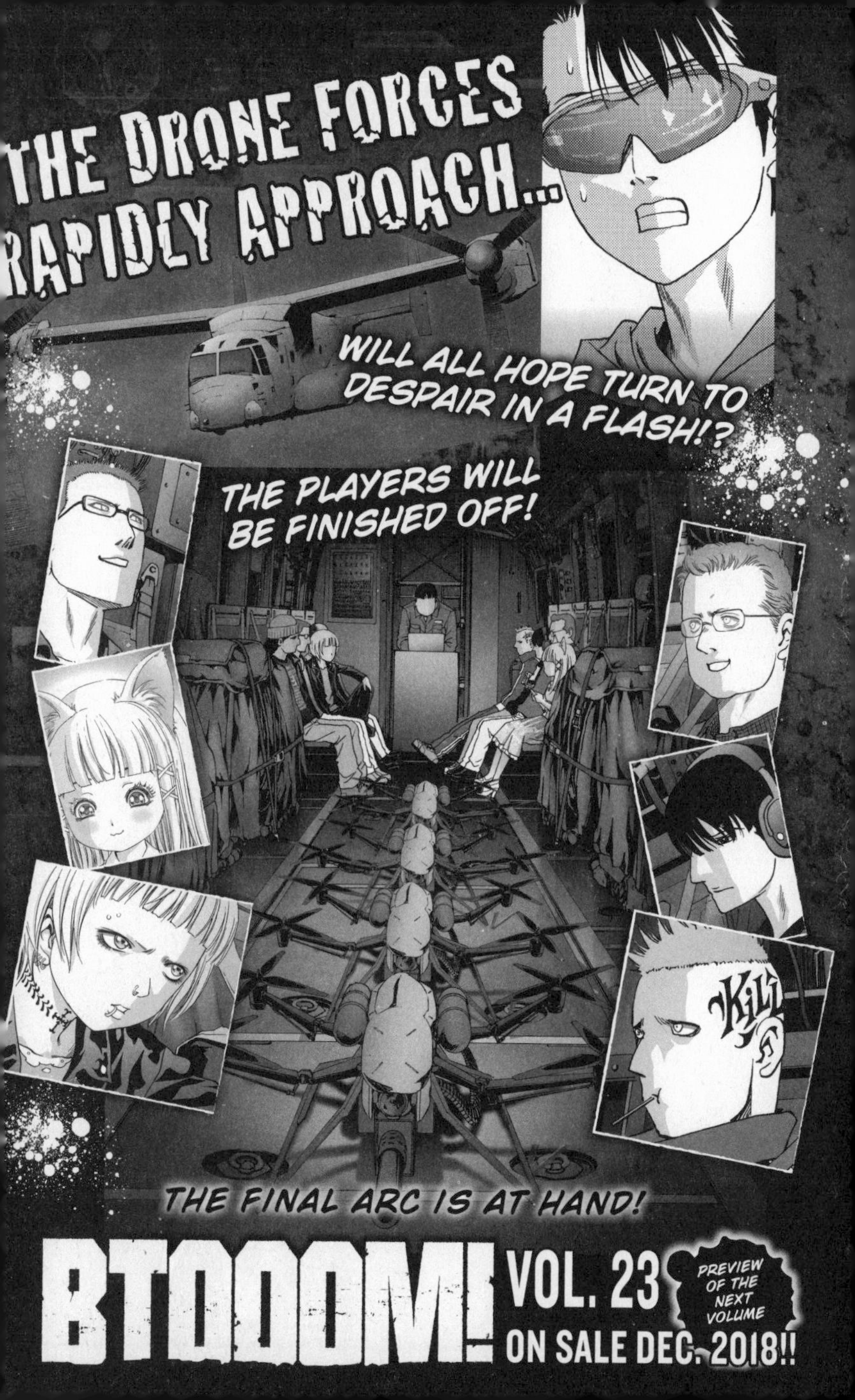
THE DRONE FORCES RAPIDLY APPROACH...
WILL ALL HOPE TURN TO DESPAIR IN A FLASH!?
THE PLAYERS WILL BE FINISHED OFF!
KILL
THE FINAL ARC IS AT HAND!
BTOOOM! VOL. 23
PREVIEW OF THE NEXT VOLUME
ON SALE DEC. 2018!!

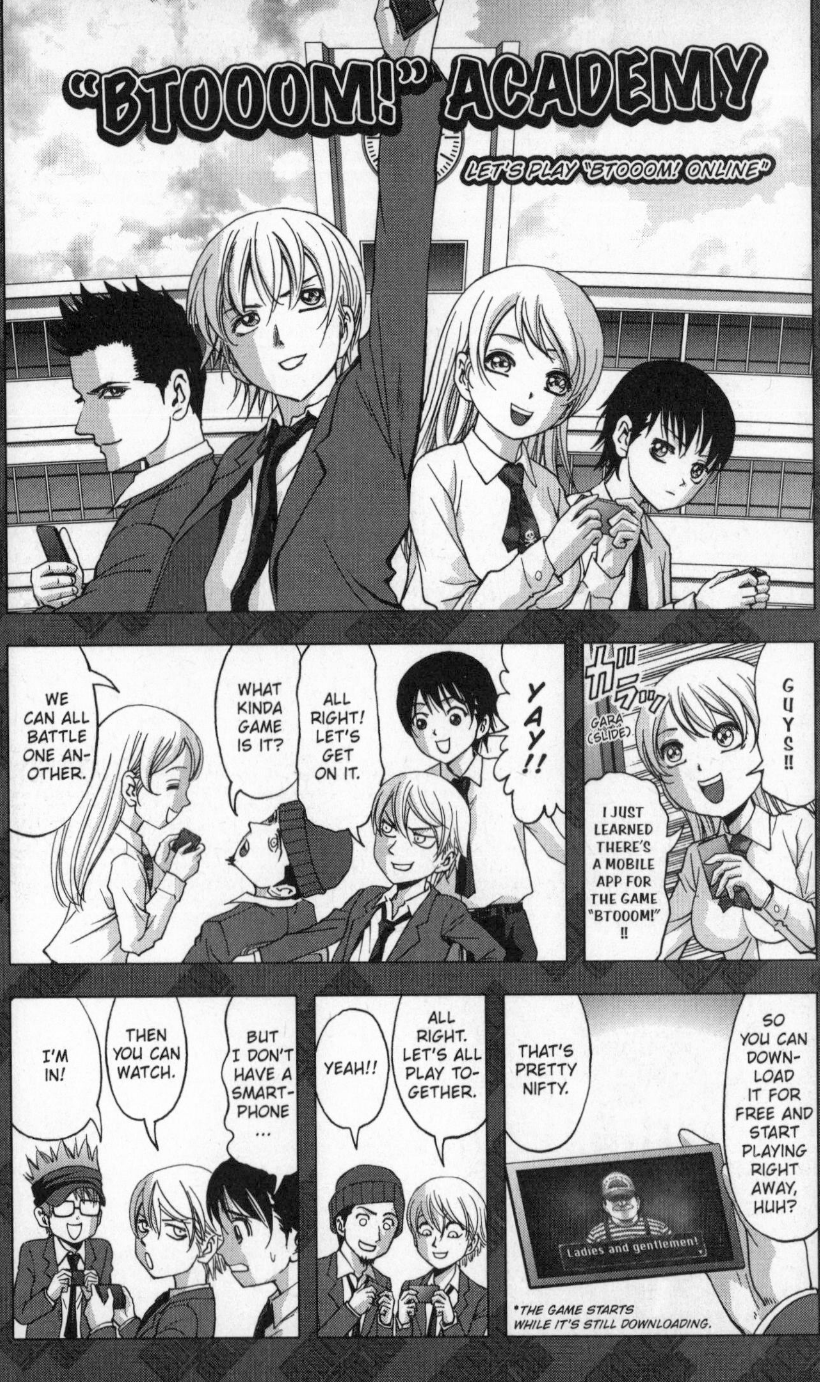
"BTOOOM!" ACADEMY
LET'S PLAY "BTOOOM! ONLINE"
GARA (SLIDE)
GUYS!!
I JUST LEARNED THERE'S A MOBILE APP FOR THE GAME "BTOOOM!" !!
YAY!!
ALL RIGHT! LET'S GET ON IT.
WHAT KINDA GAME IS IT?
WE CAN ALL BATTLE ONE AN-OTHER.
SO YOU CAN DOWN-LOAD IT FOR FREE AND START PLAYING RIGHT AWAY, HUH?
THAT'S PRETTY NIFTY.
Ladies and gentlemen!
*THE GAME STARTS WHILE IT'S STILL DOWNLOADING.
ALL RIGHT. LET'S ALL PLAY TO-GETHER.
YEAH!!
BUT I DON'T HAVE A SMART-PHONE ...
THEN YOU CAN WATCH.
I'M IN!

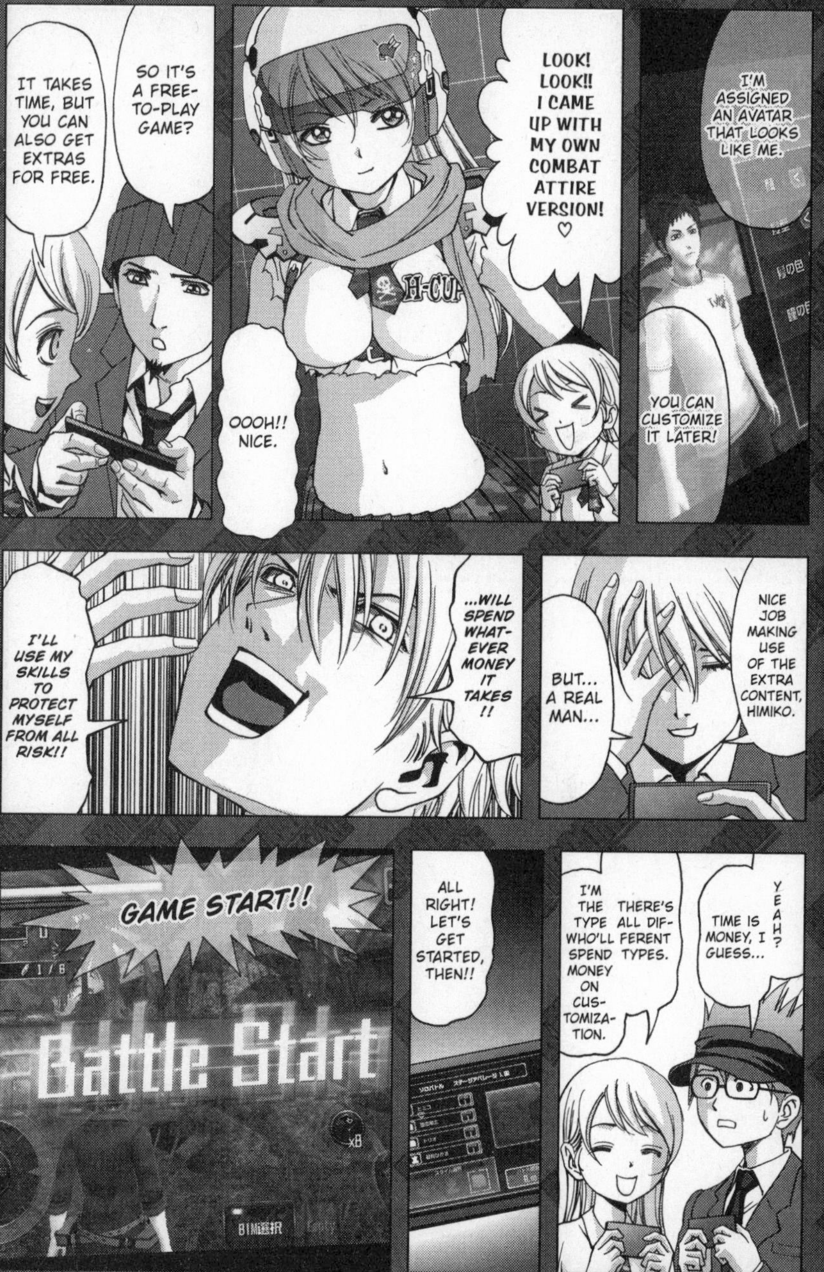
I'M ASSIGNED AN AVATAR THAT LOOKS LIKE ME.
YOU CAN CUSTOMIZE IT LATER!
LOOK! LOOK!! I CAME UP WITH MY OWN COMBAT ATTIRE VERSION! ♡
H-CUP
OOOH!! NICE.
SO IT'S A FREE-TO-PLAY GAME?
IT TAKES TIME, BUT YOU CAN ALSO GET EXTRAS FOR FREE.
NICE JOB MAKING USE OF THE EXTRA CONTENT, HIMIKO.
BUT... A REAL MAN...
...WILL SPEND WHATEVER MONEY IT TAKES!!
I'LL USE MY SKILLS TO PROTECT MYSELF FROM ALL RISK!!
YEAH?
TIME IS MONEY, I GUESS...
THERE'S ALL DIFFERENT TYPES.
I'M THE TYPE WHO'LL SPEND MONEY ON CUSTOMIZATION.
ALL RIGHT! LET'S GET STARTED, THEN!!
GAME START!!
Battle Start

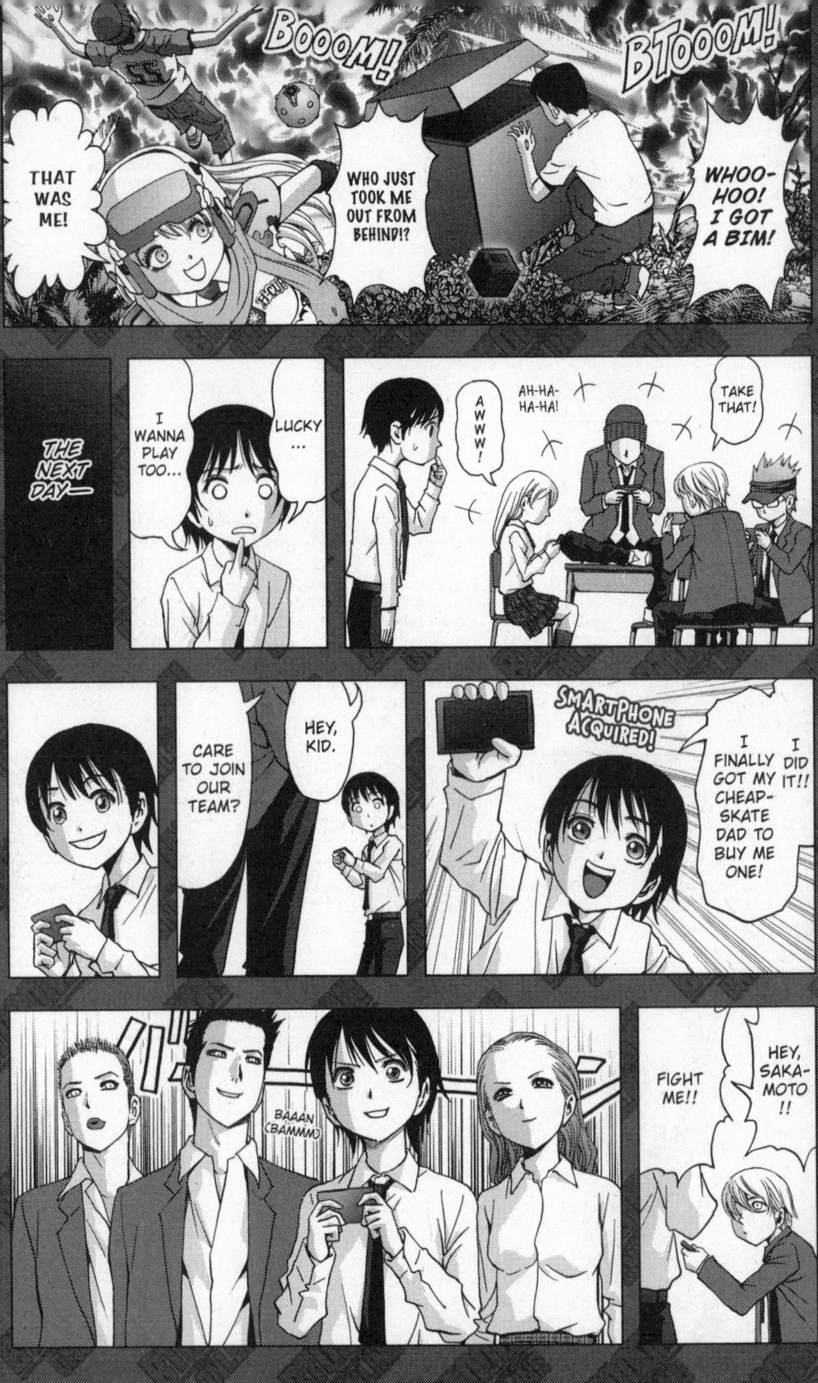
BTOOOM!
WHOO-HOO! I GOT A BIM!
BOOOM!
WHO JUST TOOK ME OUT FROM BEHIND!?
THAT WAS ME!
TAKE THAT!
AH-HA-HA-HA!
AWWW!
LUCKY...
I WANNA PLAY TOO...
THE NEXT DAY—
SMARTPHONE ACQUIRED!
I DID IT!!
I FINALLY GOT MY CHEAP-SKATE DAD TO BUY ME ONE!
HEY, KID.
CARE TO JOIN OUR TEAM?
HEY, SAKA-MOTO!!
FIGHT ME!!
BAAAN (BAMMM)

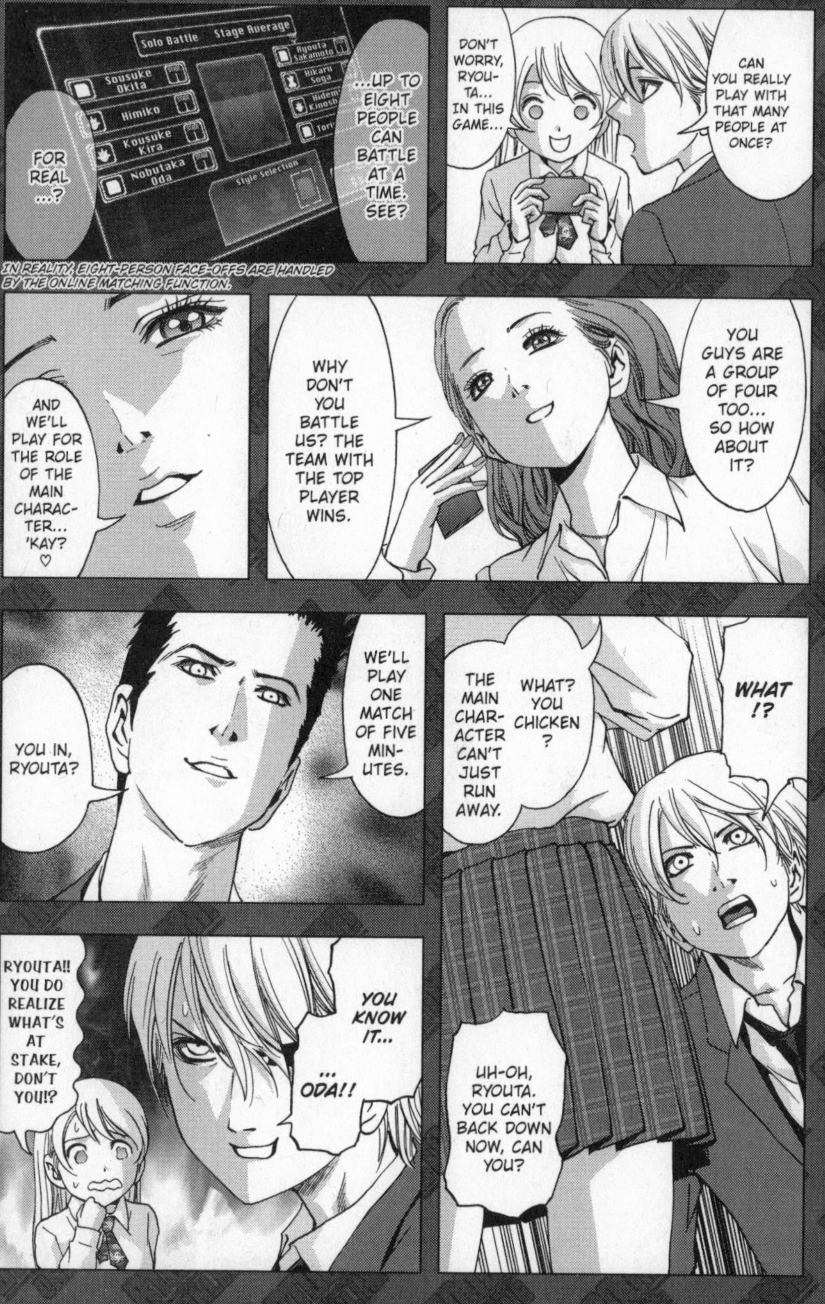
CAN YOU REALLY PLAY WITH THAT MANY PEOPLE AT ONCE?
DON'T WORRY, RYOU-TA... IN THIS GAME...
...UP TO EIGHT PEOPLE CAN BATTLE AT A TIME. SEE?
Solo Battle
Stage Average
Ryouta Sakamoto
Hikaru Soga
Sousuke Okita
Himiko
Kousuke Kira
Nobutaka Oda
Style Selection
FOR REAL ...?
IN REALITY, EIGHT-PERSON FACE-OFFS ARE HANDLED BY THE ONLINE MATCHING FUNCTION.
YOU GUYS ARE A GROUP OF FOUR TOO... SO HOW ABOUT IT?
WHY DON'T YOU BATTLE US? THE TEAM WITH THE TOP PLAYER WINS.
AND WE'LL PLAY FOR THE ROLE OF THE MAIN CHARAC-TER... 'KAY? ♡
WHAT !?
WHAT? YOU CHICKEN ?
THE MAIN CHAR-ACTER CAN'T JUST RUN AWAY.
UH-OH, RYOUTA. YOU CAN'T BACK DOWN NOW, CAN YOU?
WE'LL PLAY ONE MATCH OF FIVE MIN-UTES.
YOU IN, RYOUTA?
YOU KNOW IT...
... ODA!!
RYOUTA!! YOU DO REALIZE WHAT'S AT STAKE, DON'T YOU!?

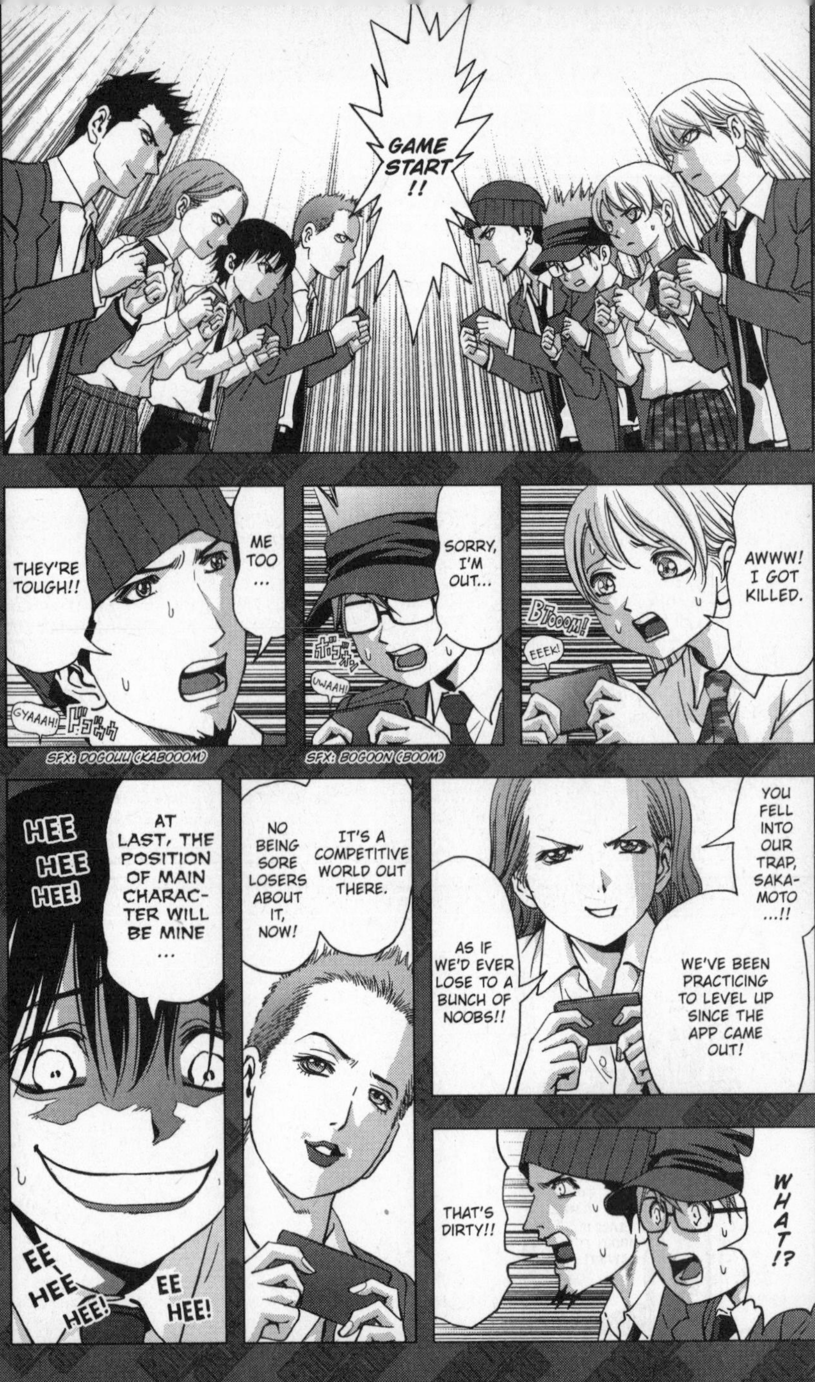
GAME START!!
AWWW! I GOT KILLED.
BTOOOM!
EEEK!
SORRY, I'M OUT...
UWAAH!
SFX: BOGOON (BOOM)
ME TOO ...
THEY'RE TOUGH!!
GYAAAH!
SFX: DOGOUU (KABOOOM)
YOU FELL INTO OUR TRAP, SAKAMOTO ...!!
WE'VE BEEN PRACTICING TO LEVEL UP SINCE THE APP CAME OUT!
AS IF WE'D EVER LOSE TO A BUNCH OF NOOBS!!
WHAT!?
THAT'S DIRTY!!
IT'S A COMPETITIVE WORLD OUT THERE.
NO BEING SORE LOSERS ABOUT IT, NOW!
AT LAST, THE POSITION OF MAIN CHARACTER WILL BE MINE ...
HEE HEE HEE!
EE HEE!
EE-HEE HEE!

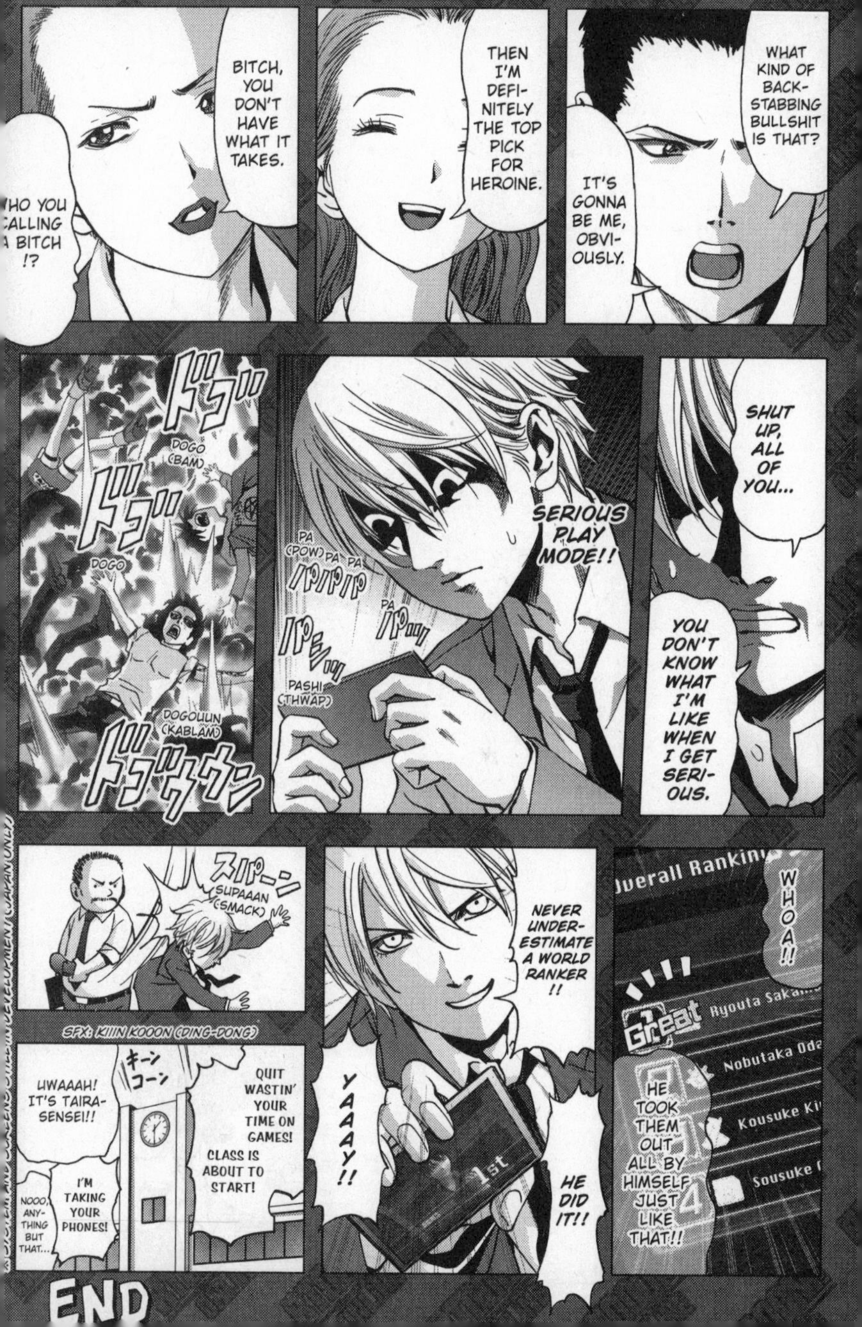
WHAT KIND OF BACK-STABBING BULLSHIT IS THAT?
IT'S GONNA BE ME, OBVIOUSLY.
THEN I'M DEFINITELY THE TOP PICK FOR HEROINE.
BITCH, YOU DON'T HAVE WHAT IT TAKES.
HO YOU CALLING A BITCH !?
SHUT UP, ALL OF YOU...
YOU DON'T KNOW WHAT I'M LIKE WHEN I GET SERIOUS.
SERIOUS PLAY MODE!!
PA (POW) PA PA
PA
PASHI (THWAP)
DOGO (BAM)
DOGO
DOGOUUN (KABLAM)
Overall Rankin
WHOA!!
Great
Ryouta Saka
Nobutaka Oda
Kousuke Ki
Sousuke
HE TOOK THEM OUT ALL BY HIMSELF JUST LIKE THAT!!
NEVER UNDER-ESTIMATE A WORLD RANKER!!
1st
YAAAY!!
HE DID IT!!
SUPAAAN (SMACK)
SFX: KIIN KOOON (DING-DONG)
QUIT WASTIN' YOUR TIME ON GAMES!
CLASS IS ABOUT TO START!
UWAAAH! IT'S TAIRA-SENSEI!!
I'M TAKING YOUR PHONES!
NOOO, ANYTHING BUT THAT...
END

TWO GIRLS REMAIN AT THE END OF THE WORLD...

GIRLS' LAST TOUR

VOLUME 1 ON SALE NOW!

GIRLS' LAST TOUR 1
TSUKUMIZU

Civilization is dead, but not Chito and Yuuri. Time to hop aboard their beloved Kettenkrad motorbike and wander what's left of the world! Sharing a can of soup or scouting for spare parts might not be the experience they were hoping for, but all in all, life isn't too bad...

BTOOOM!

JUNYA I

Translation: Christine Dashiell

Lettering: Brndn Blakeslee

Yen Press
1290 Avenue of the Americas
New York, NY 10104

Visit us at yenpress.com
facebook.com/yenpress
twitter.com/yenpress
yenpress.tumblr.com
instagram.com/yenpress

First Yen Press Edition: August 2018

Yen Press is an imprint of Yen Press, LLC.
The Yen Press name and logo are trademarks of Yen Press, LLC.

The   t) that
are

Lib

ISB

10 9 8 7 6 5 4 3 2

WOR

Printed in the United States of America